THE LONGEST BATTLE

THE LONGEST BATTLE

THE WAR AT SEA 1939-45

RICHARD HOUGH

CASSELL

Cassell Military Paperbacks

Cassell
Wellington House, 125 Strand
London WC2R 0BB

Copyright © Hough Writing Ltd 1986

First published by Weidenfeld & Nicolson 1986
This Cassell Military Paperbacks edition 2003

British Library Cataloguing-in-Publication Data
A catalogue record for this book is available from the
British Library

ISBN 0-304-36328-6

Printed and bound in Great Britain by
Cox & Wyman Ltd., Reading, Berks.

Contents

Illustrations

A picture postcard and the wreckage of the *Graf Spee* (*A. Chatham Esq.*)
Admiral of the Fleet Sir Dudley Pound (*Imperial War Museum*)
The battle-cruisers *Gneisenau* and *Scharnhorst* opening fire on the carrier HMS *Glorious*, 8 June 1940 (*Imperial War Museum*)
The French battle-cruiser *Strasbourg* escaping from Oran, 5 July 1940 (*J. Bamber Esq.*)
The French battleship *Bretagne* blowing up (*J. Bamber Esq.*)
U-570 captured intact in the North Atlantic, 27 August 1941 (*Lieutenant-Commander W. Hutton Attenborough RN Retd*)
After the sinking of the *U-39*, two of her company swim towards HMS *Foxhound*, 14 September 1939 (*C. Clifford Esq.*)
Admiral Sir John Tovey (*Royal Naval College*)
Flottenchef Admiral Lütjens (*Imperial War Museum*)
Bismarck photographed from the *Prinz Eugen* before leaving Norwegian waters (*Imperial War Museum*)
The 8-inch gun cruiser HMS *Suffolk* (*Imperial War Museum*)
A 'Hunt' class destroyer takes in bread from the battleship *Nelson* (*J. Bamber Esq.*)
An X-craft miniature submarine (*Imperial War Museum*)
The sinking of the *Tirpitz*, November 1944 (*Von der Porten*)
A German destroyer heads the German Brest Squadron in its dash up-Channel to home ports, 12–13 February 1942 (*Imperial War Museum*)
The *Prinz Eugen* ramming the cruiser *Leipzig* (*Von der Porten*)

Admiral Andrew Cunningham (*Imperial War Museum*)
Admiral James Somerville (*Imperial War Museum*)
A Malta convoy (*Imperial War Museum*)
The ubiquitous 'Stringbag' (*Imperial War Museum*)
The battleship *Warspite* (*Imperial War Museum*)
HMS *Renown* being bombed while on convoy escort (*J. Bamber Esq.*)
The battered tanker *Ohio* being nursed into Grand Harbour, Malta, 15 August 1942 (*Imperial War Museum*)

A 63-foot 'MASBY' (Motor Anti-Submarine Boat) (*Sir Walter Blount*)
D-Day, 6 June 1944: landing-craft passing the assault anchorage position
fifteen minutes before opening fire (*J. Noble Esq.*)
Monitor HMS *Roberts* bombarding beach defences (*P. Harrison Esq.*)
'Off go the good old 49th!' (*J. Noble Esq.*)

Maps

(*The maps were drawn by Patrick Leeson*)

Acknowledgements

Once again my debt to Lieutenant-Commander Peter Kemp OBE RN (Retd), who read the manuscript, put me right on a number of points, and contributed numerous suggestions, is prodigious.

Next, I wish to thank all the people, most of whom served during the war, who sent me photographs. I could not use as many as I wished, but those whose contributions are included are acknowledged in the list of illustrations.

Many ex-serving officers and ratings were good enough to relate or send me accounts of their experiences, including Vice-Admiral Sir John Collins KBE, Vice-Admiral Sir David Loram KCB, Rear-Admiral G. S. Ritchie DSC, Commander Vincent Jerram RAN, Lieutenant-Commander 'Dusty' Miller RNZN, Squadron-Leader K. Blowers, A. D. Barling DSC, Sir Walter Blount, Bart, DSC, Don T. W. Harris, Edward Firmin, Harold Larsen, Max Germains, Gary Dewhurst, Douglas Rendell, John C. Date, and many others.

Finally, for permission to quote from published sources I must thank the following authors, publishers and agents: Mr Walter Lord, *Day of Infamy* (Holt, Rinehart & Winston), *The Miracle of Dunkirk* (Viking Press) and *Incredible Victory* (Harper and Row). Mr Martin Middlebrook, *Convoy* and *Battleship*. Sir Peter Scott CBE, DSC, *Battle of the Narrow Seas*. Constable Publishers, *Savo* by R. F. Newcomb. Pelham Books Ltd, *The Hurricats* by Ralph Barker. Doubleday and Co., *Challenge for the Pacific* by R. Leckie. Holt, Rinehart, *Iron Coffins* by H. Warner. John Murrary (Publishers) Ltd, *The Attack on St Nazaire* by Captain R. E. D. Ryder VC, RN. Patrick Stephens Ltd, *Alarm Starboard* by G. Brooke. Naval Institute Press and The Bodley Head, *Battleship Bismarck: A Survivor's Story* by B. Müllenheim-Rechberg and *U-Boat Commander: A Periscope View of the Battle of the Atlantic* (published in the UK under the title *U-333: The Story of a U-boat Ace*) by Peter Cremer. Little Brown and Company, *History of the United States Naval Operations in World War Two: Coral Sea, Midway and Submarine May 1942–August 1942*, and *History of the United States Naval Operations in World War Two: The Struggle for Guadalcanal, August 1942–February 1943* by Samuel Eliot Morison, authorized 16 and 17 April 1986. *The Second World War* by Sir Winston Churchill, copyright The Estate of Sir Winston Churchill, reprinted by kind permission of Curtis Brown Ltd on behalf of the Estate of Sir Winston Churchill. Prentice-Hall, Inc., *The Great Sea War: The Story of Naval Action in World War II* by G. B. Potter and Chester W. Nimitz. Century Hutchinson Ltd, *Dieppe: The Shame and the Glory* by T. Robertson. W. W. Norton & Company, Inc., *Climax at Midway* by T. V. Tuleja. Conway Maritime Press, *Wings at Sea* by Gerard Woods. Robert Hale Ltd, *The Drama of the Scharnhorst* by Fritz-Otto Busch. A. P. Watt Ltd, *A Sailor's Odyssey* by Admiral of the Fleet Viscount Cunningham of Hyndhope. Laurence Pollinger Ltd, *Zero* by Masatake Okumiya and Jiro Horikoshi, and *The Amazing Mr Doolittle* by Quentin Reynolds.

A number of extracts proved untraceable, and no reply could be obtained from several publishers in the UK and the USA. The author apologizes for any unintended transgression of copyright.

Foreword

War at sea has no intermissions, none of the periods of recovery between advances or retreats that land warfare enjoys, no breaks safely behind the lines between air combat operations. There are many times in a soldier's or airman's war as taxing and terrifying as anything known to a sailor at sea in wartime. But it is an accepted condition of a sailor's duty that there is never a moment at sea that is free from danger. The risk of attack is always there, ever more so in the twentieth century when a submarine's torpedo can strike at any time in any part of any ocean (or even at anchor), or an aircraft's bomb can fall equally without warning from the sky.

Added to all these man-devised hazards, there is 'the cruel sea' itself; viewed, let us say, from the reeling deck of a corvette in mid-Atlantic, mid-winter, and a force 10 gale, eight days out of Halifax and the barometer falling.

The Second World War demanded more of its sailors than any other in history in endurance and the unremitting need to face danger, with increasingly lethal weapons and an ever-increasing need for vigilance by night and day.

For Britain's Royal Navy the Second World War began on 3 September 1939, and in European waters it ceased on 8 May 1945. There was no 'phoney war' for the sailors of Britain and her allies and dominions. Later, the fall of Norway and Denmark, Holland, Belgium and France, and the emergence of Italy and Japan as new enemies, all added to the burdens and dangers of keeping the sea lanes open for trade and the transport of supplies and armies.

For the US Navy and Marines in the Pacific, hostilities began in December 1941 with even greater violence than in European waters, and spanned the Atlantic and Mediterranean, too. The hazards were as great and sustained as in every other theatre. Actions included the celebrated and awesome carrier battles and gigantic fleet actions in which the gun was still the arbiter, as well as innumerable landings, from the Solomons to Iwo Jima, before final victory in September 1945.

The Second World War was indeed the longest and greatest battle of all time, extending to every ocean and sea, and with more ships sunk and more lives lost than in any earlier conflict.

The purpose of this book is to present this non-stop battle from a sailor's view and in terms of personal experience. The war at sea was a sailor's war, whether admiral or stoker, airman or submariner. The longest battle was his battle, and when viewed through periscope, binoculars, gunsight or bombsight, or the unaided human eye, the picture has a special clarity, veracity and colour.

Without control of the oceans, and the air above them, there could have been no defeat of Japan, no material support for Russia, no invasion of Italy, no D-Day landings. When the longest battle at sea was over the world was delivered from tyranny, the gas chamber and racial extermination.

RICHARD HOUGH
March 1986

CHAPTER ONE

'... business in great waters'

On 3 September 1939 the Royal Navy's battle fleet was at Scapa Flow in the Orkney Islands, while the German U-boats and commerce raiders were already at sea. The Royal Navy's first task was to transport the army across the Channel to fight with the French against the common enemy, and to ensure that the vital sea lanes to and from Britain were kept open. To this end convoys were at once instituted. Loyal support was already forthcoming from the Dominions and colonies. It was the ardent hope of every sailor that the United States would soon become an ally, too. 'That would soon fix the Hun!'

It might have been the September of an earlier German war, and many older officers and ratings remarked on the already ominous similarity between the two wars. 'It was as if time had stood still,' remarked one captain who had been a young sub-lieutenant in 1916. 'A lot of the ships were even the same, too. Ruddy uncanny, I can tell you.'

Yes, there was the battleship *Royal Oak*, and her sister ship the *Revenge* anchored not far away, both of which had fought at the Battle of Jutland; and 'V' and 'W' class lean, twin-funnel destroyers which had done sterling service on convoy duties in that earlier war. And, of course, the same drab Scapa Flow, the end beyond the end of Scotland; the same broad sheet of slate-grey water surrounded by the naked, undulating land of Hoy, Flotta, South Ronaldsay. ... It was even said that the anchorage's defences were inadequate, as they had proved to be before.

The RN's task had not changed, either. It was the same as in 1914, and in the Napoleonic and Dutch and Spanish wars of the distant past. It was to sustain the principles of sea power, even if, in this twentieth century, air power and the submarine had added new dimensions: 'to control that area of sea you need to use for any particular operation and to retain it for as long as that operation lasts',[1] be it the breadth of the Atlantic or the waters about a Pacific atoll.

The chief naval difference between 1939 and 1914 was in the relative sea power of Germany. In 1914 Germany possessed a mighty, efficient, well-trained navy, the second most powerful in the world, and a force which threatened the domination of the seas which Britain had enjoyed unchallenged since the defeat of the combined Spanish–French fleet at

Trafalgar 109 years earlier. By 1919 the German Navy had been reduced to a token force, with severe restrictions imposed by the Versailles Treaty on what warships she could build.

On assuming power in 1933 Hitler began brushing aside all these treaty humiliations and set about building a modern fleet. The programme had not been completed by the time he invaded Poland, and France and Britain had declared war, but the new *Kriegsmarine* was, on paper, a highly efficient, superbly equipped and *modern* navy by contrast with the Royal Navy's ageing fleet.

The British Navy, too, had a large programme of modernization and building, but possessed only one new aircraft carrier, and of the battle fleet's fifteen battleships and battle-cruisers all but two had been laid down before or during the First World War. However its overall strength was almost exactly equal to that of the United States Navy at the time of Pearl Harbor, and far superior to Germany's.

Besides the up-to-date quality of Germany's warships (and her armoured ships had always been so tough as to be virtually unsinkable by gunfire), Germany had two other great counter-advantages. The first was material: in guns and shells, and above all in mines, the German product was superior to the British. The second, and more important, was in thinking. German faith in air power, as Winston Churchill never failed to point out in the late 1930s, was much greater than in Britain, where a small peacetime air force had been only partly modernized and expanded by 1939. The RAF's control of the navy's air arm until 1937 led to its being given low priority. The morale and skill of the air crew was high, but their machines were antiquated and much inferior to those of the Japanese and American naval air arms.

By 1939 the German high command, largely persuaded by Field Marshal Hermann Goering, First World War air ace and now head of the *Luftwaffe*, believed that success at sea as well as on land depended on control of the sky. There were plenty of people in the Royal Navy who shared that belief but Admiralty policy, always conservative in peacetime, remained more concerned with ritual orders for the conduct of the battle fleet, as if the warplane had never been invented, than in the security of the battle fleet from bombing or torpedo-carrying aircraft.

Even more than in the United States Navy, the battleship remained the RN's capital ship. In spite of his fear of the growing strength of the *Luftwaffe* and its bombing capability, for Churchill, back at the Admiralty on the outbreak of war, the battleship was still the key to control of the sea, and like most of his admirals he believed that a well-equipped, well-handled battleship could deal with any attack from the air.

In 1914 the Grand Fleet's battleships never emerged from their bases without a heavy escort of destroyers as protection against torpedo attack from enemy submarines or destroyers. In 1939 no similar protective screen by fighter aircraft was obligatory against the threat of enemy aircraft. Anti-aircraft guns, it was thought, would suffice.

'The bomber will always get through' had been an accepted, heart-chilling truism since the phrase had first been used by Stanley Baldwin in 1934. It referred to the bombing of cities and did not apply, according to received Admiralty opinion, to battleships. Unfortunately this myopic view of air power at sea seemed to be confirmed in the first months of war. Both the RAF's and the *Luftwaffe*'s attempts to bomb the enemy's fleet were frustrated at heavy cost in aircraft, and operations at sea had a comforting *déjà vu* aspect. The process of clearing the oceans of German surface raiders went ahead with varying success, just as it had in 1914.

There was never any threat that the *Kriegsmarine* would break out and challenge the battle fleet at Scapa Flow. It had not done so in the First World War, to the chagrin of the RN and the British public. This time Germany did not even possess a battle fleet for such a challenge. Germany's new battleships were still under construction – and very formidable they would be when finished. But for the time being the RN's concern was with Germany's two powerful battle-cruisers, the *Gneisenau* and *Scharnhorst*, her three 'pocket battleships' – fast, tough and armed with heavy 11-inch guns – and her new heavy cruisers. All these modern warships could be highly dangerous when let loose among the sketchily protected convoys in the North Atlantic and unescorted ships in the South Atlantic and the Indian Ocean.

Admiral Sir William Tennant, a captain in 1939, once made this comment on the naval situation at the outbreak of the Second World War:

The Germans almost starved us to death in 1917. I believe that there was only food for about three weeks. They were operating then with U-boats not nearly as sophisticated as twenty-two years later, and although they had in service only about thirty ocean-going boats, we knew that they would be building them faster than ever as soon as they saw we were in the war seriously and not just as a temporary gesture. I feared that we were in for a bad time, and I was right.[2]

Winston Churchill, First Lord of the Admiralty as he had been in 1914 when German raiders threatened British lifelines, wrote:

Although it was the U-boat menace from which we suffered most and ran the greatest risks, the attack on our ocean commerce by surface raiders would have been even more formidable could it have been sustained. The three German pocket battleships permitted by the Treaty of Versailles had been designed with profound thought as commerce-destroyers. Their six 11-inch guns, their 26-knot speed, and the armour they carried had been compressed with masterly skill into the limits of a ten-thousand-ton displacement.* No single British cruiser could match them. The German 8-inch-gun cruisers were more modern than ours, and if employed as commerce-raiders, would also be a formidable threat. Besides this the enemy might use disguised heavily-armed merchantmen. We had vivid memories of the

---

* In fact nearer 12,000 tons.

depredations of the *Emden* and *Koenigsberg* in 1914, and of the thirty or more warships and armed merchantmen they had forced us to combine for their destruction.[3]

Two of these pocket battleships were despatched from Germany before war was declared. Their performance was a grave disappointment to Hitler and started the decline of the German leader's confidence in his surface fleet. Like Napoleon Bonaparte, Hitler had no appreciation of sea warfare or its importance, nor did Hitler share the Kaiser's fascination with the German Navy and its ships. The first of these pocket battleships, the *Deutschland*, did no credit to her name, which was subsequently changed to *Lützow*. She sank two ships in the North Atlantic, and then was ordered home and arrived back in port on 15 November 1939.

Her consort did better in the South Atlantic and Indian Ocean. She was named *Admiral Graf Spee* after the First World War admiral who created havoc in the Pacific Ocean. Spee sank a pair of British cruisers sent to intercept his squadron, and died valiantly fighting an overwhelmingly superior enemy off the Falkland Islands. The *Graf Spee*'s captain was Hermann Langsdorff, who opened his campaign on 30 September by sinking a British liner off Pernambuco. By contrast with 1914 almost every merchantman now carried radio, and the track of the *Graf Spee* could be roughly traced by the RRR calls made by the raider's victims. However, Captain Langsdorff rapidly altered his areas of operation, from the Indian Ocean to the Cape, and then back into the South Atlantic.

On 2 December she sank the liner *Doric Star*, the following day the *Tairoa*, and another big ship on 7 December. Unlike the U-boats, Langsdorff gave plenty of warning of his intentions, captured the crews and transferred them into his supply ship, the *Altmark*, without any loss of life.

The British responded by forming hunting groups, which included battle-cruisers and French and British fast battleships and no fewer than five carriers, as well as a number of heavy and light cruisers. Raider hunting at sea is governed by the advantage for the raider of surprise and easy concealment over the vast wastes of ocean, while the hunters must employ many ships spread out over thousands of square miles if they are to have any chance of tracking down their quarry. On the other hand the hunter is handicapped by supply restrictions, especially of ammunition if he is successful in his mission, and if damaged, however lightly, will have grave repair problems. For example, Spee in 1914 expended half his ammunition in sinking the British cruisers, and almost all that he had left in attempting to defend himself later.

Commodore Henry Harwood, with three cruisers which, together, were no match for the firepower of the *Graf Spee*, anticipated Langsdorff's decision to steer for the rich pickings off the River Plate, and with brilliant timing intercepted the pocket battleship just after 6.00 a.m. on the morning of 13 December 1939, twenty-five years almost to the day after Spee himself had been intercepted by the Royal Navy in South Atlantic waters.

This time, however, the advantage was with the Germans. The *Graf Spee* opened accurate fire on the largest British ship, the 8-inch-gunned *Exeter*, and was soon hitting her with deadly effect. Harwood split his force into two so that the *Exeter* and the two cruisers, *Ajax* and *Achilles*, with only 6-inch guns, engaged the enemy from widely divergent quarters.

The range rapidly closed from 20,000 to 12,000 yards, with 'David' Harwood inflicting some damage on the 'Goliath' *Admiral Graf Spee*, but the *Exeter* losing four of her six guns and most of her bridge personnel in reply. Both sides used smoke to conceal their manoeuvres, the *Exeter* eventually having to retire from the battle, burning fiercely and listing.

'We might just as well be bombarding her with a lot of bloody snowballs,' Harwood said later. However, the two little cruisers hammered away with their peashooters, aggravating and unnerving the German commander, while the *Ajax* had two of her turrets disabled. 'I therefore decided to break off the day action and try to close in again after dark,' Harwood reported. But at the same time it was observed with surprise and satisfaction that the Germany ship was evidently heading for sanctuary in the estuary of the River Plate.

Captain W.E.Parry of the *Achilles* concluded:

My own feelings were that the enemy could do anything he wanted to. He showed no signs of being damaged; his main armament was still firing accurately, the *Exeter* was evidently out of it, and so he had only two small cruisers to prevent his attacking the very valuable River Plate trade. It was therefore rather astonishing to find the enemy steaming off at a fairly high speed to the westward.[4]

The British squadron had fought gallantly against odds, and had manoeuvred so cleverly and worried at the *Graf Spee* so effectively that she was glad to leave the ring, the loser on points. It was a craven act after an incompetently handled fight. Langsdorff did not seem to understand that he had the three cruisers at his mercy. The *Graf Spee* was due back home in a week or two anyway, and what a welcome the victor of the Battle of the River Plate would have received, and what a tonic for the German people!

Instead, Captain Langsdorff received the permission of the Uruguayan authorities to remain in Montevideo for seventy-two hours to carry out repairs, bury her dead and bring her wounded ashore. The British authorities protested, then sedulously began spreading intelligence intended to demoralize the German captain, while numerous false radio messages convinced Langsdorff that if he left Montevideo he would face certain destruction at the hands of a newly arrived force comprising the 15-inch-gunned battle-cruiser *Renown* and the carrier *Ark Royal*.

After communicating with Berlin Langsdorff weighed anchor, steamed out into the river and hove to. The crew were then taken off.

Something extraordinary was about to take place [recalled the British Naval Attaché in Buenos Aires]. The great crowd immediately below us, denied their sight of a battle, was quite hushed. What was going to happen? Time passed in considerable speculation and suspense, but the truth, unlikely though it appeared, was beginning to dawn on some of us.

Exactly as the sun set behind her, a great volume of smoke billowed up – and an enormous flash was followed in due course by the boom of a large explosion. So the *Graf Spee* met her end.

Darkness comes quickly in those latitudes, and as we watched the sky darkened into a black background against which huge flames licked up against the underside of dense rolling clouds from the burning fuel-oil.[5]

Photographs of her last moments were published throughout the world, except in Germany.

Shortly after, Commodore Harwood brought his severely battered ships in as close as he could outside territorial waters. It was, he said, 'a magnificent and most cheering sight'. The *Renown* and *Ark Royal* were still a thousand miles distant.

But that was not an end to the business. Although Langsdorff had authority to scuttle his ship if he felt it necessary, the shame was too much for him. 'I can now only prove by my death that the Fighting Services of the Third Reich are ready to die for the honour of the flag,' he began his suicide note. Then he put a pistol to his head and shot himself.

The *Graf Spee* victory greatly cheered the British people at a time when spirits were low, a stalemate prevailed and the winter was particularly bleak. The navy, it was seen, was the only service doing any fighting; and this view was supported by a related action off the Norwegian coast two months later.

Captured British sailors, released from the pocket battleship at Montevideo according to international law, revealed that some three hundred more crew members were still onboard the *Altmark*. Churchill determined that this ship must be intercepted before she could reach Germany. The *Altmark* almost slipped through the net by steaming high up into the sub-Arctic and then down the Norwegian coast inside territorial waters. She was eventually spotted in a remote fjord by Captain Philip Vian of the *Cossack*, a dashing and fearless destroyer commander. Legally, the situation was tricky. Norway was neutral, and two of her gunboats stood by the *Altmark* to prohibit interference after, or so the officers in command claimed, they had confirmed that the vessel was unarmed and carried no prisoners.

Vian reported what was happening to Churchill, who told him to board and search the *Altmark*. If the Norwegian gunboats fired on the destroyer, 'you should not reply unless attack is serious, in which case you should defend yourself, using no more force than is necessary, and ceasing fire when she desists'.

Emulating Drake and John Hawkins on the Spanish Main, Vian pursued the *Altmark* when she tried to ram the destroyer, forced her to run aground, came alongside, grappled the two ships and sent in a boarding-party armed with rifles and fixed bayonets. There was a sharp hand-to-hand fight in which four German sailors were killed and others injured. The rest of the *Altmark*'s crew fled ashore, and Vian took the ship and began a search for the prisoners which the Germans and the Norwegians had denied were onboard.

Voices and banging were heard. Vian's men forced open a hatchway, crying 'The navy's here!' In all 299 men, who had faced certain imprisonment for the duration, were released.

This was all good, exciting G.A.Henty stuff in February 1940, and everyone in Britain felt the better for it. But what Churchill was to call the 'Twilight War' was growing darker; there was a whiff of menace in the cold winter winds. Poland had long since been subjugated and carved up by the two dictatorships of Soviet Communism and German Nazism. On land all was quiet on the Western Front, and had been since 3 September 1939. Aside from sporadic exchanges and raids, unlike the First World War the Allied and German armies were content to lie behind their defences, the Siegfried Line and the Maginot Line. The French, fearing another bloodbath like 1914–18, were against doing anything that might provoke the enemy, refusing to agree to the RAF dropping mines into the River Rhine, leaving British bombers with nothing to do but drop propaganda leaflets over German cities.

Only at sea was the war real and earnest. The Royal Navy despised the term 'phoney war'. 'It was never "phoney" for us,' Lord Louis Mountbatten, commander of a flotilla of extremely busy destroyers, remarked. 'It was the most strenuous winter I've ever known. And the most uncomfortable.'[6] He could have added, 'and the most dangerous'.

In Britain [Captain Stephen Roskill has written] the winter of 1939–40 was referred to as the 'phoney' or 'twilight' war; because the great armies facing each other on the continent sparred without coming to grips, and the hail of bombs which we had expected to fall on our cities did not materialise. But for the Royal Navy the period was anything but 'phoney', since from the very first day its ships were working at full stretch, contacts with the enemy were frequent, and considerable losses were suffered. Moreover, the turn of the year brought an exceptionally severe spell of wintry weather, and for weeks on end conditions in the English Channel and North Sea, let alone in the high latitudes where the Home Fleet cruised and searched, resembled those with which we were to become familiar later in the Arctic Ocean.[7]

After the sinking of the *Athenia*, ship losses continued at a level depressingly reminiscent of the First World War, though not as bad as the terrifying figures of, say, April 1917, when almost a million tons of ships were sunk. Air escort had proved to be one of the most effective means of deterring U-boats in 1917–18. This, like much else, had been forgotten. RAF Coastal Command in 1939 possessed neither the skills nor the weapons to deal with U-boats; neither was RAF Fighter Command prepared for dealing with *Luftwaffe* bombing attacks on North Sea shipping, where losses were particularly heavy.

For a while the greatest menace was the mine the German Navy had perfected – an 'influence type' magnetic mine. Also forgotten over the years of peace was the fact that the British invented and actually laid a number of these mines in 1918 for the same reason that the Germans had developed them: they were very difficult to sweep. In November 1939 the Thames estuary and the east coast of England were almost closed to shipping after twenty-seven ships were lost to these mines. Fortuitously a single magnetic mine fell intact over land, and an extremely courageous naval officer stripped it and learned its secrets. With an urgency only Churchill could have instilled during the phoney war, means were devised to deal with this menace. A 'degaussing' process was fitted to all merchant ships sailing in home waters, and 'DWI' Wellington bombers fitted with large rings beneath their fuselage made their curious appearance in the sky.

The U-boat lessons of the First World War had been expensively learned, and another one that had been forgotten was the securing of bases against them. In 1914 the first fear of the C-in-C of the Grand Fleet based largely at Scapa Flow was that U-boats would gain entry into this large expanse of water and, like a gunman in a dark crowded hall, fire off its torpedoes with a fair chance that they would find a target.

Now the Royal Navy entered the Second World War with its chief base again insecure against U-boats, or for that matter air attack just as a number of officers had feared: two old anti-aircraft guns were the only land-based air defence. On the night of 13–14 October, *U-47* succeeded in penetrating the anti-submarine defences. The battleship *Royal Oak* made a fat target; the commander sent three torpedoes into her hull and slipped away in the darkness. The *Royal Oak* went down rapidly with the loss of over 800 of her company. Again as in 1914 the fleet was forced to vacate its main base while efforts were made to secure it against further attack. It was all very depressing.

The *Altmark* affair had highlighted the difficult situation of the Norwegians in a war from which, like Denmark and Sweden, they wished to remain aloof while – especially in the case of the Swedes – they profited from it to the utmost degree. Germany was strongly dependent for its armaments industry on the high-quality iron ore produced in Sweden. No Royal Navy blockade could prevent the trade across the Gulf of Bothnia and Baltic Sea; while far to the north the ore from the Swedish mines was transported through Narvik in northern Norway, when the Gulf was iced over, thence down the long indented coast inside territorial waters.

This was a great aggravation to the Allies, just as the free passage of U-boats down this coast had cost innumerable lives and numberless merchantmen in the First World War. Now, as in 1914–18, the Scandinavian countries were prepared to leave the liberation of Europe from the threat of tyranny to others, confident that they would not be involved.

The intransigence of the Norwegian Government had been demonstrated over the *Altmark* affair. Early in 1940 Churchill had, after a long struggle with the Foreign Office, persuaded the War Cabinet that it was essential to mine Norwegian coastal waters in order to force iron ore shipping out to sea where it could be seized as contraband. As a precaution against violent German response to this operation landing forces were embarked in cruisers to occupy four of the key Norwegian ports: Stavanger, Bergen, Trondheim and Narvik.

These plans were drawn up in co-operation with the French, the date being fixed for 5 April 1940. Then at the last minute the French again got cold feet and objected. R4, as the landings were code-named, was postponed and the troops disembarked. The consequences of this cancellation were catastrophic. The mines were duly laid on 8 April. The Norwegians were still busy protesting to Britain when they were suddenly assailed by a series of blows which made the British precautionary action appear trivial.

There were many ties of friendship and culture between the Germans and Norwegians. Since the rise of Nazism Joseph Goebbels's powerful propaganda machine had been directed at the Norwegian people and institutions. Protestations of eternal amity had drawn results, and there was a strong element of pro-Nazism in the country. The shock was therefore all the more severe when early on the morning of 9 April German forces landed from the sea and from the air at key points up the Norwegian coastline, occupied all seats of administration and communication, and, with the ruthless cruelty which the Poles had already experienced and which was to be suffered by most of the nations of Europe, stamped out all opposition.

As Winston Churchill was to write, 'The rapidity with which Hitler effected the domination of Norway was a remarkable feat of war and policy, and an enduring example of Germany thoroughness, wickedness and brutality.'[8]

The Norwegian invasion and occupation was also a brilliant example of how control of the sea – albeit brief control – could clear the way for a military landing. If the Royal Navy had been in the right place and with the superior strength it could so easily have mustered, the German forces would have been annihilated. But German deception was brilliant; the Admiralty's response dilatory and fumbling.

Hitler had agreed in principle to an invasion of Norway four months earlier, and had given the green light on 1 March 1940. The planning was meticulous, down to the last detail; the risk element was reduced to the minimum, with speed as the first ingredient for success. The entire German Navy was to be involved, with ten of the most powerful and modern destroyers landing the occupying force at Narvik, the most northerly of the ports.

German security was good. Allied security – thanks to the French –

was slack. But even for the Germans, in this age of electronics and air reconnaissance, it was impossible for an invasion to take place without warning. The German ships were sighted as they sailed up the coast of Jutland, close to the scene of the great naval clash of 1916, and the Admiralty was so informed. But intelligence misinterpreted the movement as a covering action to pass the two fast and formidable battle-cruisers *Gneisenau* and *Scharnhorst* into the Atlantic to prey on convoys.

There was little that the Norwegians themselves could do to oppose the invasion. The Royal Norwegian Navy was headed by two coast-defence vessels of 3,800 tons built in Britain in the last years of the nineteenth century, supported by several modern small destroyers, aged torpedo-boats and gunboats. Surprise, bluff and treachery brought swift and almost total success to the Germans. The two old coast-defence ships were blown apart in Narvik harbour. Elsewhere there was little resistance. Only at Oslo did the Germans pay a price. Here the new powerful German cruiser *Blücher*, carrying officers of the evil Gestapo and members of a puppet administration, was fired on by coastal batteries and sent to the bottom with torpedo hits along with over 1,000 men. There was further resistance, but the Germans promptly brought into action the weapon that was to seal the success of the campaign – air power. Airborne troops were landed outside the city and immediately occupied it.

In the Norwegian campaign that raged from that fateful morning of 8 April until the final British evacuation – the first of so many – in early June, the Royal Navy showed itself at its worst and best. Its fighting prowess and courage were beyond all praise; the overall control of the campaign by the Admiralty and Supreme War Council was reminiscent of those early months of the First World War; and the expensive failure was all too reminiscent of the Dardanelles catastrophe of 1915 which had led to Churchill's downfall. Now, so it seemed, it was all happening over again. The troubles stemmed from the initial misinterpretation of German intentions, followed by a number of confused or conflicting orders which led, for example, to the loss of a golden opportunity to knock out the German naval force in Bergen harbour. 'Looking back on this affair,' as Churchill later accepted, 'I consider that the Admiralty kept too close a control upon the Commander-in-Chief. . . .'[9]

But when the initiative was left in the hands of the men on the spot, individual gallantry was matched by tactical brilliance. Take the case of the destroyer *Glowworm*, and Lieutenant-Commander Gerard Roope, part of the covering force during the initial minelaying operation. After losing a man overboard in heavy weather the *Glowworm* became separated, and on endeavouring to catch up chanced upon two enemy destroyers, themselves part of the German covering force for the seizure of Narvik. With odds of more than two to one against her – the newest German destroyers were almost light cruisers – the *Glowworm* engaged the ships. Then out of the spume and mist loomed the towering shape of the 10,000-ton heavy cruiser *Hipper*. When the *Glowworm*'s torpedoes missed the German ship, Roope ordered the helm over and rammed it, doing considerable damage. Then, lying crippled and stationary in the water, the *Hipper* blew her to pieces. Neither the gallant Roope (posthumous Victoria Cross) nor the great majority of his men survived.

By speed, surprise, bold planning and execution Germany succeeded in landing sufficient troops to gain control of the whole country. But as control of the sea was regained by Britain it became possible for the Allies to make landings to counteract this German success, belated though these landings were. As Peter Kemp has written,

It was in the support and maintenance of these military operations that, for the next four to eight weeks, the main strength of the Navy was to be chiefly engaged .... Almost at once the naval, equally with the military, side of the campaign ran into difficulties. It was easy enough for the Navy to carry the Army and its supplies across the North Sea, to put it ashore at its appointed landing-places, and to improvise the necessary base installations. That was a traditional task, carried out with all the customary skill and accuracy....[10]

But, as Kemp then points out, a new element of an alarming nature suddenly made itself evident. German fighters and bombers had occupied the Norwegian airfields as soon as they were cleared by the army, and now proved to any remaining doubters that neither armies nor navies could operate effectively without supporting air power. At the Norwegian ports of Namsos and Aandalsnes, almost as soon as the Allied armies were put ashore plans had to be made for their withdrawal owing to the almost non-stop bombing and strafing from the air. When, with prodigies of effort, a single squadron of RAF fighters was landed, using a frozen lake as their airfield, they were instantly decimated by overwhelming numbers of German bombers and fighters.

The landings had been made at Namsos on 14 April and at Aandalsnes on the 17th. Not a man had been lost. Now at the end of the month it was the navy's unhappy duty to evacuate these tired and demoralized British, French and Polish troops. The port facilities had been smashed by bombing, the dockyard fires still smouldered. The Norwegian fjords were subject to dense fog at this time of the year; and to attempt an evacuation in daylight would amount to suicide.

So, under cover of darkness and showing no lights, the cruisers and destroyers inched their way to the shore. Four light cruisers, six destroyers and a transport embarked over 2,000 men before dawn broke at Aandalsnes, and the rest of the force were rescued again without loss the following night.

It was even trickier at Namsos where General Carton de Wiart, a ferocious, fearless one-eyed soldier, commanded a mixed force of 5,400 troops who had been fighting against hopeless odds with inadequate weapons and no air support for two weeks. On the night of 1 May 1940 Vice-Admiral

John Cunningham brought his mixed force of cruisers, destroyers and transports close inshore at dusk, only to face an impenetrable fog. One of the destroyers was commanded by Captain Lord Louis Mountbatten, a household name in social circles but still to make his mark in the navy.

> I asked permission for my division of four destroyers to evacuate the first night's contingent under the fog cover [said Mountbatten]. It seemed to me to be the only way of ensuring success. The moment permission was granted, I began a mad dash along the seventy or so miles of Norwegian coast to Namsos. It was 5 a.m. Suddenly the fog cleared, like a curtain pulled aside. A hundred yards ahead was a mass of half-submerged rocks. So it was full astern, and we missed them by yards. It also meant we couldn't continue with our plans, and all that day we played hide-and-seek with the German bombers, in and out of scattered fog banks.
>
> We tried again at nightfall – or twilight, because that's all you get at this time of the year. We went up the fjord at 26 knots, between the snow-capped peaks and the lush valleys with their wooden farmhouses. It was all incredibly peaceful, and I remember saying to myself, 'This can't be war. . . .' But it was!
>
> The last turn of the fjord revealed Namsos in flames. Every building was burning from a German bombardment. It seemed impossible that anyone could be alive, but there was old de Wiart, one eye gleaming defiance.
>
> The Germans really missed a trick not putting on a raid while we were taking on board these great numbers of men. There were thousands of them lined up on the jetties.[11]

'Lord Mountbatten managed to feel his way into the harbour,' General Carton de Wiart later wrote, 'and the other ships followed him in. It was a tremendous undertaking to embark the whole force in a night of three short hours, but the Navy did it and earned my undying gratitude.'[12]

But the German raiders did appear when the naval force was at sea. Ju87 Stuka dive-bombers and He111 medium bombers attacked in large numbers and with great determination. The first ship they sank was the French destroyer *Bison*. HMS *Afridi* succeeded in picking up most of her crew and her large contingent of soldiers. Then she too was hit, turned over and sank, with heavy loss of life. It was the one blemish on a remarkable record of naval success. The remainder of this armada succeeded in returning across the North Sea some five thousand men. In spite of these two setbacks and evacuations the War Council determined to persevere with the campaign at Narvik. If the Allies could succeed in capturing and holding this port it would remain an irritant to the Germans and would cut her off from the winter iron ore supplies upon which she depended.

The first phase of the Battle of Narvik was purely naval. Almost immediately after the arrival of the German naval force of big destroyers carrying the troops to occupy the town, and the loss of the two ancient Norwegian warships, Captain (D) B.A.W.Warburton-Lee of the 2nd Destroyer Flotilla was ordered 'to send some destroyers up to Narvik to make certain that no enemy troops land'. It was a forlorn order, typical of the dilatoriness of the high command.

Warburton-Lee had a high reputation in the service. Many officers thought that he would 'go to the top'. The 'H' class destroyers with which his flotilla was equipped were modern craft of 1,350 tons armed with four 4.7-inch guns in addition to their torpedo tubes. 'The fog of war' was deeply wrapped about the five destroyers as they groped their way into the fjord: visibility was no more than a cable-length and they lacked any knowledge of what they would find if they ever got into the harbour. As Captain Donald Macintyre has written,

The shoreline was invisible behind the curtain of snow for long stretches of the tortuous passage.... The bright lights of a local passenger steamer suddenly appeared as it steamed right through the line of darkened ships. Unaware of her narrow escape as wheels were put over and turbines screamed in reverse to claw the destroyer clear of collision, the steamer passed on and vanished in the snowfall.

The first grey light was growing as the flotilla passed through the Narrows into Ofotfiord – 15 miles to go. . . ,[13]

From the pilot station it was learned that the Germans had got there before them, and that they were in some strength, too. A sailor serving in Warburton-Lee's flotilla leader, HMS *Hardy*, later told of that fearful early morning of 10 May 1940:

When we sailed up the fjord to Narvik we did not know what we were going to meet. All we knew was that there was a big German force up there, but we did not know how big. We soon found out.

Almost before dawn we sailed in, in line ahead. Near Narvik we saw two ships. One was a German whaling factory and the other a British ship. Behind them were some German destroyers, bigger than we were.

There were plenty of other ships, but we did not have time to count them. We opened up with our torpedoes at the enemy destroyers, the destroyers all releasing 'tin fish' one after the other.

Two German destroyers were hit the first time. When our torpedo hit we saw a flash, and it was just as if some huge hand had torn the German ship in half. It just split into two.

With all those torpedoes going into the harbour, nearly every ship there seemed to be sunk. It was like a shambles.

Meanwhile, on shore the Germans had opened up at us with land batteries. Then we caught sight of two more German destroyers behind the other ships.[14]

It was a promising start. The Germans had been taken entirely by surprise, and paid the price. One of the surviving German destroyers fired a salvo of torpedoes at the British ships but none hit, and Warburton-Lee after withdrawing to assess the situation and check on the number of torpedoes he had left, led his ships into the harbour for a second attack. This time the gallant Captain's luck ran out.

When we had circled three parts of the way round, three German destroyers came out from the mouth of a fjord behind us, firing at a distance of about 3,000 yards.

First they shot wide, then they got on the target. Things got hot. The Germans got direct hits on us. It was then that Captain Warburton-Lee was hit. It was a bad blow. Lieutenant Cross, our signal officer, was killed, and Captain Warburton-Lee was obviously in a bad condition. Our navigating officer, Lieutenant Commander Gordon Smith, was also badly wounded.

The skipper's secretary, Lieutenant Stanning, took command. By this time we were in a worse condition than anybody else. But we had guns left, and kept them working against the big German destroyers that had engaged us. Then came more shells. Our steam-pipe was burst by a shell and the main feed-pipe as well. Soon the steering wouldn't work.

We ran into shallow water and grounded on the rocks about 300 to 400 yards from the shore. It was then that we got our last order on the ship. It came from Captain Warburton-Lee, and it was the last order he was ever to give. It was, 'Abandon ship. Every man for himself. And good luck.'

We piled overboard as best we could and swam ashore.

It was so cold that a moment after we had got into the water there was no feeling in our hands or feet. We had 100 yards to swim and at least another 200 yards to wade before we got ashore.

And all the time we were still under fire. German shells were dropping round us. They had seen we were in trouble and they let us have it.

Our torpedo officer, Lieutenant Heppell, was a real hero. He saved at least five men by swimming backward and forward between the ship and the shore, helping those who could not swim. Finally we got ashore, about 170 of us. Seventeen of us had been killed in the fight, and another two were missing.[15]

The *Hardy* was done for, and so was her mortally wounded commander. His men managed to get him on to a raft, which was towed ashore. But he died as he reached dry land, and later some Norwegians buried him on the spot. He was awarded the VC posthumously. The *Hunter*, too, was lost, the *Hotspur* seriously damaged, the *Hostile* slightly damaged. The outcome was about even in warships lost and damaged, but the British, with many times more destroyers than the German Navy, could afford the loss more readily than the Germans, and they had sunk every supply ship they could see and blown up an ammunition ship. And this was only the first phase in the Battle of Narvik.

The German naval commander at Narvik had to face the certainty of another attack and in a more powerful form. Its imminence was confirmed when German naval intelligence, which was 'reading' British signals without difficulty, passed on the information. This time there would be no surprise. The Germans prepared their defences with all their usual speed and skill, making full use of the numerous inlets and minor fjords to lay ambushes and co-ordinating the destroyers' 5-inch guns with shore batteries. There was a strong resolve to commit as much damage as possible to the British attackers before they were overwhelmed.

Vice-Admiral William Jock Whitworth flew his flag in the 15-inch-gunned battleship *Warspite*, and on the morning of 13 April led into the fjord a force of four new 'Tribal' class destroyers even more powerful than the German super-destroyers now helplessly trapped in Narvik, and five more smaller destroyers. Preceding this hunting pack was a reconnaissance aircraft catapulted from the battleship, which was able to signal back vital information of the enemy's dispositions. This plane, as a lucky bonus, caught a U-boat on the surface, dive-bombed it, making hits with its two bombs, and sank it there and then.

The gunfight opened when the British squadron faced three of the German super-destroyers which turned into line and boldly awaited the oncoming British ships. It soon turned into a confused mêlée within the confined space of the fjord.

With ships of both sides firing independently, the German destroyers weaving back and forth in a confusing pattern, and the British swerving to avoid the flights of torpedoes whose tracks could be seen streaking past or under them, spotting the fall of shot was impossible. As the Germans retired before the advancing British, keeping at the limit of visibility, the shooting on both sides became wild and quite ineffective. Frost and snow blurred gun and director telescopes. The gunfire echoed and rolled round the steep sides of the fjord, an occasional shattering blast as the 15-inch guns of the *Warspite* found a target adding to the sound and fury. The concussions dislodged clouds of snow from the hillsides which blew blindingly across the scene.

As Narvik was approached and the German destroyers stood for a time to fight, the range came down and ships came into clearer view of each other. The Germans began to take heavy punishment while they themselves were coming to the end of the meagre supply of ammunition.[16]

Before they succumbed the German ships succeeded in severely damaging two of the British destroyers; but one by one, like rats trapped in a shed, the German ships were knocked out, run aground or battered to pieces until they sank. By the end of it all every one of the ten destroyers – half of the total German flotilla strength – had been lost in the two battles. It had been a desperate, close action all the way, with no quarter given. And now the way was open for the Allied invasion fleet to land and drive the German contingent out of the town. . . .

The first and second Battles of Narvik had been fought with guns and torpedoes, an old-fashioned slogging match. But it was the new air weapon that dominated the Norwegian campaign. covering the German invasion, driving off the Allied counter-attack, picking off British light warships and damaging cruisers; even the mighty British battleship *Rodney* was hit, although the $6\frac{1}{4}$-inch deck armour prevented serious harm.

Whenever the Allies succeeded in bringing superior air strength to bear the tide of battle swung accordingly. And the first-ever sinking by bombing of a major warship was credited to the British Fleet Air Arm. Air reconnaissance spotted the lurking German cruiser *Königsberg* in Bergen harbour on the first day of the campaign. In a hastily mounted operation two squadrons of Skua dive-bombers took off from the Orkney Islands before dawn the next morning. The target across the North Sea was at the very limit of their range but by skilful navigation all the planes made an accurate landfall. The *Königsberg* was still there in the harbour, moored alongside a jetty. Without wasting a moment the Skuas went down with their 500-pound bombs. Between them they scored three direct hits, and a number of damaging near-misses. She was already going down when the planes left.

Weeks later, when a powerful, 25,000-strong Allied force belatedly landed at Narvik, they were able to drive out the Germans and capture the town only because the RAF had established airfields ashore and were operating modern fighters from them. But for only a few days. For, even while the Allies were scoring their first major success in Norway, Narvik suddenly became an irrelevance, a trivial sideshow, by contrast with events taking place hundreds of miles to the south. The *blitzkrieg* which had broken the Western Front stalemate on 10 May 1940 had taken the German Army into Belgium and the Netherlands, then into France. It was already sweeping towards Paris. Every Allied soldier, and every airman in Norway, was needed to stem the tide.

The final evacuation from Norway was carried out over the last days of May. The weary, disillusioned troops were taken off safely. The Norwegian royal family was also embarked, and troop transports and the large number of warships involved made their way south-west towards the Scottish and English coasts.

Even now there remained a sting in the German tail.

As the last hours of the Norwegian campaign ticked by, Squadron-Leader K.B.Cross, who commanded the last fighter squadron based near Narvik, was ordered to destroy his aircraft and embark his pilots and ground crews urgently. Previous experience had shown that the Hurricane fighter, lacking the required special equipment, could not be landed on a carrier's deck. Cross thought otherwise, and knew, too, how badly needed his Hurricanes were at home. At the last minute he got permission for his squadron to make the attempt. The carrier *Glorious* proceeded to sea, steamed at full speed into wind, and Cross led his squadron to her. One by one the Hurricanes approached astern and the pilots in turn, and without any previous experience, put their machines down safely.

The carrier now headed for home, escorted by two destroyers, the *Ardent* and *Acasta*. The battle-cruisers *Scharnhorst* and *Gneisenau* and the heavy cruiser *Hipper*, all repaired now from their various damage, left Kiel on 4 June. The German warships had already made several killings when, at 4 p.m. on 8 June, the two battle-cruisers sighted smoke to the west. Hastening towards it, the German Admiral recognized the inviting chunky shape of a carrier with no more than a pair of destroyers protecting her. At 4.30 p.m., at a range of over fifteen miles, he opened fire with his 11-inch guns.

The German shooting, as usual, was quick and accurate. Time and again the *Glorious* was struck, until by 5.20 p.m. it was clear that she was finished and the order to abandon ship was given. It was a sorry end for all those who had fought so hard and against heavy odds both at sea and in the air.

A young marine, Ronald Healiss, lived to describe in harrowing detail the destruction of his great ship:

... another salvo hit, and the whole side of the *Glorious* seemed to cave in, leaving a choking cloud of smoke and a thunderous roar that echoed away to the darkening sky. The sea, so calm before the action, was now churned up and flecked with grey. God, I thought, we've nearly had our chips! Stupefied, we waited. And I wish we hadn't. For that's when I saw Ginger McColl. He was walking over from his post ... holding on to crazily twisted rails of the ship and laughing at me.

'You're a lucky lot of sods, you are. You're all right. That was our gun, that was. Lifted the whole ruddy gun right out. Last I saw was that bloke Jarvis with it, looking as if he was holding the gun in his great mitt, like he holds a water-polo ball.'

Then I saw why he was walking oddly. His uniform was ragged, what was left of it. Just a torn shirt and part of his trousers. One leg was shot off, and there was the splintered bone, dripping red and black blood, and white strings of sinews. My throat was full of spittle and I could vomit just to look at him. I thought the world of Ginger.

'I must go and get this wrapped up,' was all he said, then hobbled off guiding his way through the smoke and clutching the twisted rail.[17]

The two destroyers did what they could to shield their charge from the overwhelming power of the two big German ships, making smoke and running in to deliver torpedo attacks. The *Ardent* was soon sunk. There was, it seemed, nothing more that the *Acasta* could do. But to turn tail and flee the scene was outside consideration. Her captain, Commander C. E. Glasfurd, decided on one last attack. One of his leading seamen, C. Carter, the only one of his company to survive, described the last minutes:

On board our ship, what a deathly calm, hardly a word spoken, the ship was now steaming full speed away from the enemy, then came a host of orders, prepare all smoke floats, hose-pipes connected up, various other jobs were prepared, we were still steaming away from the enemy, and making smoke, and all our smoke floats had been set going. The Captain then had the message passed to all positions: 'You may think we are running away from the enemy, we are not, our chummy ship (*Ardent*) has sunk, the *Glorious* is sinking, the least we can do is make a show, good luck to you all.' We then altered course into our own smoke-screen. I had the order stand by to fire tubes 6 and 7, we then came out of the smoke-screen, altered course to starboard firing our torpedoes from port side. It was then I had my first glimpse of the enemy, to be honest it appeared to me to be a large one and a small one, and we were very close. I fired my two torpedoes from my tubes, the foremost tubes fired theirs, we were all watching results. I'll never forget that cheer that went up; on the port bow of one of the ships a yellow flash and a great column of smoke and water shot up from her. We knew we had hit, personally I could not see how we could have missed so close as we were. The enemy never fired a shot at us, I feel they must have been very surprised. After we had fired our torpedoes we went back into our own smoke-screen, altered course again to starboard. 'Stand by to fire remaining torpedoes'; and this time as soon as we poked our nose out of the smoke-screen, the enemy let us have it. A shell hit the engine-room, killed my tubes' crew, I was blown to the after end of the tubes, I must have been knocked out for a while, because when I came to, my arm hurt me, the ship had stopped with a list to port. Here is something believe it or believe it not, I climbed back into the control seat, I see those two ships, I fired the remaining torpedoes, no one told me to, I guess I was raving mad. God alone knows why I fired them, but I did. The *Acasta*'s guns were firing the whole time, even firing with a list on the ship. The enemy then hit us several times, but one big explosion took place right aft. I have often wondered whether the enemy hit us with a torpedo, in any case it seemed to lift the ship out of the water. At last the Captain gave orders to abandon ship. I will always remember the Surgeon Lt, his first ship, his first action. Before I jumped over the side, I saw him still attending to the wounded, a hopeless task, and when I was in the water I saw the Captain leaning over the bridge, take a cigarette from a case and light it. We shouted to him to come on our raft, he waved 'Good-bye and good luck' – the end of a gallant man.[18]

Of the three sunk warships totalling 1,561 crew, only forty-five survived besides Seaman Carter. Squadron-Leader Cross was another, after enduring extremes of suffering on a raft which took the lives of twenty-five of twenty-six of his companions.

It was a miserable blow to end a miserable campaign. But the acts of courage, the moments of glory, shine out – not least that of Commander Glasfurd. For one of the *Acasta*'s torpedoes had indeed found its mark, badly damaging the *Scharnhorst* and forcing her to head for Trondheim, accompanied by the *Gneisenau*. A few hours distant were several weakly protected convoys carrying thousands of troops, and a cruiser conveying the Norwegian royal family to Scotland. All of them were ripe game and some or all of these vessels must have been intercepted had the battle-cruisers not withdrawn.

The benefits to Germany of the conquest of Norway were almost beyond calculation. Not only were the iron ore supplies secure, but all the Norwegian ports were free to be used by U-boats and surface men o'war, bringing the German bases effectively a thousand miles closer to the North Atlantic trade routes. This was to pay extra dividends after the German invasion of Russia when the Allies attempted to supply Russia from Arctic convoys to Murmansk. Britain was also cut off from all supplies of Swedish ore and other armament industry supplies like high quality ball-bearings.

In addition the Royal Navy had suffered badly in the two months of the campaign, for besides the *Glorious* there were lost two cruisers, a sloop and nine destroyers, with damage to other ships. On the other hand the naval cost to Germany was very much higher, actually and relatively. Besides the ten destroyers lost at Narvik, the *Blücher* at Stavanger and the *Königsberg* sunk by the Fleet Air Arm, another cruiser sunk by a British submarine and three U-boats, the Germans lost the use of both the *Gneisenau* and the *Scharnhorst*, as well as the *Lützow*, leaving them with just one heavy cruiser, two light cruisers and four destroyers for the critical weeks lying ahead, including the possible invasion of Britain.

As Winston Churchill put it: 'In their desperate struggle with the British Navy the Germans ruined their own, such as it was, for the impending climax.'[19] But of even greater importance in the long term was the indisputable fact that, leaving aside individual courage as demonstrated by the German destroyer crews at Narvik, the German Navy had not covered itself with glory or shown much of the spirit of the Kaiser's Navy in the First World War. Early in the campaign the very modern and very powerful *Gneisenau* and *Scharnhorst* had fled from the single elderly and thinly armoured British battle-cruiser *Renown*, after receiving some sharp punishment. Again the *Gneisenau* had not proceeded alone with her convoy-hunting after her sister ship had been damaged by the *Acasta*; and the *Hipper* had left Trondheim too late to join the opportunity of committing severe damage to British shipping.

Hitler liked none of this. Nor had he liked to hear that when in superior strength the Narvik destroyers had not annihilated the British destroyers of Warburton-Lee, and then had been annihilated themselves three days later. He was furious at the loss of the brand new *Blücher* to the puny Norwegian defences of Oslo Fjord, and much else concerning the conduct of his navy. All this displeasure he made clear to Grand-Admiral Erich Raeder, the Commander-in-Chief of German Naval Forces.

For the British Navy, now about to face another evacuation that made Narvik seem a very small party, the lessons of Norway were as slow to sink in as they generally have been in an essentially conservative service. The fact that they had transported some 30,000 men and their equipment safely across the North Sea and brought most of them safely home; that they had lost relatively few ships to bombing and that the only battleship hit by a bomb had shrugged off the blow; that ship-for-ship they had put up at least as good a show as the more modern German Navy: all this seemed to confirm that their concept was right and that they had done well. After all, it was the gun and the torpedo which had done the most damage to both sides.

The bomber was seen now as a definite danger but not a mortal one to surface ships, and air cover was thought highly desirable, but not vital. As one destroyer commander expressed the view of the navy after it was all over:

It is [he wrote] very far from being a triumph of air over sea. In spite of the total absence of air cover, short nights and perfect weather, I do not think any essential sea or landing operation has not come off. And escort vessels, solitary and stationary in fjords, have been constantly maintained. But of course you can't go on for ever in what amounts to enemy coastal waters if he has all the air; and the wretched and undefended troops can't go on at all.[20]

The battleship, then, remained in British eyes the capital ship even after the Norwegian campaign. It was not a view shared by officers of the Fleet Air Arm, however; nor was it the view of Admiral Isoroku Yamamoto, whose plans for an all-air attack upon the main base of the American Fleet were soon to mature.

CHAPTER TWO

Amphibious Warfare

There had never before been a military campaign so swift and implacable as the descent of the German armies on Belgium, the Netherlands, Luxembourg and France in May 1940. It was indeed the *blitzkrieg*, the lightning war, with German tanks punching through demoralized armies, outflanking the forts and fixed defences of France's vaunted Maginot Line, creating chaos among civilians and soldiers alike. 'The Battle of France', Captain Basil Liddell-Hart has written, 'is one of history's most striking examples of the decisive effect of a new idea, carried out by a dynamic executant.'[1] This executant was General Heinz Guderian, and his enthusiastic sponsor, Adolf Hitler.

As in Norway, the appreciation and the use of air power in support of advancing armies had shown the world the shape of future military success. The French and British air forces in France had been overwhelmed in the first hours of the German break-out of 10 May. The small professional British Army had been harried throughout their withdrawal and continued to suffer as they reached the ultimate point of their retreat: the sea.

Ironically, and mercifully for Western civilization, the advance was so swift, and the success so bewildering, that the perpetrators could no more believe what was happening than the generals of the fleeing and demoralized defending armies. Suddenly, without logical reason, Hitler lost his nerve, removed Guderian from command, and ordered the massive and triumphant machine to slow down. Advanced tanks and motorized forces, happily refuelling from French filling stations, airborne forces which had caused cities to fall, advanced infantry well supported by mobile artillery, all lost their momentum overnight. Before they were permitted to proceed with their conquest the greater part of the British Expeditionary Force and many thousands of French soldiers were granted a stay of execution. This intermission, thanks to British sea power, they were able to use to escape from the German panzer divisions, just as the Royal Navy off Norway had succeeded in bringing home almost all the land forces from that expedition.

In less than two weeks from the first German strike the greater part of the BEF and tens of thousands of French soldiers were contemplating their annihilation on the approaches and on the beaches of the Channel port of Dunkirk. With control of the sea as well as of the air and land, there would have been nothing to halt the Germans from wiping out the British land forces and crossing the Channel. It would have been all over within days. For the first time in almost a thousand years Great Britain would be conquered and enslaved, as the Germans were to enslave the people of most of Western Europe and to the east from the Gulf of Finland to the Sea of Azov.

On 14 June 1940 units of the Germany Army marched down the Champs Elysées in Paris. They could have been marching down the Mall from Buckingham Palace to the Admiralty a few weeks later but for the sea power represented and controlled by that Admiralty, and some 600 single-seat fighter aircraft. The emergency evacuation of an army from a foreign beach was a novel, dangerous and immensely complicated operation. But by 22 May, working at a pace and with an urgency that was to seize the whole nation during the following critical weeks, plans were complete, light naval craft and hundreds of small boats assembled. This operation, reflecting the spirit of crisis, was code-named 'Dynamo'.

The hazards that lay ahead for the Royal Navy were foreshadowed by the immediate need to take off two Guards battalions and other troops from the besieged French Channel port of Boulogne. Only destroyers were suitable for this task, and in daylight and darkness, under fire from German artillery and while suffering heavy losses, all but 1,400 of the Allied troops were got away. These last were picked up from a jetty in darkness by a single destroyer, which could scarcely operate its guns for the massed humanity on its narrow decks. Five of the destroyers were damaged from the air or from shore artillery.

Operation 'Dynamo' was put into effect at 7.00 p.m. on Sunday, 26 May 1940. Across the narrow strip of Channel, which could be traversed in forty-five minutes by a destroyer and in five minutes by a fighter plane, were some 400,000 men, trapped within their own defence line, short of supplies and food, and desperately tired from an arduous and demoralizing retreat. That morning there was a service of intercession and prayer in Westminster Abbey, and up and down the land churchgoers knelt in prayer for a miraculous deliverance.

'The House', Winston Churchill was to declare in the Commons, 'should prepare itself for hard and heavy tidings.' And on that same Sunday the C-in-C of the British Expeditionary Force telegraphed to the Secretary of State for War, 'I must not conceal from you that a great part of the BEF and its equipment will inevitably be lost, even in best circumstances.' He was right about the equipment.

There was no reason to believe that this mass evacuation would be possible before the panzers overran the town of Dunkirk and its port. The Germans were bringing in more and more armour, artillery and men to batter down the puny defences. German bombers were increasingly active and – so it seemed to those on the ground – unmolested. Any ship approaching Dunkirk must brave the natural hazards of the sandbanks and the tides, the fixed minefields and magnetic mines dropped nightly by German aircraft, fast motor torpedo- ('E') boats, artillery fire from the shore, and bombs and machine-gun fire from the air.

The first vessel in the first flotilla to be despatched was the *Mona's Queen*, an Isle of Man packet-boat which had been used for some weeks on supply operations across the Channel, and now faced her most hazardous run. It was 9.15 p.m. when she steamed out from the Downs. Calais to the west was falling and the Germans already had coastal guns in position. Captain R.Duggan reported:

We were shelled from the shore by single guns and also by salvos from shore batteries. Shells were flying all round us, the first salvo went over us, the second, astern of us. I thought the next salvo would hit us but fortunately it dropped short, right under our stern. The ship was riddled with shrapnel, mostly all on the boat and promenade decks. Then we were attacked from the air. A Junkers bomber made a power dive towards us and dropped five bombs, but he was off the mark too, I should say about 150 feet from us. All this while we were still being shelled, although we were getting out of range. The Junkers that bombed us was shot down and crashed into the water in front of us (no survivors). Then another Junkers attacked us, but before he reached us he was brought down in flames.[2]

The town was blazing, too, an enormous pall of smoke rising into the sky. The ship was shelled as she entered the harbour, but she rapidly embarked 1,420 men. Her propellers were fouled, her decks strafed by another German plane – eighty-two casualties – but she got out with only superficial damage and reached Dover the following morning.

That night, the following day, and for several days and nights after, an amazing marine exodus took place from the harbours, estuaries and creeks of south-east and eastern England, manned by the boats' owners, volunteers and naval personnel, all heading for Dover and the Downs. Liners in London's docks had their lifeboats requisitioned, laid-up little skiffs, ocean racing yachts, 'anything that can float', some 400 vessels in all, assembled off the white cliffs; they were shuffled into some sort of order and despatched across the Channel.

By great good fortune the seas remained calm, and cloud cover restricted to some degree the depredations of German bombers. Among the hundreds of volunteers, many of them weekend yachtsmen who enjoyed 'messing about in boats', was Charles Herbert Lightoller, who had been involved in the *Titanic* tragedy back in 1912 and had been the senior surviving officer. He had been responsible for the rescue of many passengers. Now, as a retired Naval Reserve commander who owned a sixty-foot yacht, the *Sun-downer*, berthed up the Thames at Chiswick, he set off on another mercy mission. With his son and a Sea Scout friend they ran down river at their maximum of 10 knots. *En route* for Dunkirk they made their first rescue, the crew of a motor boat. Then Lightoller brought his yacht into the chaos and carnage of Dunkirk and began embarking the weary, filthy, unshaven men, his son Roger loading the 'cargo' below decks.

At fifty I called below, 'How are you getting on?' getting the cheery reply, 'Oh plenty of room yet'. At seventy-five my son admitted they were getting pretty tight – all equipment and arms being left on deck.

I now started to pack them on deck, having passed word below for every man to lie down and keep down, the same applied on deck. By the time we had fifty on deck, I could feel her getting distinctly tender, so took no more. Actually we had exactly 130 on board.

Whilst entering [harbour at Ramsgate], the men started to get to their feet and she promptly went over to a terrific angle. I got them down again in time and told those below to remain below and lying down until I gave the word. The impression ashore was that the fifty-odd lying on my deck plus the mass of equipment was my full load.

After I had got rid of those on deck I gave the order 'Come up from below,' and the look on the official face was amusing to behold as troops vomited up through the forward companionway, the after companionway, and the doors either side of the wheelhouse. As a stoker Petty Officer, helping them over the bulwarks, said, 'God's truth, mate! Where did you put them?' He might well ask. . . .[3]

Many of the rescue attempts were not as neat and successful as this. Several of the 'little boats' turned back at the sight of the bomb and shell bursts in the water, of diving German aircraft and of burning, sinking ships. And it was not all glorious courage among the troops, either. There was sporadic fighting among the men to get on board and officers had to use their revolvers to restore order. But one of the miracles of 'the miracle of Dunkirk', as it came to be called, was the relative order and discipline that was maintained; and the sterling efforts of the weekend yachtsmen and others who, untrained for battle, found themselves in the midst of one. A number of them died or were wounded.

None of this mass rescue would have been possible without the presence of the navy. It was the navy that provided the protection from German surface ships, the navy that fought against the German bombers and fighters, shooting many of them down, and it was the navy that carried the vast majority of those who were rescued, and suffered the most damage. All were light craft – destroyers, sloops, corvettes, gun-boats, minesweepers, trawlers and drifters, anything that could get close inshore. The destroyers, racing to and fro during the days and nights of the evacuation, into Dunkirk harbour while it was still usable, standing off the mole or offshore, were the mainstay throughout and suffered most, nineteen of the thirty-nine engaged being damaged and six more sunk.

No fewer than 226 boats of all kinds went to the bottom, including the *Mona's Queen*, some carrying their passengers down with them, others being relieved of their troops by the ubiquitous destroyers before sinking. There were cases of rescued soldiers being sunk twice on the way home.

As the days went by the numbers brought ashore rose to figures never believed possible when the evacuation was first planned: 100,000, then 200,000; 68,014 on 31 May alone. In the early hours of 4 June the last troops were evacuated. At 2.30 a.m. some French trawlers, packed with soldiers fresh from fighting the advancing Germans, emerged from the harbour and puttered towards Dover. At 2.40 a.m. the destroyer *Malcolm* with Scottish troops onboard – some playing the bagpipes – got under way. A few minutes before 3.00 a.m. the destroyer *Express* slipped her lines, and then the *Shikari*, the last of the British warships. It was all over.

Walter Lord graphically describes the final scene:

At 3.20 *Shikari* finally cast off – the last British warship to leave Dunkirk.

But not the last British vessel. Occasional motorboats were still slipping out, as Captain Dangerfield's two block ships reached the designated spot. With helms hard over, they attempted to line up at right angles to the Channel, but once again the tide and current were too strong. As on the previous night, the attempt was largely a failure. Hovering nearby, *MA/SB 10* picked up the crews.

Dawn was now breaking, and Lieutenant Cameron decided to take *MTB 107* in for one last look at the harbour. For nine days the port had been a bedlam of exploding bombs and shells, the thunder of artillery, the hammering of anti-aircraft guns, the crash of falling masonry; now suddenly it was a graveyard – the wrecks of sunken ships ... abandoned guns ... empty ruins ... silent masses of French troops waiting hopelessly on the pierheads and the eastern mole. There was nothing a single, small motorboat could do; sadly, Cameron turned for home. 'The whole scene', he later recalled, 'was filled with a sense of finality and death; the curtain was ringing down on a great tragedy.'

But there were still Englishmen in Dunkirk, some of them very much alive. Lieutenant Jimmy Langley, left behind because the wounded took up too much room in the boats, now lay on a stretcher at the 12th Casualty Clearing Station near the outskirts of town. The station – really a field hospital – occupied a huge Victorian house in the suburb of Rosendaël. Capped by an odd-looking cupola with a pointed red roof, the place was appropriately called the Château Rouge.[4]

A great tragedy and a great triumph. The obvious tragic element was the loss of those left behind, the loss of so many lives during the evacuation, the loss of war materials – most of the men came back empty-handed – and the loss of morale any defeat in the field must bring. The aftermath also brought some bitterness. Veterans of the Great War of 1914–18 who had fought off so many German attacks were scathing about what they regarded as a swift retreat in the face of the enemy. There was bitterness, too, among many of those rescued directed towards the RAF because their valiant and often successful attempts to drive off the German bombers were largely unwitnessed. Cloud or the distance from the beach-head when the German bombers fell from the sky obscured their work.

The triumphant element was witnessed in two main ways. First, the men were back to fight again: 'The boys are home!' as the newspapers proclaimed in huge headlines alongside pictures of 'Tommy Atkins', leaning out of a train window, forehead bandaged, thumb raised, fag clamped between his grinning lips. The Royal Navy's evacuation of 338,000 men from the ruins of northern France was indeed a triumph. But as Churchill warned Parliament in a speech later in the day when that last torpedo boat had quit the devastated port, 'We must be very careful not to assign to this deliverance the attributes of a victory. Wars are not won by evacuations....'

The shock of Dunkirk, the nature and extent of this defeat, the fall of France a few days later, the realization that Britain had lost her only European ally and, with her Empire and Commonwealth overseas, stood alone against the might of the new German Empire; the knowledge that the nation was more vulnerable to invasion and conquest than for 900 years: all this led to a sharpening of determination and an inspiration of warlike spirit, as mighty and memorable as that aroused in the American people by Pearl Harbor eighteen months later.

If the Royal Navy's prime task must be – as it always has been – to secure the nation's commerce against her enemies, the secondary task is to transport military forces to enemy shores, to keep them supplied and to evacuate them where this unfortunate necessity arises. It arose all too often in the early years of the Second World War. A third task, hardly less important than the first two, was to transport Imperial and Dominion forces to Britain and to the one fighting front overseas where Britain could go on the offensive in 1940 – North and East Africa.

At a conveniently safe and advantageous moment in June 1940 Italy had entered the war on Germany's side. The situation had long been anticipated, and the navy's immediate concern was to reinforce the Mediterranean Fleet, denuded in 1939, in order to keep the sea lanes to the Near and Far East open to Allied traffic, and to reinforce the army in Egypt in preparation for an offensive against the enemy forces in Italian North African possessions.

Churchill had left the Admiralty to supersede Neville Chamberlain as Prime Minister on the first day of the German offensive in the West, a day when the war in Europe suddenly became real and recognized by the rest of the world, 10 May 1940. After striving with all his will and resolve to keep France in the war, Churchill was obliged to face the reality of fighting on alone against Germany and, from 10 June, Italy also. In fact Britain was not alone, for besides the numbers of 'Free' French, Belgians, Dutch, Polish and Norwegian fighting men who had escaped from their homelands to continue the fight, powerful forces were again heading for Britain and the Middle East from Canada, Australia and New Zealand, South Africa and India, the Caribbean and other colonies.

In Churchill the Allies now had a leader who despised a defensive policy and whose martial spirit was conditioned by positivism. It was, after all, defeatism and fear of taking the offensive which had led to the surrender of the French Army to an inferior number of German troops.

'My first reaction to the "Miracle of Dunkirk"', Churchill wrote, 'had been to turn it to proper use by mounting a counter-offensive. When so much was uncertain, the need to recover the initiative glared forth.... I made haste to strike the note which I thought should rule our minds and inspire our actions at this moment.' [5]

Translated into naval action this meant that, no sooner had the last soldier been returned from France than preparations had to be considered for landing military forces back on the continent of Europe. That day might still be distant in time but Churchill recognized that an invasion and the defeat of the German Army was the only way of winning the war.

On the same day when the destroyer *Shikari* embarked the last soldier from France Churchill despatched a minute to General Hastings Ismay, head of the Military Wing of the War Cabinet Secretariat:

The completely defensive habit of mind which has ruined the French must not be allowed to ruin all our initiative [ran one passage of this minute]. It is of the highest consequence to keep the largest numbers of German forces all along the coasts of the countries they have conquered, and we should immediately set to work to organize parties on these coasts where the populations are friendly. [6]

Plans and preparations moved swiftly in that critical summer of 1940 and by July Churchill had set up a Combined Operations Command responsible for offensive operations along the greatly extended enemy coastline from north Norway to the south of France. Raids against heavily defended targets had acquired a bad reputation as a result of the Dardanelles catastrophe in 1915, and the much smaller raid in 1918 on Zeebrugge, which was intended to block up a major U-boat base and tragically failed to do so.

The leader of this 1918 raid, and a strong supporter of Churchill's Dardanelles expedition, was a fearless, ferocious sailor called Roger Keyes, in 1940 an Admiral of the Fleet aged sixty-seven years, loaded with decorations and highly frustrated by inaction. 'It is sad that in this war ... I have only been able to act offensively by word of mouth which is not my strong suit,' [7] he wrote to Churchill on 4 July. A few days later Churchill replied in the best way possible to please the old fire-eater by appointing him to command Combined Operations. It was a typically quirky appointment made out of affection, admiration and gratitude for past support. Churchill had always had a soft spot for old admirals even if one of them – Jackie Fisher – had ruined his political career in 1915. Keyes's reply was equally typical of the man: 'I must tell you how happy I am – and that I am most grateful to you for giving me this opportunity of proving that I am not as useless as my detractors, whoever they may be, would have you think.' [8]

Neither the creation of this command nor the appointment of Keyes, a man whose tact was in inverse ratio to his courage, was popular with the other services. The grabbing of a share of the inadequate supplies of almost every form of war material was already competitive enough without the intervention of a new force, and one which had the backing of the Prime Minister. Wherever he turned for men, armaments and landing-craft he was met with obstructionism. The Admiralty, which regarded him as a nuisance and a has-been, was especially hostile. No planned raids could be undertaken in 1940 because of the lack of supplies of all kinds, and Keyes's eager commandos were temporarily transferred to anti-invasion defensive duties.

In spite of Churchill's active backing the proposed seizure of the island of Pantelleria in the Mediterranean was eventually 'killed' by the Combined Chiefs of Staff and the C-in-C of the Mediterranean Fleet. Keyes continued to fume and fight until Churchill at last saw the error he had made, and with extreme reluctance replaced him with a naval captain twenty-eight years his junior.

This step marked the end of one praiseworthy naval career and the beginning of another. Captain Lord Louis Mountbatten, fresh from having his destroyer sunk under him in the Mediterranean, accepted the responsibility gladly. Mountbatten recalled:

I had been visiting Pearl Harbor [October 1941] and was in Los Angeles when I got a message from Winston. It just said, 'We want you home here at once for something which you will find of the highest interest.' I stopped off in Washington just long enough to warn Admiral Stark about the vulnerability of Pearl Harbor, and raced for home. Winston said, 'I want you to turn the south coast of England from a bastion of defence into a springboard of attack.' It was a job that suited me perfectly.[9]

In a trice Mountbatten had Combined Ops HQ reorganized from top to bottom, with new and eager staff at work, new priorities and plans, and young blood coursing through the veins of a demoralized and disappointed command. Mountbatten was ten times as clever as Keyes, five times faster in everything that he did, and possessed not only tact and charm but had access to everybody – the King (his cousin), Churchill, the First Sea Lord and all the members of the combined Chiefs of Staff, to which he was soon appointed, together with promotion to Admiral.

The first raid took place on the night of 27–28 February 1942, from the 'springboard' of the south coast to Bruneval, on the north coast of enemy-occupied France. Its object was to seize a strongly guarded, new and highly dangerous radar set from the cliff tops. It was a small operation in terms of ships, men and equipment. Its target was of importance, but immeasurably more significant was the tight co-operation between the commandos and the three other services. A naval force of gunboats and assault landing-craft transported the heavily armed troops, while paratroops were transported by the RAF to drop behind the target and assault it from the land side. It was molecular in size compared with D-Day on the beaches of Normandy two years and four months later; but it was the first proof that services which had so frequently and tragically worked in competition with one another were at last demonstrating the reality of combined operations, without which the war could not be won.

Moreover, Bruneval was a complete success: the radar station assaulted, the radar set torn from its foundations, while the navy brought the raiders safely home. A month later a much larger raid was made on the enemy naval base at St Nazaire on the Atlantic coast of France. The port of St Nazaire lies four miles up the estuary of the River Loire on the west coast of France, and 400 miles from Plymouth, the nearest British base. St Nazaire possessed the only dry dock outside Germany capable of taking the latest German battleship, the *Tirpitz*. This giant had just been completed and was expected to break out into the North Atlantic to attack convoys, falling back on St Nazaire at the conclusion of her raiding.

To counter this threat it was decided to lay on a daredevil attack from the sea in an effort to destroy this dock. How Nelson would have relished this challenge! A special force was urgently trained for the operation and on the afternoon of 26 March 1942 an odd mixed armada sailed from Plymouth. It consisted of an old 'suicide' destroyer, the *Campbeltown*, strongly armoured round the bridge, packed with twenty-four time-fused depth-charges; a motor gunboat, *MGB 314*; sixteen launches carrying a contingent of commandos; a motor torpedo-boat, *MTB 74*, and two escorting destroyers.

It seemed highly unlikely that all these vessels could make their way across the Channel and into the Bay of Biscay without being spotted from the air or the sea; and as dawn broke it revealed a U-boat on the surface not far distant, doubtless already transmitting details of this curious collection of ships and boats. The two destroyers raced towards her, firing all the way and hitting her. Then when the U-boat submerged she was attacked by quantities of depth-charges. She was believed to have been sunk but in fact was only slightly damaged; she surfaced later and the captain informed base of what had been seen. Fortunately he got the course wrong, reporting it as due west instead of east.

Commander Robert Ryder RN, the naval force commander who was to earn the VC on this operation, later described how his force crept into the estuary under cover of darkness, avoiding minefields and a patrolling vessel. The leading boats were less than two miles from their target before the trouble started.

At 01.22 hrs. all the searchlights on both banks were suddenly switched on, flood-lighting the whole force. Every detail of every craft must have been clearly visible to the enemy. In anticipation of this, however, we had taken such precautions as we could; indequate though they were, they helped. All the craft had been painted a dark colour, our dirtiest and most tattered ensigns were used, and the *Campbeltown*'s funnels had been cut on the slant, giving her a very good resemblance to the *Möwe*-class torpedo-boats employed by the Germans on that coast.

Looking back at the force following us, however, it was difficult to imagine that there could be any successful deception. Each craft, with her silvery bow-wave, stood out clear and bright, and *Campbeltown*, rising conspicuously over the smaller craft, could be seen by her funnel smoke to be increasing speed. We were challenged from the shore, first by one of the coastal batteries and later from somewhere in the dockyard. It was for this moment that Leading Signalman Pike, who could send and receive German Morse, had been attached to my staff. The challenge was accompanied by sporadic flak, aimed indiscriminately at the force. It was 01.23 hrs, we were a mile and a half from our objective; ten minutes at that speed. How long could we bluff? Although we had successfully evaded the heavier batteries at the entrance, every minute still counted.

We did not know the correct reply to the challenge, but we instructed them to 'Wait' and then gave the call sign of one of the German torpedo-boats known to us. Without waiting for them to consider this, Pike embarked on a long plain-language signal. With an 'urgent' prefix, the gist of this was, 'Two craft, damaged by enemy action, request permission to proceed up harbour without delay.' Firing ceased. Without finishing the first message we made the operating signal to 'Wait' again. We had to reply to the second station.[10]

Then fire was reopened, more heavily than before. It would take the *Campbeltown* another six minutes to reach the dock gates. Pike tried another bluff, this time using a signalling lamp to flash the international signal for ships being fired on by friendly forces. It did the trick again.

The defending gunners on both banks of the estuary and from the naval batteries of the base were clearly in a state of confusion, and it was not until 1.27 a.m. that heavy fire was renewed. Ryder declared that it was the end of bluff and the time for counter-action. Every ship opened fire, mostly with tracer, so that the wider stretch of water reflected the horizontal flight of thousands of bullets and shells and dozens of searchlights, creating a highly lethal low-level firework display. A German guard ship was almost torn apart by the MGB's pom-poms, caught fire, and became the unfortunate target for friendly guns.

But the Germans continued to hold the advantage in weight of metal, and it was through a wild criss-cross of shellfire, including 88-mm, that Ryder increased speed and guided the *Campbeltown* towards the lock gates, turning aside at the last minute. This steel-encased floating mass of TNT was hit over and over again and the bridge personnel were thankful for their heavy armour protection.

The *Campbeltown* was doing 19 knots when she hit the centre of the gates. It was 1.34 a.m. The impact shifted the depth-charges forward in the old destroyer so that, when they did explode, they would be in line with both dock gates. The gunners had kept up a steady stream of fire until the last second. Now they leapt ashore, along with the bridge personnel.

They were not the only British on French soil in St Nazaire. The commandos from the launches were conducting their own special form of destruction with explosive charges set among the dock machinery, store houses, pumping stations and other equipment essential for running an important naval base. The demolition charges began exploding soon after the *Campbeltown* struck, adding to the chaos and confusion which caused the Germans to kill more of their own men than the attackers had done. But the intensity of the defence increased as more troops were brought in and soon it became clear that the commandos who had succeeded in getting ashore could not be evacuated because so many of the launches had been sunk. The order was given to form up and fight their way through the town and out into open country, while seven of the launches withdrew, loaded with wounded men, and were picked up by the waiting destroyers.

Tragically for the Germans the delayed charge on the *Campbeltown* did not go off two and a half hours after impact (as fused), but at noon the same day when the ship was being inspected by a large party of senior German officers. Not only were they all killed by the gigantic explosion, and the dock utterly destroyed, but the German troops, already trigger-happy from the night's fighting, opened fire on one another causing frightful casualties.

For the British, and for Combined Operations Command, and the Royal Navy which had made it all possible, it was a triumphant operation with a lower casualty rate than anyone could have predicted – 144 being killed out of the 630 men in the small boats and the 'suicide' destroyer.

The biggest raid the Royal Navy was called upon to transport and support took place in August 1942, five months after St Nazaire. And it was a very different proposition from the previous Combined Operations raids. Conceived and planned by Mountbatten's Combined Operations Staff, it had from the start too many mixed motives and objectives. The first was to assault and hold for a day one of the French Channel ports in order to learn lessons and obtain experience for the eventual full-scale invasion. Second, it had the political motive of placating Russian restlessness at what she regarded as the Allies' inadequate contribution to the war effort. Third, it was intended to provide some action for the considerable Canadian forces in Britain, some of whom had been kicking their heels for almost two years. There were also subsidiary objectives, like landing tanks for the first time, learning just how effective German beach defences were, and to attack and hold a German radar station in order to discover details about the set which intelligence services badly needed to know.

This plan to land a Canadian division of 5,000 men on the beaches of Dieppe, supported by 1,000 commandos who were to make diversionary landings east and west of the town, was approved by the Chiefs of Staff in April. Everyone had been enormously encouraged by the results at St Nazaire and there was a feeling of optimism among the planners. In command of military forces was Lieutenant-General Bernard Montgomery. Then the operation experienced four successive blows. The weather turned foul, Montgomery was wanted elsewhere, it was decided (again for political reasons) to cancel the heavy bombardment from the air and the sea prior to the landing in case too many French civilians were killed, and the intelligence services learned that details of the operation had leaked through to the German high command.

Montgomery advised scrapping the whole business. Churchill and Mountbatten did not accept this advice and reprogrammed it for August. While the heavy British bombers were not to be involved, Fighter Command provided support on a big scale – fifty-six squadrons, more aircraft than had been involved in the Battle of Britain two years earlier.

Just about everything that could go wrong occurred on that bloody day, 9 August 1942. The naval force of light craft and landing-craft consisted of 237 vessels under the command of Captain Jock Hughes-Hallett RN who had served in a cruiser in the Norwegian campaign and knew something of the hazards of amphibious warfare as a result. This armada sailed from Portsmouth, Shoreham and Newhaven on the evening of 8 August, passed through a gap in the German minefields in mid-Channel which had been cleared by sweepers, and was on time when one group of craft bumped into a German convoy. Fire was exchanged – and the German defences were alerted by this pyrotechnic display just off the coast, and doubtless by warning radio messages, too.

The final approach to Dieppe's beaches was not at all like the run up the Loire estuary towards St Nazaire. It was made through a hail of fire from the defence batteries which had been installed to meet just this contingency since the summer of 1940. The supporting destroyers fired back to some effect but their guns were of no more than 4.7-inch calibre, and they too came under fire and bomber attack. The frontal assault on the beaches was a disaster in the face of murderous enfilading fire. Many of the Canadians fell even before they disembarked or within seconds of hitting the beach. The tanks, which could have turned the scales if they had got into the narrow streets of the town, arrived late and not one of them got off the steeply sloping shingle. The sea wall could not be breached by the demolition parties because of the intensity of the fire. All the courage in the world could not prevail against these sweeping curtains of steel. The order was given to withdraw. The landing-craft went in and scooped up a few of the unfortunate Canadians and Royal Marine Commandos who had been sent in to strengthen them.

I was shocked at the sight on the beach [Lieutenant-Colonel Charles Merritt declared]. Instead of finding a few scattered remnants still hanging back, the place was swarming with men, hundreds of them. That was my mistake, I should have gone down to the beach earlier to see for myself that they were re-embarking as fast as they reached the beach.[11]

But the re-embarkation was even more difficult and bloody than the delivery of the men. Lieutenant David Flory survived but was only one of many who endeavoured to carry out this lethal task:

I proceeded to the beach which lay under a thick smokescreen; and ML warned me of men in the water and coming through the smoke. I found the men swimming out from the beaches to get away from the machine-gunning at the flanks. There were some corpses in the water and those that were alive had little strength left. I picked up about 20 men from the water and proceeded into the beach.... By this time one engine was not working and the steering apparatus was defective. I stopped the boat before a group of men who had waded one hundred yards out; four were carrying a severely wounded man on a stretcher. We were now bow on to a machine-gun post and it was impossible to manœuvre the craft owing to the mechanical defect and the weight of men clambering over the bow and stern; many were shot in the back as we pulled them over the bow. When every man in the vicinity was on board we had great difficulty in dragging the injured men from the lowered door. I gave orders to go astern on one engine which was a slow process, but by this time the steering had improved and we were able to put out to sea.[12]

Some 1,000 of this force were evacuated amidst ceaseless fire, impeded by the floating bodies and equipment and the abandoned, sinking assault craft. The only military success that could be recorded was the west-flank attack which knocked out the German heavy guns and withdrew with few casualties, and the radar station assault which, in the course of a desperate adventure, succeeded in acquiring the information needed and withdrawing, though with a number of casualties. In the skies above the carnage the RAF, in a reverse role from the Battle of Britain and fighting mainly over enemy-held soil, lost over 100 fighters, twice as many machines as the *Luftwaffe*.

Over 68 per cent of the Canadians taking part became casualties on that August day. The loss of material and of vessels taking part – a destroyer and thirty-three landing-craft – was nothing compared with the demoralizing sense of failure.

In fact the word 'failure' cannot be applied in simple definition of the Dieppe raid. The lessons learned were of critical importance in the planning and execution of the invasion almost two years later, saving many times more lives than were lost in this operation. The most important was the realization that it would not be possible to attack and hold a port and use it for delivering supplies. The Allies would have to build their own port; thus the conception and construction of 'Mulberry' which served a vital need on the beaches of Normandy. It was also made (expensively) clear that no assault could be hoped to succeed without preliminary heavy sea and air bombardment support to reduce or eliminate enemy gunfire from carefully fixed positions. And, as Peter Kemp has written, 'From the experiences of Dieppe emerged the correct command and communications organizations for large-scale combined operations.'[13]

Some of the lessons of Dieppe were learned in time for 'Operation Torch', the Anglo–American invasion of North Africa in October 1942; all of them proved of vital importance in Normandy in June 1944. But there can be no doubt that these lessons could have been gained at a lower cost in lives with more intelligent planning and better luck. But, then, hard-earned lessons are well-earned lessons. Montgomery, rightly, denied all responsibility for the decision to give the green light to a postponed operation. Mountbatten, while also denying responsibility (hotly and to his dying day), suffered from a guilt that was engraved upon his heart. The most charitable excuse for the excessive expense of Dieppe was the morally well-intentioned one of concern for the lives of French civilians who would have been slaughtered in hundreds in any bombardment.

Dieppe was the last heavy raid for which Combined Operations were to be responsible in home waters. From the Royal Navy's point of view this was a profound relief. The service was already stretched to the limit in a struggle that would decide the outcome of the war in the West – a fight of unending attrition: the U-boat war.

CHAPTER THREE

U-boat Warfare, September 1939–March 1943

Twenty-five years earlier, when the depredations of German U-boats in the Atlantic had brought the Western Allies almost to their knees, Norway, Denmark and Holland were neutral and France unconquered. The massive U-boat fleet's bases in northern Europe were confined to the coasts of Germany and conquered Belgium. In 1939, with the renewal of war by Germany, Admiral Karl Doenitz, commander of the German U-boat fleet, did not even have the Belgian bases which had proved so useful in 1917. This picture was very different by June 1940. With Norway, Denmark, Holland, Belgium and France all 'under the jackboot' of the Greater Reich, Hitler controlled some 3,000 miles of coastline of northern Europe instead of 300 miles. While this state of affairs made the task of the defending German Army many times more difficult, it offered a new freedom of action to the German Navy.

In the early days of this new German war, passage through the English Channel had been as effectively blocked to Atlantic-bound U-boats as it had been in the First World War. Three U-boats which tried to penetrate the defences of minefields and patrols were destroyed, and the long and dangerous passage round the north of Scotland had again to be undertaken. Twenty more U-boats were sunk out of the total of fifty-seven with which Germany had begun the war. Ten months later, as one German U-boat 'ace' described the situation: 'The string of bases at the Navy's disposal now stretched from the Arctic Sea to the Bay of Biscay. The age-old handicap of having to operate exclusively out of the "liquid triangle" of the North Sea was thus removed. The enemy could no longer lie in ambush as German ships departed or bar their way home.'[1] On 5 July 1940 *U-30*, under the command of Fritz Lemp, arrived at Lorient. Soon there were eight flotillas operating from Brest, Lorient, La Pallice and St Nazaire, and they were soon preying on the vulnerable North Atlantic sea lanes.

With the loss of almost all of the French Navy and the threat posed in the Mediterranean by the entry of Italy into the war, this presented the Royal Navy and the Dominion navies, supported by a handful of Polish, Dutch, Norwegian and Free French vessels, with appalling new responsibilities. In that same month of July losses, almost all in the Atlantic, were thirty-eight ships. This figure was still less than a quarter of sinkings in the worst months of 1917: but the writing was on the Western wall.

As grave a danger to shipping in 1940 as the U-boats' operating bases was the unpreparedness of the Royal Navy to meet the renewed U-boat threat. Complacency, traditionalism and self-satisfaction had been the bane of the Royal Navy since mid-Victorian times, and neither Winston Churchill as First Lord of the Admiralty (1911–15), nor the handful of reformers within the service, succeeded in completely correcting these weaknesses. In spite of never winning (or losing) a fleet action in the First World War, the German challenge at sea had been defeated in the end and the virtually impenetrable Allied blockade was the greatest single factor in the surrender of Germany in 1918. By that year the U-boat had been overcome by the introduction of convoys, the deployment of adequate numbers of escorting warships and air cover. This victory was followed by the Anglo–French invention of ASDIC (Allied Submarine Detective Investigation Committee), later renamed SONAR, an echo-sounding device which could locate submerged submarines. ASDIC, in combination with the depth-charge set to explode at a predetermined depth to crush the hull of the submarine, was regarded as the complete answer to any renewal of the U-boat menace in a future war.

Navies have always disliked the threat to the status quo posed by new weapons. In the case of the battleship it had something to do with pride in the grandeur of this big fighting ship, and the threatened loss of status as well as the number of officers employed. 'Sir, who would wish to command a fleet of submersibles?' A future First Sea Lord, Admiral Sir Arthur Wilson, claimed in 1904 that submarines were 'underhand, unfair and damned un-English'.[2] Just as that double line of battleships at Pearl Harbor symbolized the continuing faith of the US Navy in the battle fleet as the supreme arbiter of sea warfare, so received opinion in the Royal Navy and the French Navy was that they had the measure of the U-boat.

In the early years of the century, when the submarine was more a curious novelty than a serious weapon, the rules on exercises were loaded against it to such a ridiculous degree that it was almost impossible for it to make a 'kill'. That it frequently did so all the same was ignored by the old shellbacks of the time. So, once again, in the years before the Second World War ASDIC was operated on exercises only in conditions that were favourable to it – not at night or in rough weather for instance – with results that seemed to confirm the comforting belief that the submarine was no longer the threat it had once been.

One of the most courageous and distinguished British naval officers who fought the U-boat (and earned three DSOs and a DSC), Donald Macintyre, was only too aware of this British overconfidence. 'Perhaps the greatest miscalculation, caused by an incomplete study of the lessons of the First World War, was that which assumed that U-boat attacks would be confined to submerged attacks,'[3] Macintyre wrote after his long and arduous North Atlantic service. Doenitz himself had commanded a U-boat in this earlier war in which a certain Kapitan-Leutnant Steinbauer had pioneered U-boat surface night attack after the defences had made daylight attack too dangerous. Doenitz himself had written and published his theories and observations on U-boat warfare which advocated this method of attacking convoys. It was freely available to the public but was not the subject of study among British naval planners before the war.

Macintyre also had this to say about the U-boat situation in 1939:

Now the ASDIC suffered from certain limitations, one of which was its poor performance against small surface targets. Thus if the U-boat commanders employed the same tactics as in the First World War [i.e. Doenitz's] – and opposed by the ASDIC they were certain to do so – the escorts would be confined to the same means of detection as in 1918, the human eye. Thus the linchpin of the Navy's confidence in its ability to combat the U-boat was knocked out.[4]

A combination of peacetime parsimony, neglect and this same overconfidence led to the Royal Navy being desperately short of escort vessels for the convoys, which were instituted for certain classes of merchantmen at the outset of war. A last-minute attempt to correct this neglect led to the ordering of numbers of corvettes and other classes of cheap, quickly built vessels. The RN possessed about 150 destroyers, some old, some (like Warburton-Lee's in the Narvik battles) almost as powerful as a light cruiser. But many of these were needed for fleet work, and in any case were expensive and took too long to build to meet the immediate needs of convoy escort.

One more lesson from the past that was forgotten at first in the Second World War was that it was useless to hunt U-boats across the broad expanses of open sea. The chances of discovering them were too remote, even with the added help of air cover. It was far more effective to protect the convoys as comprehensively as possible and wait for the U-boats to be drawn to them. If they did not discover the convoy, all well and good; if they did, there was a reasonable chance of the U-boats being discovered themselves and, if not destroyed, frightened off.

But within days of the outbreak of war, between 9 and 14 September 1939, three of the Royal Navy's precious carriers put to sea separately with destroyer escort as U-boat hunting groups. They sighted a number of U-boats and delivered a number of attacks, one of which was successful. But on 14 September the brand-new armoured fleet carrier, *Ark Royal*, was attacked. Three days later the *Courageous* was attacked and hit by *U-29* 350 miles off Land's End. She went down swiftly, and with most of her crew. The lesson had been re-learnt expensively, and that was the end of these offensive operations.

The Battle of the Atlantic, as it came to be called, began after the fall of France in 1940. Doenitz established his headquarters on the west coast of France and his flotillas sailed to attack the lifelines upon which Britain depended for her survival. The battle was to last five years, a war of deadly attrition by the U-boats against the convoy defenders, at first mainly British, then Canadian escorts and, until withdrawn to the Pacific, with increasing support by the United States Navy.

The casualties in this interminable and relentless battle were appalling on both sides, the tides of fortune and technical superiority fluctuating first one and then the other way as new weapons were introduced. The time, ingenuity and wealth expended by both protagonists were incalculable. The experiences of those engaged, whether in the foetid, claustrophobic hulls of the submarines, the decks of the storm-wracked escort vessels where survival depended upon razor-sharp alertness, or onboard the merchantmen, formed a compound of nerve-taut fear and the endurance of unalleviated discomfort and boredom. It was far removed from the sharp stab of terror and elation of the fighter pilot, the slower build-up towards crisis of the bomber crews and the sound, fury and concussion of being bombed or shelled, or the animal terror and fury of close infantry combat: it had something of the character of all these experiences, but there are those who survived the Battle of the Atlantic who believe that its sum total of demand upon the endurance of man was higher than any other. They could well be right.

On 17 August 1940, with Britain facing the imminent threat of invasion, Churchill appealing to President Roosevelt for old American destroyers to help fill the need for convoy escorts, and the Battle of Britain over the skies of southern England at its height (forty-six German machines lost the previous day), Hitler was persuaded to lift all restrictions on U-boat targets. Neutral as well as enemy shipping would be sunk on sight, a step which had eventually made the United States an enemy in 1917. Shipping losses instantly increased, especially among ships either too fast to require escort – so it was thought – or too slow to keep up. Tonnage lost rose from 382,000 in July to 394,000 in August and 442,000 in September.

The Atlantic is never a warm ocean. With the coming of the equinox and longer nights, when air escort was ineffective and therefore not operated, the life of a Merchant Navy seaman was highly dangerous. There was rarely any warning: just a violent, shuddering explosion, often fatal to the engine-room staff, and the rapid tilting of decks as the water came thundering in; then icy seas, usually oil-covered and sometimes on fire.

The ordeal of the counter-attacked U-boat crews was no less frightening when the depth-charges began to explode, throwing the men about their cramped quarters and sometimes opening up cracks in the hull to let in jets of water.

The ordeal of Convoy SC7 in October 1940 was typical of that period when the Royal Navy was still short of experience, and even more critically short of escorts. SC7 consisted of thirty-four ships with a convoy speed of 7 knots, half that of a U-boat's surface speed. By October 1940 Doenitz had been reinforced with new U-boat construction, which had been rapidly

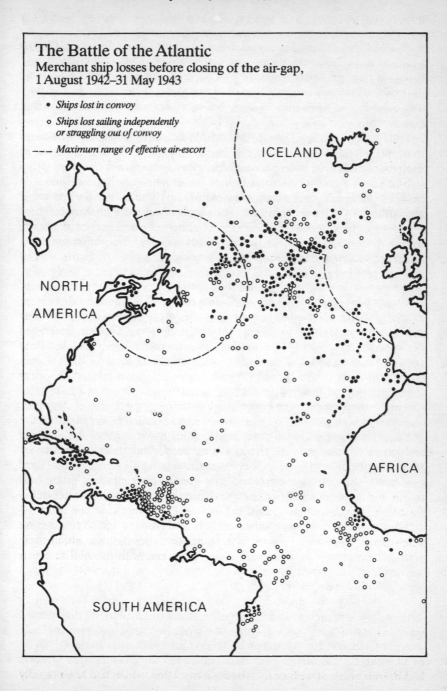

The Battle of the Atlantic
Merchant ship losses before closing of the air-gap,
1 August 1942–31 May 1943

- Ships lost in convoy
- Ships lost sailing independently
  or straggling out of convoy
- - - Maximum range of effective air-escort

ICELAND

NORTH

AMERICA

AFRICA

SOUTH AMERICA

accelerated under Hitler's orders. Doenitz had developed the wolf-pack method of attack, whereby a number of U-boats worked together under the immediate command of a leader and the more distant control of U-boat headquarters ashore. Once a convoy was located a single U-boat shadowed it during daylight hours, reporting its position and any change of course. The pack was then positioned ahead of the convoy, which it could comfortably outstrip, and when night fell worked together under a strictly controlled plan.

Wolf-pack operation, like night surface attack, had been practised in the First World War; Doenitz had written about it, too, and in detail in his book. But the first wolf-pack attacks came as a severe shock.

SC7's sole escort for the first half of the eastern crossing was the sloop *Scarborough* of just over 1,000 tons, with a maximum speed of 16 knots and armed with two 4-inch guns and depth-charges. The confidence of her captain, Commander N.V. Dickinson, and her crew, had been undermined during the course of her outward passage when the convoy she had been escorting had lost six out of nineteen ships in one night, without sight or sound of a U-boat, just the dull thud and shock waves of explosions. The weather was appalling, a southerly gale scattered the convoy and of the four ships which did not rejoin three were summarily sunk.

SC7 continued its snail-like progress in eight columns, the columns half a mile apart. At 21°30' West, another sloop and a corvette joined the *Scarborough* and reduced the danger from the night of 16 October. But on that same night Hans Rösing, *U-48*, sighted the mass of dark shapes and reported the convoy's position and course to all U-boats in the vicinity. Six of them were ordered to take up a patrol line ahead of the convoy, and in the meantime Rösing broke into the convoy, fired a salvo of torpedoes and sank two ships. The corvette stood by to rescue the crews while the other two escorts searched long and fruitlessly for the attacker, leaving the convoy unprotected until the afternoon of 17 October, when two further escorts joined to form a thin protective screen.

It was almost totally ineffectual. The U-boat pack was reinforced now by the two aces, Joachim Schepke and Günther Prien, who had taken his *U-47* into Scapa Flow to sink the *Royal Oak*. The pack moved in to the attack on the surface soon after 10 p.m. on 18 October. Another ace, Kretschmer, torpedoed four ships in short order, finishing off one of them with gunfire, undisturbed by any counter-action. Only one U-boat was sighted and attacked. It suffered no damage. Harassed, pursued and again struck by foul weather which scattered the surviving ships, Convoy SC7 'made their way individually to port, while the escorts returned sorrowfully to their base with their crowd of survivors from sunken ships. The disastrous count of seventeen ships sunk and two more damaged, out of thirty-four which started, was enough to mark October 1940 as one of the black months of the war.'[5] Thus wrote Donald Macintyre, who knew the low periods and the later high periods of the Battle of the Atlantic as well as anyone.

At the same time as S C7 was being decimated Convoy HX79 was suffering a similar fate from the torpedoes of other wolf packs. The fact that it lost 'only' a quarter of its ships was due to the much heavier escort.

All that could be recorded on the credit side of this ghastly balance sheet was the experience gained under the shock of disaster. The defence was unco-ordinated as well as inadequate: escorts went dashing off hither and thither in futile search of their prey, leaving the merchantmen without protection, or stopped, and, in accordance with peacetime practice but not harsh wartime necessity, picked up survivors from their boats and rafts. Above all, the need for air cover was once again recognized.

On 1 December 1940 Churchill convened a meeting in the Admiralty War Room to consider urgent means of countering the U-boat onslaught, which threatened to starve out the nation and fatally sever the supply of raw materials and armaments from North America and elsewhere. In some respects the position was even worse than in April 1917, for in that month the United States had thrown in its lot with the Allies with all that that implied in the way of immediate naval support. In December 1940 there was little more than sympathy, except for the United States' offer of fifty old destroyers in exchange for British bases in the Caribbean and Newfoundland. And it would be many months before these crank and inadequate little vessels could be usefully operational.

In a long telegram of appeal to the American President, finally despatched on 7 December 1940, Churchill wrote of 'the mortal danger' of 'the steady and increasing diminution of sea tonnage.... The decision for 1941 lies upon the seas,' he declared. Now, at this meeting with his naval chiefs, the role of air power in countering the U-boat came up for discussion, and not before it was time. Coastal Command was the neglected branch of the RAF – a neglected child, in fact, as it was only four years old. Its defined functions were co-operation with the Royal Navy, reconnaissance and 'trade protection'. Nothing of an offensive nature was included in its duties, its few squadrons were mainly equipped with the 1934-designed Anson with a range of 600 miles and no effective means of attacking U-boats.

Because everything learned in 1918 had been forgotten or insufficiently studied, it came as a great surprise when Coastal Command aircraft patrolling over the North Sea proved effective at observing U-boats. Before the U-boat offensive of the summer of 1940 there was no pressure to modernize, enlarge or even provide effective weapons for Coastal Command. The use of modified depth-charges was tried out and at first found wanting. The autumn sinking figures changed all that. The purchase of modern aircraft from America was speeded up, and at this 1 December meeting,

We gave orders [wrote Churchill] to the RAF Coastal Command to dominate the outlets from the Mersey and Clyde and around Northern Ireland. Nothing must be spared from this task [he emphasized], it had supreme priority. The bombing of Germany took second place.* All suitable machines, pilots and material, must be concentrated upon our counter-offensive, by fighters against the enemy bombers, and surface craft assisted by bombers against the U-boats in these narrow vital waters. Many other important projects were brushed aside, delayed or mauled. At all costs one must breathe.[6]

The enemy bombers to which Churchill referred were the Condor, and to a lesser extent the smaller and shorter-range Heinkel He111 and Junkers Ju88. The Focke-Wulf Fw200 Condor was a modified pre-war twenty-six-seat fast airliner with a long range (2,200 miles) and retractable under-carriage. In strengthened form, armed with cannon and machine-guns and carrying four 550-pound bombs, it was a very formidable anti-shipping weapon. A squadron of them was transferred to Bordeaux after the fall of France and during the early autumn began to add to the sufferings of merchantmen in convoy or travelling alone. By the end of September they had recorded 90,000 tons of enemy losses.

The Condor operated far beyond the range of shore-based fighters, and in the days when escort carriers were only on the drawing-board and anti-aircraft fire from a convoy's escort was negligible, the winter of 1940–41 was as much 'the happy time' (as German submariners later referred to this period nostalgically) for the bombers as for the U-boats. Various means of countering the Condor's depredations were considered in November 1940, among them the stationing of long-range twin-engined fighters in Northern Ireland. An ingenious alternative was thought up by an Air Ministry official at an emergency joint Navy–RAF meeting on 12 November 1940, and later received the blessing of Air Chief Marshal Sir Charles Portal, Chief of Air Staff, and Admiral Sir Dudley Pound, First Sea Lord.

The meeting had discussed the possibility of including in each big convoy a mobile sector radar station which could guide the long-range fighters from Northern Ireland on to the Condors, just as fighter squadrons had been vectored on to German bomber formations in the Battle of Britain. But then why not, suggested this unnamed officer, 'fit such a ship with a catapult so that two or three fighters could be carried for interception purposes'.

And so were born the 'Hurricat' and the 'Camship': the expendable fighter and its launching pad. The Hawker Hurricane, the backbone of Fighter Command in the Battle of Britain, but rapidly becoming obsolete in that role, was ideal for the purpose. It was available, it was tough, and it was just fast enough to catch the Condor. How badly it was needed was shown on 9 February 1941 when five Condors sank five merchantmen in the same convoy 1,000 miles from their Bordeaux base. On 6 March 1941, when a Battle of the Atlantic Committee was formed, Churchill issued a directive about the battle which included this paragraph: 'Extreme priority will be given to fitting out ships to catapult or otherwise launch fighter

---

* It did not.

aircraft against bombers attacking our shipping. Proposals should be made within a week.'[7]

They were. The catapulted Hurricane experiments proceeded rapidly. A Merchant Ship Fighter Unit (MSFU) was established at Liverpool, and volunteers called for from RAF Fighter Command. The Fleet Air Arm characteristically *appointed* their share of the pilots: to land in the sea was all part of the business of flying with the navy – or so it was assumed. Training was rushed through, and the first Camships were operating by May 1941. The very first, the *Michael E*, sailed for New York with her convoy on 28 May. Instead of bombing the convoy, Condors ironically confined themselves to spotting for U-boats, one of which sank the *Michael E* before any launch could be made.

The first Hurricat 'kill' was not made until 3 August 1941, when a launched Hurricane was involved in a long and testing battle with a Condor, which proved dauntingly fast and better armed than the fighter. The Condor eventually went in but not before severely damaging the Hurricane, which only just made it back to the convoy. The pilot was picked up after ditching. This was a highly satisfying, if freezing, experience for him.

A success like this was a rare entry in a pilot's logbook, and the second enemy – boredom and frustration – was a common and everyday experience, all too often against a background of bad relations with the Camship's skipper and crew. The pilots, in their twenties, were all individualists, restless for action and a bit cocky in their style. They were accustomed to adulation as ex-Battle of Britain types, top button undone to establish that they were fighter and not bomber pilots, all too ready for evening roughhouses as on their fighter stations.

The officers and crews of these ships, on the other hand, had been through dangerous times too, without much public recognition, and did not take too kindly to the presence of these pilots and their crews, who had no particular duties, got in the way and were outside the closed walls of a ship's community. In addition the Camship had to sacrifice a good deal of cargo space for the catapult and Hurricane and all the paraphernalia required to maintain and service the machine. The handling qualities of the ship and the visibility from the bridge were both adversely affected by the plane and its catapult; and also provided a tempting target for U-boat and Condor alike.

Finally the Hurricats were the victims of their own success. From the time the first Hurricane was spotted on deck the Condor pilots became more cautious and began to shun convoys altogether after the first launch and combat. Instead they looked for single ships or stragglers, content to report the presence and course of convoys from afar to the U-boat wolf packs.

All the same several pilots got 'kills' in spite of the slow speed of the Hurricane and its armament of .303 machine-guns against the deadly cannon of the Condors. Flying Officer Norman Taylor DFM was one, a veteran at the age of twenty-two and a good deal less flamboyant and excitable than some of his fellow pilots. He was onboard the Camship *Empire Heath* with a convoy of sixty-five ships heading north from Gibraltar on 1 November 1942.

At 10.00 a.m. action stations was sounded, and Taylor spotted a Condor circling like the great bird of prey after which it was named at a distance of some eight miles. Experience had shown that at this range, by the time the Camship had turned into wind and launched, the Condor would have escaped. Cautiously, uncertainly, the Condor continued to circle low on the horizon. When the enemy's range was no more than five miles, the alarm sounded and the *Empire Heath* swung into wind and prepared to launch.

Locking the throttle wide open, forcing his skull hard back against the head-rest, Taylor braced himself for the shock as the rockets ignited behind him, tearing the morning apart with their dazzling brightness and their ear-shattering displacement of air....

For Taylor, in the cockpit, the moment of truth had come; but he could feel the exhilarating power of the Merlin [engine] and knew it would pull him clear.

The Condor was swift to react, veering away at low level at which its camouflaged upper surfaces were difficult to see, especially in the bright sunlight reflecting on the dappled ocean. Taylor switched on his R/T only to find the channel was being jammed by the Condor so that he could not hear his controller's directions or, after the flash of the launching rockets, see where the Condor had gone. The controller therefore resorted to the simple age-old practice of pointing with his arm – and off sped Taylor.

For fully two minutes Taylor continued at full throttle on a south-westerly course. It was beginning to look like a fruitless chase. But knowing the reputation of Condor pilots for expert flying, he guessed what his adversary's tactics might be and squinted hopefully up sun.

'I see him! I see him!'

Only the Condor's size had given its position away. Against the background the pilot had chosen, a smaller aircraft might have escaped....

Keeping his height advantage, but still blinded by the dazzle off the sea, Taylor opened his throttle again and aimed a one-second burst ahead of the Condor to try to force the pilot off his course.... The Condor pilot knew his business and held on. Meanwhile, to keep the Hurricane at a distance, the German gunners were putting up a curtain of fire for Taylor to fly through....

Closing in to 150 yards and meeting continuous return fire, Taylor ruddered across the stern of the Condor from starboard to port, delivered a four-second burst from his eight machine-guns as he slid over, and dropped back to 250 yards to confuse the German gunners. This did not save him from an accurate burst from the forward upper turret that riddled his port wing; but in the clatter and judder of his own guns he noticed nothing. Neither did he know whether or not he himself had scored any hits....

Taylor, with his fixed guns, was at a disadvantage as he fought to line up astern of the Condor. The German gunners, with their free guns, had the edge on him, and they kept up a withering fire. Another 300 feet and the Condor would be safe.

The German pilot now abruptly changed his mind. That was how it seemed to Taylor. Deciding perhaps that the cloud was not quite so opaque as it had appeared from below, he thrust his control column forward and made for sea level, presumably trusting to his skill at low flying to frustrate the British pilot until either his fuel or his ammunition or his patience ran out. The manoeuvre again took Taylor by surprise, so much so that he was unable to follow up immediately as the Condor shallow-dived towards the sea.

The manoeuvre, it seemed to Taylor, was brilliantly executed. He was even more impressed as the Condor pilot kept up his dive almost to sea level. Indeed he began to wonder how he would ever pull out.

He watched astounded as the Condor, staggering helplessly at the bottom of the dive, hit the sea without completing the expected recovery. For a moment the huge bird-like machine was completely obliterated by the splash. When the foaming waterspout had subsided, and the turgid water had settled, nothing was visible of the Condor but the tail.

'He's down! He's gone down!'[8]

Taylor's was one of only half a dozen Condors shot down by the Hurricats in the two years of their operation. But this puny statistic bears no relation to the deterrent effect of their presence, or to the number of bombing runs that were broken off by the presence of these fighters, some of which had already exhausted their ammunition and had to be content with dummy attacks. They were sufficient. It was indeed a very nasty shock for the pilot and crew of one of these Condors, confident that they were a thousand or more miles from the nearest land and nearest carrier, to be suddenly confronted by a Hurricane single-seat fighter diving on them out of the sun or cloud. If the crew escaped and returned to Bordeaux safely, they had a tale to tell over their *Schnapps* in the mess that evening that led other aircrews to ever greater caution in approaching Atlantic convoys.

The Hurricats were only one of the numerous weapons brought to bear on the enemy in the relentless and seemingly endless Battle of the Atlantic. In the broader view they represented in miniature the awesome growth of air power in the *guerre de course*, the outcome of which must decide the fate of the Allied cause. The launching of Hurricats at sea, and the bombing of the main Condor base at Bordeaux, were two early and positive counter-attack operations by air power at a time when the U-boat appeared almost invulnerable and all-dominant. While weapons and experience developed side by side in this Atlantic campaign it was finally air power that provided the most feared and effective single weapon, just as it had – in its rudimentary form – in 1918.

First the machines themselves: in 1939 RAF Coastal Command took delivery of the first Consolidated PBY Catalina flying boats (later amphibians) from its American factory. The 'Cat' was a curious looking machine, with a single high-set wing carrying two radial engines, and with machine-guns sprouting from Perspex nacelles in its boat-like fuselage. It was faster than it looked – around 175 mph – and could carry a useful load of bombs or depth-charges. But its first quality as a U-boat hunter was its endurance. It could remain in the air for seventeen hours and possessed a range of almost 4,000 miles. The Catalina, looking like some marine pterodactyl, made a comforting sight for sailors as she patrolled for hours at a time over a convoy far distant from land.

Another product of the Consolidated Company of America was the B-24 Liberator, a four-engine bomber, with an even greater range and much dreaded by the U-boat crews because, with its heavy load of bombs and depth-charges, it could deliver more than one attack and had a formidable armament of guns, too.

From the start of the Battle of the Atlantic, Coastal Command operated the Short Sunderland. At first there were only a handful of these useful and massive flying boats with their range of 800 miles, one-ton bombload, and machine-gun armament formidable enough for them to be nicknamed 'the flying porcupines' by German pilots. (One Sunderland drove off eight Junkers Ju88s, shooting down three of them.)

Other aircraft contributed to the sum volume of air power over the Atlantic, machines like a long-range Wellington bomber, Northrop seaplanes, Beauforts and Whitleys; but it was the Liberator, the Catalina and the Sunderland which were most seen, most feared and most dangerous for the U-boat crews, together with the short-range aircraft of the escort carriers when they made their appearance.

After an autumn and winter of severe trial and losses the priority granted to air power, which was given further impetus by Churchill's directive of 6 March 1941, began to turn the tide in the spring. In one month the loss, with their U-boats, of Günther Prien and Joachim Schepke, and the capture of Otto Kretschmer, was a serious blow to Doenitz's command. Air patrols over the western approaches and air escorts farther out into the Atlantic had the effect of forcing the U-boats west and even beyond the reconnoitring Condor's range. Far out in the centre of the Atlantic the pickings were thinner and the operating time of the U-boats shorter, especially during the brief nights of summer. The arming of merchantmen was having a chastening effect on the U-boat commanders, too. Doenitz was ordered to give greater attention to the west coast of Africa and the convoys from the Cape and the shipping from South America, even penetrating into the Indian Ocean.

At first this new assault paid heavy dividends for the U-boats. The Condors for a while enjoyed renewed successes, and the U-boat packs found rich pickings among inadequately defended convoys on the long haul north. Convoy SL87, for example, lost all but four of eleven ships in successive night attacks, and homeward-bound convoys from Gibraltar suffered severely, too.

Coastal Command replied by despatching a squadron of Sunderlands to Freetown and Hurricats were switched from the Atlantic run. These moves eased the situation, but it was an altogether new development in air power that transformed the figures of losses. In September 1941 the first escort carrier went into action. The early escort carriers were often hastily converted merchantmen of around 5,000–10,000 tons carrying no more than twenty-five aircraft. HMS *Audacity*, 5,500 tons, Commander D.W.Mackendrick, was typical of her type and equipped exclusively with Grumman Wildcat fighters, or Martlets as they were renamed for the Royal Navy. The Grumman Company, based on Long Island, New York, had for long established a special relationship with the US Navy and supplied it with superb naval fighters – as it still does today. Thanks to political skulduggery and inter-service rivalry, the Royal Navy entered the Second World War with completely inadequate carrier fighters. Fleet Air Arm pilots suddenly found themselves in the cockpits of 300-mph well-armed fighters with excellent handling qualities. Now there would be no need for emergency boost, as all too often selected by Hurricane pilots in order to catch the Condors.

Audacity sailed with Convoy OG74 from Malta, which was escorted also by a sloop and five corvettes. The Martlets were soon in action, forcing shadowing U-boats to submerge and fending off a multiple Condor attack. The Condors did have some success, but all were shot down into the sea after their pilots had radioed the daunting news that modern, heavily armed fighters were buzzing about the convoy. The real worth of this escort carrier could be judged all too tragically by the experiences of the next convoy, which had only ship escort, leading to the loss of nine ships in night attacks.

Just as Doenitz had organized his U-boats into hunting wolf packs, so Admiral Sir Percy Noble, the RN's C-in-C Western Approaches until November 1942, was influential in forming Escort Groups trained in the specialist skills of countering them. It was inevitable, under the press of rivalry, that these groups too should have their 'aces'. Aces encouraged *esprit de corps* and the competitive spirit. One of the first of them was Commander Johnny Walker, an enterprising, skilful and non-conformist officer whose style did not always endear him to authority. But he was also the most experienced anti-submarine officer in the service, having first specialized in this branch as long before as 1921.

Walker assumed command of the 36th Escort Group in the autumn of 1941 and at once started training it intensively in conformity with his personally devised tactics.

In the ingenious Attack Teacher [Donald Macintyre has written], where synthetic submarine hunts and depth-charge attacks could be carried out, the control teams – captains, anti-submarine control officers and asdic operators – spent long hours perfecting their techniques. None of this was of any use, however, unless the submarine could be got within the very limited range of the asdic. Study of past convoy battles made it clear to Walker that only by pre-arranged, concerted moves of the escorts could this be ensured.[9]

Convoy HG76 was a large and important convoy of thirty-two ships which sailed from Gibraltar on 14 December 1941, and in clear, calm weather for most of the way suffered a series of ferocious and unrelenting attacks by Condors as well as U-boats for ten days and nights. Walker employed his own tactics of tight co-ordination between his modern sloop, *Stork*, another older sloop and seven corvettes, and reinforcement of escorts which made up the group.

When HG76 steamed out into the Atlantic there was an escort for every two merchantmen, with the *Audacity* ready to provide air cover. Doenitz knew about the convoy, its precise time of sailing and its destination from his highly efficient and well co-ordinated intelligence sources. For their part British intelligence was by now able to locate with considerable accuracy the position and course of most U-boats through the remarkable resources of 'Ultra', the cryptographic machine which began breaking the German code as early as April 1940 and rapidly developed in sophistication and effectiveness.

The advent of Walker with his brilliant new concepts of U-boat counter-attack, along with his disciples like Peter Gretton and Donald Macintyre, was matched by the development of even more sophisticated and successful code-breaking of German signals. The recent publication of the official history of *British Intelligence in the Second World War* by Professor F.H. Hinsley has made clear for the first time the immense contribution the code-breakers made to the outcome of the Second World War, requiring an entire reappraisal of both campaigns and individual battles.

It was during the Norwegian campaign in April 1940 that a small government intelligence department, based near the home counties town of Bletchley, began 'reading' Enigma, the ultra-secret German cipher machine. The operation was code-named ULTRA. ULTRA was at first only intermittently successful and for some months the lapse of time between intercepting German messages and reading them was too great to be effective. But the brilliant Bletchley team, whose work was known only to a very small chosen few, made rapid strides. By June 1941 the code-breakers were, for example, able to notify the Admiralty of the exact position, course and speed of the pocket battleship *Lützow* as she travelled from the Baltic into the North Sea. Torpedo-bombers were despatched and intercepted the big ship. Within a few hours Bletchley was able to pass on the news that, due to torpedo damage, the pocket battleship was limping back to its base under escort – where it remained out of action for months.

In the same month many transmissions to or from U-boats in the Atlantic – and they could not operate in total silence – were being deciphered. By now decryption delay was much reduced, so that not only could many situation and instruction transmissions from German headquarters be read, but the Admiralty knew the position and sometimes even the intentions of most U-boats. Convoys like HG76 were routed accordingly.

But of the three German services the navy was by far the most security conscious, and U-boat Command soon became suspicious that its code was no longer safe. In the summer of 1942 it inserted a fourth wheel into its Enigma machines. It was like a spanner in the works for Bletchley, who got no more joy after that until, after intense and exhausting work, the cryptographers began to break through again in April 1943.

Nor is it widely appreciated how comprehensively the Germans, through their own 'Bletchley', *B-dienst*, were reading the British naval code. German intelligence had been given a priceless gift during the Abyssinian crisis between Britain and Italy in the Mediterranean in 1936. At that time the Germans monitored the vast mass of British naval signals, which allowed them more or less to reconstruct the British naval code in time for the outbreak of war three years later. By this means the *B-dienst* had a considerable entrance into British naval signal procedure; the British knew nothing of this and therefore remained dangerously confident that the RN code was secure and kept it unchanged.

In 1942, then, neither the British nor the Germans knew that their codes were being 'read', although suspicions were beginning to grow. Just as Bletchley could tell Admiralty intelligence the whereabouts and intentions of Doenitz's U-boats, so *B-dienst* could give U-boat Command pretty complete information about every convoy's date of sailing, its destination, and when at sea, its course, speed, alterations of course and speed, details of its escort, and so on. It was not until early 1943 that the Admiralty recognized what they were giving away. New ciphers were introduced, plus the all-important 'one-time pad', and *B-dienst* virtually dried up for the rest of the war. At the same time Bletchley became more and more 'clever' so that almost nothing missed the cryptographers. For the last two years of the war in European waters the Allies knew almost everything the Germans were doing at sea, while they remained blind.

In spite of dark days ahead for Bletchley, in December 1941, when Convoy HG76 sailed, ULTRA was enjoying the early fruit of its labours. With information based on ULTRA intelligence, this convoy was warned of the presence of a shadowing U-boat on the evening of 16 December 1941. At dawn aircraft from the *Audacity* took off to search the area and spotted the U-boat on the surface. Walker concentrated five of his ships, ASDIC pinging, in search of the now-submerged enemy. She was found, forced to the surface, and shelled until her captain surrendered. *U-131* provided first blood for the defenders.

The same fate met *U-434* the following morning, but this double disaster did not in the least deter the pack, which closed in on the night of 18–19 December, blowing up one of the escorts, but losing another of their number a few minutes later. And so the ding-dong battle of attrition continued like a pack of hyenas following a herd of buck.

The biggest prize fell to Korvetten-Kapitän Bigalk, *U-751*, when he got close enough to the *Audacity* to put three torpedoes into the RN's first escort carrier and sent her to the bottom. That was at 20.35 hours on 21 December. By then the non-stop assault was almost over, and on the next day the off-watch men could at last relax and get some sleep. Doenitz had thrown in everything: his Condors and wave after wave of U-boats, all of them in the hands of experienced captains and supported by much increased anti-aircraft capability, which had led to one of the Martlet pilots becoming the first casualty of the convoy. From August 1942 all U-boats were also fitted with FuMB, a radar search receiver which warned when an aircraft was in radar contact, a piece of valuable equipment passed on to Germany's ally, Japan. But with the introduction of centimetric radar sets in February 1943 this device, too, became sterile, and remained so.

The destruction of HG76's carrier was a fine bonus for the German attackers, but they had sunk only two merchantmen over the six days and nights, and lost four U-boats out of the nine deployed. For the first time in the Battle of the Atlantic the Germans had lost almost half their attacking force, and twice as many U-boats had been sunk as merchantmen.

Was this the beginning of the Allies' 'happy time'? Had the U-boat menace really been mastered? There were those in the planning and intelligence divisions of the Admiralty who thought so. Others who remembered the past pendulum swing of advantage and counter-advantage were more cautious. Nevertheless, the Walker-principle of highly trained, tightly co-ordinated counter-attack, combined with air surveillance and air attack, was now making life too dangerous for the German submarines. But German U-boat architects were already working on new designs which would pose new problems for the Allies. German intelligence had been decrypting the British naval code with the same facility as Bletchley had been reading the German code.

Pearl Harbor and the declaration of war by the United States on Germany proved in the short term to be an advantage to Doenitz and his flotillas rather than the reverse, ending all uncertainty at last. Anglo–American co-operation was already so close on the Atlantic convoys that the new state of belligerency made little difference.

American participation in Atlantic naval warfare had begun, mildly enough, on 5 September 1939 when the US Navy's C-in-C, President Franklin D. Roosevelt, ordered a Neutrality Patrol as a gesture of defence of the Western Hemisphere, as he defined it. This had been followed by a meeting of Foreign Ministers of the American Republics in October which led to the passing of the Act of Panama. This defined a line down the North and South Atlantic on the west side of which the belligerent European nations were prohibited from 'conducting warlike operations'. It was really no more than a political gesture. It was not a line that could be rigorously patrolled, and when, at the Battle of the River Plate a few weeks later, German and British ships met well inside the zone, there was no hesitation about opening fire.

American participation in the Battle of the Atlantic took a giant step forward with the German seizure of the west coast of France, with all that that implied. Against a background of intense naval rearmament the American Atlantic Fleet began to engage in what was loosely referred to as a 'short of war' policy. Especially before the Battle of Britain was fought and won in the air by the RAF, there was deep anxiety in Washington about the imminent invasion of the British Isles and the surrender of the British Fleet, giving the Axis Powers – Germany, Italy and Japan – an overwhelming superiority at sea.

By the winter of 1940–41 the United States was being inexorably drawn into the European conflict. Britain, which traditionally had provided the first line of maritime defence for America in the east, was threatened with starvation, and the lucrative North Atlantic trade was close to becoming throttled by the ever-increasing U-boat attacks.

Owing to the threat to the sea communications of the United Kingdom, the principal task of the United States naval forces in the Atlantic will be the protection of shipping of the Associated Powers [Britain, USA and invaded European nations], the center of gravity of the United States' effort being concentrated in the North-western Approaches to the United Kingdom.

So ran a passage from the conclusions of a series of secret staff conversations held in Washington from 29 January 1941. In effect the US Navy would now take over a share of responsibility for the protection of North Atlantic shipping. Just how bad things were was emphasized by a statement made by Admiral Harold Stark, American Chief of Naval Operations, on 4 April 1941: 'The situation is obviously critical in the Atlantic. In my opinion, it is hopeless except as we take strong measures to save it. The effect on the British of sinkings with regard both to the food supply and essential material to carry on the war is getting progressively worse.'[10]

These strong measures included the massive reinforcement of the Atlantic Fleet at the expense of the Pacific Fleet and were taken against a background of sinkings of American ships in the North and South Atlantic. 'The war is approaching the brink of the Western Hemisphere itself,' Roosevelt declared on 27 May 1941. 'It is coming very close to home....' Early in September the first German attack was made on an American warship, the USS *Greer*, and Roosevelt let it be known that this sort of 'piracy' must lead to German or Italian warships being attacked in defence if they 'enter the waters the protection of which is necessary for American defence'.

Two months later neutrality legislation was repealed, and preparations were made for American warships to participate directly in convoy escort work. These plans were implemented in the case of Convoy HX150 which sailed from Halifax on 16 September 1941 with fifty vessels. A month later the first American warship was sunk by a U-boat. Declared war with Germany was still six weeks away; undeclared war was already in effect with the deaths of 150 officers and men of the destroyer *Reuben James*.

The formal declaration of war on Germany on 11 December 1941 coincided with the introduction by Doenitz of two new types of U-boat, the 1,100-ton long-range Type IX and the even bigger 1,700-ton 'milch cow' type, which rendezvoused with U-boats far from their base to renew their fuel stocks, food supplies and torpedoes.

Within days of the United States becoming a full instead of a half enemy, Doenitz had conceived plans to renew a campaign which, like wolf packs and surface night attacks, had been tried out in 1918. Now he intended to take the war to the American east coast. One U-boat ace, Peter Cremer, recalled how he heard to his amazement that on the east coast 'they seemed to be asleep, to put it mildly.... It emerged that the lights and buoys were not blacked out but shining as in deepest peacetime, for the guidance of friend and foe alike.' Coastal cities were not blacked out either, providing a convenient glow against which the continuous flow of traffic was silhouetted as if for target practice.

Doenitz asked Hitler if he could divert a dozen long-range boats to this area. Permission was restricted to six: they were enough to give the U-boat service another 'happy time', the happiest time of the whole war as it turned out.

The two areas of attack were between Cape Hatteras and the St Lawrence River to the north, and around Trinidad in the Caribbean. In January 1942 five U-boats sank almost 330,000 tons. Admiral King did not believe in convoys. On the old and long since discarded Churchillian principle of 'Attack. Attack!', King insisted on hunter-killer patrols. In five months they did not claim a single victim, while the slaughter, especially of British tankers, continued unabated.

Cremer did not arrive on the scene until May 1942 with his *U-333*. It had been an eventful passage, during which he refuelled for the first time in mid-ocean from a 'milch cow' and had been rammed by a tanker, which had badly damaged the U-boat's bows. Suddenly, on 4 May, they entered a new world – a new world almost of fantasy and make-believe. What they had heard about peacetime conditions off the American coast was now five months old. Surely the Americans would have learned their lesson by now!

Directly off Florida, we were in one of the loveliest holiday paradises in the world. As in quiet times, the fairway in the strait was marked with buoys, so navigation was not difficult. Everything seemed to me inexpressibly peaceful and I let my officers look through the periscope. When evening came we surfaced and, one after another, the men came up to the bridge for a breath of fresh air – and rubbed their eyes in disbelief.

We had left a blacked-out Europe behind us. Whether in Stettin, Berlin, Paris, Hamburg, Lorient or La Rochelle – everywhere had been pitch dark. At sea we tried not to show any light, even hiding the glowing cigarette in the hollow of the hand when smoking was allowed on the bridge. Not a ray of light came through the conning-tower hatch. Yet here the buoys were blinking as normal, the famous lighthouse at Jupiter Inlet was sweeping its luminous cone far over the sea. We were cruising off a brightly lit coastal road with darting headlights from innumerable cars. We went in so close that through the night glasses we could distinguish equally the big hotels and the cheap dives, and read the flickering neon signs. Not only that: from Miami and its luxurious suburbs a mile-wide band of light was being thrown upwards to glow like an aureole against the underside of the cloud layer, visible from far below the horizon. All this after nearly five months of war!

Before this sea of light, against this footlight glare of a carefree new world, were passing the silhouettes of ships recognizable in every detail and sharp as the outlines in a sales catalogue. Here they were formally presented to us on a plate: please help yourselves! All we had to do was press the button.[11]

In fact convoys had now been instituted, but the protection was sketchy and a number of ships straggled or failed to join and steamed on their own. Cremer's first victim was a 13,000-ton tanker, followed by another of 11,000 tons and a smaller freighter. Other U-boats nearby were enjoying an equally satisfactory 'happy time'. At length *U-333* headed for home, 4,500 miles distant, and almost at once encountered and sank the 7,500-ton freighter *Clan Skene*. That was on 10 May. Five days later the Navy Department at last prevailed upon the authorities to institute a complete coastal blackout, in spite of the strong lobbying of the tourist industry. Those anachronistic scenes of oil-stained, gaunt-eyed survivors landing at brightly illuminated resorts where the holiday season was in full swing were at last over. War had come – even to Miami. Convoying was tightened up along the full length of the American coast and losses dropped dramatically.

The unacceptable losses in the North Atlantic and the Western Approaches and the introduction of 'milch cows' for a time drew more U-boats to other distant hunting grounds besides the east coast of the United States. In the spring and summer of 1942 U-boats penetrated far into the South Atlantic and the Cape. They worked in widely spaced groups rather than packs, in conjunction with their big supply boats, and struck many blows at unprotected ships on distant shipping lanes. The Mediterranean was at this time virtually closed to mercantile traffic, which was forced to make the long passage about Africa. This made the Cape area a particularly lucrative killing ground, and once led to a curious and poignant incident.

Normally troopships for Egypt and the North African war sailed in convoy, well escorted, on the Cape route, but the big ships returning with few onboard had to look after themselves. No loaded troopships were sunk as a consequence, but several liners succumbed to U-boat attack on their homeward voyage when Doenitz ordered some groups south of the equator. One of these was the *Laconia*, a 20,000-tonner, which was certainly not empty: it carried over 2,000 Italian prisoners of war, besides many civilians, men and women.

U-156, Korvetten-Kapitän Hartenstein, picked up this fat target on 12 September and sank her at once. One or two survivors whom he saved he found to his horror were allies. He immediately despatched a message *en clair* calling for assistance. An international rescue mission was set in train. Two RN ships were despatched from Freetown, the Vichy French sent a sloop and the cruiser *Gloire* from Dakar, other U-boats from Hartenstein's group hastened to the spot. An American plane from the newly established base on Ascension island flew to the scene.

For more than three years of war torpedoed crews had been left to their fate, sometimes even by their fellow seamen, such were the dangers of rescue work. Now one radioed announcement that the U-boats were also promised immunity had led to this swift mercy operation.

The rescue operations were still proceeding, the French cruiser being instrumental in saving over 1,000 lives, when a Liberator flew over the scene, circled, flew off as if calling for instructions, then returned and bombed *U-156*, inaccurately as it turned out but with the immediate effect of cutting short the work of mercy. In spite of the most searching enquiries no one has ever discovered where that bomber was based and whether or not it asked for and received orders. Its attack certainly led to the loss of many hundreds of lives. In all, 450 Italians of 1,800 were saved, and 1,111 of the 2,732 passengers (many of them women) and crew. A few, after appalling sufferings, reached the coast of Liberia in a lifeboat.

When Doenitz heard this story he drafted an order which was despatched to all U-boats instructing commanders:

No attempt of any kind must be made at rescuing the crews of ships sunk. This prohibition applies to the picking up of men in the water and putting them in lifeboats, righting capsized lifeboats.... Be harsh, bearing in mind that the enemy takes no regard of women and children in his bombing attacks on German cities.

One U-boat commander, Heinz Eck, claimed that he was merely following this order when he machine-gunned in their open boats the crew of a freighter he sank on 13 March 1944. He also destroyed the boats in the hope that no trace would ever be found of his victims. Unfortunately for him three survivors eluded his machine-gunner and they were later picked up by a destroyer. Heinz Eck and his machine-gunner were, in their turn, among the survivors when their U-boat was sunk. They were both court-martialled, sentenced to death and executed by the British.

The other U-boat survivors in this case were treated as prisoners of war. Less fortunate were the crew of another U-boat sunk early in the war who were rescued, brought on board and then hunted down and shot one by one over a period of twelve hours, the last two sailors being found huddled in the ship's screw alley. Churchill was outraged when he heard and issued stern instructions to avoid a repetition.

These, however, were isolated cases in this inexorable *guerre de course*. On the whole the Battle of the Atlantic, with all its horrendous destruction and disregard for human life, was conducted on both sides with a surprisingly high regard for the unwritten rules of concern and mercy which govern sea warfare.

Doenitz's order after the *Laconia* affair almost cost him his life. At the Nuremberg Trials of war criminals he was eventually found guilty of two of the three charges arising from it, crimes against peace and war crimes, and was sentenced to ten years in prison.

But that fate for the U-boat C-in-C still lay four years ahead in September 1942, a month when he again changed tactics. He had always strongly believed that the North Atlantic held the key to victory for his command, and had obeyed orders reluctantly from Hitler to disperse his effort to distant theatres. Now, with the building rate of U-boats rising fast, increasing the operational number from ninety to 196 between January and October 1942 – even with losses – he received permission to reopen the offensive in this zone. But this time he operated his forces exclusively in the central area of the North Atlantic, where air cover was only intermittent. This was partly caused by Coastal Command's loss of priority in the supply of aircraft and air crews to Bomber Command and the Middle East. And this time, Doenitz's crews were ordered, they should revert to daylight attack, submerged.

This new offensive came at the time of the Anglo–American landings in North Africa, the first large joint amphibious operation of its kind, involving hundreds of ships, escorts and escort carriers. Thus further denuded of the protection vital to keep North Atlantic losses down to an acceptable level, the statistics soon made very grim reading. In November 1942 U-boats, mainly operating in mid-Atlantic, sank 117 Allied ships totalling 700,000 tons, and another 100,000 tons were lost by other causes – mines, bombing, etc. This was as bad as any period in the First World War, and came at a time when every ton was sorely needed for the tremendous task of feeding and supplying not only the people and factories of Britain, but also the great armies now operating in North Africa and preparing for the invasion of Europe from the south.

All over the world, too, the need was for ships, ships and more ships, from the south-west Pacific and the central Pacific where great amphibious operations were proceeding, to the Arctic north, where Russia was crying out for supplies for her beleaguered armies in the greatest land campaign of them all. And in German shipyards, in spite of heavy bombardment from the air, six new U-boats took to the water every week, and submariners graduated from training establishments to man these craft and replace those who lay entombed in their iron coffins* on the seabed.

The casualty level of U-boat crews was appallingly high throughout the

---

* 'To the seamen of all nations who died in the Battle of the Atlantic in World War II, and especially to my U-boat comrades who lie entombed in their Iron Coffins.' Dedication to the book of that title by Herbert A. Werner.

war, but rising to a terrible climax during the last year. The officers and men knew this, from sudden silences from U-boats working in their group, from the absence of friends in port and their own experience of narrow escapes. Boats were never reported missing or destroyed, and only the high command knew that on average in late 1942 and the first half of 1943 a boat would be lost on its third or fourth patrol, and that when sunk each crew member had a one in three chance of surviving.

Life at sea in the North Atlantic was like a very extended bomber mission: the same tedium, the same discomfort and buffeting, the same terror during an attack by the enemy – flak or depth-charge, there was little to choose between them – the same mixed elation and relief with the dropping of the bombloads or the launching of a spread of torpedoes, the same comradeship to sustain each crew member's spirit. An oberleutnant of *U-448* confirms the importance of this spirit:

The life on board our Atlantic operational boats was very hard because of the constricted space and the proximity of the sea; even on the bridge we were only five metres above the water. As every man on board was visible to everyone else and regardless of rank and position exposed to the same hardships, sacrifices and dangers, there had to develop quickly a strong feeling of togetherness, of sharing the same fate. It fulfilled us completely even when we were not at sea. It was our whole life. We had been put into it with all its glory and terror and we accepted it, often with joy and enthusiasm, often with anxiety and fear.[12]

But another U-boat officer also speaks of the depths to which spirits could sink when a target eluded them for a long time during their patrol – a state of affairs which became more common as convoys were routed away from them.

When a U-boat had been at sea for days or even weeks without seeing a ship [wrote Kapitänleutnant Kurt Baberg of *U-618*] morale on board was not of the best especially if we kept hearing on the wireless of other boats' successes. We were always very pleased to get the order from B.d.U. to form a patrol line; we knew from experience that this gave the best opportunity of finding a convoy. We put the best men on look-out duty; very often there was a bottle of champagne or cognac on return to harbour for the man who made the first sighting. Morale reached the depths when storms or rain blotted out visibility and went even lower if the sweep went on too long without a sighting. We felt then that the convoy had slipped through or round the line.[13]

By contrast there was the tingling excitement of stalking the enemy, positioning for the attack, and finally delivering it, the awesome destructive power shooting from the tubes and racing at 40 knots at shallow depth towards the target.

U-758 had been in contact with a big convoy for twelve hours. Her commander, Kapitänleutnant Helmut Manseck, describes the last moments:

I had shadowed the convoy all day keeping at extreme range on the starboard side, just keeping the smoke and tips of the masts in sight. I remember that the ships were doing well and not making much smoke. We had been about twelve miles out during the day and came in to four to five miles at dusk.

When I came in to make my attack I found that I had misjudged the speed of the convoy and that we were almost level with it but I decided to attack from there rather than try to get ahead again; we came in from just ahead of 90 degrees. I could see six, eight, or ten ships and selected a solid, overlapping target of the third ship in the starboard columns. We fired our four torpedoes, then turned sharply away to port and ran out.[14]

Manseck claimed a hit for all four torpedoes. It was as common for U-boat captains as bomber captains to exaggerate the damage, and it was not usually deliberate. In fact two ships were hit: a Dutch cargo ship, the *Zaanland*, and an American Liberty ship, the *James Oglethorpe*. For the crew of the *Zaanland* the extent of the German claim was irrelevant. They knew only that it was dark, that a long and dangerous night stretched ahead, that the convoy was inadequately protected, and that shortly before 9.30 p.m. there was a mighty explosion. Chief Officer P.G. van Altveer recalled:

I was just passing Number 4 hatch, when it suddenly happened. I felt the iron deckplating rattle and shake under my feet. I saw a flash of light and felt a torrent of water all over my body and then I was blasted away. At first I thought that I was swept into the sea but then I lost consciousness. After about ten minutes I regained consciousness and found out that I was lying on my back between the winches of Number 4 hatch and the mainmast. I saw the stars and clouds right above me and realized my situation. I got up very carefully and walked towards the boat-deck being well aware of the danger that the deckplating might have been torn open by the explosion of the torpedo but everything appeared to be safe to proceed. I later found that I had two broken ribs.

Captain Gerardus Franken was the *Zaanland*'s master. He heard the water rushing in through the great hole torn in the ship's side, forcing up oil from the tanks below which flooded across the decks and into the sea, where it 'calmed the troubled waters', just like the saying. He knew that it would also be a choking enemy, and that his ship must be abandoned at once. An officer, J. Waasenaar, was in command of one of the boats, and later described the scene graphically:

The boats were wildly tossing up and down. I don't remember climbing into my boat but I do remember vividly struggling with the lower davit blocks to disengage them from the lifeboat. One moment there was slack in the boat falls, the next moment they were dangerously tight; we were buck-jumping all the time. One moment our eyes were level with the ship's railing, the next moment we saw the boot-top flashing past us. When we got the afterblock free, it started to swing dangerously over our heads. It knocked my cap off and that cap seemed so damned important to me that, for a moment, I forgot that far more important things were at hand. I desperately searched for the cap without finding it. Disengaging the forward block was impossible and, in the end, we cut the falls.

We saw the other lifeboats also waiting for what was going to happen to our ship. We did not have long to wait; she sank very rapidly, stern first she went down. With her bows high in the air, we heard a rumble like thunder.[15]

This was the Battle of the Atlantic, as experienced by thousands of the protagonists, of whom these four men were fortunate to survive. In March 1943 the casualty rate among merchant seamen was still rising,* a ghastly toll in a war that featured none of the zest, glory, prestige and honours of tank warfare on land or the stabbing thrill of battle in the air. For most of the men for most of the time it was a cold, wet, miserable and hellish business.

The German invasion of Russia on 22 June 1941 soon brought new responsibilities for the hard-pressed Royal Navy, and new opportunities for German U-boats, surface raiders and the *Luftwaffe*. On the day before this invasion Churchill was at Chequers for the weekend, with – among others – the American Ambassador, John Winant, and his wife. The Prime Minister knew for certain, but had failed to convince the Russians, that war between the two great empires must soon break out, and at dinner that evening informed his guests. Hitler, Churchill added, was confident of enlisting right-wing political sympathies in Britain and in America. But when this attack took place, on the contrary, Britain and America should give all the help and support to Russia that they could. On behalf of the United States, Winant agreed.

When, later in the evening, Churchill's private secretary expressed some surprise to him that an ardent anti-Communist should take such an attitude, Churchill replied, 'Not at all, I have only one purpose, the destruction of Hitler, and my life is much simplified thereby. If Hitler invaded Hell I would make at least a favourable reference to the Devil in the House of Commons.'[16]

On the following day, Sunday, 22 June 1941, Churchill returned to London to make a long, rousing, highly emotional broadcast to the British people. In the course of one particularly fighting passage the Prime Minister stated that 'any man or state who fights on against Nazidom will have our aid ...'. Even before Harry Hopkins, America's roving Ambassador, returned from Moscow the following month with pleas for help, Roosevelt had decided that America, too, must make every effort to ship war goods to Russia.

The only effective means of getting supplies to Britain's new ally at this stage was by sea, around the North Cape to the north Russian ports. These Russian convoys, from the beginning, were extremely hazardous and physically demanding. The long winter nights provided concealment from U-boats, aircraft and surface warships stationed in Norway. But conditions at sea were as frightful as anywhere in the world, and from the New Year

---

* In all the British Merchant Navy lost 30,248 men; the Royal Navy 51,578 in the U-boat war.

until mid-March the pack-ice line moved steadily south, forcing shipping to steer closer to the North Cape and to German bases. But the summer months were even more dangerous as almost perpetual daylight exposed convoys to non-stop German air and sea reconnaissance.

The Royal Navy prepared itself philosophically for this new task. It could not have come at a worse time, when the Atlantic convoys were demanding all the escort vessels that could be spared, and the duties and losses of warships in the Mediterranean were at their height. Nevertheless, Churchill had said Russia 'will have our aid' and steps were at once taken to implement this promise. While Churchill himself was crossing the Atlantic in early August 1941 in the battleship *Prince of Wales* to meet Roosevelt at Newfoundland (and high on the agenda of their discussion was aid for Russia), the first convoy set off for Russia. Russian losses of fighter aircraft had been appalling in the first weeks of war, and now two dozen Hurricanes were squeezed into the old carrier *Argus*, and more were stowed, crated, into a number of merchantmen, along with other munitions. Every ship arrived at Archangel safely. So did fifty-five more ships later, all packed to the gunwales with armaments and raw materials. Britain could ill spare these fighters, tanks, trucks, etc., all badly needed in the Middle East, but considering the scale of Russian losses and Russian suffering at the time, it was the least that could be done, practically and politically. It would just have been a happier business if the Russian authorities had been more gracious, co-operative and efficient and less carping at the scale of the operation. Perhaps their attitude would improve later? It never did.

In retrospect it seems remarkable that the *Luftwaffe* and the German Navy allowed these valuable first supplies to pass by their back door without any interference. For not only were the Russians receiving the supplies but the Royal Navy was gaining invaluable experience for the rougher days that lay ahead.

During the early weeks of 1942 Enigma decrypts at Bletchley indicated more and more clearly that serious counter-measures against this passage of armaments to Russia were being put in hand. Surface ships, *Luftwaffe* aircraft equipped with bombs or torpedoes, and strong forces of U-boats were all being alerted.

Outgoing Russian convoys were code-named PQ, returning convoys QP. PQ13 set sail on 20 March, and QP9 the following day from Murmansk, so that there would soon be rich pickings. Ten U-boats were deployed for these operations, and Enigma was able to provide Admiralty intelligence with the details of their patrol areas and to warn that attacks of all kinds could also be expected.

Without this intelligence the losses among the merchantmen of PQ13 must have been much higher. As it was, the five victims were either stragglers or ships which had been scattered by atrocious weather; and the price Germany paid – three destroyers sunk or damaged – was a great deal higher than had been anticipated. Subsequent convoys through the early summer of 1942 suffered worse, and the loss of escorting ships, including two cruisers, was a further grave worry. The twenty-four-hour days at the most northerly and most dangerous leg of the voyage made life desperately difficult for the escorts, which had no respite, while attacking aircraft, destroyers and U-boats slipped to and from their Norwegian bases and airfields in relays.

The Admiralty request for permission to call a halt to the Russian convoys until the days became shorter and there could be greater reliance on foul weather and fogs to help conceal their passage was rejected. The reasons were political as well as strategic. Marshal Stalin could – and did frequently and vehemently – claim that while the Russian armies and people were bearing nine-tenths of the burden of the German war the West should be prepared for the loss of a few ships in supporting the common cause.

On 6 May 1942 Stalin wrote to Churchill asking him to release what he believed to be as many as ninety merchantmen loaded with supplies for Russia but awaiting an adequate escort. 'Please', he wrote 'take all possible measures in order to ensure the arrival of all the above-mentioned materials in the USSR in the course of May, as this is extremely important for our front'.[17]

Churchill replied on 9 May pointing to the dangers, especially from surface ships, and concluding with a hint that the Russians themselves might contribute to the protection of these convoys.

Prime Minister to Premier Stalin   *9 May 42*

I have received your telegram of May 6, and thank you for your message and greetings. We are resolved to fight our way through to you with the maximum amount of war materials. On account of *Tirpitz* and other enemy surface ships at Trondheim the passage of every convoy has become a serious fleet operation. We shall continue to do our utmost.

No doubt your naval advisers have pointed out to you the dangers to which the convoys are subjected from attack by enemy surface forces, submarines, and air from the various bases in enemy hands which flank the route of the convoy throughout its passage. We are throwing all our available resources into the solution of this problem, have dangerously weakened our Atlantic convoy escorts for this purpose, and, as you are no doubt aware, have suffered severely.

I am sure that you will not mind my being quite frank and emphasizing the need for increasing the assistance given by the USSR naval and air forces in helping to get these convoys through safely.[18]

As a direct consequence of Marshal Stalin's appeal the biggest of all Russian convoys assembled in Iceland and sailed on 27 June 1942. It consisted of thirty-four ships, a close escort under Commander 'Jackie' Broome of six destroyers, two anti-aircraft ships, two submarines and eleven smaller craft, including 'rescue' ships. These vessels of mercy had recently been included in convoys and were equipped with medical teams and all the necessary equipment to comfort and care for half-drowned, half-frozen merchant seamen, who were dragged from the sea by specially rigged nets.

This was highly dangerous work that had been previously conducted – often too late – by the escorts themselves, diverted from their primary function of hunting and destroying U-boats.

This convoy carried the identification PQ17. The ships were of mixed origin, but with a high proportion of American vessels, Liberty ships. Two American heavy cruisers, the USS *Wichita* and USS *Tuscaloosa*, also contributed to the support force of four 8-inch-gun warships and three destroyers under the command of Rear-Admiral Louis Hamilton. As distant back-up there was, as usual, the Home Fleet, again with a substantial American contribution in the form of the new battleship *Washington*, with the C-in-C, Admiral Tovey, flying his flag in the *Duke of York*, a carrier and destroyer.

Tovey's task was a dual one of ensuring that the heavy German surface ships did not break out to attack the Atlantic convoys, and to protect the incoming and outgoing Russian convoys in the remoteness of the Barents Sea. These double duties were a consideration that weighed heavily with the Admiral at sea and the Naval War Staff in the Admiralty, and with Sir Dudley Pound, First Sea Lord.

There was a fair chance of this large convoy fighting through to Russia, like its predecessors, with an acceptable number of losses so long as it did not become the target for the powerful German surface ships in north Norway. In that event it was recognized that Admiral Tovey was unlikely to arrive in time to help, and Admiral Hamilton was much too weak to deal with 11-inch guns. U-boats were also a major threat, as were the numerous land-based German bombers, especially at this time of perpetual daylight. But these last were a known quantity and the escort was well equipped to deal with both.

At first everything went smoothly and there was a distinct air of optimism. This increased further when the first air attack was beaten off without loss. Broome was delighted and wrote 'in my diary in the charthouse of HMS *Keppel* that the convoy was going like a train, and if the ack-ack ammunition (which to date had been sprayed rather extravagantly) lasted out, I reckoned that we could get anywhere'.[19]

Godfrey Winn, the journalist, was serving as a seaman on this convoy and gave a most graphic account of what it was like to be on Arctic convoys, and PQ17 in particular. The mass attacks by Heinkel III torpedo bombers were more nerve-testing than the stealthy U-boat. These were no 'Stringbags' either – all doped canvas and struts and 90 knots maximum – but twin-engined 280-mph machines, bristling with machine-guns as well as two torpedoes. Winn watched another attack developing – an attack which, like the others, was touched with triumph and tragedy.

They did not hesitate or hover on the horizon, like the previous relays of Heinkels – all part of a deliberate strategy, presumably, to weaken our concentration, to keep us hanging about at Action Stations, to fill us with false confidence that they had no real desire to come in and mix – but these specially chosen squadrons came bang into the attack at mast height. And everything going up at them, right across the whole sweep of the convoy, everything. It was like a Brock's* Benefit Performance, in daylight.

Aferwards, I heard that the destroyer *Offa* had only time to send a Signal, '25 Heinkels approaching', before the first wave was on their starboard quarter. From our position on the port side of the convoy, we had a dress circle view, and in the isolation of our intense excitement to witness the drama, one lost all sense of approaching danger. Some of the enemy, picked pilots though they were, turned away, unable to face the curtain of fire from the escorts. Others were brought down before they reached us. But their leader seemed to have a charmed life. Deliberately on and on he came, weaving in and out of the columns, as though conscious that by his example he could compel the others to follow, and all the time it was obvious he was making a dead set at the tanker *Aldersdale* which, in relays, had been oiling the destroyers. Even so, he found time – and the precision – to drop a couple of bombs athwart the conning-towers of *M.614* and her sister 'sub' who had surfaced in the middle of the convoy. As for the tanker, his main objective, I wish all those who are now brave enough to boast openly of their black market hauls on shore could have been forced to see the instantaneous sheet of flame that shot up far higher than the level of the attacking machines, swallowed in turn by a huge bellyful of belching black smoke, completely obscuring its subsequent fate. A funeral pyre.

At that moment, fresh cheering broke out round me. And no wonder! We were truly in the battle ourselves now, blazing away with all our pom-poms and Oerlikons, and look, there's our first bag, falling to starboard of us, in the water, sizzling like burning cooking fat, as it hit the Drink ... and there's our second ... you can see it better from the bridge (which I had now reached) away to port of us. The second was the leader, and yet another cheer rose at that, but what I remember most vividly of all was PO Hynes's epitaph. He is with Peter now, he said, and got six iron crosses into the bargain.

Certainly the Nazi pilot had led a suicide attack with great courage, I agreed as I stared at the burning wreckage on the water.[20]

Jackie Broome's optimism was not reflected in the Admiralty 2,000 miles to the south, where London was experiencing fine, warm summer weather. All was gloom in the operations room where, as usual, they were receiving an amazingly comprehensive picture of German activities, but this time flawed with gaps caused by the delay in decrypting several German signals due to new German code settings. What was starkly clear was that the battleship *Tirpitz* and the heavy cruiser *Hipper* had left their base at Trondheim and were proceeding north, and the pocket battleship *Scheer* was also ordered to move north from Narvik. The pocket battleship *Lützow* was also involved in these movements, but precisely how was not known until later.

Clearly, these four powerful ships with 15-inch, 11-inch and 8-inch guns, working together could mutilate or destroy the entire escorting force with impunity and then set about the convoy long before the Home Fleet could

* The well-known fireworks company.

get among them. What even Enigma could not do was to penetrate the mind and 'read' the conclusions of Adolf Hitler at this critical moment. Nor could this magical machine make allowances for the gross incompetency of the German navigators which led to all three of *Tirpitz's* escorting destroyers grounding in a fjord and the *Lützow* running aground so badly that she was unfit for sea, later having to return to Germany for repairs.

Hitler, who was prepared to hurl hundreds of tanks into a Russian counter-attack with the near certainty of suffering 90 per cent losses; who, at Crete the previous year, had sacrificed almost his entire strength of airborne forces; who had shown himself a risk-taker over and over again – this same war leader was not prepared to risk elements of his fleet even with the fair prospect of annihilating the biggest Russian convoy of them all, unless the danger element was virtually nil. The reason for this timorousness, which was reflected down the ranks of the surface fleet, had its origins in the policy of the high command in the First World War, when, by keeping the High Seas Fleet 'in being', it had tied down the British Grand Fleet for the duration of hostilities. There are no braver warriors than the Germans but in its brief history the German Navy has never shown much of the Nelson spirit, believing, perhaps subconsciously, that wiliness and the waiting game bring better results than blind aggression.

On this occasion Hitler was not prepared to allow his big ships to proceed against PQ17 without positive assurance that there was no carrier within range, or if it were, before it was put out of action by the *Luftwaffe*. No such positive assurance was forthcoming, so that, while every preparation for a surface fleet attack was made, and the big ships moved north in readiness, nothing further could be done. The officers and men of these idle ships – some 5,000 of them – who had been bored and frustrated for so long holed up in their sanctuaries, reconciled themselves to sinking back into inactivity. 'It was hard for us to bear,' complained one gunnery officer, 'especially after we had been brought to a knife edge of expectation and knew what a juicy target there was not far away.'

With the weather remaining poor for aerial reconnaissance, and Enigma offering information on the German preparations for putting to sea, the Naval War Staff at the Admiralty were in a quandary. Then at a meeting on the evening of 4 July 1942 the drastic and, as it turned out, catastrophic decision was made to withdraw PQ17's escort and order the convoy to scatter.

Hamilton and Broome were appalled when they received this signal. They thought they were doing rather well and, while suffering some losses, were giving the *Luftwaffe* a rough time. With the convoy held tight together under the disciplined control of the navy with its sophisticated defence against U-boat attack and exceptionally heavy anti-aircraft capability, both officers were confident of getting through. Then, like a thousand-kilogram bomb from a Heinkel, the Admiralty signals were taken in, couched in terms that indicated the need for utmost urgency. An officer in the *Norfolk* made these observations at the time:

At 26 knots the four cruisers and all the destroyers swept close past the convoy. Our last sight of the merchantmen showed them slowly opening out and separating. The effect on the ship's company was devastating. Twenty-four hours earlier there had been only one thought – that at last we were going to bring enemy surface ships to action. I had never known the men in such good heart.... Then in the space of a few hours ... we abandoned the convoy. The ship was in a turmoil; everyone was boiling, and the Master at Arms told me he had never known such strong feelings before.... It was the blackest day we ever knew – sheer bloody murder.[21]

Admiral Hamilton had no alternative but to obey with equal urgency. This huge and valuable convoy was suddenly bereft of the protection that had so far been so successful at fighting off the enemy. As one officer has put it, 'By simply shifting her anchorage the *Tirpitz* had done what massed U-boats and aircraft had failed to do. She had broken the cohesion of the convoy, the principal defence against both these methods of attack.'

The consequences were dreadfully predictable. When the isolated, demoralized survivors eventually reached Russia the count was just eleven out of thirty-seven ships which had left Iceland on that late June afternoon.

So ended one of the most controversial and melancholy naval incidents of the war. The arguments blaming and defending Admiral Pound and members of his Staff (none of whom dissented in his decision to scatter the convoy) have raged ever since. Others have blamed Admiral Hamilton, and one historian who hinted at cowardice in Broome was taken to court some twenty-five years later and had to pay £40,000 damages.

There was no cowardice over the PQ17 catastrophe; indeed there was much sublime courage exhibited by the men of many of those ships that were picked off by bomb or torpedo after the escort was withdrawn. Tovey, Hamilton and Broome all blamed Pound, as have most authorities since. Broome himself in his memoirs has written,

The order given in the final signal either had to be obeyed or ignored. To my dying regret I obeyed it. Having done so, it triggered off a sequence of events which (as Admiral Tovey agreed later) were inevitable, by accepted naval procedure. ... What the result would have been had the order to scatter not been given, no one knows. But with the *Tirpitz* and her consorts then almost regarded by the Germans as 'sacred cows', the result could hardly have been worse. The responsibility for what actually did happen must therefore for ever rest on the shoulders of the man who gave that order, and his advisers.

And yet a strong case can be made for Admiral Pound's decision, too. In no naval operation was the formula of probabilities more complex.

Chance and imponderables certainly ruled at this time. If the heavy German warships had departed on their mission of destruction, patrolling British and Russian submarines, never absent, might damage one or two and force them to return, and PQ17's own submarines might do the same. By clever manoeuvring of the heavy cruisers and the use of smoke and deployment of the destroyers, an attack on the scattering merchantmen would be postponed. The 8-inch guns of Hamilton's cruisers might cause enough damage to deter the big ships and, on the past evidence of German nervousness, lead them to shy off entirely, especially as the Admiralty believed (rightly) that the enemy naval commander had no certain knowledge of the whereabouts of the Home Fleet.

On the other hand if, as the Admiralty believed to be almost certain, the German heavy ships had already left Norway and could therefore be on top of the convoy in a few hours they could, equally, sink all four heavy cruisers before the British could get within range, then deal with Broome's escorting light ships, and finally the merchantmen before they could scatter. The loss of four more heavy cruisers in addition to the *Edinburgh* and *Trinidad* in early May in PQ15 was a serious consideration. Moreover two of them were American, and the consequences of their loss took considerations into the arena of politics and future Anglo–American naval co-operation, especially as the admiral was British.

The order to a convoy to scatter was an accepted contingency in *The Merchant Navy Signal Book*. The manœuvre was the subject of diagrams and was even rehearsed.

This was a pre-arranged manœuvre [writes one senior naval officer], in which each ship had a course to steer differing from that of its neighbours. Thus, on the order to scatter, the convoy would open up like the petals of a symmetrical flower. By the time the raider had dealt with the escort, the ships of the convoy would be steering away to every point of the compass, making it a lengthy business for the raider to round them up one by one and sink them.[22]

There was, after all, the early precedent of the *Jervis Bay*, whose Captain's order to scatter while he engaged the enemy resulted in a remarkable escape. But that was different in many respects from PQ17's situation on 4 July 1942.* The *Jervis Bay*'s ships scattered into the long winter night in the broad expanse of the Atlantic; PQ17's ships faced twenty-four hours of daylight and were confined to the narrow breadth of the Barents Sea.

The most important difference was that the *Jervis Bay*'s decision was taken by the captain on the scene who had the enemy in sight and firing at him; the PQ17's by an admiral in London who was unaware of the prevailing optimism and determination of the convoy after early successes. And Admiral Pound made his decision on surmise – not on the evidence of shell bursts from an attacking enemy.

Much criticism has been levelled at the First Sea Lord not only for his decision but for the fact that he did not even consult with Admirals Tovey or Hamilton before making it. This is quite unjust. There was no

---

* The American merchantmen in the convoy all simultaneously ran out large new national flags in a gesture of defiance and celebration on this, Independence Day. These Stars and Stripes had a tonic effect on all those who beheld them after the initial shock of seeing the old colours lowered as in surrender after an enemy air attack.

time for consultation, so urgent did Pound consider the decision to be. Interference, or distant orders from on high, were nothing new in the British and other navies. In the German Navy control was absolutely rigid.

Control by the Admiralty, the navy's operational headquarters, of campaigns at sea was established far back into the mists of time. It had merely become more efficient with the development and refinement of submarine cables, later long-range radio, and above all the massive increase in the volume of accurate intelligence. With the keen encouragement of Winston Churchill as First Lord of the Admiralty in 1914–15, and his personal intervention at critical moments, this long-range control, *without complete trust between the First Sea Lord and his admirals*, could have baleful and sometimes disastrous consequences. It was just the same in the Second World War. All Pound did was to conform to a long-established practice, which worked when there was confidence and trust. No admiral was then ever blamed for making decisions contrary to advice or direction from the Admiralty.

As another naval officer who worked in the Operations Intelligence Centre during the war has written: 'Admiral Tovey had proposed, should there be strong evidence of the *Tirpitz* and *Scheer* leaving their bases, that the convoy should be turned back towards his advancing ships in the hope of reaching their protection in time. The First Sea Lord, however, had decided that the convoy must go on.'[23]

Undoubtedly Admiral Tovey's opinion was the correct one. He was there, he knew his enemy, he was highly experienced and he had as much recent information as the First Sea Lord. Had PQ17 turned back, *Luftwaffe* reconnaissance planes would have reported the fact, just as they had already reported the distant presence of units of the Home Fleet. In the face of two modern battleships and a carrier there was no doubt what the German commander on the spot would have done, even without the prohibition of Adolf Hitler. He would have turned tail and fled.

The real lessons of PQ17 were: leave the initiative to the commander at sea not the officers back at base; and however brilliant your intelligence penetration, remember that it can never penetrate the mind and fighting spirit of the enemy.

'Convoy Slaughter in the Arctic Sea', German propaganda crowed, for once with justification. The Russians were deprived of all but a fraction of their desperately needed supplies. And they would get no more, anyway for the time being and by this route. The Admiralty view at last prevailed, and Stalin had to be told that the disaster of PQ17 meant the end of Arctic convoys for the time being. 'It is therefore with the greatest regret', Churchill signalled to the Marshal, 'that we have reached the conclusion that to attempt to run the next convoy, PQ18, would bring no benefit to you and would only involve dead loss to the common cause.' A multitude of causes had led to this considerable German victory, among them, paradoxically, Allied will to get at the enemy and German reluctance to take risks.

CHAPTER FOUR

Folly and Infamy

Every Japanese naval officer knew the story from 1905 of Captain Narikava of the *Sinano Maru*; how he had heard the enemy's radio chatter, faint and fading in a roar of static, then the message slowly coming clearer and louder, until human eyes took over from primitive electronics and the vast spread of the enemy fleet could be seen a mere seven miles distant. Japanese schoolchildren were later told how Captain Narikava had tapped out in Morse the message to his C-in-C that the enemy was steaming slowly north-east towards their homeland.

In sight at last! After the weeks of anxious preparation and waiting, the enemy had been located, and Admiral Togo, it was said, smiled for the first time in the war. 'Having received warning that the enemy fleet is in sight,' the Admiral telegraphed to Japanese headquarters, 'the combined squadrons will go out to meet and defeat it....' And so they did, all but annihilating the powerful Russian Fleet sent to destroy the fledgling Japanese squadrons, in the most decisive victory in modern naval warfare: the Battle of Tsu-Shima.

That was a mere thirty-six years ago. Now, in the first light of 7 December 1941, 'the combined squadrons' were again about to 'meet and defeat' the enemy – not with the gunfire of 10,000-ton ironclads but the bombs and torpedoes of almost 400 naval aircraft, manned by crews as dedicated and skilful as the sailors of 1905. Just as Captain Narikava had groped his way towards the Russian Fleet, guided by the apprehensive chatter of Russian wireless operators, Commander Mitsuo Fuchida, by adjusting the radio direction-finding controls in his plane, could locate his target, far ahead and far below. By contrast with the anxious Russian messages of 1905 Commander Fuchida was listening to the strains of Hawaiian guitar music, broken by commercials for Coca-Cola and Camel cigarettes, broadcast by the Honolulu radio station KGMB. It sounded cheerful and inviting, and innocent. He found he was five degrees off course, and led his armada of torpedo-bombers, dive-bombers, horizontal-bombers and the escorting fighters above into a slight correcting turn.

The first planes had taken off from the six carriers at 6 a.m., climbing slowly with their heavy load into the pre-dawn sky and then into the premature sunrise, a reflection of the scarlet-painted suns on the wings of every plane; then forming up into groups on a southerly heading. They made the greatest force of shipborne aircraft ever to set off on a mission, and certainly it was the most important mission upon which the Imperial Japanese Navy had ever embarked, more important even than Tsu-Shima.

First conceived in 1909, just one year after Wilbur and Orville Wright had taken their flying machine to Europe to prove their claims, the mission was, no less, to destroy in a surprise attack the American Fleet at its main base, Pearl Harbor, on Oahu, one of the Hawaiian islands. Thirty-two years before it was to have been a bombardment from the sea and a suicide attack by submarines and torpedo-boats. With the development of air power Admiral Isoroku Yamamoto, C-in-C First Fleet, had persuaded his superiors that he could cripple the American Pacific Fleet from the air, without a single man-o'-war coming within sight of shore.

In the event one feature of the original conception remained: the torpedoing of American warships inside Pearl Harbor by Japanese submarines. In 1909 they would have been imported submarines from the United States and Great Britain. By 1941 the Imperial Japanese Navy possessed a formidable force of home-built submarines, five of which were fitted with pick-a-back miniature two-man submarines which were to attempt an entry of the inner harbour.

Hostilities in the greatest naval war in history began before Commander Fuchida sighted the Hawaiian islands. The periscope of one of these midgets was sighted two miles off the harbour entrance buoy and was attacked by a patrolling American destroyer. It was sunk with gunfire and depth-charges at 6.45 a.m.

The alarming report on this incident was passed to Admiral H.E.Kimmel, C-in-C Pacific Fleet. 'I will be right down,' he answered and hastened to his headquarters. Unknown to him until later, at least one of the midgets penetrated the anti-torpedo net protecting the habour; but all five were eventually lost without committing any damage on their 'day of infamy', as the American President described 7 December 1941.

Commander Fuchida knew nothing of this setback far beneath him, nothing of the first loss of Japanese lives. He was preoccupied with making the correct landfall and was much concerned with the eight-tenths cloud reflecting the brilliant early morning sun. He was reassured to hear the forecast for the day's weather broadcast from station KGMB during a brief break in the music. It should be all right – a few clouds, and these mostly over the mountains, good visibility: 'a great day for barbecues and the beach'. And within minutes the Japanese commander could see for himself the accuracy of this conveniently timed information. The clouds below broke up and between the gaps he caught sight of the northern coastline of Oahu from Kahuku Point west to Kawela Bay, the surf marking a strong white jagged line.

The first wave of over 213 planes, at heights between 9,000 and 15,000 feet, thundered south across the island, over the soft valleys and hills, the farmhouses and villages, the winding dirt roads, over a lake dotted with a few early morning fishing boats. Like any Japanese tourist, one of the bomber pilots, Lieutenant Toshio Hashimoto, snapped the scene with his little camera.

Minutes later the main features of Pearl Harbor itself could be seen ahead and below. Its configuration was familiar to all the Japanese air crew, who had had unlimited opportunity to study the large-scale model prepared long ago for this moment, the aerial photographs taken from light aircraft and mailed from the Japanese consulate in Honolulu. It was like reading from a story book and suddenly finding it was really happening. There was Ford Island, looking like a foetus within a womb, the indented outline of the harbour with Waipo peninsula extending south, the naval dockyard, the oil tanks like serried ranks of balls in a bowling alley; the long, broad stretches of runway of the air base on the land, and the clearly defined umbilical cord of the railway to Honolulu, curving past Hickham Field air base, one of the primary targets.

And there were the ships themselves, the ships they were to destroy within the next minutes, appearing a lighter shade of grey than they had expected, and in their numbers and position sure proof that surprise had been total. All but the fighter pilots who were too high for certain identification could distinguish the battleships, in neat peacetime formation along the east side of Ford Island – one, two, four more in pairs, another detached and to the south-east, in dock the eighth, making up the entire Pacific Fleet of battleships. While on the other side of Ford Island, moored in line with two cruisers and a big seaplane tender, was a big ship they identified as an aircraft carrier.

Nothing appeared to be moving, not a car on the roads, not a vessel in the harbour. At just before 8.00 a.m. on this fine December morning Pearl Harbor might have been a ghost of a naval base, a life-size enlargement of the model back home at their own naval base.

No radio message passed between group leaders and their pilots. Everything had been rehearsed and the planes took up their correct positions as if for an air pageant over Tokyo. Just one message was expected, and Commander Fuchida now made it, seizing his signal pistol and firing it from his cockpit – a single 'black dragon' flaming into the sky. Attack now!

To the few people on the ground who heard the thunder of the oncoming armada and saw the massed little crosses like a Flanders war grave high in the sky, this was an exercise by the navy or the Army Air Corps to test the island's defences. No one, civilian or serviceman alike, was able to accept that this was a hostile attack by the Japanese. A screen of conformity, protective and comforting, separated the normality of a quiet Sunday morning from the unacceptable reality of massive and sudden violence.

The only witnesses to the arrival of the attacking aircraft who were forced to accept the truth were a handful of civilian pilots in light planes up for an early morning flip or instruction. Three planes, including one piloted by an experienced woman, Cornelia Fort, found themselves engulfed by more planes than they had ever seen in the air at one time. Their unfamiliar shape, their yellow colour, their sheer numbers, and then the recognition of the red ball of the rising sun – the 'meatball' as it came to be known – on the wings and fuselage of the planes destroyed any last illusions. One of the little planes was fired at briefly, and the pilot dropped his machine like a stone towards safety.

Commander Fuchida's signal pistol shot was echoed innocently by the regular morning signal to all the ninety-five naval ships in the harbour. It was a hoist of bunting which fluttered out from the top of the signal tower, a white square on a solid field of blue, the Prep, which at 7.55 a.m. precisely indicated that morning colours would rise in just five minutes, at 8.00 a.m. On this morning the 'P' unknowingly marked more than the beginning of another day; it marked the beginning of a Sunday of devastation and death, for at that moment the bombs began to fall.

It was like the rumbling overture of the timpani in a Wagner opera. Far to the east the bombers fell upon the flying-boat base and then swept west across Oahu, wrecking the air bases of Bellows, Wheeler and Hickham fields as a precaution against fighter opposition. It was a good tactical move but no planes were standing by to scramble on this quiet Sunday morning. They were all in conveniently neat lines, ripe for destruction by long bursts of cannon and machine-gun fire.

A number of early risers saw the Japanese planes circling overhead, orbiting in groups which split into smaller formations before coming in to the main attack. Other people rose from their beds and came out on to verandahs or front lawns, some with binoculars to observe what was clearly a spectacular exercise. A few of these civilians were not best pleased at this early awakening, but most were reassured by the demonstration of America's power to defend the islands. 'I never knew we had so many planes!'

No one seriously expected an attack so distant from Japanese bases, but these past weeks had been anxious ones of threats and accusation. The international scene was critical, with Britain fighting in North Africa, in the North Atlantic and the Mediterranean, and defending herself from more air raids, and Russia fighting for her life on a 1,000-mile front. Even when the first shudder of exploding bombs was felt and then heard, punctuated by the ripple of machine-gun fire like tearing calico; even when the first black puffs of anti-aircraft fire spotted the sky, there were still plenty of people who only remarked on the realism of this mock attack. One boy out fishing told his father that the colour of American planes appeared to have been changed; another that he had seen the Japanese insignia of the rising sun on the wings of one low-flying plane. The observation met with indulgent laughter.

'It was hard to grip the truth of what was going on,' the wife of a serviceman recounted later. 'It just didn't seem possible. Next I felt affronted, and then furiously angry so that I wanted to throw something at them.'

On Ford Island, and onboard the ships that were in the eye of the storm of high explosive, the reaction was violent and sudden. Here were the men who had been trained, many of them for ten years or more, to react to a crisis. There were some, inevitably, who were for a time paralysed with fear, but for the most part the response of ships' companies was instant and altogether creditable.

Both dive-dombers and torpedo-bombers struck first at the battleships: this is what they had come all the way for – to destroy the battle fleet, the beating heart and the main source of strength of the American Navy, and any carriers in the harbour. The torpedo-bombers came in low from the east, dropping lower over the water, each to its appointed target, unopposed by so much as a single bullet in these first seconds. The big 'pickles' were released at around 50 to 100 feet, struck the water with no more of a splash than a good diver, and tore at 40 knots towards the vulnerable hulls of the battleships, tracing a tell-tale white line of bubbles.

The speed of destruction was the next shock, like a great second wave that breaks over a man before he has recovered his breath. The first bombs and torpedoes exploded at between 7.56 a.m. and 7.59 a.m. – there is no more precise record than that. At 7.58 the alarm was broadcast to all ships, 'Air raid, Pearl Harbor! This is no drill! This is no drill!'

Lieutenant C.V.Ricketts of the USS *West Virginia* recalled:

I was sitting at breakfast table in the wardroom when assembly was sounded and the fire and rescue party called away. Almost immediately thereafter, as I was leaving the wardroom, general quarters was sounded. As I went up the ladder to the starboard side of the quarter deck, I heard the word being passed by word of mouth that, 'The Japs are attacking.' As I reached the quarterdeck I felt the ship being hit. She was shaken some but I was not knocked from my feet. I thought then that instead of actual hits the vibration might be caused by bombs falling close aboard. I went up the starboard side of the boat deck to the anti-aircraft battery which was being manned. Ensign Hunter was present on the starboard battery and I told him to open fire as soon as possible. I then went to the Fire Control tower as I was the senior officer in the gunnery department aboard. The tower was locked so we broke it open. The Captain then appeared and as the ship was listing rapidly to port and I knew probably few C&R officers were aboard I said, 'Captain, shall I go below and counterflood?' He replied, 'Yes, do that.'[1]

Disbelief was not yet dead, even though men were already dying. Interservice rivalry was as keen at Pearl Harbor as anywhere and there were some who thought that the Army Air Corps was pulling a fast one on a Sunday morning to prove how unprepared the fleet was. 'They're only dummy torpedoes,' one sailor was heard to declare. And when the bombs began exploding on Hickham Field, a bosun exclaimed, 'The crazy bastards, they're using live ammunition!'

On the destroyer *Phelps* a chief gunner's mate, charging down the after gangway, was shouting that this was real war; but all the response he got from his shipmate, William Taylor, was the unspoken complaint, 'You mumbling jackass, isn't this drill enough without added harassment from you?' [2] And when someone on the *Pennsylvania* cried out that the Japs were attacking, Machinist's Mate Felsing retorted sceptically, 'So are the Germans.'

The captain of the *West Virginia*, in keeping with his rank and responsibilities, accepted the news and took it calmly. Recalling the Japanese sneak attack on Port Arthur which had opened proceedings in the Russo–Japanese War, he commented, 'This is certainly in keeping with their history of surprise attacks.' Then his ship took the first of six torpedoes. Lieutenant Ricketts continued his account:

We went to the main deck and aft on the starboard side and down to the second deck through the escape scuttle in the hatch in front of the Executive Officer's Office. The hatches in this vicinity were closed with escape scuttles open. Wounded were being brought up the hatches forward. The ship was now listing so heavily that on the linoleum decks it was impossible to walk without holding on to something. I reached the third deck by the ladder at frame 87 starboard and went forward to the first group of counterflood valves. Billingsley went aft and got a crank for operating the valves. When he came back Rucker and Bobick, ship-fitters from Repair III, came with him. Billingsley and I started B-163 counterflooding while the other men assisted at other valves. When I was assured that counterflooding was well underway, I told Rucker to counterflood everything on the starboard side until the ship was on an even keel.[3]

The 'Weevie', as the *West Virginia* was known to her crew, was deep in the heart of the high-explosive storm. 'The torpedoes virtually opened up the whole port side,' according to the subsequent report. Besides the torpedoes and bombs that were tearing her apart, she was also being affected by flames from the *Tennessee* alongside her, and this 32,000-ton battleship was also squeezing against her side as that ship wedged against the quay.

Commander R.H.Hillenkoeter, the 'Weevie's' Executive Officer, felt the first two torpedoes hit while he was dressing. Seconds later the marine orderly rushed into his cabin and shouted unceremoniously, 'The Japanese are attacking us!' The ship was listing heavily to port by the time Hillenkoeter reached the quarterdeck. There was a fire burning on turret three caused by the catapult seaplanes. The commander tried to organize a fire party, but another heavy explosion threw him to the deck.

Almost simultaneously the *Arizona*, just astern of the *West Virginia*, suffered two explosions, the second flash of flame shooting even higher than the first – higher than the foretop. It was like one of Nelson's battles – like the *L'Orient* at the Nile, with burning debris falling in lethal abundance on to the decks of the nearby ships.

By this time the stern of the *Tennessee* was burning [continued Commander Hillenkoeter], and a wall of flame was advancing towards the *West Virginia* and the

Tennessee from oil on the water from the *Arizona*. I looked around and saw no one else aft on deck and then I dove overboard and swam to the *Tennessee*. On getting on deck of the *Tennessee* I found about ten *West Virginia* people gathered under the overhang of the *Tennessee*'s Number Three Turret. As the *Tennessee* people were busily engaged in fire fighting but in no need of any extra help, I took the *West Virginia* people over the starboard side on to the pipe-line to help in extinguishing the fire that had started in the rubbish and trash and oil covered water between the *Tennessee* and Ford Island. Several of our people that were hurt were loaded into a truck and taken to the dispensary. I then brought the truck back to that part of Ford Island opposite the *Tennessee* and kept on with efforts to extinguish the fires among the trash and oil on the water. More and more *West Virginia* personnel kept arriving at this point, some by swimming, some by hanging on to wreckage, and, I think one whaleboat load.[4]

Where the battleships were moored in pairs the outside vessels took the torpedoes while damage to the inside battleships was mainly limited to bomb blasts. The *Oklahoma* was berthed forward of the *West Virginia*, and her sufferings were even more acute and dreadful in their toll of death. In spite of the experience gained in the First World War, and for all their internal and external protection, it was remarkable how swiftly a single torpedo hit caused these stationary vessels to list. A series of three in quick succession sealed the fate of the *Oklahoma* within minutes – seconds almost – of the explosions; as confirmed by Lieutenant Commander William M. Hobby Jr:

I started up the ladder from the main deck aft to the anti-aircraft gun platform on the starboard side; at this point I felt what I believe was the first torpedo hit – a dull thud and a powerful reverberation, on the port side, and the ship began listing to port. I started back down with the idea of getting to Central and directing the flooding of the starboard blisters, but almost immediately there was a second torpedo hit and then a third and the ship listed more; at this time streams of men were pouring up through hatches to the topside. A second or so later, at about the time I was back down to the main deck aft again, came the fourth torpedo hit, and the ship continued to list to port – at least a twenty degree list at this time, I estimate, and still listing. I directed petty officers near me to spread out over the length of the ship and keep the men as orderly and calm as possible. I sighted Commander Kenworthy on the starboard catwalk and made my way to him and told him that I thought the best now was to save as many men as possible, that it was now impossible to make further watertight closures and establish any further watertight integrity. He agreed and we both passed the word to abandon ship. I called to men on main deck aft to attempt to get to work on the loud speaker.

Although there were now hundreds of men on the starboard side, the general conduct of all hands was quiet and calm. There was an explosion around the port side of the forecastle, which I thought was a bomb hit. I worked my way forward and Commander Kenworthy worked his way aft. There was another shock and concussion and vibration and fuel oil splashed in streams over everything topside. This was either another torpedo hit or a large bomb hit close aboard. The ship continued to list over to port, now about 30 degrees, or more, I thought.

I entered # 1 casemate to see about the escape of men from below to topside. Men were still coming out through casemates, and thence out through gun parts to the catwalk and onto the side. When no more men were to be seen in casemates, I climbed up through a gun port and out over the side; the ship was capsizing and the angle was about 90 degrees. I pulled myself along the side and bottom as the vessel keeled over; the ship finally settled when the mast and stack apparently hit bottom, with an angle of approximately 145 degrees, starboard side uppermost.

I sat on the bottom at about frame 60; hundreds of men were along the hull making their way to the water's edge. Keenum C.W., CBM, joined me and rendered much aid in steadying the men. The air attack continued and bombs were dropping nearby, but none struck the *Oklahoma* after she capsized.[5]

There had been no time to set the emergency Condition Zed (close up all watertight doors) or to counterflood as on the *West Virginia*. The *Oklahoma* had been built in New York between 1912 and 1916, and two years later she was on convoy duties in the North Atlantic. At the end of that war she had escorted President Wilson on his trip to France, and in 1936 had rescued American citizens trapped by the Spanish Civil War. Now, on this early Sunday morning, she seemed to decide upon retirement and turned slowly on to her side until her masts caught in the mud of the harbour bottom. Hundreds of her crew were trapped inside her hull, and many more who had escaped incarceration were lying on her hull.

For these men the ordeal was not yet over, however, as the Japanese planes which had completed their attack were now, in increasing numbers, diving low to machine-gun survivors. Of the total complement of the *Oklahoma* of 1,272 men and eighty-two officers, twenty officers and 395 men were trapped or killed outright. The figures would have been even worse but for the efforts of a civilian yard worker who, with amazing speed, organized a rescue team which returned to the capsized battleship and succeeded in cutting a hole in the bottom. Thirty-two men scrambled out, unhurt, blinking in the bright sunlight.

For most of the battleships it was the torpedoes that did the worst damage. Many of the bombs were modified heavy armour-piercing shells. The dud-rate was high and a lot of them did little damage in spite of the accuracy of both dive-bombers and horizontal-bombers. But when these big bombs did explode, and in vulnerable places, their effect was devastating. The USS *Arizona*, after being struck by several torpedoes, was hit by one of them beside the second turret, where it penetrated the forecastle and exploded in one of the forward magazines. The whole fore part of the battleship blew up, killing her captain, Rear-Admiral IsaacC.Kidd and several hundred officers and men. Eight more bombs struck various parts of the ship, which can claim the doubtful honour of being the first battleship to be destroyed in action by aircraft bombs.

There was not even time for the *Arizona* to capsize. She was just blown apart, and within minutes was a funeral pyre for over 1,100 of her officers and men.

By contrast the *Nevada*, moored next astern of the *Arizona*, had an easy time of it; but it was thanks in part to the skill of her acting commander and his men that she was saved. She was not one of a pair, which was a blessing, as she was able to manoeuvre as soon as she had acquired the power to do so, and her anti-aircraft gunners were as quick as any to get into action, which led her at first to be given a wide berth by the attacking planes. However, this battleship took one torpedo hit before she got under way, and later suffered six bomb hits, none of them fatal.

The *Nevada*, assisted by two tugs, grounded herself near the entrance to Waipo Point, opposite the southern end of Ford Island. Later her commander, Captain F.W. Scanland, praised his officers and men who 'without exception performed their duties in a most commendable manner and without regard to personal safety. The courage and spirit of the anti-aircraft gun crews, where bomb hits caused most of the casualties, was of the highest order. Every man on the ship carried on in accordance with the best traditions of the service.' [6]

The *Utah* was the only battleship moored on the west side of Ford Island, alone and defenceless as she had been converted into a target ship and had nothing to fire at the enemy. Within minutes of the first attack the old vessel was listing 40 degrees and the order was given to abandon ship: 'All hands on deck and all engineroom and fireroom, radio and dynamo watch to lay up on deck and release all prisoners.' She was not an easy ship to abandon as her decks were covered with lengths of heavy timber to insulate the ship from the shock of dummy bombs and shells. These broke loose, obstructing the struggling men, or shot up like projectiles when submerged.

Like animals of prey about a wounded buck the Japanese planes clustered about the doomed vessel, machine-gunning the hundreds of men swimming or lying on the upturned ship's bottom. There were men trapped inside. The sound of knocking was reported to the ship's acting commanding officer, Lieutenant-Commander S.S.Isquith. 'At this time planes were still strafing and dropping bombs,' he recounted later. 'I called for a volunteer crew.' Four men returned to the ship and located the tapping. Still under intense fire, Machinist Szymanski procured a cutting torch and cut a hole in the ship's bottom. Through it emerged a single sailor, one of the luckiest men of the battle, who reported that he had been the last man in that part of the ship.

As in any great battle the fates worked capriciously, dealing severely here, more mercifully there, on both sides. One Japanese plane might be shot down by a single, haphazard rifle shot; others would pass unscathed through the most intense shell- and machine-gun fire – which in fact became fully effective during the second strike some forty minutes after the first.

A number of men escaped even from the *Arizona* with no more than a wetting from their swim; in a Honolulu suburb far from the action the splinters from a stray bomb killed three civilians in their car, while another car driven by a naval officer frantic to reach his ship was pursued half way from Honolulu by a fighter yet escaped every burst of machine-gun fire.

The loss of life during the attack was remarkably small considering its ferocity and that there was no time to prepare for it: 1,763 officers and men of the fleet were killed, only a few hundred more than had died when HMS *Hood* had been lost in action in the Atlantic seven months earlier, and less than the toll of a few hours' fighting in the siege of Moscow then raging. Another 900 or so were killed ashore, and many men were grievously wounded. But the holocaust presented by Pearl Harbor at 10.00 a.m. when the last Japanese planes had left and black smoke towered higher than the mountains, the scene of shattered or capsized ships and planes, burning hangars and shore installations, suggested death on a catastrophic scale.

Secretary of the Navy Frank Knox did not reach Pearl Harbor for some days, but he noted, 'Some of the damaged ships were still smoking,' and on Ford Island 'the destruction was thorough and complete'. At the hospital Knox 'saw hundreds of wounded, and more hundreds suffering from shock. The worst cases, though, were the men who had been burned. Some of them were charred beyond recognition.'[7]

It is not to belittle the sufferings of these men or diminish the seriousness of the losses to point out that in harsh statistical terms it was a near-miracle that so few of the thousands of sailors onboard their ships that morning became casualties.

On the material side the figures are not less surprising. Of the battleships the *Arizona* was sunk at her berth, split in two and later deemed too danger-ous to salvage. She lies in the same spot today, a steel memorial to her dead, most of whom remain entombed in her hull. The capsized *Oklahoma*, *California* and *Utah* were eventually salvaged, although it was not considered cost-effective to repair the first for active service again. The other four battleships were all repaired and rejoined the fleet. A few light cruisers and destroyers and auxiliary craft were also damaged but none was lost.

The overestimate factor in air actions, which was already deeply entrenched in the European war, both in aircraft claimed shot down and in damage caused by bombing, played its part in no mean measure at Pearl Harbor. Commander Fuchida and every one of his air crew were convinced that they had destroyed or incapacitated the entire American battle fleet, sunk one of the US Navy's few fleet carriers, and knocked out the air force and its facilities; all at a cost of twenty-nine planes, fewer than had been lost in practice for the operation.

But the price of optimism was much higher. So strong were the claims transmitted during the attack – 'Another battleship sunk!' – that a second follow-up operation was cancelled. When Commander Fuchida landed back on the flight deck at 1.00 p.m., the last plane to do so, the first planes were already being rearmed and refuelled for take-off. But by now the First Carrier Striking Force's commander, Admiral Chuichi Nagumo, had been so convinced of the effectiveness of the dawn strike and concerned for the safety of his task force that it was cancelled. At 1.30 p.m. the six carriers and their escort swung back on a northerly heading for home.

No operation in naval history with such high expectations was so ill-starred as the Japanese operation against Pearl Harbor. It was a disaster in every department except in its demonstration of the prowess and superb equipment of the Japanese naval air arm. The Americans learned vital lessons at negligible cost. Only one ship, the *Arizona*, had been permanently sunk. Even the destroyer *Shaw* which had had its bow blown off was speedily equipped with a makeshift bow which allowed her to make her own way to west-coast repair facilities. The badly damaged battleships were rebuilt to modern standards, much to Japan's disadvantage, with enough anti-aircraft firepower to defend themselves against any future air attack.

The temporary loss of the battle fleet was considered at the time a greater blow than it turned out to be. All the battleships were unfit for carrier warfare. If they had been at sea, unsupported by a strong carrier force, there can be little doubt that they would all have been sunk by Nagumo's task force, sunk irrecoverably and with terrible loss of life. And they would certainly have been at sea if Pearl Harbor had received warning of the attack. Thus, for the loss of one old and obsolete battleship and the temporary disablement of the Pacific battle fleet, the US Navy had gained the pricelessly valuable knowledge that the old-style ship-of-the-line was finished as a fighting unit and that battleships could survive only with air cover and a bristling array of anti-aircraft guns. It had been a violently induced birth, but the new age of sea warfare had taken over and the centuries-old fleet action between heavy guns mounted on big ships was belatedly recognized as dead – from midday, 7 December 1941.

Within a relatively short space of time the Americans also gained a new battle fleet, made up of the new construction which was completing, now at even greater speed, in American shipyards. Their role was a new one, but so fit for the air age were these battleships that not one was to be lost in the long war that lay ahead.

Aside from the material bonuses of Pearl Harbor, the 'treachery' (a much-used word in those more fastidious times) element of the Japanese attack united the most powerful nation in the world and ensured, in one fell stroke, that America would discard at once her pacific stance and her muted semi-belligerency and throw all her strength and resources into all-out war until the unconditional surrender of Japan and Germany.

When Commander Minoru Genda, the inspired Japanese aviation specialist, learned from intelligence sources before the attack that, while only battleships were known for certain to be berthed in Pearl Harbor, two carriers might soon arrive, he is reported to have remarked, 'If that happened, I don't care if all eight battleships are away.'[8] Here was an officer who already appreciated the irrelevance of the battle fleet in modern sea warfare.

According to combat reports one carrier at least had been in harbour – the *Saratoga* – and moreover she had been bombed and torpedoed so effectively that she had capsized. If the second carrier had slipped through their fingers, then at least they had sunk one of America's biggest fleet carriers, and there was much comfort in that at the outset of war. In fact the Japanese had misidentified the *Utah* as the *Saratoga* because she occupied the berth usually reserved for carriers and the heavy timbers gave her the appearance of having a flight deck. And so she became an unintended dummy, and the priceless American fleet carriers, at sea on various missions, escaped unharmed.

But if Nagumo's force had found all the carriers at Pearl Harbor, upon which the main attack would have then concentrated; and if he had destroyed instead of ignoring the base's fuel and docking facilities, and followed up the second with a third attack on a stunned and mainly helpless naval base – there was now scarcely a fighter fit to fly – the Japanese could have congratulated themselves on a great victory. It would have justified the triumphant, but hollow, 'Tora, Tora!' which Commander Fuchida had cried out over his radio.

CHAPTER FIVE

Battleships in the North Atlantic

Time and again since the end of the First World War theorists had claimed 'The battleship is dead.' The bomber 'school' in Britain, fighting for restricted funds from the exchequer, advocated air fleets in place of battleships. You could, after all, build some 700 bombers for the cost of a £7 million battleship. In the United States the debate was more public and spectacular, with that showman-aviator General William 'Billy' Mitchell actually bombing and sinking an ex-German dreadnought, the *Ostfriesland*. (The battleship was stationary and undefended.) Admiral William Sims, lately C-in-C US Fleet in European waters, supported Mitchell; while the Assistant Secretary of the Navy and future President, Franklin D. Roosevelt, was on record as declaring that 'later on in the future, aviation may make surface ships practically impossible to be used as an arm'.[1]

During the 1914–18 war at sea neither the German nor the British battle fleets could leave harbour without a screen of destroyers for fear of torpedo attack, and at the epic Battle of Jutland the evolutions of the fleet and the final outcome were conditioned more by the threat of the torpedo than the big bang of the big gun. Twenty-five years after Jutland and the crippling of the American battle fleet, the fighter plane had become the battleship protector replacement to the destroyer.

All this was recognized at the end of 1941 but it did not mean the end of the battleship; only a radical change in its role, from one to several duties. Now the battleship in its turn became a protector of the new capital ship, the carrier, a protector of convoys; and also, latterly, a bombardment vessel.

The C-in-C of the German Navy, Admiral Erich Raeder, had great faith in his battleships, pocket battleships and heavy cruisers working in harness with the U-boat fleet, in the North Atlantic especially. The early failure of the *Admiral Graf Spee* and the *Deutschland* did not in any way affect his confidence, and he awaited impatiently the commissioning of his battleship reinforcements. And what battleships! The *Bismarck* and *Tirpitz* had a speed of over 30 knots, were faster and also bigger and more comprehensively protected than any British or French battleship. They were, in the definition of one admiral, 'the twin terrors of the Atlantic'.

The commerce raider of the 1940s possessed many advantages, and some disadvantages, over its counterpart of the First World War. When the *Admiral Graf Spee* left Germany on her ill-fated mission shortly before the outbreak of the war in 1939, she had not only effective radar but seaplanes to locate her prey and warn of pursuers. She had a much greater operating range than the ships of 1914 commanded by the admiral after whom she was named. Moreover, being oil-powered she could refuel at sea, and in a much shorter time than her coal-fired predecessors. But efficient long-range radio carried by her victims helped to seal her fate.

At the end of 1940 Admiral Raeder had the pocket battleship *Scheer*, the battle-cruisers *Gneisenau* and *Scharnhorst* and the heavy cruiser *Hipper*. These four fast armoured warships, let loose among the convoys of the North Atlantic, represented a danger of which the Admiralty was fully aware. There was one consolation, even though it carried with it a tinge of sadness. The fate of the French Fleet after the surrender of France earlier in the year was of critical importance to Britain's one-time ally. Under the pressure of her conquerors, any French reassurance that her navy would not be handed over to Germany could not be trusted.

Powerful units of the French Navy were at Toulon in the south of France, at Alexandria in Egypt, Oran in Morocco and Dakar on the African west coast. After some delicate negotiation the French commander at Alexandria agreed to immobilize his ships, but no pleas or threats would prevail upon the C-in-C at Oran to do the same, or to surrender them or hand them over to a neutral party. Vice-Admiral Sir James Somerville therefore was ordered to resort to the unpleaant task of putting the ships out of commission by shellfire. With the loss of many French sailors' lives one battleship was sunk, and two more run aground and disabled. Only the fourth escaped, while at Dakar the most powerful and modern battleship, the *Richelieu*, was put out of action by carrier aircraft.

It was a sorry business which left much bitterness. But the harsh realities demanded this drastic action, which also emphasized to the Spanish authorities, who were very delicately poised neutrals enduring strong German pressure at the time, that Britain had both the power and will to resist. It also made the Americans sit up and take notice. Five additional battleships, three of them modern, powerful ships, might well have turned the scales in the Battle of the Atlantic soon after it began.

The first German raider to break out into the Atlantic in the autumn of 1940 was the pocket battleship *Scheer*. The earlier spell of bad luck seemed to have broken when she sighted a homeward-bound convoy of thirty-seven ships escorted by a lightly armed converted merchantman, the *Jervis Bay*. A few 6-inch guns could surely not be expected to delay the destruction of every one of these unfortunate ships. Instead, the *Jervis Bay* came out to meet the pocket battleship's challenge, firing fast and accurately, while her charges made smoke, behind which they scattered.

The fight was not a long one. The *Scheer*'s 11-inch shells tore the ex-merchantman apart, but the *Jervis Bay* delayed and diverted the attention of the raider almost until nightfall, when many of the ships escaped in the darkness. Only five of the convoy succumbed to the German gunfire, and Captain E.S.F.Fegen, the *Jervis Bay*'s captain, was awarded the Victoria Cross posthumously for his courage and sacrifice.

There was one curious aftermath to this engagement. The tanker *San Demetrio*, with 12,000 tons of high-octane aviation fuel, suffered a hail of shellfire which holed her tanks and smashed her bridge, killing all those on it. The surviving crew took to a boat, among them an American, Able Seaman Oswald Preston, who had been at work painting the masts and funnels when the ship was attacked. All that night and through the following day the men rowed their boat in hope of finding and being picked up by one of the other ships of the scattered convoy. There were several false alarms, and then late in the afternoon they found themselves close to a ship that was ablaze and appeared to be drifting out of control.

As they rowed nearer the bosun suddenly cried out, 'Yank, you never finished chipping and painting the funnel!' Now they all recognized that they were seeking refuge in their own ship, which had not yet sunk. The sea was running too high and darkness was too imminent for them to board the *San Demetrio*, so they passed round her stern and kept on her weather side during the night.

It was a dreadful night and they were all suffering from exposure when dawn broke to reveal an empty sea. But later in the morning they sighted her again, still blazing, on the horizon. By now the boat's crew were prepared to take any risk to get back on board. Able Seaman Calum MacNeil takes up the narrative:

There was no argument now as to whether we should board her. After a while someone said he thought he saw her, and was accused of dreaming. But sure enough there she was still blazing and smoking and still slipping away from us. This time we meant business, and, despite the Atlantic gale, sail was hoisted and we soon began to close down on her. Hopes ran high through the boat's company. It would not be long now before we could get aboard a blazing vessel with a cargo of oil. She was the only thing we could see in all the wide circle of ocean and she looked good. At least very warm. She might blow up at any time, but that was quick and painless death compared with this slow freezing and sickness, this forced labour of failing muscles. And, besides, she was our own ship, still floating in spite of what she had suffered. She meant home to us, she was ours and had not failed us. She had looked for us and by some miracle had found us. We could not fail her. . . .

I took charge of the sailing and had to nurse the boat and manoeuvre her very carefully in the strong gale, and purposefully, instead of with the jerky progress of tired rowers, she leant over and made for our parent vessel.

A little before noon we drew to her and once more passed round her stern, this time to get to leeward of her. We approached her from the starboard side where the remains of a boat-ladder were hanging over her quarter. We put the boat's blankets over the gunwale to prevent any sparks striking from the possible clash of steel, then the Yank was up the ladder and on board making our painter fast. I unshipped the rudder while the rest climbed on board.[2]

It was a nightmare experience to survey the wreckage of the ship which twenty-four hours earlier had been their home and was now largely smashed and burned, with the bodies or ashes of some of their shipmates lying where they had been at the time of the attack. The ship's provisions had been destroyed, the engine-room partially flooded – and the fire still blazed.

The manner in which this handful of men, weak and half-frozen, succeeded in dousing the fire, and after a superhuman effort of salvage, got the engines going and eventually brought the tanker to Glasgow, without charts, compass or steering, was typical of the gallantry, determination and endurance of those who fought the Battle of the Atlantic.

After the *Jervis Bay* encounter the *Scheer* moved down to the South Atlantic, and there refitted at a rendezvous used also by several armed merchantmen which the German Navy was employing with some success in more distant seas. Her cruise lasted in all five months, and in that time she sank or captured sixteen merchantmen with a total tonnage of 99,000, not a big enough 'catch' to justify the investment of time and expenditure. On the other hand it had cost the RN a heavy sum in diversion of convoys and despatch of ships to attempt to locate and destroy her. She certainly had better luck in the Indian Ocean and South Atlantic than her sister ship *Admiral Graf Spee*, and succeeded in passing through the Denmark Strait to arrive back at Kiel on 1 April 1941.

Admiral Raeder had meanwhile already despatched the heavy cruiser Hipper on a similar operation. These 8-inch-gun cruisers were not so suitable for the *guerre de course* as the pocket battleships, although they were only marginally smaller. Ships like the *Scheer* and *Lützow* not only had 11-inch armament, which called for a battleship or battle-cruiser to secure their destruction, but they had a far greater endurance. The *Hipper*'s first cruise in December 1940 was a miserable affair. By chance rather than good judgement or intelligence she sighted an enormous troop convoy bound for the Middle East, which she shadowed from a distance for some time with every expectation of making a spectacular 'killing'.

The *Hipper* planned to pounce on Christmas morning. But she had failed to spot an escorting carrier, an 8-inch-gun cruiser and two more cruisers, which at once engaged her and drove her off. The *Hipper* limped into Brest for repairs, the first surface raider to make use of these invaluable facilities.

The cruiser was luckier when she sailed again on 1 February 1941, for eleven days later she sighted a convoy steaming north from Freetown. The escort had not yet arrived, and the *Hipper* sank seven of their number before low fuel reserves forced her to return home.

A few weeks earlier British intelligence had got wind of the imminent departure from Germany on a similar errand of the *Gneisenau* and *Scharnhorst*. These two battle-cruisers, many times more formidable than the *Hipper*

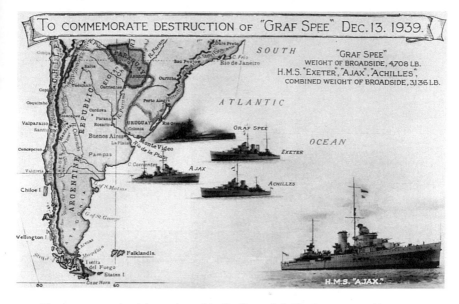

"GRAF SPEE"
WEIGHT OF BROADSIDE, 4,708 LB.
H.M.S. "EXETER", "AJAX", "ACHILLES",
COMBINED WEIGHT OF BROADSIDE, 3,136 LB.

GRAF SPEE

EXETER

AJAX

ACHILLES

H.M.S. "AJAX."

The picture postcard, and the wreckage of the *Graf Spee*, tell all. The victory gave equal heart to the people of Britain in 1939 as the Battle of the Falkland Islands in 1914 when the squadron of Admiral Graf Spee (after whom the pocket battleship was named) was virtually annihilated.

Left: Admiral of the Fleet Sir Dudley Pound, who led the Royal Navy through the dangerous years until shortly before his death on Trafalgar Day 1943.

Below: The battle-cruisers *Gneisenau* and *Scharnhorst* opening fire on the carrier HMS *Glorious*, 8 June 1940.

The French battle-cruiser *Strasbourg* escaping from Oran, 5 July 1940, guns trained on the unseen British squadron.

The French battleship *Bretagne* blowing up, a scene reminiscent of the destruction of *L'Orient* at the Battle of the Nile in 1798.

Above left: U-570 (right) captured intact in the North Atlantic by a Hudson aircraft, 27 August 1941, is brought alongside two British submarines in Holy Loch. After careful study she was renamed HMS *Graph* and did sterling service.

Above right and below: After failing to sink the carrier *Ark Royal, U-39* was sunk by three destroyers on 14 September 1939. Two of her company swim towards HMS *Foxhound*, and later they all gathered together to smile at the cameraman before facing five years and eight months in a POW camp.

Admiral Sir John Tovey (*left*) and Flottenchef Admiral Lütjens, chief protagonists in the *Bismarck* action, May 1941

Bismarck photographed from the *Prinz Eugen* before leaving Norwegian waters.

The 8-inch gun cruiser HMS *Suffolk*, which, with the *Norfolk*, shadowed the 8-inch gun *Prinz Eugen* (*below*) and the *Bismarck* in the northern reaches of the Atlantic until the Royal Navy could deploy the strength to destroy the latter and drive the cruiser into Brest harbour.

Below: Victualling at sea: a 'Hunt' class destroyer takes in bread hot from the ovens of the battleship *Nelson*; *Rodney* astern.

The threat posed by the giant German battleship *Tirpitz* tied up a large part of the British surface fleet in home waters, and some American heavy ships, too. She was several times crippled, in September 1943 by miniature submarines, X-craft, one of which is here shown on her trials. But she was not sunk until November 1944 when she received three direct hits by 12,000-pound bombs dropped by RAF heavy bombers.

A German destroyer heads the German Brest Squadron in its dash up-Channel to home ports, 12–13 February 1942. The *Scharnhorst* is next in line, followed by the *Gneisenau* and *Prinz Eugen*.

The *Scharnhorst* was sunk in northern waters by shellfire and torpedoes, 26 December 1943; the *Gneisenau* never recovered from the mine damage sustained during the Channel dash; while the *Prinz Eugen* ended up in this *impasse* with the cruiser *Leipzig*.

or the pocket battleships, had completed repairs after their damage in the Norwegian campaign. They were under the command of the able and determined Admiral Günther Lütjens, who was to be a very sharp thorn in the Admiralty's flesh for many of the middle months of the war. His ships kept turning up again like some pestilential plague, actually claiming relatively few victims but causing a great deal of trouble.

On 23 January 1941 their low, dark, sleek shapes were observed by a British agent as they steamed out of the Baltic. It did not take long for the Admiralty to conclude that the *Scharnhorst* and *Gneisenau* were heading for the North Atlantic convoy routes. This time, unlike April 1940, there could be no doubt. Eighteen 11-inch guns between them, a speed of 32 knots, 32,000 tons, 13-inch armour belt: these figures represented a very difficult proposition for the new C-in-C of the British Home Fleet, Admiral Sir John Tovey.

Tovey sailed his entire fleet from Scapa Flow to a position south of Iceland while radar-equipped reconnaissance vessels searched to the south and east. Success on 28 January: the light cruiser *Naiad* got a radar contact on the German ships, then a brief visual before Lütjens flinched away, rightly fearful of what this single warship represented. The battle-cruisers sped north, as deep into the Arctic as the ice allowed.

A week later the German Admiral was back on the convoy routes, ever watchful for signs of the battleships of the British Home Fleet. He might comfortably outpace the *Rodney* and *Nelson*, for example, but he knew the price he would pay if he suddenly faced their 16-inch guns between snow storms. But the reward to be gained from finding a lightly escorted convoy, as the *Scheer* had done, was worth the risk. And just such a reward appeared imminent when on 8 February his radar picked up numerous blips which indicated a convoy for sure. The two big ships sped towards their intended victims. First a visual on two merchantmen, plodding through the high seas, then several more in a clear patch, and then more still; but then one of the look-outs reported something else: a distant tripod mast.

Every German sailor knew the story of how Admiral von Spee, back in 1914, had been approaching the Falkland Islands with his all-conquering squadron when one of his look-outs reported seeing tripod masts rising above Port Stanley – and tripod masts could mean only British battleships or battle-cruisers. Later that same day, many years ago, all but one of Spee's ships was at the bottom of the ocean.

And now, twenty-six years later, Admiral Lütjens made a similar sighting and correctly drew the same conclusion. As a precautionary move the Admiralty had scraped the bottom of the battleship barrel and found enough old 15-inch-gunned battleships to provide one for all the largest and most valuable Atlantic convoys. Lütjens was 3,000 miles from his nearest base, and a single hit by a heavy shell was all that was needed, through a loss of speed, or of fuel, to ensure his destruction. He left in a hurry.

But this was to be no abortive cruise. Already his presence in the Atlantic had created disruption to the carefully timed and routed convoys, and on 22 February, after steaming farther west, Lütjens picked up a recently dispersed convoy, accounting for five ships. There were more rich pickings off Newfoundland, but fuel was running low, and the two battle-cruisers now rendezvoused with a tanker before turning south-east for the African convoy routes. Here he was on the point of intercepting a massive homeward-bound convoy, SL67, when he sighted that other dreaded distant object – a reconnaissance plane. It was a Walrus amphibian, catapulted from the escorting battleship *Malaya* carrying out its intended role, just as those Japanese seaplanes were to do when the search for the *Prince of Wales* was at its height.

Again, the battleship was briefly sighted. The *Scharnhorst* and *Gneisenau* were 300 miles north of the Cape Verde islands; and again they left the area at speed. Dangerous as well as difficult hunting so far!

Lütjens returned to the North Atlantic convoys' most vulnerable area, and the long trip paid off high dividends. He caught a convoy just as it was dispersing and virtually without protection. It was 16 March 1941, and he sank sixteen ships to match the date.

The German Admiral's course since 28 January had been more or less accurately plotted by the Admiralty and these last series of RRRs had led to an even greater intensification of the hunt. Conditions were appalling and British resources strictly limited, but success came to the pilot and observer of a reconnaissance aircraft from the carrier *Ark Royal* which spotted the two raiders still far out in the Atlantic as they were preparing to head for Brest. Darkness was approaching and there was no time for the *Ark Royal*, 160 miles distant, to launch a torpedo-bomber attack. Nor was it possible in this foul weather to sustain a night patrol from the air.

Lütjens did not know it, but the next hazard was the battleship *Rodney*, which missed him by only a few hours. It was with a great deal of relief that the Germans steamed into Brest harbour on 22 March 1941. It had been, by any reckoning, a pretty successful voyage, a raiding operation as Admiral Raeder had envisaged before the war, and a bad dream if not a nightmare for the Royal Navy, just as it had feared: 115,600 tons of shipping captured or sunk in two months.

Raeder sent a note of congratulation to Lütjens, Hitler sent a note of congratulation to Raeder. Yet this figure was no higher than what a pair of U-boats might accomplish within the same period – an investment of 150 officers and men instead of 3,000, two boats that cost £100,000 each instead of £10 million and took six months to build instead of three and a half years. And the risks the *Gneisenau* and *Scharnhorst* had run were infinitely higher than those of U-boats at that stage of the war.

The thorn in the Royal Navy's flesh was still deep and painful, and these two fine fighting ships – nicknamed 'Salmon and Gluckstein' after the tobacco company – were to engage the expensive attention of the navy, and the RAF too, for a long while yet. It was, however, their last dual participation in the *guerre de course*. Admiral Raeder was already completing plans for an even bigger Atlantic raid.

The Germans were reading many British naval codes in 1941. The British had the advantage of the more traditional human network of intelligence agents on enemy-held territory and in neutral countries, while German agents filtered into Britain were, one and all and immediately, picked up and either disposed of in the usual manner or 'turned round'. 'Our man' in neutral Sweden was Captain Henry Denham RN, who had arrived from Narvik via Finland in June 1940. On 20 May 1941 Denham learned through a Norwegian and Swedish contact that there was important German naval activity in the Baltic. He did not, for obvious reasons, ask about the source, which was in fact an officer in the Swedish cruiser *Götland* (4,700 tons) which had been out on exercises when she had met German warships in an area which had been cleared of all other shipping. Within an hour, Denham had transmitted in cipher to the Admiralty in London:

Kattegat today 20th May. At 1500 two large warships, escorted by three destroyers, five escort vessels, ten or twelve aircraft, passed Marstrand course north-west. 2058/20.

The ships could only be the battleship *Bismarck* and heavy cruiser *Prinz Eugen*, both new and extremely formidable, hellbent for the North Atlantic. The *Bismarck* had been laid down in 1936 and commissioned on 24 August 1940, the subsequent period being devoted to sea trials and working up her fighting efficiency. The last battleships Germany had built were the *Baden* and *Bayern*, completed after the Battle of Jutland in 1916. They were coal-fired vessels with a maximum speed of 22 knots and a displacement of 28,000 tons. The *Bismarck* and her sister ship *Tirpitz*, completed later, were 52,000 tons full load and had a similar armament of eight 15-inch guns disposed in four turrets. They were no stronger or more heavily protected than the earlier ships, but were 10 knots faster.

The high speed reflected the new role of the battleship as envisaged by German naval thinking. Like the earlier pocket battleships and the recent battle-cruisers, the *Bismarck* and *Tirpitz* had been designed for the *guerre de course*. And if the Royal Navy had few ships that could outpace *and* outgun the *Scharnhorst* and *Gneisenau*, it had none with the dual capacities to deal with these new monsters, with their fuel capacity of almost 9,000 tons of oil and operating range of over 8,000 miles.

The captain of the *Bismarck* was Kapitän zur See Ernst Lindemann, a gunnery officer and dedicated careerist, one of the few officers who served through the First World War and remained in the *Kriegsmarine* through the lean years and the advent of Hitler. His personal adjutant was Baron von Müllenheim-Rechberg, the only surviving officer of the *Bismarck* alive today. Lütjens himself was to fly his flag in the *Bismarck*. Tall and lean, fifty-one years old, dour, withdrawn, 'taciturn as a Cistercian monk',[3] a destroyer man in the old High Seas Fleet, Lütjens belonged to the Tirpitz-inspired school of the early years of the century. Although stoutly patriotic, he was strictly non-Nazi and always answered the Nazi salute with the naval salute.

Under Lindemann were 103 officers and midshipmen and 1,962 petty officers and men, including those who would be deputed as prize crews of captured ships. Morale was immensely high and all believed with some reason that their ship was the finest in the world, and indestructible.

The *Prinz Eugen* was a miniature *Bismarck* and like all the new German armoured ships similar in profile to confuse the enemy: low on the water, single-funnel, a towering fortress-like unbroken mass amidships, 11,000 tons, eight 8-inch guns and very heavy anti-aircraft protection.

Admiral Raeder's original plan called for a combined assault on the North Atlantic convoys by the *Scharnhorst* and *Gneisenau* as well. These four very fast ships, working together, the *Bismarck* dealing with any battle-ship escort, could have created mayhem, severing entirely Britain's sea links both with North and South America and with the Middle East via the Cape. Well supplied with tankers, this squadron might have operated for weeks on end.

The timing was full moon in April. It was an appalling prospect of which Churchill and the Admiralty's Naval Staff were fully aware.

Once again air power came to Britain's rescue in the nick of time. From the moment they arrived in St Nazaire, the two battle-cruisers were subjected to bombing attack. Bomber casualties were heavy because the dockyard was ringed with flak but raids were driven home with great courage. As a result, a torpedo-bomber captained by a Canadian, Flying Officer Kenneth Campbell RCAF, succeeded in putting a 'tin fish' into the side of the *Gneisenau*. Campbell (awarded a posthumous VC) and his crew were killed. The explosion smashed a propeller shaft, flooded two engine-rooms, and put the ship out of commission for months. That was not all. Towed into dry dock, she was hit no fewer than four times by heavy bombs. Meanwhile, it was discovered that her sister ship had serious boiler trouble which would take a number of weeks to repair.

Almost at a stroke the operation had lost half its strength. Lütjens wanted to postpone; Raeder wanted to go ahead, keen to gain credit for his surface fleet in the eyes of Hitler, who was rapidly losing confidence in its effectiveness. So operation 'Rhine Exercise' went ahead, lacking the benefit of the moon and with the prospect of only brief nights in the far north.

Hitler, busy with his plans for another and bigger operation to the east, with Moscow as the first target, still agreed to come to inspect the ships at Gdynia and bid them Godspeed. Were there any risks attached to the cruise? the Fuehrer asked Lütjens. None at all, he was assured. What about torpedo-bombers? Well, that was a risk that had to be considered, Lütjens agreed, but the tremendous flak could cope, of that he was confident.

The Briton who carried the greatest responsibility for intercepting and destroying the *Bismarck* and her satellite cruiser was Admiral Sir John Tovey at his base in Scapa Flow. The youngest of eleven children, Tovey came from a military family. He had preferred the sea, and like Raeder had been a destroyer officer at Jutland. He was mentioned in despatches and awarded the DSO in that earlier war. Now, with fully stretched resources, he faced the biggest challenge of his life. He was a small man, blue-eyed, easily roused to laughter, and was generally known to people who did not care for him (including Churchill) as stubborn, and by everyone else (the majority) as tenacious. He had a quick brain and was quite unflappable.

Tovey had under his immediate command the new battleship *King George V* (28 knots, ten 14-inch guns) and the even newer *Prince of Wales*, the only ships in service capable of meeting the *Bismarck* on almost equal terms, except that the *Prince of Wales* was so new she still had workmen on board trying to cure faults in her main armament, and she could by no stretch of the imagination be described as fully worked up. The only other big ship immediately available was the battle-cruiser *Hood*, the pride of the navy since her completion twenty years earlier, the quintessence of warship handsomeness, quite as fast as the *Bismarck*, as heavily armed and almost as big.

But the *Hood* was more like a tin can while the *Bismarck* resembled a Tiger tank. It was not that the *Hood* was all that lightly armoured, and there had been additions to her armour over the years, but she had never been designed for a slogging gun duel any more than the earlier battle-cruisers, three of which had been blown up at Jutland at the time she was laid down. Her horizontal armour particularly was insufficient against plunging fire and aerial bombs alike.

These ships were quite inadequate to provide for a successful search, which required a multiple division of resources, and certain destruction of the *Bismarck* and *Prinz Eugen*. So the carrier *Victorious* and the battle-cruiser *Repulse*, which was smaller and even flimsier than the *Hood*, were called from a troop convoy; two old 'R' class battleships, laid down before the First World War, and the 16-inch gun, 1920s battleship *Rodney*, were also detached from their other duties. Finally Force H, consisting at that time of the *Repulse*'s sister battle-cruiser *Renown* and the armoured carrier *Ark Royal*, was ordered up from Gibraltar when radar contact with the enemy was lost.

This all added up to a considerable total of gunpower and air power, and reconnaissance prospects were much improved from earlier months in the war by the presence of long-range Coastal Command aircraft based in Iceland, Northern Ireland and the west coast of Scotland. Speed was the missing factor and the hunting pack's enemy was the vast extent of the Atlantic Ocean itself, with its vagaries of weather, especially to the north in the sub-Arctic.

There were three corridors into the Atlantic that the *Bismarck* might use: one running between the Shetland Islands and the Faeroes, another between the Faeroes and Iceland, or the Denmark Strait north of Iceland. The first was dangerously close to Scapa Flow, the second was permanently patrolled by cruisers, the third was very narrow owing to the pack-ice line and the minefields the British had laid against this eventuality.

British intelligence knew that the *Luftwaffe* had had daily patrols out over the Denmark Strait for the past week, and 90 per cent of successful break-outs had been through this strait in the past. It was therefore calculated that it was 90 per cent certain that the enemy would use that exit once again.

The captain of one of the British cruisers claimed afterwards:

The trouble about Lütjens was that he made life so darned difficult for himself. Why on earth did he come out through the Skagerrak at all? He was bound to be seen by someone and the sight of this great big battleship where you normally only saw fishing boats was not something you forgot. If he had gone through the Kiel Canal and gone north out of sight of the Jutland coast he had a ten to one chance of getting away with it. As it was we were forewarned with plenty of time and my Admiral [Rear-Admiral W.F.Wake-Walker, Commander First Cruiser Squadron] and I had the *Norfolk* on patrol while the *Bismarck* was somewhere off the Norwegian coast.[4]

In Scapa Flow Tovey waited for news in his flagship *King George V*, unfussed and patient, occasionally using the scrambler telephone to the Admiralty or answering calls from London. All his contingency plans had long since been worked out in the smallest detail. For the present it was up to 'the air boys'. The PRU (Photographic Reconnaissance Unit) of the RAF was in an early stage of development. They used mainly specially developed Spitfires, stripped of armour and armament and equipped with camera and extra tanks. Two of these machines took off from Wick in north Scotland on 21 May 1941, one flying east for the Oslo area, the second north-east towards Bergen and the adjacent fjords. As Lütjens's luck would have it, the weather was perfect. The pilot was able to take several crystal clear photographs of the big ship and attendant vessels inside Grimstadfjord near Bergen, while farther north the *Prinz Eugen* lay alongside what could only be a tanker. The cruiser and battleship were obviously topping up their fuel before setting off on their mission.

The weather was not so favourable the next day, and over Norway it was 10/10ths cloud down to 200 feet. But another intrepid pilot, wave-hopping through intense flak and aware of the fjord's cliffs closing about him, succeeded in penetrating deep enough to report confidently that the birds had flown. So, now the hunt was on. Admiral Tovey despatched his two fastest ships, the *Hood* (Vice-Admiral Lancelot Holland) and *Prince of Wales* (Captain John Leach), to Iceland to support the patrolling cruisers, while he took the *Repulse* and *Victorious* on a more westerly heading. He was fully aware of the shortcomings of the *Prince of Wales*; he also knew that, apart from the senior flying officers in the *Victorious*, that carrier's air crews were fresh from training school, keen to be on their first operation so soon after joining the ship but with little, and in some cases no, experience of landing on and off a carrier. Nor were their 90-knot Swordfish biplanes the ideal instruments for attacking the strongest-defended battleship in the world.

The two German ships with destroyer escort left the Norwegian coast at midnight, 21–22 May, the *Prinz Eugen* with full bunkers, while the *Bismarck* did not bother to refuel. Her captain's adjutant, Müllenheim-Rechberg, later wrote, 'As we lay at anchor the entire day, I was perplexed – this is not hindsight, I remember it very clearly – as to why the *Bismarck* did not make use of what seemed like ample time to refuel, as did the *Prinz Eugen.*'[5]

Four hours later Lütjens shed his destroyers, and the two big ships proceeded alone at 24 knots in hazy weather with low scudding cloud, perfect conditions for the break-out. It was only now that Lütjens finally decided to use the Denmark Strait passage. By 6.00 p.m.,

it was raining and a south-westerly wind was blowing at Force 3 [according to Müllenheim-Rechberg]. Visibility fell to between 300 and 400 metres, and patches of fog appeared. A damp cold gripped us, and the *Bismarck* glistened all the way to her foretop under a silvery sheen of moisture.... In order to maintain contact and station, both ships turned on their signal lights or small searchlights every now and again.... We were now in the northern latitudes, where the nights are almost as light as the day, so we could stay in a tight formation and maintain 24 knots even in poor visibility. Our passage was truly ghostly, as we slid at high speed through an unknown, endless, eerie world and left not a trace. The setting might have been created for the 'perfect' breakout.[6]

The Denmark Strait patrol was not the most popular activity with the cruisers of the Home Fleet. Even in the third week in May the weather was bitter and in heavy seas spume froze as it struck flesh, fogs clamped down with an alarming suddenness, and off watch it was hard to sleep against the severe movements of the ship. Although adequate sea boats, the 'County' class cruisers *Suffolk* and *Norfolk* were more at home on tropical peacetime stations, showing the flag in the West or East Indies. They were 'Washington Treaty' cruisers, built to the limit of 10,000 tons, with a good turn of speed and eight 8-inch guns, but only very lightly armoured. Almost twenty years older, they were no match, ship for ship, for the *Prinz Eugen*.

The two British cruisers met close to land off the north-west corner of Iceland in thick fog on the morning of 23 May, when Wake-Walker ordered Captain Robert Ellis of the *Suffolk* to take up a patrol line close to the pack-ice on the northern limits of the Denmark Strait, while his flagship patrolled fifteen miles to the south of her. All through that long Arctic day the *Suffolk* cruised up and down, look-outs covering every point of the compass, and the aerial of the radar rotating inexorably. Who said war was nine-tenths boredom?

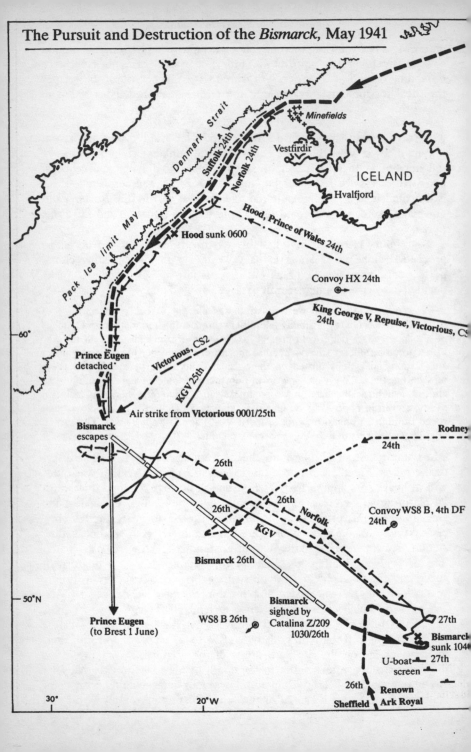

The Pursuit and Destruction of the *Bismarck*, May 1941

Denmark Strait

Minefields

Vestfirdir

ICELAND

Hvalfjord

Suffolk 24th

Norfolk 24th

Hood, Prince of Wales 24th

× Hood sunk 0600

Pack Ice limit May

Convoy HX 24th

King George V, Repulse, Victorious, CS?
24th

Prince Eugen
detached

Victorious, CS2

KGV 25th

Air strike from **Victorious** 0001/25th

Rodney

Bismarck
escapes

24th

26th

26th

26th

Norfolk

Convoy WS8 B, 4th DF
24th

KGV

Bismarck 26th

Prince Eugen
(to Brest 1 June)

WS8 B 26th

Bismarck
sighted by
Catalina Z/209
1030/26th

27th

× **Bismarck**
sunk 104?

U-boat
screen   27th

26th   **Renown**
Sheffield   **Ark Royal**

60°

50°N

30°   20°W

0°

↑ **Weissenburg** (tanker)

Narvik

23rd

Bismarck & Prince Eugen

10°E

NORWAY

Bismarck's destroyers to
Trondheim

Trondheim

Faeroe Is.

22nd **Wollin**
(tanker)

GERMAN

OCCUPIED

60°

Shetland Is.

Air reconnaissance

Bergen

Orkney Is.

23rd
23rd

23rd

Scapa Flow

Kristiansand

Marstrand

21st Skagerrak

Kattegat

20th

BRITISH ISLES

Kiel

19th

Gdynia
(Gotenhafen)
Bismarck, Prince Eugen
sailed 2130, 18 May

Hamburg

GERMANY AND

GERMAN OCCUPIED EUROPE

50°N

Brest

U-boat bases

Lorient

St Nazaire

British submarine patrol
th-27th

La Rochelle

0°

0   100   200   300

Nautical miles

10°E

At 6 p.m. precisely the other-tenth came up, and Lütjens's luck ran out again. Able Seaman Newell, the starboard after look-out on the *Suffolk*'s bridge, with his eyes glued to his big binoculars and bored out of his mind, observed a very large shape emerge from a fog bank like a monster from the wings of a pantomime. It was no more than seven miles away, and was the biggest battleship in the world. 'Ship bearing Green One Four Oh!' he shouted in a wonderfully steady voice, considering. Then before anybody had time to respond: '*Two* ships bearing Green One Four Oh.'

All over the cruiser the alarm bells rang out with shrieking insistence. Hardly a man below believed it was the real thing: war *was* false alarms. But they had to run anyway, grabbing lifebelts, tin hats and everything else they needed for their duties. The turbines were already whining on a higher note, vibrating in tempo, the ship listing hard over as Captain Ellis raced for the nearest fog bank. You did not share the stage with a 50,000-ton battleship if you were a 10,000-ton cruiser. The *Suffolk* just made it in time.

The sighting report was picked up by Wake-Walker but not by Admiral Tovey. Jerry Phillips, too, ordered full speed for the *Norfolk* and headed through mist and freezing drizzle to close the gap with his consort. 'We came out of all the muck in something of a rush,' Phillips recounted later. 'It was like drawing a curtain aside in the early morning, but I didn't much like the view. What's more, the *Bismarck* boys had woken up themselves now and started to throw everything at us.'

The *Norfolk* emulated the *Suffolk* and dipped back into the fog. Unlike *Suffolk*, though, he could get no radar reading on the enemy. His was an old fixed-aerial type by contrast with the *Suffolk*'s. And how cock-a-hoop Bob Ellis had been, showing it off proudly to Jerry Phillips! Very few ships yet had it; it was Admiral Lütjens's luck that the first ship to sight him was one of them, though this did not become apparent until later.

There now began the finest piece of shadowing by a RN cruiser since Captain John Kelly had 'tailed' the *Goeben* through the Mediterranean in 1914. In and out of fog banks, which sometimes cleared unpredictably, through sleet and rainstorms, dangerously close to ice floes, through the long hours of daylight and brief hours of semi-darkness, always at the risk of being blown out of the water by *Bismarck*'s 15-inch guns, the *Suffolk*, accompanied by the half-blind *Norfolk*, held on, even through the brief tragic spectacle of the forthcoming violent gunnery duel.

If the *Norfolk* was half-blind because of her primitive radar, the *Suffolk* was at first half-dumb because of ice on her aerials, a contingency not sufficiently studied by the wireless specialists before the war. For some reason the *Norfolk*'s aerials were unaffected, and it was her sighting report that was heard first both by Admiral Tovey and Admiral Lütjens, whose cryptographers now proceeded to decode every message signalled by the enemy cruisers for the duration of the pursuit, to the German ships' considerable advantage.

Admiral Holland was also handed the sighting report on the bridge of the *Hood* within a minute of its receipt. He was 300 miles away and conveniently on a converging course. For the first time in the mighty *Hood*'s long career it seemed not only likely but almost inevitable that she would before long be in action against a battleship.

It was heavy going for the *Hood* and *Prince of Wales*, with the wind freshening from the north off the Arctic pack. With awesome regularity the *Hood*'s great bows dipped deep, her four screws each with 36,000 horsepower thrusting her north-west at 27 knots. If the *Prince of Wales* and *Hood* were taking it green almost continuously, the destroyers of the screen ahead of them had become racing semi-submersibles. Lieutenant T.J.Cain, the *Electra*'s gunnery officer, remembered this sight all his life,

with *Electra*, at maximum revs, slicing through the waves, the waters rising like green-white walls around her bows, and sheets of spray shooting up and over the ship like heavy rain. Our sisters, the rest of the destroyers, were often quite invisible beneath the water they displaced, and the battlewaggons rose and fell with the sound of thunder as they pressed majestically on, jettisoning great streams of water from around their cable chains, and steaming around their 'nostrils' – the gaping hawse-holes that flanked their bows – like a pair of angry dragons.[7]

All through that night of 23–24 May 1941 the two big ships with their acolytes drove through the seas south of Iceland, course 295°, the steady reports from the cruisers requiring no deviation. Very few of the 3,500-odd men of the Home Fleet squadron got much sleep that night. One of the *Prince of Wales*'s officers, the actor Esmond Knight, retired to his cabin to write letters and make things shipshape for action, which meant wrapping up breakables and securing pretty well everything else. 'All the time', he recalled, 'there was a persistent little voice crying out from every nook and cranny in the ship that we were to be in action before many hours, and that nothing could avoid it.'[8]

Before dawn the whole squadron went to action stations and the huge white battle ensigns were hoisted – as they had been before Jutland and Trafalgar and St Vincent and the Saints, way back into the mists of British naval history. At 3.00 a.m. the *Suffolk*'s reports showed that *Bismarck* was not far distant to the north-west. Admiral Holland had already turned his ships on to a south-westerly heading in anticipation of the interception. As the first touch of daybreak tinted the grey sky lighter, two battleships, a battle-cruiser, three heavy cruisers and six destroyers in all were on a south-west-by-west heading, gradually closing their antagonists a mere thirty-five miles distant.

At half this range the destroyers could still see nothing of the racing enemy, but from the bridge of the *Prince of Wales* the upper works and masts of the *Bismarck* and *Prinz Eugen* were now visible to the north-west, and from his Air Defence position above the bridge Esmond Knight could make them out clearly. The distance between the squadrons had closed to seventeen miles. In less than a minute the *Hood* in the van hoisted the signal 'Blue Four' – alter course 40 degrees to starboard. Holland was clearly anxious to close the range rapidly, even though it meant that half his guns could not bear on the enemy, nor four of the *Prince of Wales*'s ten 14-inch guns. Moreover, his flagship, the weaker-protected of the two, would for certain be the first target of the *Bismarck*'s big guns.

At 25,000 yards, or 14 land miles, the *Hood* fired her first four-gun salvo; thirty seconds later the *Prince of Wales* opened fire. The 35,000-ton ship shuddered from the recoil; the cordite blast was an assault on the ears of those exposed on deck, a thunderous rumble deep down in the engine-rooms. The *Bismarck* and *Prinz Eugen* replied almost at once, and for a minute the air between the four big ships was rent asunder by the passage of projectiles, some weighing almost a ton, in opposing directions.

The effect of these early salvoes at long range was very similar to heavy-gun engagements between British and German ships twenty-five years earlier. Then, at Jutland and the Dogger Bank and elsewhere, the German stereoscopic rangefinders led to initial accuracy which never failed to impress the British, many of whom died very soon after. British co-incidental rangefinders led to guns being a good deal slower on to the target, but having once achieved a straddle the gunnery tended to improve, whereas in a sustained action (as in the battle-cruiser phase at Jutland) the quality of German gunnery tended to fall off. The reason for this was that stereoscopic rangefinding required immense concentration and wearied the eyes after a relatively short time.

It was the same story in May 1941 as in May 1916. Lütjens's first salvoes were deadly accurate. The *Hood* was at once surrounded by a forest of waterspouts like tall pines in snow. Within seconds – or so it seemed to onlookers from the untroubled *Prince of Wales* – the flagship sustained a hit amidships, followed by leaping flames: 'a glow that pulsated like the appearance of a setting, tropical sun,' as Jerry Phillips graphically described it. It was not fatal, and a signal could be read at the *Hood*'s yardarm ordering a turn to port in order to bring all the squadron's guns to bear.

Captain Leach was greatly relieved. He had not understood why his admiral had offered the enemy such a relatively easy target while almost half their guns were incapable of bearing on the German ships. Meanwhile the *Prince of Wales* had lost one of her big guns forward because of mechanical failure. Now the four guns in the turret aft could open fire.

Considerations of this kind, and every other thought for that matter, were blasted from the minds of eyewitnesses by the blowing up of the flagship. For those in the *Hood* there was no time to register more than horror and perhaps a flash of recognition that this was what it was like to die; for Captain Leach and his staff, the yeoman of signals and helmsman, for Esmond Knight above them, and the few others above decks who were not wholly concentrated on the enemy – like the rangefinder ratings – the eye took in the ghastly wonder of the scene while the brain, like a suddenly defective computer, refused to record it.

A full broadside of 15-inch shells had descended upon the flagship, and one or perhaps two (one was enough) had struck the old battle-cruiser somewhere between her two after main battery turrets. It had pierced the 3-inch deck armour as if it were cardboard and plunged down towards the main and secondary magazines where it exploded. It was as if a volcano had suddenly erupted in those Arctic seas, flames rising to three times the height the *Hood*'s mainmast had once been, carrying with them the massive detritus of an exploding man o'war. For a second or two huge chunks of gun turret, superstructure, derricks and masts and funnels, hundreds of tons of tortured steel, hung in the air before crashing back on to the remaining ruins, while 15-inch shells exploded in brighter yellow flashes within this wall of flame, symbols of futile defiance.

Above this holocaust the secondary eruption was of grey-black smoke billowing higher still, its top lost in the clouds, a funeral pall above the broken ship which for a while stood in two broken sections, headstone to headstone, out of the water. When the *Prince of Wales* came thundering by half a minute later the forward section was still there, its jagged tip high above the bridge of the battleship, a battered steel coffin for hundreds of trapped men. This, too, disappeared beneath the waves; the flames extinguished as rapidly as the lives of 1,400 sailors, the smoke already fading as it was blown south-east while all that remained to be seen was a fast-growing mass of flotsam and an ocean surface deformed and oil-black.

HMS *Electra*, one of the destroyers which had earlier been detached from the squadron, now raced towards the scene of the catastrophe, rigging scrambling nets, preparing the sick bay for casualties. But what did she find?

... a large patch of oil ahead, a tangled pile of small wreckage ... *and that was all*.

But where were the boats, the rafts, the floats ...? And the men, *where* were the men? I thought of how we'd last seen *Hood*; and I thought of her impressive company. Like a small army they'd looked as they mustered for divisions. Then I thought of my words to Doc ... 'We'll need everyone we've got to help the poor devils inboard.'

But, almost immediately, came another hail, and far over to starboard we saw three men – two of them swimming, one on a raft. But on the chilling waters around them was no other sign of life....

Chiefie exclaimed incredulously as we looked again: 'But there *must* be more of them – there can't be only *three* of them! Where the hell are all the others?'

But there were no 'others' ... those scattered specks were all that remained of the *Hood*'s brave complement. Just three men now remained, three out of 1,419; three men who had lived through a catastrophe that had destroyed 42,000 tons of steel in less than four minutes of flame and shock.

It was a moment never to be erased from the memory. It was a revelation of horror.[9]

*   *   *

Some hours earlier, with the *Bismarck* leading, closely followed by the *Prinz Eugen*, the German squadron had faced the most dangerous part of their attempt to break out into the Atlantic on the evening of 23 May 1941. The corridor between the known minefields off the northern tip of Iceland and the pack ice was narrow off the Greenland coast, and much would depend on the weather. The forecast from Germany spoke of cloud, rain and at the best moderate visibility, and radar gave them the great advantage of being able to run blind close to the ice. In fact, long before the light began to fade, scattered ice floes could be seen ahead and the two ships began zig-zagging in and out of them as if fearful of submarine attack.

Unlike the *Suffolk*'s look-out, the Germans made no early visual contact. It was the *Bismarck*'s radar and hydrophones which warned that they were being watched, and by the time Lütjens had his powerful Zeiss binoculars trained on the distant shape, the cruiser was already fading into her protective fog bank. Half an hour later in this game of hide and seek, and at closer range, the *Norfolk* was seen in good time as she emerged from the fog.

Captain Lindemann called out over the ship's loudspeakers, 'Enemy in sight to port....' The rangefinder ratings were on to the target within seconds, and for the first time the *Bismarck* opened fire on an enemy. The cruiser, identified as 'County' class by her three tall funnels, disappeared again surrounded by the white spouts of near-misses. But the only damage was self-inflicted. The blast of the heavy guns beneath the *Bismarck*'s bridge had smashed the radar aerial, a design fault that had failed to be picked up during the many weeks of trials. So the big ship was now half-blind, and Lütjens was obliged to order the *Prinze Eugen* with her intact radar into the van.

The Admiral was more bothered about the radar damage than that he had been seen and identified. As the night closed in he felt confident that with his high speed and in this uncertain weather he would be able to throw off his shadowers. Both of them were behind him now, visible only to radar and out of range. He took advantage of a rain squall at 10.00 p.m. to make a 180-degree turn, hoping either to throw off the cruisers or locate them at such short range that he could blow them both out of the water. The manoeuvre appeared to have done the trick: at 5.00 a.m., with daylight well advanced and visibility clear, there was no visual or radar sign of the enemy.

It must have been around 0545, the rising sun having already lit up the horizon [wrote Müllenheim-Rechberg] when the smoke plumes of two ships and then the tips of their masts came into view on our port beam. General quarters was sounded on the *Bismarck*. Through my director, I watched as the masts in the distance grew higher and higher, reached their full length, and the silhouettes of the ships below them became visible. I could hear our first gunnery officer Korvettenkapitän Adalbert Schneider, speaking on the fire-control telephone. His hour had come, and all our thoughts and good wishes were with that competent, sensible man.[10]

Schneider had already identified the two ships as cruisers, cruisers apparently intent on self-immolation. His number two thought otherwise, and there was time for a telephone argument before the first enemy salvoes were indicated, as if they were giant signal lamps, by orange-yellow flashes from the fore part of the two ships. '*Donnerwetter!* Those flashes couldn't be coming from a cruiser's medium calibre guns,' exclaimed Müllenheim-Rechberg. The junior officer had been right.

The *Hood* was almost as well known to the German Navy as to the Royal Navy, the biggest enemy ship, the fastest capital ship too, and packing a punch as powerful as the *Bismarck*'s. The *Hood* had been the first antagonist in peacetime war games, and now here she was, barely 12.5 sea miles away, already firing her 15-inch guns, and this time it was no game. With the *King George V* (as the *Prince of Wales* was mis-identified) in support, they were up against a formidable foe before they had been able to get near to any convoy.

The *Kriegsmarine* had never been able entirely to throw off the inferiority complex under which it had laboured through the First World War. But the dreaded *Hood* was firing not at them but at the *Prinz Eugen* in the van, so confusingly similar were their silhouettes: perhaps that radar failing had been a blessing in disguise. In the *Bismarck*'s charthouse the navigator and his assistant were punctiliously plotting their course, listening to the loudspeaker which was giving a commentary as if they were at the Kiel football stadium playing Hamburg. At the words 'We have just straddled the enemy . . .', the two officers could not resist taking a look:

We put our instruments down and hurried to the eye-slits in the forward conning-tower, looked through, and asked ourselves, what does he mean, straddling? At first we could see nothing but what we saw moments later could not have been conjured up by even the wildest imagination. Suddenly, the *Hood* split in two, and thousands of tons of steel were hurled into the air.[11]

The jubilation among the men of the *Bismarck* and *Prinz Eugen* was intense but brief, for the fight was not yet over. Already the main armament of both ships had turned on the *Prince of Wales*, and soon hits were being scored on her, too. After a few minutes the battleship turned away. Soon she was out of range behind a smokescreen.

There were three courses of action that Admiral Lütjens could now pursue. He could continue with his raid, he could turn after the *Prince of Wales* and finish her off too, or he could bring his ships home to a hero's welcome for sinking the enemy's proudest man o'war. 'The men below', claims Müllenheim-Rechberg, 'found it absolutely incomprehensible that, after the destruction of the *Hood*, we did not go after the *Prince of Wales*.' Having blown up one of the enemy's big ships with five or six salvoes, and driven off the second after another dozen or so, was not this the time to follow up defeat with annihilation?

If that was the opinion below decks, it was also certainly the opinion of the captain on the bridge. Lindemann argued that the sinking of the *Hood* alone had justified the operation and the sinking of two would be an unprecedented triumph, and at the same time bring even greater success to a later combined break-out with the *Gneisenau* and *Scharnhorst*.

The captain's view was supported by information he was now receiving on the condition of his ship. The *Prince of Wales*, with her 'green' gun crews and faulty guns – all four in the aft turret had become unserviceable as she turned away – had in fact made hits on the *Bismarck*, three in all though not everyone had felt them. The first had hit forward and had led to the flooding of the forecastle with some 2,000 tons of water. The second had done considerable damage amidships, smashing bulkheads and severing fuel lines. All the third did was to splinter a boat without even exploding. But the *Bismarck* was down at the bows by 3 degrees and had a 9-degree list to port, her speed cut to 28 knots, and most serious of all, she had in effect lost 1,000 tons of fuel in the forward tanks, and this was leaking out, scoring a black tell-tale trail on the ocean's surface. This made the earlier failure to top up supplies from the tanker even more serious.

But the *Bismarck* remained a fast fighting ship, her magazines almost full, all her guns serviceable. Therefore, why not turn on the more gravely damaged *Prince of Wales*? No, said Admiral Lütjens. They would proceed into the Atlantic as a squadron, detaching *Prinz Eugen* to attack shipping while the *Bismarck* headed for St Nazaire, disposing of any enemy shipping met *en route*.

Within minutes of breaking off the action the Admiral signalled, 'Battle-cruiser, probably *Hood*, sunk. Another battleship, *King George V* or *Renown*, turned away damaged....' And later: 'Intention: to proceed to St Nazaire. *Prinz Eugen* cruiser warfare.'

He also added, more ominously, 'Two heavy cruisers maintain contact.'

The effect of the combined fire of the two German ships on the *Prince of Wales* was devastating. The *Bismarck*'s secondary 5.9-inch guns as well as the *Prinz Eugen*'s 8-inch were all comfortably in range, and the ship was hit again and again. One 15-inch shell struck and passed clean through the bridge, killing everyone except the Captain and Yeoman of Signals, who were thrown half-stunned to the deck. It almost did for Esmond Knight, too:

From this moment everything seems hazy, except that I remember again hearing that great rushing noise, like the approach of a cyclone, and having quite an irrelevant dream about listening to the band in Hyde Park, and then being conscious of a high ringing noise in my head and slowly coming to. I had the sensation that I was dying. It was a strange feeling, and one that made me feel rather sad – no more. There was a lot of water swishing about – I was lying on my side with a great weight on top of me. What on earth had happened? ... Again the deck below me was shuddering under the vibration of another salvo; there were muffled voices, and shouts of 'Stretcher-bearer!' and 'Clear the way there!' I remember being able to raise enough breath to let out a squeaky, 'Georgie, old boy, can you get me out?' Strong hands lifted the dead men off me; there was a horrible smell of blood, and the uncanny noise that men make when they are dying. Somehow or other I fumbled down those ladders I knew so well – everything feeling quite unfamiliar and dream-like. Below decks I was conscious of water rushing in the passages, the smell of the sick-bay, and the efficient bustle of the ship's doctors as they attended to that sudden, rather unnerving rush of casualties. 'Hallo! What are you doing here? ... Open your eyes, old boy.' I did so with difficulty, but I could not see him.[12]

Yes, the actor was blind.

Admiral Wake-Walker was now in command of the squadron, and the *Norfolk* the flagship, and it was he who gave the order for the *Prince of Wales* to join him in shadowing the enemy until reinforcements arrived. Admiral Tovey with the *King George V*, *Repulse*, *Victorious* and five cruisers was about 350 miles away now, to the south-east, and fast closing. The 16-inch-gun *Rodney* was also on her way, and Force H with a second, and highly experienced, carrier and the battle-cruiser *Renown* were on their way from Gibraltar. Not for the first time the Royal Navy was revealing herself as a many-headed hydra which no Hercules could ever destroy.

The *Suffolk*'s radar operators had been on duty for so long now that the rotating white line stroking at every circle the faint blip of the *Bismarck* was engraved on the retinas of their eyes to the exclusion of almost everything else, and they reached for their mugs of coffee like men as blind as Esmond Knight. They lost her for a while later in the day when the battleship slowed down (for temporary repairs, in fact) and simultaneously visibility fell.

As soon as he heard the news Jerry Phillips ordered over the helm and the *Norfolk* made a majestic complete turn through 360 degrees. 'We had a hunch it might work'; and it did, almost too well. 'We resumed our earlier course for only a few minutes when the mist suddenly cleared, and there she was, dead ahead, about eight miles.'

The *Bismarck* had turned on to a southerly heading. Wake-Walker signalled Tovey, who was relieved because it suggested that the battleship was heading for France rather than back to Norway. But it was still possible for her to increase speed during the night in a bad patch of weather, throw off her pursuers and join the two battle-cruisers at St Nazaire. To let her get away now would only prolong and intensify the nightmare of decimated Atlantic convoys. Tovey decided he must use every means to slow her up. For the present only air weapons could do it. If he detached the *Victorious* now her aircraft might be just within range before darkness fell. If they could find her the final outcome might depend on how well those 'green' pilots had been trained, and how courageous they were.

The next sighting of the *Bismarck* was made not by any of the numerous warships now searching for her in mid-Atlantic, nor by the long-range flying boats from Iceland. She was spotted by a neutral, the United States coastguard cutter *Modoc*, a perky little single-funnel vessel armed with a couple of 5-inch guns, a unit of the Greenland Survey Expedition, itself a euphemism for a patrol to discourage a German attack and occupation. American neutrality was rapidly becoming less neutral, and the *Modoc* was currently engaged in searching for survivors from the badly mauled convoy HX126. Instead of finding open boats with soaked and half-frozen sailors, she found the world's biggest battleship. It was now the evening of 24 May; the captain of the *Modoc*, Lieutenant-Commander H. Belford USCG, had heard on the radio of the destruction of the *Hood* at dawn, and how she had been destroyed. Now, carving her way south through heavy seas, the *Bismarck* swept arrogantly by, guns trained fore and aft, disdaining to acknowledge the cutter's existence.

It was not the end of an eventful day for the coastguardsmen, who were hardened to one day following another with nothing more than the North Atlantic and an occasional ice floe to break the monotony. Out of the cloud there now appeared like wind-tossed skuas a squadron of biplanes. For Commander Belford the sight was like going back to American fleet manoeuvres of the 1920s when the Marine Corps was flying biplane Curtiss F8Cs. He did not know that the British Navy pilots nicknamed their Swordfish 'Stringbags', but the word would come to anyone's mind watching these tubby biplanes with fixed undercarriage being buffeted about in the strong north-westerly. Each plane had a big torpedo slung under its belly. Watching with some relief as the Swordfish flew off, the cutter's crew, who had noted the serried ranks of the *Bismarck*'s anti-aircraft guns, gave them a nil out of ten chance of survival if they were foolhardy enough to take on that mountain of steel, still in sight to the south.

Seconds later a multiple display of muzzle flashes told them that the killing had begun. And it was the real thing, not fancy fireworks, for some of the heavier shells ranged as far as the *Modoc*, bursting unpleasantly close. The ridiculously uneven battle faded into the distance and was soon gone, while Commander Belford listened to the sound of heavier guns, like some ominous overture.

Minutes later three more warships hove into sight on the same course as the *Bismarck*, and clearly in tense pursuit: a battleship almost as big as the German, and two three-funnel cruisers. They, by contrast, were taking too much notice of the *Modoc*. To the dismay of Commander Belford, he saw the battleship's guns trained on his puny cutter. However, recognition came in the nick of time. Like their quarry, the hounds disappeared into the grey and the mist to the south.

The German gun crews, closed up about their guns, were as astonished as the Americans at the sight of the Swordfish, unsteady in high wind, coming slowly towards them very low above the waves. They made easier targets than any towed drogue on exercises in the Baltic.

Müllenheim-Rechberg watched incredulously:

Our anti-aircraft batteries fired anything that would fit into their barrels. Now and again one of our 38-centimetre [15-inch] turrets and frequently our 15-centimetre turrets fired into the water ahead of the aircraft, raising massive waterspouts. To fly into one of these spouts would mean the end. And the aircraft: they were moving so slowly that they seemed to be standing still in the air, and they looked so antiquated. Incredible how the pilots pressed their attack with suicidal courage, as if they did not expect ever again to see a carrier.... [The helmsman] who was steering from the open bridge, did a brilliant job.... The enemy's tactics were such that torpedoes were coming in at us from several directions at the same time and, in trying to avoid one, we were liable to run into another. Back and forth we zig-zagged. All at once the sharp, ringing report of an explosion punctuated the roar of our guns and the *Bismarck* gave a slight shudder....[13]

Miraculous good fortune blessed both sides during that furious fifteen-minute engagement. The successful Swordfish's undersized 18-inch torpedo had struck the ship where she was best able to resist the explosion, leaving little more than a dent in the midships armour. The concussion had hurled a sailor fatally against a heavy metal object, and several others were injured. Again the worst damage was self-inflicted. The high-speed violent evasion had smashed the temporary repairs to the earlier damage by shellfire, and water was pouring into the ship at an increasing rate. As for the Swordfish, to their own astonishment only one or two of them suffered damage, none of it serious. Having discharged their duty, and their torpedoes, they flew back through the advancing night fifty miles to their carrier. Some of the pilots had never made a night landing; the *Victorious*'s deck was soaking and pitching violently, but one by one the newly battle-seasoned pilots landed safely with their crews, not a man wounded.

An hour later, more as a warning threat, the *Prince of Wales* fired a salvo at the *Bismarck* in the gathering darkness; and like a schoolboy's defiant tit-for-tat, the *Bismarck* replied in kind. The double reports signalled the end of violence for that day, which had witnessed so much death and destruction.

With the prospect of lost speed during the night, and the need to repair the damage below, Lütjens determined to throw off his pursuers. This was easier now, without the *Prinz Eugen*, which increased the size of the radar blip as well as their visual size. At 3.00 a.m. Captain Lindemann ordered the helmsman to turn the ship slowly through a complete circle, and then a further 20 degrees, so that an hour later the *Bismarck* was on a slightly east of south course.

The turn fortuitously coincided with one of the zig-zags Wake-Walker had ordered as a precaution against U-boat attack. These entailed *Suffolk* losing temporary radar contact, and picking it up again on the inward leg. But this time there was no *Bismarck* to smudge the radar screen when she turned to the point where she should have been. The big bird had flown.

At 5.00 a.m., two nights and a day after that blip had first appeared on the screen, Captain Ellis had to accept defeat. 'Have lost contact with enemy,' he signalled his Admiral. Wake-Walker, who had become almost a sleep-walker, was at last stretched out on a bunk: just a quick cat-nap which had become essential before he faced another critical day. Jerry Phillips was on the *Norfolk*'s bridge where heavy doses of adrenalin demanded from the ship's doctor kept him awake. 'It was a disappointment, yes – of course it was,' Captain Phillips commented on this moment of the operation. 'But it wasn't the end of the world. I passed the news on to John Tovey in case he hadn't heard and set about finding her again.'[14]

CHAPTER SIX

'A bloody tumult of destruction ...'

The *Bismarck* lost! The three words were heard with dismay amongst the senior officers on the bridge of many British warships, at Scapa Flow and Gibraltar, in the operations room and the Operational Intelligence Centre in the Admiralty. New dispositions, new moves and courses and considerations of all kinds were debated, swiftly but with the cool practicality for which senior naval officers were admired. The First Sea Lord, Dudley Pound, the Vice-Chief of Naval Staff, Tom Phillips, John Tovey, Wake-Walker and James Somerville – all these admirals pored over charts while navigators calculated speeds and compass bearings and points of interception, and engineers worked on ships' fuel supplies and rate of consumption at this speed and that.

As soon as word was passed round the German battleship that they had thrown off their shadowers, there was great relief and jubilation.

Contact has been broken! Broken after thirty-one long, uninterrupted hours! It was the best possible news, a real boost to confidence and morale. Exactly how this blessing had come about and where the British ships were at the moment, we did not know.... We probably would not even have wanted to know that much detail. Content with the momentary respite, we kept expressing to one another the hope that we would not catch sight of the enemy again before we got to St Nazaire.[1]

In this prolonged battle of wits, after Lütjens had fooled his pursuers by brilliant evasive action, it was he who made the next mistake. After retaining radio silence for so long, in the late morning of 25 May he suddenly transmitted a long radio message to Germany recounting in some detail his action with the *Hood* thirty hours earlier, and describing the efficiency of British radar. Unless the German Admiral believed he was doomed, and had determined to pass on all the intelligence he could before he was engulfed, there was no possible justification for this dangerous indiscretion.

Predictably, his message was picked up by British direction-finding stations. It was a very indefinite 'fix' because it was distorted by a cold front in the Atlantic, but the bearings did indicate that the *Bismarck* was on course for a French Biscay port.

Before sailing Admiral Tovey had asked the Operational Intelligence Centre to signal individual direction-finding bearings instead of the position because he expected to have with him two destroyers fitted with high-frequency direction-finding receivers which might give him a cross bearing if plotted in the flagship. But as it happened, these destroyers were absent, while Tovey failed to cancel the arrangement, and the bearings were plotted in his flagship on a navigational instead of a gnomonic chart, which gave a false position well to the north. Tovey then quite reasonably concluded that the *Bismarck* was heading for home by way of the Faeroes Gap and altered course accordingly.

Thus, at midday on 25 May, the *Bismarck* was heading south-west for France at 20 knots, unobserved, while all the hounds were off on a false scent, steering north and east. It was not until later that day that the Admiralty realized the mistake that had been made, and Tovey, when informed, signalled: 'Act on the assumption that the *Bismarck* is making for a French port.' According to Admiralty calculations the most likely ship to find and intercept the *Bismarck* also happened to be the most powerful, the battleship *Rodney*, her decks piled high with stores relating to the refit in America for which she had been heading, and with a passenger list of some 500 troops and a number of American officials and officers. Her engines were in poor condition, but her 16-inch magazines were full of shells. Her Captain was Frederick Dalrymple-Hamilton, a large, aggressive and highly capable Scot. And his battleship would make a formidable adversary.

But all through that day, and through the night of 25–26 May, no visual or radar sighting was made of the *Bismarck*. On the German side, hopes began to rise that they might succeed in making it to port, in spite of her low fuel reserves and heavy list; while the British in the Admiralty as well as those taking part in the search began to despair. 'A day of fearful gloom ensued. The PM [Prime Minister] cannot understand why the *Prince of Wales* did not press home her attack yesterday',[2] wrote Churchill's Assistant Private Secretary in his diary.

Late that evening there was a meeting at HQ RAF Coastal Command between two Admiralty operations officers and the C-in-C Coastal Command, Air Marshal Sir Frederick Bowhill, in order to plan the next morning's air patrols. Bowhill was of the opinion that the *Bismarck* might continue farther south than was anticipated, in order to avoid the attention of RAF bombers, and make a last-minute turn east towards the French port. As a result, one of the very long-range Catalinas was given a patrol to cover this contingency.

This particular flying boat took off from Lough Erne in Northern Ireland in the early hours of 26 May. By happy chance its crew included, as co-pilot, an American, Ensign Leonard 'Tuck' Smith, from Higginsville, Missouri. He was one of several experienced Catalina pilots loaned, extremely unofficially, to the RAF to help air crews accustom themselves to the relatively new machine. The Catalina had already been airborne for over six hours and was operating just south of the 50th parallel far out into the Atlantic. The crew had had a bacon and egg breakfast, and the American had just taken over the controls from the British pilot, Flying Officer Dennis Briggs. The weather was foul, the cloud down to 500 feet in places, the sea very choppy. It was almost time to head for base. Then, out of the murk – 'Harry clampers' the RAF called it – there appeared at extreme visual range a vague, dark shape. It was, without doubt, a big ship, but unidentifiable. Tuck Smith took the Catalina up into the clouds, turned in the direction of the ship and a few minutes later, as the cloud too suddenly lifted, found himself right above the biggest warship he had ever seen. And it was not friendly. Within seconds, muzzle flashes sparkled and the air was full of tracer and lethal shell bursts.

As the Catalina was thrown about by high explosive and the violent evasions of her pilot, Briggs managed to get off a preliminary sighting report before what appeared to be their inevitable destruction: 'One battleship bearing 240 degrees five miles, course 150 degrees, my position 49°33' North, 21°47' West. Time of origin 1030/26.'

Badly damaged, the Catalina and her Anglo–American crew survived. And the Royal Navy had the news for which it had been so anxiously waiting.

The *Ark Royal* was a similar carrier to the *Victorious*, a few years older and with a very much more experienced company of air crews. But her main strike aircraft were the same lumbering Swordfish flown by the *Victorious*'s courageous green pilots. She had been flying patrols since first light, and one of these long-range Swordfish spotted the *Bismarck* only twelve minutes after the Catalina's first report. What was more, the Stringbag held on to her, just out of flak range.

Lütjens knew now that it was only a matter of time before they were subjected to another torpedo-bomber attack, and Captain Lindemann's reassurance to Adolf Hitler would be put to the test again. The German Admiral calculated that if they could survive that day and the following night without suffering any further damage they had just enough fuel to make port the following day. But if they were slowed down again it was almost inevitable that they would be in action with surface ships again. He also knew with almost as great accuracy as Admiral Tovey the strength and nature of the searching forces, and that if the gathering warships cornered him they must bring about his destruction.

Conditions were so awful that they were beyond the accepted limit for flying operations from carriers. The rise and fall of the flight deck of the *Ark Royal* was 60 feet and there was a 40-knot wind. A Swordfish's stalling speed was 55 knots so that the carrier had to steam into wind at no more than 8 knots if the aircraft were not to be blown backwards, and this low

speed increased even further the pitch and roll. The spray was like a hurricane, slashing the deck crew who already found it hard to keep their feet
on the soaking and lurching steel deck. The biplanes had to be held from
being swept over the side until the very last second before take-off.

But the need for an attack was desperate and one by one the first of
the fifteen Swordfish got away safely, though several of them dipped their
wheels into the water as they dropped with their 18-inch 'tin fish' before
staggering up again at full throttle. A case of mistaken identity led to near-
tragedy. With adrenalin racing, the squadron-commander led the planes
on to the *Sheffield* which had now taken on the task of maintaining radar
contact with the enemy. No one knew that the *Prinz Eugen* had been
detached, and in spite of the British cruiser's twin funnels, one heavy
cruiser was not unlike another in this visibility.

Luckily the cruiser's skipper had had Fleet Air Arm experience, recognized what must have happened, and was a fine handler of a ship, too.
The *Sheffield* combed all the torpedo tracks, despatched a rude signal, and
that was that. On landing back the crestfallen commander reported: 'It
was a perfect attack, sir. Right height, right range, right cloud cover, right
speed, and the wrong f——ng ship!'

A second attack by another fifteen Swordfish took off under equally
dangerous and foul conditions at 7.10 p.m. The observer in A4 C 'Charley'
was Gerard Woods, and he later recounted his personal experiences on
one of the 'hairiest' and certainly the most important of operations in which
he ever participated.

The plan was to climb to around 5,000 ft above *Sheffield*, and to make a co-ordinated
attack by sub-flight. Thus, five sections of three aircraft each would attack simultaneously from different bearings, dividing the enemy fire, so giving us better prospects of hitting and getting away scot-free. At least, that was the theory.... After
a few minutes we realized that in these conditions formation flying was dangerous,
but it would be even more dangerous to try to break out of it. So onward, ever
upward we climbed 'hanging on the prop'. Just what happened inside those clouds
will never be known but it seemed on comparing notes later that each aircraft
came out independently of the others, each pilot taking a look round, deciding
he'd lost his fellows and diving back through the dark grey cotton wool. Miraculous
to relate, as we came out of the perfect cloud cover at about 1,000 ft, we were
almost back in sub-flight formation! ...

The minute or so which followed will be forever engraved on my memory.
There she was, a thousand yards away, big, black, cowled funnel, menacing, with
every close-range weapon stabbing flame as we steadied on our approach, 100
knots, 100 ft, 1,000 yards just as the textbook says. 'Flash' Seager, the TAG, was
sensibly crouching down in the cockpit, sitting on a lead-covered codebook. Later
he told me I was shouting my head off as we ran in, probably true, but what
it was I have no idea. All I do know is that as we dropped our 'tinfish' A4 'Charlie'
almost leapt into the air, and as we turned away aft tightly, we were suspended
motionless for a split second that felt like an eternity as every gun seemed to concentrate upon us. The flak ripped through the fabric-covered fuselage like peas on

a drum. 'Flash' yelled, and then Alan said 'Christ! Just look at this lot' as *Bismarck* put her 15 in guns on a flat trajectory, firing ahead of us, either intending to blast us off the face of the earth, or as happened in fact, to make a Beechers' Brook of water-splashes 100 ft high through which we must fly. . . .[3]

Under those chaotic conditions none of the Swordfish crews could be 100 per cent certain of making a hit although a number of claims were made. 'Estimate one hit amidships,' the *Ark Royal* signalled modestly to Admirals Somerville and Tovey; and later, after studying all the reports again: 'Possible second hit on starboard quarter.' Regardless of what damage these fifteen Stringbags had done to the battleship, the near-miracle was that everyone had come safely back to the carrier, even if a few of them were wounded – none seriously.

At about the same time *Sheffield* reported that the *Bismarck* was firing at her and that the battleship was on a northerly heading. This was confirmed a little later: 'Enemy steering 340 degrees.' This made no sense at all; why, when the *Bismarck* was so close to escape, should she steer straight towards her pursuers?

Müllenheim-Rechberg, an eyewitness to this last desperate air strike on his ship, knew the answer.

Once more, the *Bismarck* became a fire-spitting mountain. The racket of her anti-aircraft guns was joined by the roar from her main and secondary turrets as they fired into the bubbling paths of oncoming torpedoes, creating splashes ahead of the attackers. Once more, the restricted field of my director and the dense smoke allowed me to see only a small slice of the action. The antique-looking Swordfish, fifteen of them, seemed to hang in the air, near enough to touch. The high cloud layer, which was especially thick directly over us, probably did not permit a synchronized attack from all directions, but the Swordfish came so quickly after one another that our defence did not have it any easier than it would have had against such an attack. They flew low, the spray of the heaving seas masking their landing gear. Nearer and still nearer they came, into the midst of our fire. It was as though their orders were, 'Get hits or don't come back!'

The heeling of the ship first one way and then the other told me that we were trying to evade torpedoes. The rudder indicator never came to rest and the speed indicator revealed a significant loss of speed. The men on the control platforms in the engine rooms had to keep their wits about them. 'All ahead full!' – 'All stop!' – 'All back full!' – 'Ahead!' – 'All stop!' were the ever-changing orders by which Lindemann sought to escape the malevolent 'eels'.

We had been under attack for perhaps fifteen minutes when I heard that sickening sound. Two torpedoes exploded in quick succession, but somewhere forward of where I was. Good fortune in misfortune, I thought. They could not have done much damage. My confidence in our armoured belt was unbounded. Let's hope that's the end of it!

Soon after the alarm, Matrosengefreiter Herzog, at his port third 3.7-centimeter anti-aircraft gun, saw three planes approaching from astern at an oblique angle, while the talker at his station was reporting other planes coming from various directions. Then, through the powder smoke, Herzog saw two planes approach on the port beam and turn to the right. In no time they were only twenty metres off our stern, coming in too low for Herzog's or any other guns to bear on them. Two torpedoes splashed into the water and ran towards our stern just as we were making an evasive turn to port.

The attack must have been almost over when it came, an explosion aft. My heart sank. I glanced at the rudder indicator. It showed 'left 12 degrees'. Did that just happen to be the correct reading at that moment? No. It did not change. It stayed at 'left 12 degrees'. Our increasing list to starboard soon told us that we were in a continuous turn. The aircraft attack ended as abruptly as it had begun.[4]

Just as one 14-inch shell forward had partially disabled the *Bismarck* shortly after dawn on 24 May, now at dusk on 26 May a single torpedo had crippled her beyond repair. It had exploded right aft, damaging her propellers and making her steering engine unserviceable. Captain Lindemann was forced to reduce speed to 8 knots and put the *Bismarck*'s bows into the wind. The Atlantic rollers came thundering over her low forecastle, and now that she was scarcely moving through the stormy waters it was as if the *Bismarck* was in an attitude of supplication.

At that moment a new enemy arrived to add to her ordeal. Captain Philip Vian, of *Altmark* fame and much other subsequent action, had as usual taken the initiative without orders. He had picked up the Catalina's sighting report and broken off to intercept. His arrival could not have been more timely. Darkness was falling, and all through the night Vian's destroyers harried and struck at the *Bismarck*, firing off starshells and real shells to deprive the Germans of any chance of rest, closing in from time to time to launch torpedoes, two or three of which made hits.

Like a condemned prisoner the *Bismarck* awaited her last dawn. The ubiquitous *Norfolk*, her tormentor for so long, had her in sight and flashed a signal to the nearest battleship, the *Rodney*. A gale was now blowing, and out of the grey gloom, taking it green along her vast deck forward with all three of her massive 16-inch triple turrets, the *Bismarck* came into sight through Admiral Wake-Walker's glasses. It was 8.20 a.m. 'Enemy bears 130 degrees, 16 miles,' signalled the *Norfolk*.

'Yes, we were pretty tired by then,' admitted Jerry Phillips. 'Not much sleep for three nights. But the dear old *Rodney* made off in the right direction, and about half an hour later we heard her guns.'

Rain squalls whipped across the sea between the two ships. The *Bismarck* answered the fire and for a few minutes it seemed as if a classic gun duel between the two battleships might develop. 'We shall fight to the last shell,' Lütjens signalled home. 'Long live the Führer!' But the German ship demonstrated none of the gun-laying skill nor spirit of the earlier engagement, and as soon as the *King George V* brought her 14-inch guns to bear the accuracy and frequency of her fire fell off.

The *Rodney*'s gunnery was superb, her third salvo scoring a hit. Hits followed in rapid succession when *King George V* joined in, and the giant battleship was rapidly reduced to a shattered wreck.

Some men were trapped below [Müllenheim-Rechberg wrote]. The hatches leading to the upper deck were either jammed shut or there was heavy wreckage lying on top of them. In Compartment XV near the forward mess on the battery deck, two hundred men were imprisoned behind jammed hatches. They were all killed by shell fire. Flames cut off the whole forward part of the ship.... The task of the doctors and corpsmen became overwhelming as one action station after another was knocked out and the men who were no longer able to take part in the fight crowded the battle dressing stations.[5]

The *Bismarck* never lowered her colours, and like Admiral von Spee's flagship in 1914, she was pounded to pieces by an overwhelming mass of high-explosive. 'I can't say I enjoyed this part of the business much,' Captain Dalrymple-Hamilton said afterwards, 'but didn't see what else I could do.' Still she refused to sink, until the heavy cruiser *Dorsetshire* pumped two torpedoes into her starboard side, steamed round her bow and launched two more into her port side. The *Bismarck* heeled over to port and sank by the stern.

In all just 107 of a total complement of more than 2,000 officers and men of the *Bismarck* were saved, the great majority by the *Dorsetshire* and the destroyer *Maori*, three by a U-boat and two by a German weather ship later. The *Dorsetshire* could probably have added at least another 150 to her total but there was a U-boat alarm, probably false, and a warning from other nearby ships of a German bomber attack, which was real enough. The cruiser was forced to steam away leaving many unfortunate men in the water. It was a cruel end for them after all that they had endured.

The destruction of the *Hood* three days earlier had stunned the British people and greatly alarmed the American naval authorities, not least President Franklin D. Roosevelt. No details of the pursuit were made known during the following days, which made international anxiety and especially British anxiety all the greater. Fortunately the Canadian people had no knowledge of a convoy of Canadian troopships in mid-Atlantic and highly vulnerable to destruction, especially in the early stages of the pursuit. In Britain trust in the navy had taken a blow but there was ultimate confidence that the German battleship would be tracked down and destroyed.

On the morning of 27 May 1941 Churchill addressed the House of Commons on the subject, reporting that the *Bismarck* had been found and was being attacked. That was about all he could say to allay anxiety. Then he sat down and was almost at once passed a piece of paper, which led him to rise to his feet again. 'I asked the indulgence of the House', he wrote, 'and said, "I have just received news that the *Bismarck* is sunk." They seemed content,'[6] he added in a masterly understatement.

The *Prinz Eugen* succeeded in refuelling in the Atlantic and heard of the end of her senior consort. The North Atlantic had never been so full of hostile ships, and the cruiser's captain and crew, utterly dispirited, made their way to France and arrived safely at Brest on 1 June, with a damaged propellor from hitting the ice.

The long-term consequences of the sinking of the *Bismarck* were far more profound than the loss of one battleship. It signalled the further disillusionment of Hitler in Raeder's surface fleet, and the eventual rise to supremacy in the German Navy, in early 1943, of Admiral Doenitz and his U-boats. 'The sinking of the *Bismarck*', Doenitz later wrote with some relish, 'had ... shown that the enemy had improved his system of patrolling the Atlantic to such a degree that our own surface vessels could obviously no longer operate in these sea areas.'[7]

At the same time, with the *Bismarck* gone and the *Scharnhorst* and *Gneisenau* non-operational and incarcerated in Brest, the Royal Navy, and soon the United States Navy, could concentrate their resources on their first enemy in the Battle of the Atlantic. The *Bismarck*'s sister ship *Tirpitz*, soon to be completed, was to become a thorn in the flesh, but for the present, as Churchill signalled to Roosevelt, the position was much eased: 'She was a terrific ship, and a masterpiece of naval construction,' he told the President. 'Her removal eases our battleship situation, as we should have had to keep *King George V*, *Prince of Wales* and the two *Nelsons* practically tied to Scapa Flow to guard against a sortie....'[8]

A further consequence of the sinking of the *Bismarck* was a sudden increase in Hitler's fear of a British counter-invasion of Norway. As Churchill had told Roosevelt, the British Home Fleet was now at liberty, and Hitler knew full well that the four British battleships would not be idle for long. The German Chancellor prided himself on his military intuition, which had indeed proved right on a number of occasions. He also shared Kaiser Wilhelm II's love of large men o'war, which was why he had put in hand such a big naval building programme soon after he seized power in 1933. So far he was disappointed in the surface fleet's performance, but not yet wholly disillusioned.

Hitler judged that the only way of deterring a British amphibious attack on north Norway, with Narvik again as the key target – so his intuition told him – was to station all the heavy units of the German Navy there. This would prevent Britain seizing Swedish iron ore and getting supplies through to Russia more easily. Overcoming Admiral Raeder's opposition, the Führer ordered the *Bismarck*'s sister ship *Tirpitz* to Trondheim as soon as she was completed and ready for sea. This was in the late autumn of 1941. On 13 November he raised for the first time the question of bringing the *Scharnhorst*, *Gneisenau* and *Prinz Eugen* back home from Brest, and thence to Norway. Raeder pointed out the dangers of attempting to do this by the northern route, with the *Bismarck*'s fate as a sound lesson, which led Hitler to ask why they should not use the English Channel. This was tantamount to asking a bank robber to walk down Threadneedle Street.

When the Admiral raised his hands in horror and cried 'Impossible!', the Führer's response was predictable.

It is not on record but it is quite reasonable to suggest that Hitler then said in uncompromising terms something like this: 'Those three big ships of yours at Brest are nothing but a liability to the war machine. We have fighter squadrons there to protect them which are badly needed in Russia, countless flak and gunners, more guns and men to defend the harbour from raids like the costly one on St Nazaire. What do they do to justify themselves, these ships of yours? Do they make daring attacks on Atlantic convoys? They do not. Are they immune from bomb attack? They are not. Do they get hit from time to time and damaged so that more resources are used to repair them? They do. So we will bring them home, then send them to Norway where they can work for their living and be ten times safer from bombing attack.'

By 12 January 1942 Raeder had completed plans for sending the two battle-cruisers and the heavy cruiser up the Channel under the nose of the Royal Navy and the RAF, as the Fuehrer desired. It was all worked out in meticulous Germanic detail, so that the ships would be escorted by minesweepers, E-boats and destroyers, and in the air by a standing patrol of fighters. They would await really bad winter weather, leave in darkness without any suspicious preliminaries, and pass through the narrowest (twenty-three miles) Dover–Calais stretch in full daylight at full speed to fool the British, who would expect a night dash.

The British Chiefs of Staff had for long formulated contingency plans for such a dash home, and during those short winter days of January and early February PRU Spitfires flew over Brest whenever the weather permitted. Three patrol lines of radar-equipped Coastal Command aircraft kept a constant watch, while others prepared for mine and torpedo dropping. Agents in France were alerted, Bomber Command ordered to have aircraft on constant readiness. By 2 February 1942 the Admiralty was certain that the attempt was imminent.

Vice-Admiral O. Ciliax commanded the German squadron which put to sea late in the evening of 11 February. From the start he was blessed with good fortune, whilst in almost every department the well-laid British plans went awry, partly through bad luck and partly through incompetence and lack of imagination and co-ordination. For instance, the German ships pierced all three of the airborne radar screens: the first because either the operator or the machine was at fault, the second because the aircraft had been withdrawn through faulty radar and had not been replaced due to shortage of aircraft, and the third because the aircraft was withdrawn shortly before she would have picked up the German squadron because thick fog was forecast at her base. The navy was not informed of any of these failures by the RAF, which really was inexcusable.

Shore radar began picking up the German ships at 8.30 a.m. on 12 February but the controllers thought they must be air/sea rescue operations.

Only when it was noted that the blips were travelling at a steady 25 knots almost two hours later were suspicions raised. Then at 10.10 a.m. two Spitfires had taken off by chance and, 'to enliven one of the quiet days of the war', had flown over to the French coast 'with the idea of picking up a stray Hun'. They found what they wanted quite quickly. In a moment half the *Luftwaffe* (or so it seemed) was about their ears, and as the British pilots endeavoured to extricate themselves, observed beneath them large warships screened by numerous escorts.

These Spitfire pilots, a station commander and wing commander, had not been told of the likely breakout. They thought what they had seen was important, but not important enough to put out over the R/T. It was, therefore, not until they landed at 11.10 a.m. and made a telephone call that the authorities learned not only that 'Salmon and Gluckstein' were out, but were already past Le Touquet and near Calais. The effect of this news on the Admiralty was devastating.

Admiral Ciliax could scarcely believe the luck that had held all the way so far. Certainly the weather had been on his side, with low cloud and sweeping rainstorms, but for three ships, totalling almost 80,000 tons, with their wide screens of fast light craft and with fighters accompanying them through all these daylight hours – for this considerable armada to come all this way undetected was scarcely credible. They had traversed the whole length of the English Channel without any hostile move being made against them, and the weather was closing in as they approached the North Sea with its notorious winter mists.

Even off Dover, Ciliax's luck held. Raw recruits under instruction had recently taken over the long-range British batteries – and the shooting was ragged. At this late hour, with the short February afternoon ahead and the cloud base so low, only torpedo-bombers seemed likely to have any chance of damaging the big ships, or possibly some of the destroyers immediately available. These squadrons were based at various airfields along the south coast in anticipation of an early warning of the ships' approach, and had now been by-passed. Only six Swordfish at Manston and seven more modern Beauforts were immediately available, and were scrambled.

Commanding the Stringbags was Lieutenant-Commander E. Esmonde, a highly experienced airman who had led that first attack against the *Bismarck* from the *Victorious* with his green pilots. This was an even stickier proposition for with only six aircraft he faced the flak of three ships, plus the destroyers and E-boats; and, worse still, single-seat fighters – scores of them. Most of Esmonde's promised Spitfire support failed to turn up, and the few that did were far too busy defending themselves against huge odds to be of any help.

So the Fleet Air Arm air crews were harried by Messerschmitt Me109s and Focke-Wulf 190s almost all the way from the English coast to their target where they were met by an impenetrable stream of flak of all calibres, the 11-inch and 8-inch heavy guns firing ahead of them into the sea to create a solid curtain of white water.

Some of the Stringbags survived long enough to launch their torpedoes but all of them crashed in the vicinity of their targets, torn to pieces or hurled into the sea by the wall of water. Esmonde died at the controls, along with all the other young air crew except five, and three of these were seriously injured when they were picked out of the sea. Esmonde was later awarded a posthumous VC, and Admiral Sir Bertram Ramsay, Flag Officer Commanding Dover, described the desperate attack as 'one of the finest exhibitions of self-sacrifice and devotion to duty that this war has yet witnessed'.

Other brave efforts were made to halt or slow up the German ships in the gloom and the rising seas. Destroyers from Harwich forced their way through, braving minefields as well as the powerful escort. Over 200 bombers sought them out as they raced up the Dutch coast, but few of them found their targets and none made a hit. Nor did any of the Beaufort torpedo-bombers. Suddenly it seemed to the amazed German Admiral that he was going to get through unscathed. But not quite. The two big ships passed through some recently laid British mines, detonating three of them. The *Gneisenau* never recovered and the *Scharnhorst* was badly holed and had shipped over 1,000 tons of water by the time she reached Wilhelmshaven. Many months passed before she was fit to go to sea again.

'The Channel Dash', as it came to be called, was a severe blow to the navy and the RAF, and there was an official enquiry into the failures revealed. There was no attempt to censor the story and the newspapers waxed indignant. At least Queen Elizabeth's navy had located Medina Sidonia's armada in 1588 before it had even entered the Channel, one newspaper indignantly declared, and had destroyed much of it before it reached the North Sea, actually an exaggeration. German propaganda made the most of the occasion. But in strategical terms it was much more convenient to have the three warships tucked away in Germany, or in various Norwegian fjords, than in western France where they could at any time break out in tip-and-run raids against Atlantic convoys and where they diverted a substantial proportion of Bomber Command's strength from targets in Germany.

When Roosevelt heard the news of the escape he did his best to cheer up Churchill. 'I hope you will be of good heart,' he signalled. 'I am more and more convinced that the location of all the German ships in Germany makes our joint North Atlantic naval problem more simple.'[9]

The surviving German heavy warships remained an intermittent nagging nuisance for some time to come, requiring continual observation and constituting a lurking threat to North Atlantic and Arctic convoys. But after the loss of the *Bismarck* never again did a battleship, battle-cruiser or heavy cruiser break out and engage in the interminable *guerre de course* in which the U-boats were by contrast steady and deadly dangerous participants.

The greatest of the German ships, the *Tirpitz*, spent almost her entire career in various Norwegian fjords, camouflaged, screened by nets and mines, protected by numberless anti-aircraft guns and nearby fighters, and the butt of numerous sour German jokes: every day she rose higher on her empty tins of herring and bottles of beer, and so on.

She was at once a strange sight, as poignant a symbol of shattered German naval aspirations as the surrendered High Seas Fleet in Scapa Flow in 1919, and yet also a potentially menacing wounded beast of prey. For much of her ill-starred career, the *Tirpitz* had as company the *Scharnhorst* and the *Lützow*. By the beginning of 1943 the three ships were tucked away with the most elaborate protection in their north Norway sanctuary. By now Raeder, the battleship exponent, had been replaced by Doenitz. Although first and last a U-boat man, Doenitz could recognize a strategical place for these three surface ships, especially in terms of the northern convoys to Russia. Hitler was now thoroughly and finally disillusioned with his big armoured ships and wanted nothing more to do with them, but reluctantly allowed Doenitz to have his way.

The problem of destroying this powerful trio was a difficult one for the Royal Navy to solve. Bombardment by battleships was impossible because of the sharp configuration of the intervening land. And as for heavy RAF bombers, the range was so great that they would be able to carry only a very restricted bomb load. Submarine attack, deep up narrow mine- and net-defended waters, would be suicidal.

However, midget submarines might do the trick. At this time – late 1941 – experiments had already begun in Britain on prototype X-craft of 35 tons, with an overall length of 51 feet and a crew of four. Their offensive power consisted of two detachable time-fused charges each containing two tons of Amatex explosive, which were designed to be placed on the sea bed directly under the target.

The RN took delivery of six of these craft in January 1943. Their arrival was timely and training of the crews went ahead swiftly. On 11 September six full-size submarines, each towing an X-craft, sailed from Loch Cairnbawn in Scotland to attack the *Tirpitz*. They had 1,000 miles to go, with the moonlit night of 20 September as the chosen date of attack. Two of the midgets snapped their tow *en route*, but the surviving four slipped their tows successfully close to the Norwegian coast and continued their attack alone.

The original plan called for an attack on all three ships, but this had to be modified due to losses, and when one of the four survivors broke down the remainder, *X5*, *X6* and *X7*, concentrated on their chosen target, the *Tirpitz*. All three negotiated the minefield at the entrance to the fjord and assembled off an island soon after midnight. The big ship was now only six miles distant, but there were numerous obstacles and dangers to be overcome before they could sink beneath her hull and drop their charges.

Lieutenant Godfrey Place, commanding X7 and today a retired admiral, had already become entangled in one set of the nets and extricated his submarine with great difficulty when she struck another net at 7.05 a.m. Again she managed to wrench herself free.

When X7 next came clear and started rising, the motor was stopped lest she run up the beach or on to the top of the nets and fall into enemy hands. When she broke surface I saw we were inside the close-net defences (how we got underneath I have no idea) about thirty yards from the Tirpitz's port beam – 'group up, full ahead, forty feet'.

We actually hit the target's side obliquely at twenty feet and slid underneath, swinging our fore-and-aft line to the line of her keel. The first charge was let go – as I estimated, under the Tirpitz's bridge – and X7 was taken about 200 feet astern to drop the other charge under the after turrets. The time was 0720. It was just as we were letting go the second charge that we heard the first signs of enemy counter-attack – but, oddly enough, we were wrong in assuming they were meant for us.

In X7 we had to guess a course that we hoped would take us back to that lucky spot where we had got under the nets on our way in; but we were not lucky. We tried in many places within a few feet of the bottom, but in vain, and rapidly lost all sense of our exact position. The gyro was still chasing its tail and the magnetic compass could not be raised for fear it foul some wire or a portion of a net; we did use the course indicator (a form of compass that remains steady during alterations of course but does indicate true position) but the noise it made was most tiresome so we switched it off again.

The next three-quarters of an hour were very trying; exactly what track X7 made I have no idea, but we tried most places along the bottom of those nets, passing under the Tirpitz again more than once, and even breaking surface at times, but nowhere could we find a way out. We had to blow each time we got into the nets and the HP air was getting down to a dangerously low level – but bull-in-a-china-shop tactics were essential as our charges had been set with only an hour's delay – and those of others might go up at any time after eight o'clock.... We dived to the bottom and at once started to get under way again to put as much distance as possible between us and the coming explosion. Sticking again in a net at sixty feet was the limit, as this confounded my estimate of our position relative to the nets. But we were not here long before the explosion came – a continuous roar that seemed to last whole minutes.[10]

X7 should have been blown to pieces. Instead she still floated and could be manoeuvred, but there was no question of making the passage down the fjord again, to be picked up by her submarine. Place had no alternative to surrender, and after what they had just done to their precious battleship, he did not expect a warm welcome from the German crew. 'X7 was surfaced and I, gingerly, I must confess, opened the fore hatch just enough to allow the waving of a white sweater. Firing did immediately stop, so I came outside and waved the sweater more vigorously.' Almost at once, the little sub. swung round, hit an obstruction which caused her to dip her bow, and water poured in through the open hatch, upsetting the buoyancy so that the craft immediately began to sink. Place could do nothing. While he was taken on board the *Tirpitz*, his crew of three struggled to save themselves. Only one of them did so.

X6 had also succeeded in penetrating all the *Tirpitz*'s defences and lay her charges. Her commander, Lieutenant D. Cameron RNR, and her crew, were forced to scuttle their miniature, too, and were all picked up safely. *X5* appears to have failed to get through to the ship and was sunk by shellfire and depth-charges, without survivors.

The cost of the operation was high in human life but the value of the attack was incalculable. All three of the *Tirpitz*'s engines had been put out of action by the massive explosions, hundreds of tons of water had poured into her hull, and rudders and steering gear – the *Bismarck*'s Achilles' heel, too – were gravely damaged. Place and Cameron were both awarded the VC.

At the time the Allies had no means of calculating what damage had been done by this daring operation. All they knew, and Place and Cameron knew while they were being taken away for interrogation, was that the *Tirpitz* was still afloat.

Early in 1944, four months after the X-craft raid, secret agents in Norway passed the information to London that the *Tirpitz*'s repairs were almost complete. It was, therefore, time to put the monster out of action again.

The Fleet Air Arm's equipment was very different from the 100-mph biplanes flown against the *Bismarck* almost three years earlier. The bombers were Barracudas, fine Rolls-Royce-powered monoplanes with retractable undercarriages and capable of carrying almost a ton of bombs in place of a torpedo, and with a top speed more than twice that of the Swordfish. What's more, there were modern American fighters like the Corsair and Hellcat available in numbers to escort the bombers; and, at last, plenty of carriers.

The brilliant attack on the *Tirpitz* on 3 April 1944 marked the high point of Fleet Air Arm successes in northern waters. It was gained only after the most thorough training over a Scottish loch, and was carried out at first light as a complete surprise to the German defenders. The first strike of twenty-one bombers and forty-five fighters came in under the radar, climbed and then dived down in cannon and machine-gun attacks on shore-based flak, the anti-flak ships and the *Tirpitz*'s own guns, causing numerous casualties. They completed their work seconds before the Barracudas came down. A second wave of nineteen more Barracudas followed.

At a cost of two Barracudas the upper decks of the *Tirpitz* had been smashed into a tangled mass of torn wreckage by at least fifteen direct hits, while fires below added to the damage. Three hundred of her crew lay dead, hundreds more wounded. The bombs carried by the Barracudas were not powerful enough to penetrate the 8-inch lower armoured deck, but it would again be many months before the battleship could be made fit for action again.

In due course this most-battered battleship was again repaired, and the fact that she was moved to another anchorage suggested that she could make one last bid to justify herself by sallying forth against Atlantic convoys. By this time – the autumn of 1944 – RAF Lancasters were carrying 12,000-pound bombs, and the Chiefs of Staff decided to employ two squadrons of them against the *Tirpitz* when conditions were right, in order, once and for all, to send her to the bottom. Carrying extra fuel and overloaded by two tons, with specially beefed-up Rolls-Royce engines, at the third attempt thirty-two Lancasters took off from Lossiemouth in Scotland and caught the battleship in clear weather. Bombing from a great height, the Lancasters made three hits. One might have done the trick. The 12,000-pounder, which had devastated so many German cities, made light of the *Tirpitz*'s armoured deck. The first hit exploded deep inside the battleship and steam and smoke rose high into the air.

The cruel, spectacular scene might have been a set piece for the battleship-versus-bomber scenario which had been played almost non-stop between the wars. After the next hits, the 50,000-ton vessel turned turtle and sank into the cold deep waters of her fjord.

In the course of the extensive repair work on the *Tirpitz* after the successful Place–Campbell X-craft attack, the Admiralty felt that the time had come to deal with the ubiquitous *Scharnhorst*, which had escaped the attention of the 'mini-subs'.

After all the losses and suffering endured on those dreaded Arctic convoys of 1942, it was with the utmost satisfaction that Admiral Sir Bruce Fraser weaved his spider's web to gobble up the German battle-cruiser for Christmas 1943. 'Mind you, it wasn't all plain sailing on the Murmansk run at that time,' an officer who had witnessed the horrors of PQ17 recalled. 'There were still plenty of U-boats around that winter, and Jerry planes. But the November convoy had got through safely, and so had the first half of JW55. And for JW55B we could easily spare fourteen destroyers, two sloops and a minesweeper.'

Fraser, attempting to read the mind of his adversary, calculated that Doenitz would be so infuriated by his failure to sink a single merchantman on the Arctic run during this period that he would make an all-out assault on JW55B, led by the *Scharnhorst*. Fraser made his own arrangements accordingly. His flagship was the *Duke of York*, sister ship of the *Prince of Wales* and *King George V*, armed with ten 14-inch guns and with a maximum speed almost matching the *Scharnhorst*'s 32 knots. With the cruiser *Jamaica* and four destroyers this battleship was to be responsible for the distant support of the convoy, and then the knock-out punch.

The heavy cruiser *Norfolk* and the 6-inch-gun *Sheffield* of the *Bismarck* battle, with the 6-inch-gun *Belfast*, under Vice-Admiral Robert Burnett, would provide close cover. Bruce Fraser had been a gunnery officer in the battleship *Resolution* in the First World War, and was the first to appreciate the advances in intelligence-gathering which made the task of tracking the enemy that much more sophisticated.

In the *Bismarck* chase his predecessor, Tovey, had enjoyed the advantage of radar and air reconnaissance, and a little help from Enigma decrypts. Since then the boffins at Bletchley and in the radar laboratories had been working overtime on speeding up and making more comprehensive the decrypting of German signals and refining ultra short-wave radar. Both these developments were to have a major influence on the operation which lay ahead.

For a start, Enigma decrypts informed Fraser that the convoy had been sighted by a German plane at 10.45 a.m. on 22 December and that a U-boat had been ordered in to the attack. On the same day Bletchley also learned that the *Scharnhorst* had been brought to three hours' notice. The Operational Intelligence Centre at the Admiralty and then Fraser knew of this and had drawn their obvious deductions, within an hour or two.

Admiral Fraser continued to receive this priceless intelligence: that eight more U-boats had been ordered to the convoy, that in view of possible British intervention with heavy surface ships, the German command had decided that air reconnaissance must be carried out. Then at last, at 2.17 p.m. on 26 December, Admiralty intelligence was able to give Fraser the news he had been awaiting, '*Scharnhorst* probably sailed 1800 on 25 December': a late Christmas present, but not too late.

Early on Boxing Day, then, the *Scharnhorst* was racing north through the Barents Sea with her five destroyers fanned out in search formation and expecting soon to sight the convoy; Admiral Burnett's cruisers were steering north-west to intercept the force, while, more distantly, Fraser with the *Duke of York* and *Jamaica* was steering north-east. A full gale was blowing, the seas were mountainous, the cold indescribable.

Rear-Admiral Bey, commander of the grandly named First Battle Group, had been awaiting orders to put to sea for some time now. Reports of enemy activity had been coming in since 21 December 1943, and Convoy JW55B was at first suspected of being an invasion force, such was the continuing German obsession with an Allied counter-invasion of northern Norway. After months of inactivity it did seem that at last the battle-cruiser's company might see action again. Morale remained surprisingly high, by contrast with that of the men of the disabled *Tirpitz*. The *Scharnhorst* had always prided herself on being the queen of the Third Reich's new navy.

The *Scharnhorst* definitely had a soul [a German writer has claimed]. Furthermore, she was beautiful, and she sailed with that wonderful, gently swaying motion characteristic of a battleship in a following sea. She seemed always a happy ship, and her spirit pervaded the whole crew, giving rise to a certain fierce pride which was felt by all old *Scharnhorst* men from the captain down to the humblest rating.[11]

Her first captain had been Ciliax, who later had led the three big ships up the Channel from Brest in February 1942. *Scharnhorst* and *Gneisenau* were the first fighting ships ordered by Hitler, flouting the restrictions imposed by the Treaty of Versailles. Laid down on 3 October 1936, she was commissioned and worked up during the months before war broke out. Since then, the 'Salmon' of 'Salmon and Gluckstein' had with the *Gneisenau* been more active than any fighting ship in Hitler's navy.

Christmas of 1943 had been celebrated on board the *Scharnhorst* on Christmas Eve, with the traditional toasts and food, officers, petty officers and men together in the various messes, all decorated with Christmas trees. The trees were not difficult to find ashore, and the extreme latitude of their anchorage, and the climate, seemed appropriate to the mythology of the season. Korvetten-Kapitän Busch has written of Christmas Day in Alta Fjord:

Up in northern Norway between Tromsoe and Hammerfest there was at this time of the year almost perpetual night. The waters of the fjord were blue-black and icy cold. For some days past a south-westerly gale had been sweeping over the snow-covered mountains. It hurled itself down the steep cliffs on the south shore of Lang Fjord, a western arm of Alta Fjord, as a fall-wind, and whipped up the normally calm waters of the fjord into whirls of white foam.[12]

Christmas Day was employed in completing preparations to put to sea, and the *Scharnhorst* with her destroyer escort emerged from the relative calm of the fjords and struck the full force of the Arctic gale shortly before midnight. Among Admiral Bey and his staff, and the battle-cruiser's captain and his staff, there was an awareness of the dangers involved in their mission, but no serious apprehension. The *Scharnhorst* had been bruised and battered so often and (as one officer put it) 'had always come up smiling', that a belief in the immortality of their beloved ship had grown up. She had proved her superior gunnery so often, and her speed had got her out of danger so nippily in the past, that there was every confidence that they would seriously maul this convoy and return to Norway within the next forty-eight hours.

At 9.20 a.m., one and a half hours before dawn in this extreme latitude in December, a salvo of shells fell about the *Scharnhorst* without any warning by sight or by sound, out of the darkness, the snow and the raging wind. This was naval warfare in which electronics had provided an entirely new dimension of surprise.

Almost at once came the sound of the *Scharnhorst*'s alarm bells and the deep delayed boom of the guns that had aroused them. The *Scharnhorst*'s radar had now picked up the enemy and the main armament replied in three-gun salvoes. The gunnery duel lasted for almost fifteen minutes, illuminated now by a continuous succession of starshells: like the *Graf Spee* battle four years earlier, Admiral Burnett's 8-inch and 6-inch guns mounted in three cruisers against German 11-inch guns. But the *Scharnhorst* no more wanted an engagement to interfere with her anti-convoy operations than had the *Graf Spee*, and the battle-cruiser turned away, increased speed and laid a smokescreen to cover her movements and whereabouts.

Unlike the earlier battle, however, the British cruisers were unscathed and the German ship badly hit. The British shooting was superb, scoring two hits early on, starting a fire below decks and knocking out the forward radar. Admiral Bey reported his contact to headquarters, and received in reply a message of exhortation from Doenitz himself, who was intent only on proving to Hitler his confidence in the big ships' capacity to damage convoys. 'Strike a blow on behalf of the troops fighting on the eastern front,' he told the Admiral. Bey gave instructions for a cheering message to be broadcast over the ship's loudspeakers: 'Lull in action. We are trying once more to get at the convoy, the destroyers from the south, we in the *Scharnhorst* from the north.'[13] According to Busch, that made everyone feel better. But after the action Doenitz was critical of Admiral Bey's failure to sink all three of the cruisers before attacking the convoy which 'would have fallen like ripe fruit into the *Scharnhorst*'s hands'.[14]

The *Belfast* had first picked up the radar blip at eighteen miles, and Admiral Burnett had closed the target rapidly through the terrible seas which were threatening to overwhelm the destroyers. Then, when the *Scharnhorst* had steamed away at high speed to the north-east, evidently intent on getting round the head of the convoy, Burnett did the clever thing: he did not attempt to pursue the big ship, which would probably have outpaced him anyway in this weather. Instead, he cut north himself, calculating that if the German got close to the head of the convoy he would pick him up again, and that if he had changed his mind and made for home, he was lost anyway.

Urged on by Doenitz's message, Bey continued north while the fire was put out. But there was no chance of repairing the radar, and when the British cruisers found themselves in radar range they again caught the *Scharnhorst* by surprise. It was midday, and the 11-inch guns thundered out in the Arctic twilight at the British ships seven miles to the west.

The old *Norfolk* had had an eventful war career. Built on the River Clyde and launched on 12 December 1928, this 'Washington Treaty' 10,000-tonner, elegant with her three tall funnels and 8-inch gun turrets, had been battered by interminable Atlantic gales, escorted Arctic convoys, been attacked by enemy aircraft, U-boats and by the *Bismarck* and *Prinz Eugen*. Now, pitching acutely in the heavy seas and taking it green along the length of her forecastle, she trained her guns on the fleeing *Scharnhorst* and opened fire again. The German ship replied with rapid salvoes from her aft triple 11-inch turret and at once began straddling the cruiser.

It might have been with the fourth or fifth salvo that the *Scharnhorst* scored her first hit in this phase of the engagement. An 11-inch shell struck the barbette at the base of the *Norfolk*'s third turret, putting it out of action and killing or wounding a dozen men. A few seconds later another shell struck the cruiser amidships, doing much more damage and knocking out the ship's radar. The *Sheffield*, too, was being straddled. German gunnery, even in these appalling conditions, was living up to its high reputation.

Petty Officer Göddes of the *Scharnhorst* later recalled:

Shortly after 1230 I and several others sighted three shadows ahead and reported accordingly. The alarm had already been sounded as the result of a previous radar report. But before our guns could open fire the first star shells were bursting over the *Scharnhorst*. The enemy's salvoes were falling pretty close to the ship. The first salvoes from our own heavy guns straddled the target. I myself observed that after three or four salvoes a large fire broke out on one of the cruisers near the after funnel, while another cruiser was burning fiercely fore and aft and was enveloped in thick smoke.

After further salvoes I saw that the third cruiser had been hit in the bows. For a moment a huge tongue of flame shot up and then went out. From the dense smoke that enveloped her, I presumed the ship was on fire. The enemy's fire then began to become irregular, and when we altered course, the enemy cruisers turned away and disappeared in the rain and snow squalls. During this action the enemy had been ahead and visible on both sides. Our A and B turrets had been firing as had also for a while the two forward 5.9-inch turrets. I did not hear either by telephone or through any other source of any hit received during this phase by the *Scharnhorst*. While the enemy had been scarcely discernible during the first action, this time with the midday twilight we could easily distinguish the cruisers' outlines. The range, too, was much shorter than it had been in the morning.[15]

Admiral Burnett sensibly ordered his cruisers to reduce speed. His business was to shadow the enemy, not to get himself sunk. Moreover, signals from the *Duke of York* indicated that the battleship, driving through the tremendous seas from the west at full speed, with the *Jamaica* and her four destroyers, could soon be within range.

As the Arctic twilight gave way to total winter darkness about this storm-lashed pursuit, the British battleship's radar picked up the *Scharnhorst* at a range of twenty-two miles to the north-east. It seemed now to Admiral Fraser that his trap had worked and that nothing now could save his adversary. Half an hour later, working as a team in perfect co-ordination, the *Belfast* to the north and the *Duke of York* from the west, both fired starshells which exploded high above the *Scharnhorst*, illuminating her as if a midday sun had suddenly spotlit the ship. 'At first impression the *Scharnhorst* appeared of enormous length and silver grey in colour,' ran the report of the *Duke of York*'s gunnery officer. The range was no more than six and three-quarter miles, and hits were at once obtained on the battle-cruiser's quarterdeck.

At the first sign of this new enemy from the west, Admiral Bey ordered a 90-degree turn to the north-east, at once opening up the range and causing the enemy fire to fall short. But this move only led to closing the range with the pursuing cruisers. So the *Scharnhorst* next turned on to a due east heading, hoping to throw off her tormentors by the high speed which had so often saved her in the past. But it was by now a faint hope. His earlier indecision, which had been caused by Doenitz's appeal to try again to reach the convoy, had almost certainly settled his fate.

Franz-Otto Busch wrote of this phase of the battle:

A continuous stream of starshell was exploding over the *Scharnhorst*. The flares hung over the ship for minutes on end like so many huge floodlights exposing everything with stark, pitiless clarity, the cruel brilliance sharpened by the fiery flashes of the German's own salvoes. The whole battle-cruiser from bridges to foretop, masts and funnels was bathed in a ghastly pink to blood-red light. Smoke and cordite fumes clung to the ship, driven now by an almost following wind, and at times completely obscured visibility in the direction of the enemy. Through the thunder of the German salvoes the British shells could be heard screaming over and thudding into the sea, while those that met their target caused the ship, already rocked by the recoil of her own guns, to tremble from stem to stern.[16]

On the bridge of the *Duke of York* Admiral Fraser was showing signs of concern. The range did not appear to be closing, and after those early hits the battleship had failed to do any further damage to the enemy although starshells showed that they were constantly straddling the target. The engines were at full revolutions; speed 30 knots. At 5.15 p.m., almost half an hour after he had opened fire, Fraser ordered his destroyers to close the enemy in the hope that a hit would slow him down.

The four destroyers were already suffering in the heavy seas, and although their maximum speed was 36 knots it was all they could do to keep up with their flagship. An hour later they were still struggling but had gained less than a mile. Meanwhile the *Duke of York* was firing steady salvoes from her two forward turrets, and at 6.20 p.m. scored the hit that was to seal the fate of the *Scharnhorst*.

By contrast with the *Bismarck*, which had been slowed by a single torpedo hit which allowed the guns to get into range, this 14-inch shell allowed the destroyers to close in for the kill.

Still the *Scharnhorst* kept up a steady rate of fire. From the 4-inch director of the *Jamaica*, a Royal Marines lieutenant watched the rapid disintegration of the enemy after that fateful hit.

'She's hit! My God, we've got her!' I was yelling like one possessed. We were cheering in the director. All over the ship a cheer went up, audible above the gun-fire. I had risen half standing in my seat as the wild thrill took hold of me. Again the dull glow, and in its light the sea was alive with shell-splashes from an outpouring of shells. Great columns of water stood out clearly in the brief instant of light, and I could see smoke hanging above her. I was mad with excitement until I realized that my ravings must be an incoherent babble of enthusiasm to those below as the telephones were still hanging round my head. I straightened my tin hat, sat down, and told them as calmly as I could that we could see that our shells had set her on fire, and that both the *Duke of York* and ourselves were hitting, and hitting hard.

She must have been a hell on earth. The fourteen-inch from the flagship were hitting or rocketing off from a ricochet on the sea. I had no coherent thought. The sudden knowledge that we were beating her to a standstill had gone to my head. My crew were just as bad. Nothing seemed to matter. Great flashes rent the night, and the sound of gun-fire was continuous, and yet the *Scharnhorst* replied, but only occasionally now.[17]

For many of the men of the *Norfolk* and *Sheffield* it was like the ghastly end of the *Bismarck* all over again, 'a bloody tumult of destruction'. By 7.50 p.m. the *Scharnhorst* was almost stationary, still firing defiantly at the destroyers which were like persecuting matadors.

As soon as they withdrew the *Duke of York* and *Jamaica* began pounding her with 14-inch and 6-inch shells until her flames seemed to reduce the light of the starshells so that they were no more than candles in the sky.

'We shall fight to the last shell,' signalled Admiral Bey in a personal message to Hitler. That last shell was fired at around 7.30 p.m. 'By now all that could be seen of the *Scharnhorst* was a dull glow through a dense cloud of smoke which the starshell and searchlights of the surrounding ships could not penetrate,' wrote Admiral Fraser in his report. 'No ship therefore saw the enemy sink, but it seems fairly certain that she sank after a heavy underwater explosion which was heard in several ships at about 19.45 hrs.'

This battleship action was the last of its kind in European waters, and one of the few engagements between armoured ships without the intervention of air power, which played no part from the beginning to the conclusion. With the *Gneisenau* and the *Tirpitz* both out of action, the Allies were now free for the first time from the threat of the big gun to their Arctic and Atlantic convoys. At the cost of a dozen lives the pride of the German Navy was at the bottom of the icy seas of the North Cape, and with all but thirty-six of her company of 2,000 drowned or killed by high explosive.

Convoy JW55B arrived safely at Murmansk two days later, nineteen ships loaded with aircraft, tanks, guns and raw material for the Russians. This was what victory in the *guerre de course* meant.

CHAPTER SEVEN

Catastrophe in the Far East

Just forty-eight hours (local time) after the Imperial Japanese Navy pilots had been aroused from their bunks for their attack on Pearl Harbor, two submarine operations were taking place on opposite sides of the world from each other. One concerned the German *U-208*, Korvetten-Kapitän Schlieper, which was stalking a convoy west of Gibraltar in the Atlantic Ocean; the other the Japanese *I-65*, Captain Masao Teraoka, which spotted a British battleship in the Gulf of Siam. Neither of these submarines was to survive the war. *U-208* was sunk two days later by the 'Flower' class corvette, HMS *Bluebell*; the Japanese boat was instrumental in bringing about the destruction both of the battleship she eventually located and her accompanying battle-cruiser. This is what happened.

The threatening weeks of the late autumn of 1941, which had exploded amidst the detonating bombs and torpedoes of Pearl Harbor, had aroused equal anxieties in the British Admiralty and in the Navy Department in Washington. On 4 November 1941 Churchill wrote to Marshal Stalin, his ally since the invasion of Russia by Germany on 22 June, that 'with the object of keeping Japan quiet we are sending our latest battleship, *Prince of Wales*, which can catch and kill any Japanese ship, into the Indian Ocean. . . .'[1] The fact that Japan possessed two efficient and more powerful 16-inch-gunned battleships and was about to commission the largest battleship in the world armed with 18.1-inch guns, against the *Prince of Wales*'s 14-inch armament, was not very important. A little hyperbole to give cheer to a hard-pressed ally is always quite legitimate. What is important about this message is that the British war leader still believed that the presence of a battleship was going to alter the balance of power and influence the Japanese Government at this critical time.

If this message did not smack of 'Send a gunboat!' its tone and spirit certainly reflected obsolete naval beliefs. Only a year earlier, on 11 November 1940, twenty British naval aircraft, none of a modern type, had flown off a carrier in the Mediterranean to attack the Italian Battle Fleet in Taranto harbour, sinking at their moorings three Italian battleships in a precursor of Pearl Harbor. In spite of this example of the changing face of naval warfare, a year later Churchill was also reassuring the Commonwealth Prime Ministers that 'In my view, *Prince of Wales* will be the best possible deterrent'[2] to Japanese aggression.

Then came Pearl Harbor, and the immediate confirmation that war must soon engulf British and European possessions in the Far East, including Malaya and Singapore. 'We had only one key weapon in our hands,' Churchill pronounced. 'The *Prince of Wales* and the *Repulse* had arrived in Singapore. They had been sent to these waters to exercise that kind of vague menace which capital ships of the highest quality whose whereabouts is unknown can impose upon all hostile naval calculations.'[3]

A modern fleet carrier was at one time to have accompanied these two big ships, providing some measure of air cover for Force Z, as it was code-named. When he was deprived of this vessel at the last minute, the C-in-C of Force Z, Admiral Sir Tom Phillips, made no protest.

Tom Phillips is a puzzling figure. A navigator by profession, his only recent command experience at sea was eight months before the war as Rear-Admiral Destroyers with the Home Fleet when he had the misfortune to become involved in a collision. He had also taken part in exercises to test the efficiency of modern anti-aircraft gunnery against air attack on ships at sea. At the best of times such exercises could bear little relation to the real thing. But in the late 1930s the big-warship lobby – the battleship men – were very keen to prove that multiple-barrel anti-aircraft guns, supplemented by adequate numbers of heavy H/A (high-angle), could deal with any number of attacking aircraft. The favourite target was a radio-controlled target plane flying at a known fixed speed on a steady course.

Tom Phillips was Vice-Chief of Naval Staff when Churchill re-entered the Admiralty in September 1939, with a reputation for being a bit of a 'brain'. Churchill took to him at once and the two men worked well together for many months, and continued to do so when Churchill became Prime Minister. Things began to go sour when Phillips disagreed with Churchill's policy over Greece, which led to such heavy naval losses in the eastern Mediterranean. These losses were caused by lack of protective air power but even that still failed to change Phillips's opinion that well-co-ordinated gunnery defence could deal with any air attack.

Six months after the Norwegian lesson emphasizing the importance of fighter air cover for ships at sea, Phillips was briefing Admiral Sir John Tovey about his new command, C-in-C Home Fleet. Tovey remarked that the need for fighter cover was a lesson he had just learned in the Mediterranean. According to one officer present at this meeting, Phillips then 'blew his top and virtually accused Tovey of being a coward'.[4] As Tovey had a record of being one of the bravest destroyer commanders of the First World War, this remark, spread widely inside the Admiralty, did Phillips no good at all. The man was becoming a damn nuisance to everybody.

When Admiral Sir Dudley Pound learned that Force Z was to sail, against his judgement, he took this opportunity of appointing Tom Phillips as C-in-C, thus 'getting him out of our hair'. This had Churchill's warm approval.

Few other people approved. Admiral Sir Guy Grantham, one-time Naval Assistant to the First Sea Lord, today recalls the decision as a complete mystery. And Admiral Sir Andrew Cunningham, C-in-C Mediterranean and Britain's best fighting admiral of the Second World War, wrote of Phillips's appointment, 'What on earth is Phillips going to the Far East Squadron for? He hardly knows one end of a ship from the other,' Peter Kemp quoted, adding that 'I am by no means alone in thinking that this appointment of Phillips sealed the fate of the two ships from the moment it was announced.'[5]

When Force Z arrived at Singapore on 2 December 1941 Phillips asked for Hurricane fighters for protection in any local operations against the Japanese. He was told there weren't any, but that there was a squadron of Brewster Buffaloes. This was an Australian squadron, whose pilots had little experience with their machines and no operational training. Moreover their machines were slow – about 225 mph at sea level – inadequately armed with four machine-guns and generally obsolescent.

Without even the promise of these lame ducks, Phillips sailed from Singapore at 5.35 p.m. on 8 December. Japanese forces were reported to be landing up the Malayan coast and it was his duty, he believed, to surprise, intervene and smash this invasion before it obtained a grip upon the peninsula.

The Japanese submarine *I-65* formed part of a screen intended to protect the operations in the Gulf of Siam and the South China Sea from just this kind of interference. The invasion of Siam and Malaya was launched from French Indo-China, recently occupied by Japanese forces. Vice-Admiral Nobutake Kondo, C-in-C of these operations, was very conscious of the threat posed by the presence of the *Prince of Wales* and *Repulse* at Singapore. If they were emphatically not the deterrent Churchill supposed they would be, Kondo and his staff feared for what these two big ships might do to break up the invading forces and their subsequent supplies.

The Japanese navy had virtually been created by Britain, its early ships built in British yards, its officers trained by the RN in Britain. The Imperial Japanese Navy still held a respect and considerable admiration for its father figure, even though by Imperial decree it was their enemy.

Admiral Kondo lacked both the ships and the element of surprise which Admiral Nagumo had enjoyed in the Pearl Harbor attack. He had no carriers, and his surface ships were two old, but modernized, battleships, one of them built by the British company of Vickers before the First World War when the Treaty of Friendship existed between the two powers; and a number of cruisers, smaller ships and submarines.

Besides the submarine screen, minelayers were despatched and laid 1,000 mines across the likely course of the two British ships if they headed for the invasion beaches to the north. Finally, Kondo acquired substantial reinforcements of land-based aircraft which arrived at Saigon shortly after it was known that the *Prince of Wales* and *Repulse* were at Singapore.

The highly efficient and well-equipped 22nd Air Flotilla was under the command of Rear-Admiral Sadaichi Matsunaga, who could call upon at least 100 bombers – torpedo and high-level – and thirty-six fighters. The fighters were of the same Zero type used at Pearl Harbor; the bombers, twin-engined Bettys and Nells* (as they were code-named by the British and Americans), carried a heavier load, had a longer range and were altogether more formidable than the carrier-borne single-engine Vals and Kates which had wrought such havoc at Pearl Harbor.

I-65's sighting of Force Z with its escorting destroyers led to an accurate report which Captain Teraoka transmitted at about 2.00 p.m. on 9 December. It was exactly the news that Admirals Kondo and Matsunaga had been anxiously awaiting. There was no reason to believe that the British force knew that it had been spotted, and moreover *I-65* was now shadowing the two big ships and regularly reporting their position, until a particularly intense rain squall blotted out the ships and the submarine was at the same time forced to dive because of the suspicious attention of a Japanese seaplane.

Matsunaga despatched reconnaissance aircraft, and later a force of bombers to relocate the target. The mission was abortive, the aircraft returned, still bearing their bombs or torpedoes. There was no question of following common practice and dropping them into the sea. There were no reserves at Saigon, so the weary air crews who had been searching through stormy weather for some hours were kept in the air until the moon rose at 10.38 p.m., illuminating the blacked-out airfield and permitting all the aircraft to land safely. It was what the RAF called 'a dodgy do'.

Despite the exhaustion brought on by the harrowing flight [reported one squadron commander, Lieutenant Sadao Takai], the long hours spent in the air, and the nerve-racking landings with armed torpedoes, we were not given a chance to rest. Calling on our reserve stamina and courage, we worked through almost the entire night preparing for the next day's mission.[6]

On board the *Prince of Wales* on that evening of 9 December Admiral Phillips was still unaware that Force Z had been located and that an attack had already been mounted and then aborted. His plan was to detach his four escorting destroyers during the night. Benefiting from the experience of Dunkirk, Phillips decided that they were too vulnerable to air attack; and, besides, their operating range was restricted, especially at high speeds. Meanwhile the big ships would make a swift raid on the Japanese invasion forces on the Siam coast at Singora before returning to Singapore. He had little idea what he would find, and knew that he ought not to tarry because he did not want his ships to be damaged and require docking for repairs at this early stage of operations against Japan. But at least the

---

* Betty: 265 mph, 1 20-mm cannon, 3 mgs
  Nell: 232 mph, 1 20-mm cannon, 7 mgs

Royal Navy would not be on record as having shirked its responsibilities, and with his sixteen heavy guns – 15-inch and 14-inch – he was confident of destroying any likely opposition.

The odds on surprise and success changed suddenly just before sunset on 9 December when the *Prince of Wales*'s radar picked up a blip to the north, which rapidly developed into a visual on a seaplane. In this locality it could only be hostile, and its presence called for an urgent reappraisal of their situation.

We stood on the upper deck and watched the Jap float-plane in the now fading light [an officer reported]. Our 5.25 in guns traversed silently and menacingly, but the range was too great and, alas, we had no fighter aircraft available. We could well imagine the excitement, the conjectures, and of course the preparations the Japanese airman's radio messages would arouse at his base.[7]

Admiral Phillips's dilemma was sharpened on receipt of a signal from Singapore informing him that a number of escorted transports had been seen off the Malay coast at Kota Bharu, farther south than Singora. The temptation to take his ships in among this armada was very great. But Phillips was no hot-blooded buccaneer in the tradition of Hawkins and Drake, however confident he might be of dealing with air attack. Even a battleship man did not welcome the prospect of a night action against enemy destroyers with none of his own, and against enemy torpedo-bombers without fighter cover. It was too much of a risk-taking venture. Phillips knew all too well how the entry of Japan into the war had increased even further the navy's responsibilities. In recent weeks Britain had lost the services of three battleships, one of them sunk in the Mediterranean and two more incapacitated for several months. Force Z was therefore precious beyond calculation.

At 8.55 p.m. Phillips signalled by lamp to Captain William Tennant, who commanded the *Repulse*: 'I have most regretfully cancelled the operation because, having been located by aircraft, surprise was lost and our target would be almost certain to be gone by the morning and the enemy fully prepared for us.'

The two big ships, still with their destroyer escort, therefore put over helm and headed back to base. Every mile gained on this new southerly heading reduced the risks of attack by land-based Japanese aircraft and brought Force Z closer to the maximum range of protective RAF land-based fighters. Nor would the Japanese be aware that the ships had reversed course; indeed, they would assume that they were heading for the invasion beaches, their obvious target from the beginning of the operation.

But once again Phillips's luck was out. Shortly before midnight the Japanese submarine *I-58*, Lieutenant-Commander Sohichi Kitamura, while on the surface observed two enormous dark shapes approaching him fast. The night was clear and moonlit. Kitamura crash-dived after confirming that these were the two wanted ships, and attempted a torpedo attack. Perhaps his men were not drill-perfect and the torpedo crews mismanaged the launch in their excitement, or there was a fault in the firing mechanism of his elderly submarine. He launched at last, but too late, five torpedoes, all of which missed. Then he surfaced and started to shadow Force Z, transmitting reports on its position, course and speed.

So now Admiral Matsunaga knew that any intention to attack the Japanese invasion forces had been negative and that the two ships were on their way back to Singapore, and acted accordingly. His conclusion was only half correct. For at 2.55 a.m. Phillips had altered course from south to southwest and increased speed to 25 knots, tempted by a report that a landing was taking place at Kuantan. This small port was only one-third the distance from Singapore as his original target, Singora, making the diversion relatively risk free.

The second of *I-58*'s three signals told of this change of course. It was the only one of the signals which was not picked up, leaving Matsunaga ignorant of the fact that his chances of destroying the *Repulse* and *Prince of Wales* before they got home were now much improved – should he find them.

And so through this warm and tranquil tropical night Force Z raced towards its target, ignorant that the enemy knew of its reversal of course but not the subsequent south-westward turn, crews at second-degree readiness. The buzz on the lower deck was that they were going to see action after all, and they were quite right. For the men of the *Prince of Wales* it was just over six months since they had last been in action, and it had not been a pleasant experience.

By 5.00 a.m. the light in the sky astern began to brighten, the temperature to climb. When the sun lifted above the eastern horizon the men manning the exposed anti-aircraft guns felt at once the first flush of sweat in a day that was to be unusually hot.

An hour later, at 6.30 a.m., one of the *Repulse*'s look-outs identified a small dot just above the horizon. It remained poised, scarcely seeming to move. Captain Tennant put his glasses on it. 'I can't make out any detail but I'll wager it's a Jap seaplane,' he remarked. He was right. It was still there, no larger, no smaller, thirty minutes later. They were being shadowed. It was a disquieting feeling, with its implied threat of unknown destructive power.

At the Saigon airfield before dawn, Admiral Matsunaga addressed the bomber aircrews, stressing the importance of their mission, 'painstakingly and kindheartedly', according to one pilot. These were crack airmen, every one of them, who had been on operations over China after being very highly trained. They had, with reason, complete faith in their machines and their weapons. They had 24-inch torpedoes, and they knew what the British Fleet Air Arm had accomplished with miserable little 18-inch torpedoes at Taranto. And their design allowed them to be dropped at 500 feet, almost ten times the height at which British and American torpedoes could be launched. Their twin-engine Mitsubishi-built aircraft had been designed with just this type of operation in mind, with a long range and heavy load capacity.

The first reconnaissance machines had left before dawn, fanning out over the South China Sea, with visibility strongly favouring success. But Admiral Matsunaga, without awaiting their reports, ordered off the first bombers at 6.25 a.m., in all fifty-one torpedo-bombers and thirty-four high-level bombers, formed into three groups. The orders were that the bombers were to attack first, with the intention of knocking out the anti-aircraft crews before the torpedo-bombers went in, attacking simultaneously port and starboard in order to split the defences. The Japanese had a healthy respect for British anti-aircraft capability, knowing that the German *Luftwaffe* had failed to sink a battleship in more than two years of war.

Lieutenant Takai's squadron was within distant sight of the southern tip of the Malay peninsula by 9.00 a.m., almost beyond their point of no return and still with no sign of the enemy. Visibility remained perfect, and at 10,000 feet they could clearly see the curvature of the earth; and from horizon to horizon only empty sea. It was also ominously clear that calculations of the enemy's position were far out.

It was not until 10.15 a.m., when the main Japanese force had already turned for base, engines on the leanest mixture and lowest revs that would keep them airborne, that one of the reconnaissance machines made a sighting. Midshipman Masame Hoashi had reached the limit of his flight and turned on to a north-west heading which would bring him close into the Malay coast, far beyond the suspected area. At 10.15 a.m. he caught sight of two large white slashes and three smaller ones on the ocean surface, the wakes of speeding ships. He at once radioed the position and course, adding to the information when he had correctly identified the big ships as a *King George V*-class battleship and the *Repulse*.

The young midshipman carried out his task correctly. His signal was not picked up clearly in the air, though perfectly back at base. He was therefore ordered to repeat his report *en clair*. By the time all the air crews had received the sighting report correctly the squadrons were widely scattered and a co-ordinated attack as originally conceived was no longer possible. The Genzan Air Corps, of which Lieutenant Takai's squadron was a unit, had overshot the target and had to turn north-west to have any hope of making an interception.

With Lieutenant-Commander Nakanishi leading the group, the ships were at last sighted at twenty-five miles from an altitude of 8,000 feet. In scarcely suppressed excitement, Nakanishi ordered first 'Form attack formation!' and then 'Go in!'

The design of the *Prince of Wales* embraced the most up-to-date thinking in naval architecture and incorporated comprehensive protection against bomb and torpedo attack. The torpedo had been a threat to the battleship's survival for more than fifty years, and a great deal of thought had been given during this time to structural strength, bulkheading and pumping facilities. As a result, it could be fairly argued, not a single Dreadnought, German or British, had been sunk by a torpedo in the four years of the First World War, and the *Prince of Wales*, if not the *Repulse*, was many times better equipped to deal with this underwater weapon today.

A detonating torpedo, especially when travelling at high speed, was expected to be an unpleasant experience, but everyone from the Admiral downwards had full confidence that these magnificent vessels would be able to withstand a number of hits in the unlikely event of an enemy plane surviving the dense weight of shot and shell the *Prince of Wales* and *Repulse* could put up as protection.

Captain C.D.L. Aylwin, Royal Marines, commanded the 8-barrel multiple pom-pom sited on the top of the aftermost heavy gun turret of the *Prince of Wales*. Like all others who witnessed the opening of the attack he was surprised at the modern appearance of the Nells, their sleek lines and good turn of speed. Many men, including the Admiral, believed that they were about to be subjected to a bombing attack so high and swift was the approach, by nine planes from two sides simultaneously.

First the 5.25s opened up, the crack of eight of them firing simultaneously, almost more than the eardrum could bear. The Nells flew through the numerous black puffs imperturbably and took equally little interest when the Bofors and pom-poms added to the cacophony. For a moment it appeared impossible for any machine to penetrate this curtain of fire and observers prepared to count their victims. But only very briefly. For, contrary to all logical reasoning, the bombers came on as if on automatic pilot and sheathed in impenetrable armour, which was almost supernaturally dismaying to the defenders.

A deafening crescendo of noise erupted into the heavens [one seaman recalled]. ... I watched the shells burst – but not a plane was hit.... They came on remorse-lessly as all the pom-poms, machine-guns and the Bofors gun opened up. All hell seemed to be let loose at once but nothing seemed to stop them and, as they passed over the masts, I could see the faces and goggles of the Japanese pilots looking down at us.[8]

In fact one Japanese plane was hit, but only after the pilot had released his torpedo. As the Nell lost height the pilot, Petty Officer Katsujiro Kawada, attempted to bring his machine in on a suicide course against the battleship, but crashed into the sea.

Captain John Leach prepared to comb the tracks of the torpedoes racing towards his ship. 'Hard a-port!' he ordered the helmsman, and the giant vessel responded with marvellous agility, heeling over acutely – which added to the gunners' difficulties, too. It would be about two minutes before they would know whether they were hit.

We awaited the approach of the nine torpedoes with bated breath [said Captain Aylwin] knowing that the Captain on the bridge would be doing his best by alterations of course to avoid all. Suddenly there was the most terrific jolt accompanied by a loud explosion immediately where I was standing on the port side. A vast column of water and smoke shot up into the air to a height of about 200 feet, drenching the quarterdeck, and a vast shudder shook the ship. At least one torpedo had hit us. The jolt received was just as though the ship had encountered a rock below the surface and, though hitting it, the ship's momentum was sufficient to clear it. When the smoke and spray had dispersed it was evident that the ship had taken on a 10-degree list to port and speed was considerably reduced.[9]

The damage caused by that one torpedo which Captain Leach could not evade was appalling – far worse than anyone could have predicted. Speed was down to 15 knots, the list soon almost 13 degrees, and half of the electrics were lost, which meant no power for half the guns, no light or ventilation below decks. How could a single Japanese plane cripple one of the most modern and powerful battleships in the world? It was just not possible.

Captain Tennant watched the first torpedo attack on the flagship with grave concern. Like everyone else he was amazed at the high standard of flying, the modern appearance and speed of the aircraft, and watched with wonder as the pilots took their Nells through the dense fire without jinking or taking any evasive action, and then virtually knocked out the battleship with one hit. He had been at Dunkirk and witnessed many attacks by the *Luftwaffe* but he had never seen anything so brilliant, determined and formidable as this.

'If there are many more of these planes around,' he remembered thinking, 'then we are in for it – no mistake.' There were more, many more; and at that moment nine bombers in tight formation were seen approaching high, while the Nells which had completed their attack on the *Prince of Wales* flew low and close to the *Repulse*, their gunners sweeping the big ship's decks, killing and wounding a number of the anti-aircraft crews.

Tennant refused to be distracted and kept his eye on the approaching bombers in their arrowhead formation. At Dunkirk you could see the bombs actually leaving the racks of the dive-bombers and trace the line of their trajectory all the way. These Japanese bombs, released close to 10,000 feet he estimated, became visible only near the end of their flight, a scattering of black shapes like carelessly thrown rocks tumbling out of the sky. He ordered the helm hard over and watched them with professional objectivity. Of the nine bombs seven fell in the water well clear, the eighth was a near miss on the starboard side, sending up a tall geyser of white water and spray which came crashing back on the ship as if they had suddenly hit a force 10 gale. The ninth created no splash, for it hit the *Repulse* almost dead amidships on the aircraft hangar and exploded in the marines' mess on the armoured deck below, starting a fire. The ship gave a little shudder of mixed dismay and disgust while the debris thrown up high clattered back on to the deck. Not too serious.

Not too serious for the ship, but there were dead to be dealt with and wounded to be cared for, while the damage-control parties ran out hoses and played them on the fire. The fully fuelled Walrus amphibian on the crippled catapult had suddenly become a fire hazard. Its bearded New Zealand pilot was struggling to get the machine over the side, calling for assistance.

For the historical record of her last hours, the *Repulse* had the curious advantage of numbering among her complement two journalists, Cecil Brown of CBS and O'Dowd Gallagher of the London *Daily Express*. Both men survived, and Gallagher was able to provide *Express* readers with a scorching exclusive on the contest:

At 11.18 the *Prince of Wales* opened a shattering barrage with all her multiple pom-poms. Red and blue flames poured from the eight-gun muzzles of each battery.

I saw glowing tracer shells describe shallow curves as they went soaring skyward surrounding the enemy planes. Our 'Chicago Pianos' opened fire; also our triple-gun four-inch high-angle turrets. The uproar was so tremendous I seemed to feel it.

From the starboard side of the flag-deck I can see two torpedo planes. No, they're bombers. Flying straight at us.

All our guns pour high explosives at them, including shells so delicately fused that they explode if they merely graze cloth fabric.

But they swing away, carrying out a high-powered evasive action without dropping anything at all. I realize now what the purpose of the action was. It was a diversion to occupy all our guns and observers on the air-defence platform at the summit of the mainmast.

There is a heavy explosion and the *Repulse* rocks. Great patches of paint fall from the funnel on to the flag-deck. We all gaze above our heads to see planes which during the action against the low fliers were unnoticed.*

They are high-level bombers. The first bomb, the one that rocked us a moment ago, scored a direct hit on the catapult-deck through the one hangar on the port side....

Cooling fluid is spurting from one of the barrels of a 'Chicago Piano'. I can see black paint on the funnel-shaped covers at the muzzles of eight barrels actually rising in blisters big as fists.

The boys manning them – there are ten to each – are sweating, saturating their asbestos anti-flash helmets. The whole gun swings this way and that as spotters pick planes to be fired at.

Two planes can be seen coming at us. A spotter sees another at a different angle, but much closer.

He leans forward, his face tight with excitement, urgently pounding the back of the gun swiveller in front of him. He hits that back with his right hand and points with the left a stabbing forefinger at a single sneaker plane. Still

---

* They were, as we have seen.

blazing two-pounders, the whole gun platform turns in a hail of death at the single plane. It is some 1,000 yards away.

I saw tracers rip into its fuselage dead in the centre. Its fabric opened up like a rapidly spreading sore with red edges. Fire. . . .

It swept to the tail, and in a moment stabilizer and rudder became a framework skeleton. Her nose dipped down and she went waterward.

We cheered like madmen. I felt the larynx tearing in the effort to make myself heard above the hellish uproar of guns.[10]

There was a brief lull before the torpedo-bombers switched their attention from the flagship to the *Repulse*. Captain Tennant recalled:

I never reckoned we could do much about a mass torpedo attack with the guns. We had some recently installed Oerlikons and some pom-poms but we didn't have the modern H/A [high-angle] heavy stuff like the *Prince of Wales*'s 5.25s. We had twenty 4-inch but not all of them elevated enough and none of them could be depressed to keep track of low-flying torpedo-planes. No, evasion was our only chance, and thankfully the *Repulse* was an unusually manoeuvrable big ship.

Two squadrons of Nells now came in through the scattered cloud to attack the battle-cruiser almost simultaneously. The *Prince of Wales* opened fire on them, but the barrage was distinctly less vigorous and sustained than before, as so many of the guns had lost their power and most of those could not be hand-operated. Tennant realized that he was going to get only limited help from his flagship and gave his whole attention to manoeuvring his own ship while his gunners did as best they could.

The art of combing torpedo tracks demands instant responses, a keen sense of anticipation and timing, and above all decisiveness. Speed was an essential ingredient of success and Tennant maintained the *Repulse* at 25 knots, later raised to 27½ knots: 'I maintained a steady course until the aircraft appeared to be committed to the attack, when the wheel was put over and the tracks providentially combed.'

The Captain spoke of 'our good fortune in dodging all these torpedoes', well over a dozen of them, and gave credit to 'the valuable work done by all bridge personnel in calmly pointing out approaching torpedo-bombing aircraft', but he was the master of this remarkable demonstration of evasion, with his 32,000-ton ship swinging this way and that like a 1,500-ton destroyer, engines at almost full revs and the guns rattling away with scarcely a break.

Meanwhile, in the conning tower the quartermaster and the helmsman, Leading Seaman John Robson, were working strenuously to meet the Captain's orders.

The conning tower rapidly filled with officers and ratings. I was not relieved at the wheel and the PO Quartermaster stood by the bridge voicepipe passing wheel orders to me as we took avoiding turns. The noise was terrific when the guns fired. I always remember the PO Quartermaster only a foot from me shouting the wheel orders to me – his face red with the effort to be heard above the noise all around us.... The whole ship shuddered with the effect of twisting to port and starboard.[11]

Lieutenant Takai, who led in his squadron on this abortive attack, was doubly frustrated. He began his attack at 1,000 feet and, he calculated, one and a half miles from the *Repulse.*

The sky was filled with bursting shells which made my plane reel and shake. The *Repulse* had already started evasive action and was making a hard turn to the right. The target angle was becoming smaller and smaller as the bow of the vessel swung gradually in my direction, making it difficult for me to release a torpedo against the ship.... I descended to just above the water's surface. The airspeed indicated more than 200 knots.... I pulled back on the torpedo release. I acted almost subconsciously, my long months of daily training taking over my actions.[12]

Clear of the target, Takai saw his observer working his way forward down the slim fuselage. 'Sir, sir, a terrible thing has happened!' he cried out. 'The torpedo failed to release.'

The Lieutenant was not pleased. 'We will go in again,' he told his crew. Feeling that he was really pushing his luck this time, Takai took his Nell down again, through the fading clouds of old flak bursts, and the new ones aimed at him, feeling and hearing the rattle of splinters against his wings and fuselage, and catching the stench of high explosive as he was rocked from side to side. He never saw the result when he pulled the release lever again, this time with a wrench. In fact, he missed. As he flew clear, not greatly damaged, and his engines running sweetly, he heard a report going out to base: 'Many torpedoes made direct hits....'

These hits were still all on the *Prince of Wales*, whose condition was now lamentable, with no steering and few operating guns to defend herself, the hoisted balls stating the obvious – 'Not under control' – although she could still make some 15 knots. Tennant could get no reply to his enquiries about the flagship's condition, even by signal lamp, as if the ship's company were too preoccupied with survival to have time for the outside world. At least Admiral Phillips must have called to Singapore for fighters, but where were they? The *Repulse* had so far, and amazingly, suffered only one bomb hit, but the Japanese would be back for the *coup de grâce*, even if they had to return to base to rearm; Tennant doubted his ability to survive another torpedo attack as fierce as the last one. He recalled:

Yes, we needed fighters desperately at this stage.... We knew that there was an Australian squadron of Buffaloes available, and just a few would make all the difference. Even if they did not shoot any Japs down, their presence would deter them and put them off their run. I called for a report from my Chief Yeoman of Signals on what messages had been sent earlier. I was horrified to hear from him that none at all had been picked up by the ship's wireless.

On his own initiative, and despairing of setting up any sort of communication with his flagship, Tennant called for help: 'Enemy aircraft bombing. . . .' Meanwhile the attack was about to be renewed. The *Repulse*'s radar had picked up more blips to the north, and soon the now familiar silhouette of the Nells and Bettys could be made out among the scattered cloud. It was a few minutes before noon and very hot.

The Japanese were clearly giving first priority to finishing off the flagship, a ripe, wallowing target now, incapable of manœuvre and with even fewer guns operating. It was target practice, except that no practice target would ever be as easy as this. One after another the Nells dropped, turned and slammed in torpedo after torpedo. It was like kicking a dying animal.

And then it was the *Repulse*'s turn. Once again Tennant began twisting and turning, and again frustrating attack after attack. He was finally caught out – it was inevitable – by one torpedo-bomber which seemed set on the *Prince of Wales*, banking and turning steeply at the last moment. The *Repulse* was already combing other tracks and now the alternative was to risk three hits from port or one from starboard. 'I watched it coming, and this time there was nothing I could do.'

The old-fashioned First World War 'bulge' fitted along and under the waterline of the battle-cruiser appeared to provide better protection than the *Prince of Wales*'s more sophisticated anti-torpedo arrangement. The explosion was no more than a jolt, and although water came in, counter-flooding soon put the ship back on an even keel. 'We could still make 25 knots,' the Captain noted, 'and I thought that we still might make it.'

But not for long. Yet another squadron came down like birds of prey. A flight of three banked steeply and headed low for the *Repulse*'s port side. The anti-aircraft gunners were still priding themselves on blowing up two of the earlier attackers when this very close assault settled the fate of the old battle-cruiser. All three made hits, and this time the shudder was pulverizing. It was followed by two more as distantly launched torpedoes which had not been observed struck the starboard side.

'I wasted no more time,' Tennant recalled, 'and gave the order for all who could to come on deck and cast loose the Carley floats.'

We all troop down ladders [Gallagher wrote], most orderly except for one lad who climbs the rail and is about to jump when an officer says: 'Now then – come back – we are all going your way.' The boy came back and joined the line. . . . The calmness was catching. . . . Nervously opening my cigarette case, I found I hadn't a match. I offered a cigarette to a man beside me. He said, 'Ta. Want a match?' We both lit up and puffed once or twice. He said: 'We'll be seeing you, mate.' To which I replied: 'Hope so. Cheerio.'

We were all able to walk down the ship's starboard side, she lay so much over to port.

We all formed a line along a big protruding anti-torpedo blister, from where we had to jump some twelve feet into a sea which was black. . . .[13]

Yes, it was oil, inevitably oil, sticky, choking, blinding, filthy muck that made you retch when you needed every breath you could draw, converting everyone, senior officers, lieutenants, midshipmen, petty officers and ratings – and journalists – into anonymity, funeral black for their imminent death.

Captain Tennant was on his bridge clutching the rail against the sudden 40-degree list. Below him on the forecastle were two or three hundred men. He put a megaphone to his lips and called out, 'You've put up a good show. Now look after yourselves and God bless you.'

In less than a minute the list was 70 degrees. Tennant clambered down to B gun deck.

I just let the sea come up to me – there was not much else to be done [he recounted a few years before he died]. I went down with my ship, but luckily came up again. After a very long time. The old *Repulse* turned right over on me. The thought passed through my head – 'Why not take one big gulp to finish things off?' but luckily I did not. The black about me changed to dark green as I came up fast like a bit of flotsam. And another bit of flotsam hit me hard just before I surfaced. I was nearly knocked out, and would have been if I hadn't still been wearing my tin hat.

'Here you are, sir,' were the first words he heard before being dragged into a Carley float. He was the one man not black with oil.

Of the four destroyers which had formed the battleships' escort, one had been ordered home earlier due to fuel shortage. The other three had done what they could with their anti-aircraft guns and had been heavily machine-gunned for their pains. But no pilot was prepared to waste a torpedo or bomb on such puny prey and the officers and men, including those in the Australian *Vampire*, were little more than anxious spectators. When their nominal role as protectors ceased, they became vessels of mercy. But the *Repulse* went down quickly and it took time to get to the scene and commence rescue work. For this reason the casualties were very heavy, many men drowning in the warm oily water and many more trapped below decks by the rapid succession of torpedo strikes. Of a total complement of 1,309, 513 officers and men were lost in that contest, nearly all of them after the final five torpedo hits.

The *Prince of Wales* lasted almost fifty minutes longer, allowing the destroyer *Express* to come alongside and take off first the wounded and then as many as could make the hazardous crossing before the destroyer had to cast off. It was an agonizing equation for the *Express*'s captain, Lieutenant-Commander F.J.Cartwright, the rescuers on the destroyer's deck and those stranded on the *Prince of Wales*'s upper deck, the angle of which steepened every second and the length of line to be traversed increasing in proportion.

One of those awaiting his turn was Geoffrey Brooke, who described Cartwright as 'a picture of coolness as he leant on his forearms at the corner of the bridge, watching the side of the *Prince of Wales*'.

On the deck beneath, a seaman stood at each line, knife poised over the taut rope, eyes on his Captain. At last there was no one in front of me. I gave my precursor a few feet and went too, the half-inch diameter rope biting into my hands with considerable intensity. It was surprisingly tiring work, now with the nightmare element that, as the battleship heeled increasingly away, the men at the other end of the rope had to pay it out, nullifying most of one's efforts. When the last few yards became a steep uphill haul – the weight of bodies kept the rope well down – I felt for a moment too exhausted to go on but a glance at the oily water in which men were already struggling provided the spur of desperation. A last effort put my wrists within the grasp of eager hands and in one exhilarating heave I was over the destroyer's rail. Crawling out of the way to regain my breath, I saw the man after me come safely over and then 'Slip!' roared the destroyer Captain.

The row of knives flashed and, as I struggled to my feet, all the ropes swung down, heavy with men, to crash sickeningly against the battleship's side. 'Starboard ten, full astern together', came from the bridge above and, as the engine-room telegraph clanged, the grey wall opposite began to roll inexorably away. There was a heavy bump and we began to heel violently outwards. Grabbing at something I realized that the *Prince of Wales*'s bilge keel had caught under the destroyer. Her skipper had left it too late! But the next instant she swung back, the powerful propellers began to bite, and gathering sternway we surged clear. The destroyer stood off a cable or so and in silence except for the hum of her engine-room fans, we watched aghast.

The great battleship continued to roll slowly away; as her upperworks dwindled and then vanished.[14]

There were some agonizing scenes on the battleship at the very end. An awesome silence had descended after a last bombing run. The skies were empty, the guns silent at last. But when the ship heeled over steeply before going down, cries from the men still trapped deep in the bowels of the ship arose in an agonizing chorus through the quarterdeck ventilators.

Captain Leach and Admiral Phillips remained on the bridge to the end. Someone reported that the Admiral had called for his best hat to be brought up; it would be in character. In accordance with a ridiculous tradition, neither man made any move to save himself. Captain Tennant by doing so lived to do great work later in the war, including commanding the vital Mulberry harbours during the invasion of France. Leach and Phillips had priceless experience to offer, too. What a waste!

As the *Prince of Wales* was sinking at 1.20 p.m. the first of the Australian fighter pilots appeared on the scene, flying low above the wreckage, the bobbing heads, the rafts and the ever-widening slick of oil. Of the flagship's total complement of 1,612, 327 officers and men died, in the water or in the ship.

By becoming the first modern battleship to be sunk at sea by air power, the *Prince of Wales*, proud, newest battleship of the Royal Navy, signalled the end of her kind in the role in which her breed had always served – in the line of battle, in a gunnery duel with the enemy, the outcome deciding the control of the sea.

The sinking or disabling of the battleships at Pearl Harbor three days earlier could be ascribed to unreadiness and the sneak nature of this attack opening an undeclared war. Besides, it could be argued, the battleships were moored and bunched together in a neat row, incapable of manoeuvre. This alibi could not be applied to the *Prince of Wales* and *Repulse*. They had good-to-average anti-aircraft protection by the standards of the time and all the manoeuvring room they could wish for. What they did not have was air cover.

There were some of those unfortunate sailors struggling in the oily water after their ships went down who managed a gesture of contempt and a curse at the Australian fighter pilots wheeling low above them. (The pilots thought they were being greeted and cheered, and reported this as proving the defiant gallantry of the men.)

Why were they not sent for sooner, at the moment when the first radar sighting was made? It has never been properly explained. Captain Tennant expressed amazement when he learned far too late that the flagship had not called up the fighters: 'I could not believe my ears!'[15] Why was he not told earlier – or why did he not enquire earlier for that matter? As for Admiral Phillips, is it possible to believe that he did not give thought to fighter support when it was available even if he did recognize that the planes were old and the pilots inexperienced? Alas, the truth almost certainly is that it is not only possible but probable. An admiral who could suggest to another that he was a scrimshanker and lacking in courage in complaining about air attack, and had expressed his belief over and over again that properly equipped capital ships could head off any air attack, was unlikely to rush to call up help from another service when he thought he could do the job himself.

Peter Kemp, who worked closely with Phillips and knew him well, thinks that he 'was a bit contemptuous of air attacks on ships and reckoned that any ship worth her salt could shoot any aircraft out of the sky'. Kemp continues: 'I am forced to the conclusion that, when the Japanese aircraft were sighted, Phillips believed the ships could defend themselves adequately with their own A/A fire. A decision not to ask for air cover seems to me to be entirely in character with the man as I knew him.'[16]

However, in the broad historical context the two ships were almost certainly doomed to be engulfed in the inexorable tidal wave of Japanese military and naval power over the following months. They could not have been brought home while the political need for their presence remained, and, with the puny air protection upon which they would have been forced to rely, they would almost certainly have been sent to the bottom. Eleven Buffalo fighters, slower and less well armed than their combat-experienced foe, could have done very little to help.

To conclude where it all began, with Winston Churchill, the man most responsible for the despatch of Force Z: when he heard the news,

I was thankful to be alone. In all the war I never received a more direct shock. ... As I turned over and twisted in bed the full horror of the news sank in upon me.[17]

Besides overrunning the Malay peninsula and Singapore, the Japanese strategic plan called for the invasion of Sumatra, Java, Timor, Borneo, the Celebes, New Guinea and the Solomon Islands – a vast archipelago of rich conquest which would also include the Philippine Islands, the islands of the south-west Pacific, and then south again into northern Australia via Port Darwin and west into Burma and India. It was an operation that was outrageous in scale, brilliant in conception, and so far successful in execution. By January 1942 the 'Greater East Asia Co-Prosperity Sphere', as the Japanese super-euphemism had it, looked well on the way to completion.

The removal of the two British capital ships from the South China Sea settled the conquest of the Malay peninsula and Singapore, although the city did not finally fall until 15 February 1942. Only one obstacle at sea remained to be dealt with before the invasion forces could feel free to overwhelm the Dutch East Indies, rich in oil, rubber, tin and much else. This was a multi-national fleet under several commanders made up of mainly second-line ships ranging from 8-inch-gunned cruisers to First World War destroyers similar to those which the Americans were happy to trade with the British for Atlantic and Caribbean bases.

The Netherlands naval force was not the most powerful but was the most homogenous, while the United States Asiatic Fleet, traditionally the Cinderella of the American fleets, was commanded by the elderly Admiral Thomas C. Hart. In addition there was a British–Australian naval force under the command of Admiral Sir Geoffrey Layton with a heavy cruiser, two Australian light cruisers and three destroyers.

After suffering some damage during the early Japanese attacks on key points in Borneo and the Celebes, a last-ditch American–Australian–British–Dutch Command was set up under Field-Marshal Sir Archibald Wavell, the Allied national commands being under Hart for the Americans, Commodore John Collins, Royal Australian Navy, for the British and Australians, and Vice-Admiral C.E.L. Helfrich for the Netherlands naval forces.

By the end of February the naval strength of this combined force had been whittled down to the American heavy cruiser *Houston*, which had lost its after 8-inch gun turret in an earlier engagement, the British heavy cruiser *Exeter*, veteran of the Battle of the River Plate, the Australian light cruiser *Perth*, two Dutch light cruisers, the *De Ruyter* and *Tromp*, and nine destroyers of mixed age, nationality and quality. In overall sea command was Rear-Admiral Karel Doorman, a sturdy Dutchman conscious of his responsibilities and of the Dutch naval tradition recalled in the fighting prowess of the seventeenth-century admirals after which his ships were named.

But as in the South China Sea ten weeks earlier, Doorman was virtually without air support, the *Tromp* dated from the First World War, and the motley collection he commanded had never operated together nor had they any signalling uniformity, let alone common language. What could be expected of them against the powerful Japanese forces lurking about these East Indies islands – numerous heavy cruisers, modern light cruisers, destroyers and submarines armed with the deadly long lance torpedoes?*

In addition to powerful land-based bomber forces, the Japanese made full use of the reconnaissance seaplanes carried by their cruisers, which had already proved so effective in the hunt for Force Z and its subsequent shadowing. The Japanese had no ship-borne radar, but the numerous seaplanes of the IJN proved an effective substitute in the early months of the Pacific War. The Dutch officer appreciated the extent of the odds stacked against him, and that his duty was to delay for as long as possible the landings along the Dutch archipelago.

Slowly but surely the threat of a large landing on Java increased [wrote one of his officers, Lieutenant J.N.van Huern of the Dutch destroyer *Kortenaer*]. During the night of Thursday 26th and Friday February 27th [1942] the squadron of five cruisers and nine destroyers was cruising north of Madura, but there was still no enemy in sight. At dawn we cruised farther out into the Java Sea, in a westerly direction. At first a short air attack kept us keyed up. The hostile reconnaissance planes never let us out of their sight, so that we had something to look out for. Nevertheless, our attention flagged. Exertion and lack of sleep began to weigh more heavily upon us. The Admiral gave the order to return to Sourabaya and informed Batavia that the staying-power of his men had been stretched to its limit.

Doorman had selected Sourabaya, on the north coast of Java, from which to operate and make a last effort to prevent the Japanese invasion forces from landing. They were known to be in great strength and heavily supported. As his squadron was about to enter harbour the British destroyer *Electra*, a Force Z survivor, sighted distant smoke. Lieutenant van Huern continues his narrative:

After the fall of Singapore we no longer had any illusions about our 'chances'; in the event of a landing on Java, the fleet was to be staked in its entirety. That was exactly what we wanted, but we did not expect to come out of it alive.

When the facts about the enemy concentrations had been received, we knew our day had come. As by a miracle, heat and fatigue were forgotten. The whole squadron turned in the passage through the minefield at the western fairway and advanced to meet the enemy. 'Course 33, speed 25' was the order. It was fortunate that the speed ordered did not exceed 25 knots since only two of the *Kortenaer*'s

* The Type 93 Japanese torpedo had a range of 22,000 yards at about 50 knots. It was propelled by oxygen, a fuel so volatile and dangerous that the British Navy, first to experiment with it in 1924, discarded the idea. The less fastidious Japanese, at great cost in lives, persevered, to their enormous advantage.

three boilers were in use. This was enough for running away, which actually did not come into our plans anyway. During the short hours of stay in Sourabaya the repair of the third boiler had not been possible.

At about 4 p.m. the *De Ruyter* announced by ultra-short wave: 'Many ships 2 points on starboard bow.' It sounded just as businesslike as ever, and yet I shall never forget the deep voice which yelled these words down from the bridge of the *Kortenaer*. You could hear it right down in the mess since the loudspeaker was switched on to maximum volume.[18]

The most that poor Admiral Doorman could hope to do was to attack the vulnerable Japanese landing-craft and damage the enemy in order to reduce the odds in the unlikely event of his receiving reinforcements.

It was the second time that the *Exeter* had engaged in a gunnery duel against a more powerful enemy. She opened 8-inch fire with the *Houston* at long range, too great a range for the light cruisers' 6-inch. The Japanese heavy cruisers, outnumbering the British–American ships two to one, replied. The *Exeter* was soon hit by shellfire that was almost as good as the *Admiral Graf Spee*'s. This time it was the engine-room that was hit, with heavy casualties and the loss of one of the boilers.

There were in the end so few survivors of the Battle of Java Sea that the sequence of events is unclear. But it appears that, while Doorman's destroyers tried to protect the *Exeter* with a smokescreen, the Japanese destroyers counter-attacked. One of the lethal Japanese 24-inch torpedoes blew up a Dutch destroyer and another brought the *Electra* to a standstill. The whole Japanese destroyer force closed about the poor *Electra*. Though she fought back manfully, one by one her guns were knocked out, and she was crushed and sunk while Doorman retreated with the crippled *Exeter*.

The resolute Dutchman had not given up the fight, however. Leaving the *Exeter* to complete her laboured passage back to Sourabaya, as night fell he attempted to work round the Japanese force to strike at the transports he suspected were behind the enemy. He never had a chance. The transport armada was tucked well away and fully screened by reinforced Japanese naval forces. Doorman remained blind; the Japanese followed every one of his moves.

Nor did fortune favour the brave: the British destroyer *Jupiter* ran into a Dutch minefield and blew up, and one of the Dutch destroyers was seriously damaged when a depth-charge fell overboard and exploded close to her stern. In the course of a hair-raising night action around midnight, the sky lit by searchlights, calcium flares and starshells, the Japanese made full use of their long lance torpedoes, sending the two Dutch cruisers to the bottom. Now, apart from surviving destroyers, only the *Houston* and *Perth* remained operational, while the Japanese began their landings.

The remnants of the Allied force attempted to make their way to Batavia during the following day and night, the *Exeter* escorted by two destroyers. The two groups were followed by Japanese seaplanes without interference. On 28 February and some twelve hours later look-outs on the war-scarred

British cruiser and her escorting destroyers sighted large surface vessels, supported by a heavy force of destroyers. They had no identification problems: they were all familiar with the silhouette of Japanese heavy cruisers with their heavy pagoda-like superstructure, steeply inclined funnels and numerous gun turrets – oriental, provocative and fearsome.

The *Exeter*, crawling along on two boilers, opened fire for the last time. No one survived to report her accuracy. The engagement was mercifully brief. Japanese 8-inch shells rapidly overwhelmed all three ships, and one by one they turned over, the seas extinguishing the flames.

With their disappearance the Allies lost a further thousand and more men, and their last chance of stemming the Japanese tide of conquest in South-East Asia. Burma was already being overrun, resistance in Rangoon ceasing on 8 March, the same day that Java surrendered. Just one month later the conquest of the Philippines, which had begun within minutes of Pearl Harbor, was virtually complete, the island fortress of Corregidor holding out for four more weeks.

How many lives were to be lost, how much suffering and cost were to be endured, before the ruthless, tyrannous military forces could be driven from the conquered soil of South-East Asia and the west and south-west Pacific Ocean?

CHAPTER EIGHT

'The lowest ebb . . .'

Shortly after 4.00 p.m. on 4 April 1942 Squadron-Leader L.J.Birchall, captain of a reconnaissance Catalina flying boat, caught sight of a large Japanese fleet 350 miles south-east of Ceylon (today Sri Lanka) on a westerly heading. He at once ordered his wireless operator to transmit this information. He succeeded in doing so, without details, before the flying boat was 'jumped' by a swarm of Zero fighters which tore the machine to pieces with 20-mm cannon shells and machine-gun bullets. The Catalina had been spotted by keen-eyed look-outs first and the fighters, already lined up on a carrier's deck for just this contingency, were scrambled, gained height with a speed that no other fighter could match and came in out of the sun in the long-established attack approach.

Admiral Chuichi Nagumo, four months almost to the day since he had attacked and rendered impotent the American Battle Fleet, was about to embark on another Pearl Harbor. This time his target was British. If land-based bombers could deal so swiftly and fatally with the *Prince of Wales* and *Repulse*, he had no doubt that he could knock out the British Eastern Fleet, which was, in the judgement of a Naval Air Arm admiral, even more formidable than the battle fleet at Hawaii.

Not for one moment had the self-confidence and drive of Admiral Nagumo lost its momentum. Nor for that matter had the fleet itself lost its momentum. The six carriers had returned to Hiroshima Bay on 23 December 1941 to be greeted by Admiral Yamamoto himself, and fêted by a war-frenzied crowd. Every man in sailor's uniform was a hero after the destruction of the American fleet, and only Admirals Yamamoto and Nagumo and senior members of their staff recognized the irony, and the anxiety, implicit in the fact that these carriers, which had crowned themselves the new sovereigns of the ocean, had in fact failed to find, let alone damage, a single enemy carrier.

On 5 January 1942 Nagumo departed from Hiroshima with four of his carriers, including the giant *Akagi* and *Kaga*, and headed at high speed to support the assault and landings at Rabaul and on the north-east coast of New Guinea, the southernmost battle areas in the first phase of Japanese conquest. For the first time in its history Australia's mainland had become a military target, and on 19 February Commander Fuchida led thirty-six fighters, seventy-one dive-bombers and eighty-one 'level' bombers of Nagumo's carrier aircraft in an attack on Port Darwin.

'Our fighters wiped out an opposing force of eight enemy fighters,' reported one pilot. 'We wrecked or set aflame an additional fifteen planes on the ground. Our bombers sank two destroyers and eight other vessels, some seven smaller ships received bomb hits or near misses, and low-level ground attacks set three aircraft hangars aflame.' [1]

The old American carrier *Langley*, carrying a load of fighters to assist the Dutch defenders on Sumatra, was also sunk at this time by land-based Japanese naval bombers. Other raids in Dutch East Indies waters led to further savage destruction of enemy transports and light warships participating in the sealing off and conquest of the whole of the East Indies. Not once during all these operations was a single one of Nagumo's carriers sighted let alone attacked by the ABDA (Australian–British–Dutch–American) forces.

In order to protect the long western flank of newly conquered Japanese territory and secure it while the south-west Pacific was conquered and occupied, the Japanese High Command decided that the time had come to destroy once and for all British naval power in the Indian Ocean, which had been strongly reinforced since the loss of the *Prince of Wales* and *Repulse*.

Admiral Nagumo's timetable was characteristically hectic, and he left Kendari in the south-east Celebes and headed for the Bay of Bengal on 26 March 1942. His fleet had no match in the world: fast, equipped with the finest naval aircraft, battle-hardened and with sky-high morale. He now had five fleet carriers, only one fewer than he had had for the Pearl Harbor operation, four modernized and formidable battleships with a heavy broadside totalling thirty-two 14-inch guns, two heavy 8-inch-gun cruisers of around 13,000 tons, a light cruiser and nine destroyers; all supported by six tankers with their own escort of three destroyers, which granted the whole force self-sufficiency and freedom of movement across the oceans.

The Japanese generals had opposed the admirals' wish to send a force to invade and occupy Ceylon, believing that the logistics of supply when they were fully extended elsewhere would be too burdensome. But the navy believed that, with the example of a crushing naval victory, the army would be forced to change its mind.

On 30 March the armada was south of Java, on 2 April south of Sumatra on a north-west-by-west heading. H-hour for the attack on the British fleet in Colombo harbour was 8.00 a.m. on 5 April, when Nagumo had the highest expectations of achieving surprise and a victory at least as comprehensive as the one he had gained back on 7 December 1941.

Then came the sighting of that Catalina. It was still a long way from the fleet and its destruction had been marvellously swift. But had it been swift enough? If the reconnaissance machine had got off a message before being shot down the Admiral could not expect to have the great advantage of surprise he had enjoyed last time; and intelligence had informed him

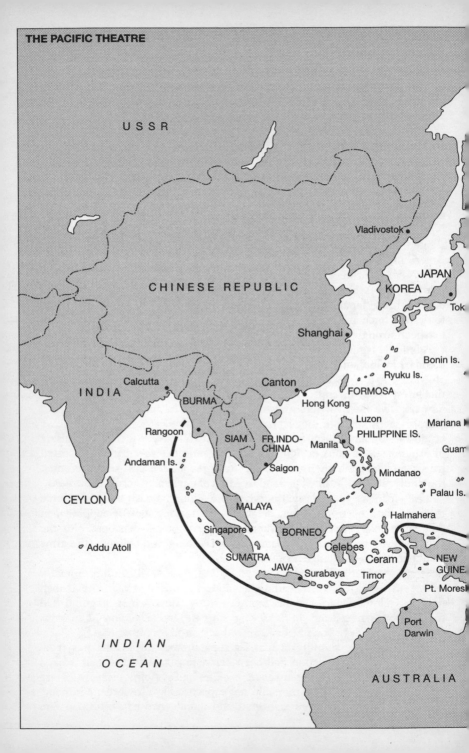

THE PACIFIC THEATRE

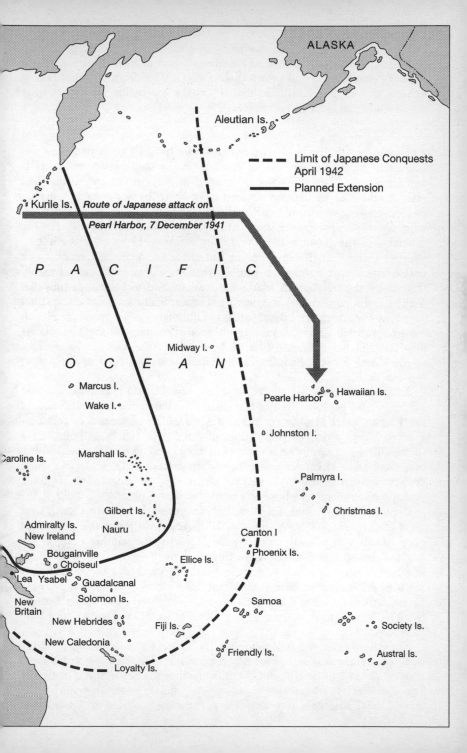

ALASKA

Aleutian Is.

- - - Limit of Japanese Conquests
April 1942

——— Planned Extension

Kurile Is. *Route of Japanese attack on*

Pearl Harbor, 7 December 1941

P   A   C   I   F   I   C

O   C   E   A   N

Midway I.

Marcus I.

Wake I.

Caroline Is.   Marshall Is.

Gilbert Is.

Admiralty Is.
New Ireland   Nauru

Bougainville
Choiseul

Lea   Ysabel   Guadalcanal

New
Britain   Solomon Is.

New Hebrides   Fiji Is.

New Caledonia

Loyalty Is.

Pearle Harbor   Hawaiian Is.

Johnston I.

Palmyra I.

Christmas I.

Canton I
Phoenix Is.

Ellice Is.

Samoa

Society Is.

Friendly Is.   Austral Is.

(incorrectly) that there were as many as 300 British fighters in Ceylon and at nearby bases in India: 'This time we had to expect greater losses but our Zekes [Zeros] had shown themselves far superior to all other enemy fighters and we had no doubt that we would win in the air and destroy the fleet and this great British base....'[2]

The build-up of British naval strength in the Indian Ocean had been the subject of much deliberation in London and debate between Roosevelt and Churchill. If the Japanese succeeded in occupying Ceylon, the vital artery to the Middle East up the east coast of Africa would be put at risk, and as a pre-emptive move Churchill determined to do what he had planned long ago – occupy French-held Madagascar, and reinforce the pitiable remnants of the Eastern Fleet with part of Force H based at Gibraltar. But the Vichy French Government had already shown itself much more enthusiastic about fighting its old ally than its old enemy, and Churchill feared that the invasion of Madagascar might lead to a counter-move by Vichy naval forces at Dakar against Gibraltar. Will you please, Churchill asked the President, send naval forces to Gibraltar to deter any such French move? Roosevelt declined, valuing his good relations with the Vichy Government, but helped just the same by sending American reinforcements to the Home Fleet, which could then spare warships for the defence of this vital base.

Admiral Sir James Somerville, a jaunty, popular and highly capable flag officer, whose exploits had, unfortunately, included the bombardment of the French Fleet at Oran in 1940, was placed in command of this new Eastern Fleet, which by the middle of April 1942 had been built into a formidable force comprising one modernized and four older battleships, one small and old carrier and two modern armoured fleet carriers, eight cruisers, fifteen destroyers and five submarines: no match for Nagumo, perhaps, but also a fleet whose loss would be catastrophic.

Besides Colombo and Trincomalee in Ceylon, this Indian Ocean fleet enjoyed the use of a base at the atoll of Addu, no more than a ring of coral islands surrounding a deep-water lagoon at the southern end of the Maldive Islands, 600 miles from Ceylon. This base, with a wide range of facilities, had been built secretly and with an efficiency strongly contrasting with the Singapore base shambles, by the Mobile Naval Base Defence Organization of the Royal Marines. It was a far-sighted move which Admiral Somerville was to have every reason to bless. The Japanese had no knowledge of it.

The Admiral arrived at Colombo in the carrier *Formidable* on 24 March, two days before Admiral Nagumo steamed out of Kandari with his fleet, bent on Colombo's destruction. At the same time the modernized battleship *Warspite*, which had been sorely damaged at Jutland twenty-six years before, and at the Battle of Crete only ten months ago, arrived in the nick of time from its American repair yard. The scene was set for a massive confrontation.

It was to be their biggest raid since Pearl Harbor. Nagumo's pilots were instructed to concentrate first on the British carriers, then the battleships and cruisers, and the shore installations which had been a disastrous omission from the American targets. The dive-bombers were to go in first, protected by top-cover Zeros, and, having thoroughly strafed shore and ship anti-aircraft guns, were to withdraw to allow the level-bombers to come over.

On all five carriers, steaming fast into wind, the scene was reminiscent of 7 December: the eager deck crews helping the air crews into their planes, and holding wingtips and tailplanes, backs turned to the slipstream; the Zero pilots with canopies open, white silk scarves fluttering, goggles pulled down before take-off; propellers a grey blur in the half-light of dawn. The captain and his staff watching from the bridge above, until the first machine was released, engine screaming at maximum revs, slowly, faster down the deck, lifting off well before the bows.

One after another in rapid succession the carriers launched their bombers, the fighters last but gaining height much more swiftly. It was a brave sight that never failed to impress any onlooker. The Japanese had learned much of naval flying from their one-time allies, and some of the veterans could remember when all the aircraft were British, mostly made by the Blackburn company, when the Japanese Navy's only carrier conformed exactly to British practice. There was a strong sentimental feeling as well as respect towards the Royal Navy in the IJN, unlike the genuine hatred they felt towards the Americans. This was not going to diminish by the smallest degree their commitment to the success of this raid: but a great number of these air crews wished the enemy this morning were American.

It was 7.00 a.m. From 5,000 feet the coastline of Ceylon, dark and undulant in the uncertain light, could be made out to the north-east. The light was variable, intermittently clear but broken by thunderstorms and curtains of driving rain. There were a few fishing boats below, nothing more. At 7.45 a.m. the first of the Group of Vals, Zeros hovering behind and above, sighted Colombo harbour. The pilots were confident now that they had achieved surprise as complete as at Oahu.

But if the skies were empty of any sign of defence – gunfire or fighters – so Colombo was empty of any warships. The British Eastern Fleet had disappeared into the broad wastes of the Indian Ocean. Expecting to find battleships and cruisers and carriers (if not lined up as neatly as the American battleships at Pearl Harbor, at least as easy targets for their bombs), all that the Group Leader could see as he flew over Ratmalan airfield at 7,000 feet was a scattering of merchant ships, mainly small, a few fishing boats – and one warship, no larger than a destroyer.

Bitterly disappointed, the Val pilots overflew their target, and at the signal of a raised arm from the Group Leader, turned their machines over on their backs and settled into their 65-degree dive, half of them aiming at the docks – the sheds and jetties, the stores, workshops and dry docks – the other half picking out the stationary ships inside and outside the breakwater.

On their way down in their hectic dive they suddenly became aware of the anti-aircraft fire coming up to meet them, the dark puffs of heavy shells, the long curving lines of tracer, criss-crossing in front of them. It was a second unpleasant surprise, especially as the fire was accurate and heavy. And that was not all. Even before the point of bomb release, there was fire coming from above, too, and the pilots and gunners were aware of a number of fighters diving with them and on their tails – unfamiliar, hunch-back, fast and evidently highly manoeuvrable monoplanes.

The time of greatest danger for a dive-bomber is when the pilot pulls out of his dive after releasing his bomb load. For a moment he is a sitting target, and as he climbs away, however harshly he jinks his machine, he remains especially vulnerable. Several of the Vals were hit before they could release their bombs and one blew up in a flash of flame at less than 1,000 feet over the centre of the harbour.

This peaceful Easter Sunday dawn was torn apart by the sound of exploding bombs, the thunder of dozens of heavy guns, the scream and roar of aero engines and the rattle, like tearing linen, of dozens of machine-guns and cannon. Aircraft were diving and climbing, twisting and turning, low over the water, while a ship burst into flames and columns of water rose tall and white from exploding bombs.

The Vals could be distinguished by their fixed undercarriage, the defending Hurricane fighters by their sharp nose in contrast to the heavy nose of the radial-engined Zeros, which were now mixing in with the fights, and shooting several of them down while they were on the tail of a dive-bomber. 'You've never seen anything like it,' one eyewitness recorded. 'An absolute shambles – planes on fire, ships on fire, buildings on fire, the guns crashing away at some high bombers which had broken out of cloud in perfect formation, just like a Hendon Air Show.'

How had it come about that the cupboard was bare? After that first Catalina's report the previous afternoon there had been further sightings of the Japanese armada, and orders were issued to clear the harbour of all shipping. Every exertion was made but there were still a number at anchor when the first Japanese wave descended at about 7.45 a.m. As for Admiral Somerville's battleships and carriers, they were, mercifully, nearly all tucked safely away at Addu Atoll. Only the poor little *Tenedos*, which back in December had been detached by Admiral Phillips before the Japanese bombers overwhelmed him, and had been the lonely target of a whole group of Japanese bombers, was left behind because she was refitting. This time her luck was out, and she was sent to the bottom, along with an armed merchant cruiser and the submarine depot ship *Lucia*.

The timing and the direction of the Japanese attack were as predictable as the rising sun on this storm-wracked morning. Even the radar, so recently installed, confirmed the imminent arrival of the enemy, and in all forty-two fighters – nearly all of them Hurricanes – were in the air or taking off when the first Vals came into sight. The Hurricane was not really a match for the Zero, in speed, manoeuvrability or armament. But it could take more punishment than the Japanese machine and its eight machine-guns could knock out the unarmoured Zero with a short burst. In the ferocious dogfights which continued for more than half an hour 258 and 30 Squadrons lost seventeen Hurricanes – a number of the pilots saved themselves – but they shot down at least nineteen of the attacking bombers and fighters. It was the first time the Japanese naval pilots had come up against a relatively modern fighter, and it gave them a considerable shock.

While Admiral Somerville appreciated the need to keep his fleet intact as the nucleus for an eventual counter-attack, he had no intention of skulking at his atoll without making any effort to counter-attack the Japanese raid on Colombo. He rightly considered that the most effective way to damage him was to follow Admiral Nagumo at a close enough distance to be able to launch a torpedo-bomber attack at night while keeping far enough away to remain undiscovered. He therefore took his fleet to sea at 12.15 p.m. on the morning of the raid, intending to rendezvous with the two heavy cruisers, *Dorsetshire* and *Cornwall*, which had left Colombo after hearing of the imminent arrival of the Japanese Fleet.

Shortly after noon on 4 April these two cruisers sighted a shadowing reconnaissance plane. It was like a repeat performance of that fateful 10 December when Admiral Tennant had put his glasses on the distant dot in the sky which had heralded the end of his ship and his flagship. These ubiquitous seaplanes, catapulted from Japanese cruisers, had become a recognized and nerve-testing harbinger of battle. An hour later, with awful inevitability, the first swarm of aircraft came into sight from the north-east. They were the same Vals which had raided Colombo that morning and, rearmed and refuelled, were now racing for this golden opportunity of avenging their losses. The Vals came down in threes, tight together out of the sun, dropping their bombs at around 1,000 feet, treating the gunfire with the utmost contempt. The *Dorsetshire* took six direct hits within the first minute, and in another seven minutes – no more – the 10,000-ton cruiser capsized. The *Cornwall* went down by the bows, shattered mainly by underwater damage from near misses. Brisk and businesslike, the bombers did not bother to machine-gun the survivors in the water, but made off back to their carriers, less dissatisfied now with their day's work.

Wreckage was sighted by a reconnaissance plane from Somerville's force later that afternoon but it was the next day before survivors, already parched and burned by the sun, could be rescued from the shark-infested waters.

Under the circumstances, it was a fine reflection on the men's discipline and endurance that 1,122 were dragged alive on board a cruiser and two destroyers, more than twice as many as had succumbed to the swift annihilation of their ships.

Four days later, after searching far and wide for the British fleet, Admiral Nagumo made a similar attack on the second British base in Ceylon, Trincomalee. It was the same story again: a virtually empty harbour, with the shore installations as the only useful targets. Again there were Hurricanes to meet them, to mix in with the fighters and bombers, with about a dozen losses on both sides. But the Trincomalee raid produced an antidote to the frustration of the Japanese pilots, too, when the old light carrier *Hermes* – the first-ever carrier to be built from the keel up – was found creeping close inshore and was treated with the same ruthlessness as the heavy cruisers.

Then Admiral Nagumo called it a day and went home, rightly to be fêted for one of the most devastating and superbly conducted odysseys of modern times. Since the morning of 7 December 1941 the Japanese Admiral had made a triumphant progress from Pearl Harbor to a point south-west of Ceylon. He had, as one naval officer has written,

careered like a whirlwind across one third of the globe, leaving a trail of destruction behind him – at Wake, Rabaul, Amboina, Darwin, Tjilatja, Colombo and Trincomalee. Harbour installations, merchant ships, warships and enemy aircraft had gone down before the guns and bombs of their planes. The two most powerful navies in the world had been neutralized, leaving the Japanese free to pursue their ambitions unopposed. In all this time Nagumo's ships had suffered no loss or damage and, indeed, except for brief glimpses during the operations off Ceylon, they had not even been sighted.[3]

What was possibly worse at the time was the trail of gloom and pessimism – hopelessness almost – that he left in the wake of his swift, brilliantly manned ships. Field Marshal Sir Archibald Wavell, C-in-C India, felt that things could hardly get worse. Churchill had never been so downhearted. In general terms, he wrote to Roosevelt, 'When I reflect how I have longed and prayed for the entry of the United States into the war, I find it difficult to realize how gravely our British affairs have deteriorated since December 7th.' And American affairs, Roosevelt might have riposted.

On 15 April Churchill even wrote of the possible loss of Ceylon and the invasion of eastern India, which would have meant the loss of the last link with the Chinese, leading to 'the collapse of our whole position in the Middle East', the interruption of oil supplies and other disasters. Admiral Somerville had already ordered his old battleships to African bases, recognizing that they could only be a liability in the face of Nagumo's aircraft and the modern or modernized Japanese armoured ships. Now Japanese domination of the oceans stretched from the Bay of Bengal to the central Pacific, and south to Australia. Seen through the eyes of the British and American high command – to say nothing of the New Zealand

and Australian high command – there seemed to exist no hope of breaking this Japanese vice-like grip until Allied and especially American shipyards could deliver the vessels, and training establishments the skilled crews to man them. And perhaps, even then, they would be too late.

With the advantage of hindsight, detached from the pressures and desperate anxieties of the time, it is possible to recognize through the rubble of bomb blasts and the flames of burning ships, some gleam of hope for the future of the war at sea in the Pacific and Indian Oceans. The first and most immediate item on the credit side was that Admiral Nagumo had quit the Indian Ocean, anyway for the time being, without destroying the British Eastern Fleet. Admiral Somerville had been extremely lucky not to have had his entire force sunk under him.

Then, the first substantial loss of Japanese aircraft in the face of modern fighters manned by experienced pilots had broken the spell of invincibility which they had enjoyed over the past four months.

Finally, not only was the British Eastern Fleet largely intact, but so were the American carrier forces – five large fast carriers, equipped with modern aircraft (which made Admiral Somerville's Albacore torpedo-bombers look like something Wilbur Wright dreamed up) and manned by highly trained air crew. Even as Admiral Nagumo was returning home to be met with another great patriotic chorus of praise and adulation, two of these American carriers were on their way to carry out one of the most daring and spectacular raids of the war.

No simultaneous operations in the Japanese war more completely emphasize the vast arena in which the conflict was taking place, and its international nature, than the Nagumo and Doolittle carrier raids of early April 1942. The war against Japan was just four months old and in this brief period apocalyptic events, military and political, had already taken place from Australia in the south to Burma in the north, from the Andaman Islands in the Bay of Bengal in the west to Pearl Harbor in the east.

On the morning of 2 April Admiral Nagumo was racing west across the Bay of Bengal with his five crack carriers *en route* to his raid against Ceylon, while 10,000 miles away Colonel James Doolittle was at sea out of San Francisco with a carrier-borne bomber force whose target was Tokyo. Over the following days hostilities involved the navies of Japan, the United States, Britain, the Netherlands, India, Australia and New Zealand, the US Army Air Force, the Japanese Air Force and Japanese Army. It had indeed become a World War.

After the US Navy had recovered from the shock of Pearl Harbor and tidied up the mess, it became clear in the highest naval echelons that some kind of offensive retaliation was urgently necessary, if only to reassert the navy's self-respect. There were plenty of other reasons, too, not least the sustaining of civilian morale at home and the denting of Japanese pride and self-confidence. When things were at their worst in the summer of

1940 the British had managed to cobble together a scratch bomber force to drop some bombs on Berlin. It made the British feel much better and enraged Hitler. A month after Pearl Harbor the Chief of Naval Operations, Admiral Ernest J.King, his operations officer, Captain Francis S.Low, and the air officer of King's planning staff, Captain Donald Duncan, who had once been a carrier Group Commander, sat round a table and contrived a plan to hit at the heart of the Japanese Empire.

The target was far beyond the range of heavy bombers from any American base, at home or in the Pacific. Because it was known that there was a day and night patrol at sea some 400–500 miles off the Japanese coast, there was no chance of sailing carriers to a point within range of the navy's single-engine bombers without being spotted, and no doubt as quickly sent to the bottom as the *Repulse* and *Prince of Wales* by shore-based Japanese torpedo- and high-level bombers.

But, remarked one of these officers, why not train an elite force of pilots to fly long-range army bombers off a carrier outside the protective ring of Japanese picket boats? But they could not be landed back, it was argued. Utterly impossible! Was it being suggested that the air crews should crash land in the sea on return, to be picked up, or bail out over the carrier like those Hurricane pilots in the Atlantic? No, this would be a one-way mission – one way from one ally to another, just as the British had bombed north Italy in 1940 and then, because of the extreme range, landed in France. These carrier-borne bombers would attack Tokyo and fly on to bases in China. That was the answer.

The plan was accepted in principle by Admiral King, and talks were opened in secret with the Commanding General of the Army Air Force, H.H.'Hap' Arnold. He leapt at the idea, and it was quickly decided that the aircraft ideal for the job was the new North American B25 Mitchell, a twin-engine machine with a normal combat range of 1,300 miles and a bomb load of 3,000 pounds. The concept of the Mitchell was a typical example of American ability to meet a critical need with the right formula at breakneck speed. In January 1939 the North American Aviation Company had been asked for a medium bomber design; in August the Army Air Corps approved and ordered the design into production. Exactly a year later the prototype was in the air and proving it could fly at more than 300 mph.

It was the B25B variant that was selected for this daring role, with modifications for carrier take-off, removal of the heavy Norden bomb-sight (they would be going in at 1,500 feet anyway), extra fuel tanks to increase the range, a dummy tail gun and bomb load reduced to 2,000 pounds, high explosive or incendiary cluster. The volunteer air crews did a month's training on a specially marked-off airfield in Florida, practising short take-offs. Their leader was Lieutenant-Colonel James H.Doolittle, a veteran flyer from the First World War, and the ship selected was the *Hornet*, a brand new 20,000-ton, 33-knot carrier, whose captain was Mark A.Mitscher USN.

On 2 February 1942, to the puzzlement of her crew, the *Hornet* embarked a pair of Mitchells, which looked ridiculously over-size on her narrow flight deck. Once at sea off Norfolk, Virginia, the carrier turned into wind. Puzzlement turned to amazement when the pilots climbed aboard and took off, without any difficulty, even though there was only six feet to spare between wingtip and the carrier's island.

During March the *Hornet* sailed through the Panama Canal up the west coast to San Francisco, and still in the utmost secrecy (even President Roosevelt knew nothing yet) embarked sixteen Mitchells on her flight deck. Then on 2 April 1942, with 134 air crew members on board, the *Hornet* departed for Midway Island. Of the ship's company only Captain Mitscher knew their final destination. When he finally gathered together his officers and men and told them, 'Cheers from every section of the ship greeted the announcement and morale reached a new high.' [4]

By 13 April the *Hornet* reached Midway where she joined the carrier *Enterprise*, which was to provide air combat cover because the *Hornet*'s own regular complement of aircraft could not be flown off until the deck space occupied by the bombers became available. Other warships forming Task Force 16 under Admiral William F.Halsey were four cruisers and eight destroyers. The weather was vile for most of the voyage across the North Pacific, and the condition of the secured bombers had to be constantly checked. A 40-knot gale was blowing, with 30-foot waves, when the Task Force suddenly sighted a Japanese patrol boat more distant from the Japanese coast than they had calculated. Rapidly, one of the cruisers opened fire and sank the vessel, but, like the Catalina which had spotted Admiral Nagumo off Ceylon, the Japanese crew managed to get off a message before they were blown to bits.

Now what should they do? Abort, or proceed at once with the launch even though they were more than 600 miles from Tokyo? And it was questionable now whether the Mitchells could reach Chinese-held territory after leaving their targets. Halsey decided they must go ahead, and at 8.00 a.m. on 18 April Colonel Doolittle, with just 467 feet of deck in front of his Mitchell's nose, opened the throttles while retaining full brake on the wheels (the Mitchell had a tricycle undercarriage), then, on release, shot down the deck and into the air with seemingly wonderful ease. Lieutenants Travis Hoover, Robert M.Gray, Davy Jones (in that order) and the other pilots had marginally more space for take-off, and, by 9.20 a.m., all rose safely into the murk of a dirty morning in spite of the sharp movements of the carrier.

The Japanese command, on hearing the report of the picket boat's sighting, made their calculations on the reasonable assumption that it would be some seven hours before the naval bombers would be within range to launch, and the defences were so informed. Now it so happened that Tokyo was having one of its air-raid exercises that morning, and by an odd stroke

of fate the first Mitchell came in low over the city just as it was finishing
and the all-clear sirens were sounding. The result was that, while the
civil population thought they were witnessing only an unusually realistic
extension of the exercise, the defences were caught completely by surprise.

Doolittle kept his eyes straight ahead, and there suddenly was Tokyo. His target
was a munitions factory.

Doolittle lifted the plane to fifteen hundred feet. 'Approaching target,' he told
Sergeant Fred Braemer, the bombardier.

And Braemer called back cheerfully, 'All ready, Colonel.'

The bomb bay was opened and Doolittle made his run. It was up to Bombardier
Braemer now. A small red light blinked on the instrument board and Doolittle
knew that the first five-hundred-pound incendiary cluster had gone. In quick succession the red light blinked three more times, and the airplane, relieved of two
thousand pounds, seemed to leap into the air. Up to now he had been too intent
upon finding the target to notice whether the anti-aircraft guns had been firing.
He swung the plane toward the coast. Now, looking around, he saw that the sky
was pockmarked with black puffs. Through the intercom he called to Sergeant
Leonard, 'Everything okay back there, Paul?'

'Everything fine,' Leonard said cheerfully.

'They're missing us a mile, Paul,' Doolittle told him.

Just then a blast rocked the ship and peppered it with bomb fragments. A shell
had burst some hundred feet to the left.

'Colonel, that was no mile,' Paul Leonard laughed.

'We're getting out of here,' Doolittle said, giving the engines full throttle and
shooting down to the relative safety of a hundred feet.[5]

The other Tokyo-bound Mitchells found their military targets, and so
did the aircraft assigned to other industrial cities, with the added bonus
that one bomb struck the carrier *Ryujo* undergoing a refit at Yokohama
naval yard. Nor did the hastily summoned fighters anticipate that the
bombers would continue right on clear across Japan. All sixteen bombers
left the Japanese west coast with minimum damage. Some of the Mitchells
landed safely at Chinese airfields, other crews bailed out in the dark when
their fuel was finally exhausted, one of the bombers headed for Vladivostok
and the crew was promptly interned by America's gallant allies (they eventually escaped to Persia). Eight crew members were picked up by Japanese
army patrols in China and were eventually tried for crimes against humanity,
three of them being shot.

The material damage done by Doolittle's gallant sixteen was negligible,
as anticipated, and the Japanese tried to capitalize on this by calling it
'Doolittle's Do Nothing Raid' in their propaganda. But it shook the Japanese
high command to the core and frightened and affronted those Japanese
civilians who understood its implications. Could this be a harbinger of
terror from the skies like the air raids on Warsaw and London, Amsterdam
and Leningrad, which they had read about?

The military effect of the raids was profound and immediate. Just as
the early raids on Berlin led to the withdrawal of fighter squadrons to

airfields closer to the city, leaving less-distant targets with reduced protection, as a consequence of the Doolittle raid, no fewer than four fighter groups were assigned to home protection from service on the fighting fronts in China and the south-west Pacific.

But much more important than this was the effect the raid had on Japanese grand strategy in the Pacific. April and May 1942 were to be months of consolidation for the Japanese military machine, a period when reinforcements could be fed to the areas where further offensives were to be opened, from New Guinea to Burma, Samoa to the Aleutian Islands; when Admiral Nagumo's carriers could be refitted and their crews rested after their marathon voyages; when plans for further conquest could be prepared in detail, and supplies brought up over the immense distances created by the sheer extent of recent conquests. And now suddenly, and with alarming speed and secrecy, the enemy had gone over to the offensive when the US Navy should still be reeling from the shocks of the weeks between December 1941 and March 1942. The Japanese were not adept at altering their plans and adjusting unexpectedly to new considerations. They were now thrown back on their heels and forced to reappraise their situation and their timetable. Above all, they had to act fast to complete the destruction of American naval power in the Pacific before raids like Doolittle's could be written off as 'do nothings'; and that meant destroying the American carrier forces, which had escaped the attention of Nagumo's bombers over Pearl Harbor.

The Nagumo raid, on a scale many times greater than Colonel Doolittle's, was merely one more addition to the string of spectacular successes achieved by Japanese arms in four months of all-out war, and it had no political consequences whatever. But those sixteen Mitchells were seen at the time as sensationally halting a string of disasters and proving that in this grim game the opponents were not invincible and the home side could score too. Doolittle had indeed done much.

In April 1942 Japan lay like an egg cocooned within the nest of her own conquests. This protective nest had been briefly pierced by those Mitchell bombers, but the map of South-East Asia and the western Pacific hanging in Japanese supreme headquarters was a satisfying enough spectacle. Now, it was calculated, a further heave south and west, during which, by means of oriental wiliness, the American carrier force would be trapped, was all that was needed to bring forth a cry for peace from the demoralized and battered Americans, British, New Zealanders and Australians. This was the new offensive whose timing had been accelerated by 'victory fever' and the Doolittle raid. Among the targets were Port Moresby on the south coast of New Guinea, an island a mere 100 miles from the north coast of Australia, the Solomon Islands, the Fijian Islands, and – the key to Pearl Harbor and the central and eastern Pacific – Midway Island.

It was the proposed capture of Port Moresby that led to the first fleet action of the Pacific war. The outcome was to be governed by scouting and intelligence as much as by the more popularly recognized factors of material, human skill and courage.

In the European war Britain had begun on about equal terms with Germany in radar development. The old myth that the Germans did not know the purpose of the radar towers along the English coast during the Battle of Britain has long since been exploded. German ship-borne radar at first was slightly superior to the Royal Navy's, which, however, like airborne radar, was developed and refined more swiftly than German radar. British intelligence-gathering was also far ahead of its German counterpart, although the Germans during some periods were reading British naval signals as fluently as Bletchley was decrypting German coded signals; and, incidentally, the Germans had no difficulty at all in intercepting transatlantic telephone conversations between Churchill and Roosevelt.

By contrast, in the Pacific war American intelligence superiority was overwhelming. Not only did the Japanese lack any ship- or land-based radar in 1941, but the American Office of Naval Intelligence in Washington under Rear-Admiral Theodore S.Wilkinson was far superior to its Japanese counterpart. The organization OP-20-G, part of the Office of the Chief of Naval Operations, was a cryptographic unit which broke and could read the Japanese code with the same speed and facility as Bletchley read German signals.

In addition there was the Mid-Pacific Direction-Finding Net with stations stretching across thousands of miles of ocean, taking bearings on enemy vessels and following their movements, just as the British had done over the far narrower confines of the North Sea in 1914–18. The Germans were less garrulous in the Second World War, but the Japanese chattered away, identifying themselves and leaving a trace of their movements of priceless value to American Naval Intelligence. (The notable exception was the Nagumo raid on Pearl Harbor, with total two-way radio silence throughout.) By April 1942 the Americans were monitoring 60 per cent of all signals made by the Japanese Navy, from overall planning to seemingly trivial ship-to-ship messages.

In total, then, the US Navy possessed a massive advantage over the IJN in intelligence-gathering at the outset of this entirely new form of naval warfare. Now the major contestants might never see one another, and the 16-inch gun firing hit-or-miss at extreme range had become a half-ton projectile with a range limited only by the fuel capacity of its plane, and an accuracy dependent on the human eye at a few hundred feet instead of the human eye at twenty miles.

American intelligence was able to give warning of Japanese activities in the Coral Sea area by 16 April 1942, and also that they would involve invasion forces from Rabaul in New Britain attacking Port Moresby. The anticipated D-Day was 3 May. This gave time for Admiral Chester W. Nimitz, C-in-C Pacific Fleet, to make his dispositions accordingly. He has written:

The only carriers immediately available were Rear-Admiral Frank Fletcher's *Yorktown* force [Task Force 17], which had been in the South Pacific for some time, and Rear-Admiral Aubrey W.Fitch's *Lexington* group [Task Force 16], fresh from Pearl Harbor. From Nouméa, New Caledonia, came the American heavy cruiser *Chicago*, to join Rear-Admiral J.C.Crace RN with the cruisers *Australia* and *Hobart* from Australia. The Japanese, overconfident from their long series of easy successes, assumed that a single carrier division was sufficient to support their new advance. The two American carrier groups, which had been ordered to join under Fletcher's command, made contact in the south-east Coral Sea on 1 May....[6]

The *Lexington*, 'Lady Lex', with her sister ship *Saratoga*, was the biggest fighting ship in the American Navy, a giant among carriers and only marginally smaller than the British battle-cruiser *Hood*, destroyed just a year before in the *Bismarck* chase.

The USS *Lexington* was the joint product of both the frenzied American–Japanese naval competition of the First World War and its aftermath, and the Washington Treaty which had brought about a compromise slow-down of naval building in 1921–2. The *Lexington* and *Saratoga* were to have been ultimate battle-cruisers of 38,000 tons, mounting eight 16-inch guns and with a speed of over 30 knots. In this form, the *Lexington* was laid down in January 1921 but, as a result of the Treaty, eighteen months later was converted while on the stocks into a 41,000-ton carrier, her funnels combined into one great block of smokestack, armed with eight 8-inch guns and with accommodation for over eighty aircraft.

'Lady Lex' was finally commissioned at the end of 1927, the cynosure of American naval aviation for the next fourteen years. While her sister ship spent months being repaired and refitted after a Japanese submarine – the same *I-65* which had tailed the *Prince of Wales* and *Repulse* – torpedoed her on 11 January 1942, *Lexington* was in the war zone almost from the beginning and was, mercifully, delivering aircraft to Midway Island at the time of Pearl Harbor.

Back in the early weeks of 1942 the *Lexington* acted as flagship for Vice-Admiral Wilson Brown commanding Task Force 11, which was due to make a full-scale attack on Rabaul on 21 February. But on the previous day she had been the target of a fierce attack by eighteen enemy bombers, all but one of which her gunners or fighter pilots shot down. So that was a good start.

The *Yorktown*, sister carrier to the *Hornet* and *Enterprise*, was as new as the Japanese fleet carriers and almost as fast (32.5 knots). As an important unit in Franklin D.Roosevelt's rearmament programme, the *Yorktown* was laid down on 21 May 1934 at Newport News and launched by the President's wife two years later. She was commissioned on 30 September 1937, Captain Ernest D.McWhorter, but early shake-down cruises and exercises revealed serious mechanical defects which eventually involved complete replacement of the reduction gearing and some 1,200 boiler tubes.

The carrier was ready for sea again late in 1938 and, as flagship of the

2nd Carrier Division, took part with the *Enterprise* in elaborate war games in the Caribbean. Roosevelt, as C-in-C of the US Navy and lifetime navy enthusiast, watched a part of these exercises from the cruiser *Houston*. The *Yorktown* was based on Pearl Harbor at the outbreak of the European war, but was called back to the Atlantic on so-called 'Neutrality Patrols' in May 1941. There were numbers of U-boat alarms and attacks on them by escorting destroyers, and the carrier flew numerous defensive scouting operations. As a result, the *Yorktown* considered herself war experienced when she put into Norfolk on 2 December 1941. Five days later, on news of Pearl Harbor, she sailed fast for the Pacific where she became flagship for Fletcher's Task Force 17.

The Japanese operational plan, with Rabaul as its starting-point, was to seize and occupy the port of Tulagi on the island of New Britain and set up a base there, while five more transports escorted by the light carrier *Shoho* and four heavy cruisers headed through the Louisiades (an archipelago of reefs and islets off the eastern tip of New Guinea) to Port Moresby. Two fleet carriers, drawn from Nagumo's recently returned Indian Ocean sortie, the crack new 30,000-ton, 34-knot *Zuikaku* and *Shokaku*, supported by two heavy cruisers, commanded by Admiral Chuichi Hara, provided long-distance cover; and the whole naval operation was under the command of Vice-Admiral Shigeyoshi Inouye.

This powerful presence, Japanese naval high command decided, was more than adequate to deal with any likely interference from American naval forces in the south-west Pacific – a single carrier, some cruisers and a mixed bag of Australian units. And so it would have been, but for the intelligence miscalculation of the number of American carriers.

By means of an elaborate series of evolutions, Admiral Inouye planned to crush the American Task Force between his heavy cruisers and his big carriers as the Americans entered the Coral Sea. The Japanese pre-operational charts resembled one of their elaborate screen engravings such was the complexity of the plan, which also involved yet another force of cruisers and a seaplane carrier which was to set up a reconnaissance base in the Louisiades.

The long-drawn-out naval–air Battle of the Coral Sea opened with a sighting report from an American Australia-based B-17 bomber that Japanese transports were disembarking troops at Tulagi, north of Guadalcanal, in the Solomon Islands. The time was 7.00 p.m. on 3 May. Fletcher headed north with the *Yorktown*, planning a dawn launch, and relishing the prospect of a major strike to counter the many island defeats the Americans had so far suffered. Speed 27 knots, weather deteriorating. Fletcher followed the edge of heavy cloud cover to ensure surprise; all his ships at flank speed, smooth seas, high curving bow waves. At 6.30 a.m., sunrise 6.40 a.m., Fletcher turned his carrier into wind and launched his first flight of Dauntless bombers, so confident of surprise that he held back any escort of Wildcat fighters.

The skies were clear over New Britain and the target easy to find. Fletcher was right: the Japanese were entirely unprepared and opposition was negligible. The excited air crews observed the shock waves circling out from the blasts, the mixed columns of water and debris, a capsized ship, running figures on shore, the criss-cross pattern of tracer fire: all heady stuff to these navy aviators.

But, as so often happens in bombing raids, especially among green pilots, the damage inflicted was much exaggerated. Canny Admiral Fletcher guessed that this was so and sent out three more strikes even though pilots of the first strike declared there were no useful remaining targets. The sum total of sinkings for the morning were three minesweepers and a destroyer. Hardly an annihilating victory, but then these air crews still had much to learn.

Anyway, everyone was in good heart as the Task Force sped off south again to rendezvous with the *Lexington* and refuel from tankers. Expectation of a full-scale clash was now high in all the ships, while the carriers, which must decide the outcome, readied for the inevitable contact.

Hangar- and flight-deck crews gassed the aircraft, and ordnancemen broke out bombs, hanging them from aircraft bellies. Torpedomen went over each fish, checking its detonator and the air pressure in its flask. Gunner's mates checked their ready ammunition lockers and exercised their guns. Fire controlmen removed range finder covers and wiped the lenses clear with soft tissue paper. Signalmen checked their flag bags to be sure all halyards, hooks, and rings were clear for free running so that signal hoists could be snapped to yardarms smartly.[7]

In spite of numerous intelligence reports, and reconnaissance flights from his carriers, Fletcher received no firm news of the main body of the enemy until the evening of 6 May. Again it was an American shore-based bomber that brought him the report of an invasion force heading for Port Moresby, covered by heavy cruisers. He at once flew off scout planes and was rewarded by a report at 8.15 a.m. from one of them: two carriers and four heavy cruisers, distance 225 miles, north of Misima Island in the Louisiades.

Admirals Fletcher and Fitch, with their big fleet carriers and escorting cruisers and destroyers, turned their carriers into wind and launched a massive attack of seventy-five dive- and torpedo-bombers, with an eighteen-strong fighter escort. This seemed like the real thing at last, the first opportunity to reverse the series of Japanese victories. From the admirals, through operations officers, deck crews, down below decks where some 2,000 men, all of whom knew that great events were looming, the excitement was keen and hopes were high.

Now it was the turn of the scouts to land back, among them the Dauntless which had made the sighting report. Only then did it become clear that there had been a decoding failure, that the radio operator had in fact signalled 'two heavy cruisers and two destroyers'.

On both sides it was to be a day of false sightings or no sightings, of misidentification and correct identification, of confusion and speculation. They were in the heart of a cold-front weather system of intermittent cloud, sometimes dense and impenetrable, seconds later thin and semi-opaque, and then with flashes of complete clarity and unlimited visibility. All battles, it is said, are fought partly in fog and confusion; at times in the Coral Sea it seemed that it was sometimes fog and all confusion.

Fletcher was now receiving more reports from the land-based bombers. Yes, the Japanese invasion force *was* heading for Port Moresby and, yes, there was a carrier – a carrier for sure, but just one, not two. Fletcher's strike was already heading in that direction, so this determined him not to recall his aircraft, in spite of the danger that his two carriers were almost entirely defenceless until the fighters returned.

The Japanese were suffering just as badly from a veritable barrage of misinformation. Admiral Inouye, orchestrating the multiple operations from Rabaul, had already received reports of two American carrier forces by 9.00 a.m. on 7 May, and had had to react rapidly to that unpleasant news. But before he could do so another report arrived that there was a third American carrier force in the eastern Coral Sea. Not one, not two, but three! At the same time one of Admiral Hara's scouts reported a carrier and a cruiser south-south-west 200 miles. He immediately launched sixty bombers and eighteen escort fighters, only to learn an hour later that the 'cruiser' was a destroyer, the 'carrier' a tanker.

So, at this time both sides were engaged upon wild-goose chases due to wrong information, and as a consequence both main carrier formations were now in a highly vulnerable situation. Of the two, Fletcher's pilots were the luckier. They chanced upon the carrier *Shoho* – not a big fleet carrier, it is true, but a prize target none the less, especially as they had become reconciled to an aborted mission. Out of a clear blue sky from 18,000 feet poured the Dauntless dive-bombers, while the Devastator torpedo-planes came in from all directions at sea level. Lieutenant-Commander Bill Burch led his sixteen dive-bombers down on to the carrier first. 'The skipper laid one right in the middle of her flight deck,' Lieutenant Stan Vetjasa recounted. 'It was a beauty. I got a hit right after that. So did Hugh Nicolson, Art Downing, Roger Woodhull and Charlie Ware.'[8]

The *Shoho* had time to launch her Zeros but the Wildcats were there, too – and, for the first time, showing themselves to be superior in fighting qualities. Eight Zeros plummeted into the sea against the loss of three Dauntless. And as for the *Shoho*, no fewer than thirteen direct bomb hits and seven torpedoes tore her to pieces and sent her to the bottom in a few minutes – as quickly as Nagumo had done for the *Hermes*.

Much more fighting was to occur in the Coral Sea over the following hours, but this brief, ferocious engagement was an even more significant moment in the history of the Pacific sea war than Doolittle's raid on Tokyo. Admiral Nagumo's myth of invincibility during his four-month triumphant cruise had revealed a quality of material in his ships and planes, a superiority in the skill of his airmen and their weapons, and a level of strategical, tactical and logistical professionalism which had been grossly under-estimated. Now, suddenly on this May morning off the coast of Australia, flaws had become exposed, and the memorable radio call from the American Group Leader, 'Scratch one flat-top!' echoed through the whole US Pacific Fleet. The Japs were beatable after all!

Lieutenant-Commander Kakuichi Takahashi, veteran of Pearl Harbor, Wake Island, Darwin, Colombo and many more raids, commanded the Japanese strike which had been so seriously misinformed. When his planes reached the tanker and destroyer he was undecided over what to do next. In the end he compromised by dividing his force, half of which continued to search for a juicier target while the rest dealt with the ships below. The destroyer *Sims* put up a gallant fight in protection of her valuable charge but was soon overwhelmed while the bombers set about the tanker, which promptly shot a Val down into the sea.

The Japanese left the tanker ablaze and clearly doomed. But in fact some of the crew fought the fires, got them under control, and for five days drifted, powerless, before the trade winds until sighted by a scouting aircraft. The crew were later taken off but their tanker had to be sunk.

By early evening on 7 May all the fleet carriers, Japanese and American, had recovered the aircraft they had earlier launched on faulty information, with a score of one tanker and one destroyer to the Japanese, and one carrier to the US Navy. Both sides still did not know where the other's carriers were in spite of non-stop scouting. This was partly because of the dirty weather with only intermittent brief clearances in the drizzle and low cloud.

Admiral Inouye had temporarily recalled the fleet of transports heading for Port Moresby and had ordered an all-out strike by land-based bombers against Admiral Crace's cruisers, which effectually barred the route to the transports' destination. From 2.00 p.m. the cruisers were subjected to a ferocious and prolonged attack by squadrons equipped with machines simi-lar to those which had so rapidly disposed of the *Repulse* and *Prince of Wales*. But by putting up a dense barrage of anti-aircraft fire and evading bombs and torpedoes with consummate skill, none of the cruisers was hit – even when some American bombers from Australia joined in. The Japanese pilots claimed a battleship sunk, a second battleship seriously damaged and a cruiser left in flames. No wonder they so often got their numbers wrong.

So what were Fletcher and Inouye to do now? The weather remained dirty, daylight was fading. Fletcher, with the decisiveness and self-discipline which were to mark him out as one of the really great admirals of the Second World War, decided to close down for the night and prepare for the morrow, which would certainly bring about a resolution. His Task Forces had lost few planes and were buoyed up with self-confidence as a result of what they had already achieved. But the loss of that tanker was a serious blow which restricted the Task Force's mobility and made it not only likely that he would be engaged in battle the next day, but absolutely necessary that he should win it. By contrast with the days of sail, oil supplies now governed the duration of operations.

Admiral Inouye, however, was stung into making one last effort during the evening in a desperate endeavour to avenge the first loss of a navy carrier and to save the face of his Task Force. At 4.30 p.m., therefore, he launched twenty-seven bombers and torpedo-bombers – without escort as the Zero pilots, like the American fighter pilots, had not been trained in night flying. Takahashi again led the attack.

The air crews were weary from so much flying, their concentration dimmed – even Takahashi's. Anyway they saw nothing, turned at the limit of their patrol, dropped their bombs and torpedoes, and flew back right over one of the American carriers, which meanwhile had launched a squadron of Wildcats. For the American fighter pilots it was a dream end to a long day. Unseen in the half-light, they jumped a group of torpedo-bombers and shot down eight of the fifteen Kates, as well as a Val dive-bomber.

Masatake Okumiya and Jiro Horikoshi take up the account of the tragi-comedy:

Our aircraft soon fell victim to the delusions and 'mirages' brought on by exhaustion. Several times the pilots, despairing of their position over the sea, 'sighted' a friendly aircraft-carrier. Finally a carrier was sighted, and the remaining eighteen bombers switched on their signal and blinker lights as they swung into their approach and landing pattern.

As the lead aircraft, with its flaps down and speed lowered, drifted toward the carrier deck to land, the pilot discovered the great ship ahead was an American carrier! Apparently the Americans also had erred in identification, for even as the bomber dropped near the carrier deck not a single enemy gun fired. The Japanese pilot frantically opened his throttle and at full speed swung away from the vessel, followed by his astonished men.

Our aircrews were disgusted. They had flown for gruelling hours over the sea, bucked thunder squalls and, finally, had lost all trace of their positions relative to their own carriers. When finally they did sight the coveted American warship, cruising unsuspecting beneath eighteen bombers, they were without bombs or torpedoes.[9]

This was not the last act in Takahashi's dusk tragedy. Now thoroughly disorientated and scattered, the surviving air crews struggled through the rain and low cloud to locate their carriers, the needle of their fuel gauges knocking the zero pin. Admiral Hara ordered searchlights to be played on the cloud in a desperate and dangerous attempt to guide home his charges. Takahashi made it, with just a few remaining drops of fuel, and five more eventually landed safely, one with engine spluttering as it touched down. Six out of twenty-seven returned, and every man lost was a veteran of Nagumo's all-triumphant troupe. With the additional loss of a carrier, this added an even deeper gloom to the squally darkness of the night of 7–8 May 1942.

The state of tension in the American carriers – and no doubt in the Japanese carriers, too – in the late evening of 7 May 1942 had been built up as if from a prepared scenario designed to test every sailor and aviator to the utmost. So many days and nights had passed in expectation of full-scale combat, with false alarms and real alarms, aborted missions and operations that had not lived up to expectation, distant sightings of enemy scouts and despatching and recovery of their own reconnaissance planes – all these happenings that raised hopes and fears to a scarcely bearable pitch before the seemingly inevitable anti-climax.

In medieval times the knights and the common soldiery would be sharpening their lance tips and broadswords. For these twentieth-century knights of the air, with their planes readied, their weapons checked and re-checked down on the hangar decks, it was the spirit and fighting eagerness that was so important and had to be kept buoyant. This was a time when the squadron commanders especially showed their mettle and leadership.

Among them was Lieutenant Jo-Jo Powers, commanding Bombing 5 in the *Yorktown*, an Irishman from Brooklyn with a broken nose to mark his record as a boxing champion at the Navy Academy. Powers was already a bit of a legend, respected and admired by his young pilots.

Powers, that night, strode up and down as he spoke, his dark eyes burning. He recounted to [his aircrews] details of the strike on Tulagi and the attack on *Shohu*. He reminded Bombing 5 that there were still two Japanese carriers on the loose. He concluded with these words: 'Remember what they did to us at Pearl Harbor. The folks back home are counting on us. As for me, I'm going to get a hit on a Jap carrier tomorrow if I have to lay my bomb right on her flight deck.' [10]

The events of 8 May 1942 form a classical shape and sequence that contrasts with the confusion and false alarms of the build-up to battle. Not only does the climax of the Battle of Coral Sea have a tidiness quite lacking in the overture but possesses a majesty and coherence like that of few other naval battles.

Just as the *Hood* and *Bismarck* had opened fire on each other almost simultaneously in Arctic waters just a year earlier, their 2,000-pound shells passing each other in their trajectory, so in these tropical waters the aircraft of the *Lexington* and *Zuikaku* with their half-ton bombs and torpedoes passed one another *en route* to their targets. Some groups of opposing sides even sighted one another distantly between rain clouds, like mobsters hellbent on their own errands of destruction. The principle had been the same since the spears and slings of Salamis, the Spanish Armada or Trafalgar;

only the range had changed, from a few yards to 20,000 yards and now here, in the Coral Sea, to close on 200 miles.

One of Admiral Hara's scouts, despatched before dawn, had been the first to sight the big flat decks of the *Lexington* and *Yorktown* and send back the critical signal for which the Japanese had been waiting for so long. At almost the same time Lieutenant J.G.Smith from the *Lexington*, far to the north and in a rainstorm, caught a brief glimpse of the *Zuikaku* and *Shokaku*. The *Lexington* and *Yorktown* turned into wind and began launching a few minutes after 9.00 a.m. – forty-six Dauntless dive-bombers, twenty-one Devastator torpedo-bombers and fifteen Wildcats as escort.

The weather was foul all the way and some of the pilots, including Lieutenant-Commander Joe Taylor leading Torpedo Squadron 5, wondered if they were going to miss their target again. Others were more confident. 'I felt in my guts that this was going to be the real thing at last,' one pilot recalls, 'and we were all feeling pretty good after we'd put that little flat-top at the bottom of the sea the previous day.'

If the weather was tricky, the American air crews held one advantage. The two big Japanese carriers had still not closed on one another after turning to launch their aircraft and were still eight miles apart. This meant that the American strike force could concentrate on one target and face the air-patrol and anti-aircraft fire of only one carrier instead of two. By now the *Zuikaku* was obscured by cloud anyway, so it was her sister ship that the dive- and torpedo-bombers attacked, the Wildcats hovering above ready to throw themselves against any defending Zeros.

Joe Taylor lumbered in with his slow Devastators, 'flat on the deck and jinking like crazy against the tracer'. They were not all that much faster than the British Swordfish and were terribly vulnerable as they steadied for the launch. One after the other their 'tin fish' splashed, but the gunfire was so ferocious that they launched beyond accurate range, and the carrier had no trouble in turning to avoid the 30-knot projectiles, some of which were turning in circles anyway because of faults in the steering mechanism. It was a typically disheartening business for the American aviators to go through all this and be let down by their weapons. But at least the Wildcats were keeping off the Zeros in furious low-level dogfights, and they all got through the gunfire safely, if badly pock-marked by bullets and splinters.

Up above at 17,000 feet the Dauntlesses, each with a 1,000-pounder under its belly, were turning on to their backs for the long dive, a more exhilarating experience than fumbling your way through the flak just above the waves. But they had their problems, too. Owing to the freak disturbed weather conditions with erratic temperature variations, their sights and screens misted up in the dive. For a moment it was like dive-bombing blind at night; then at around 10,000 feet the glass mercifully began to clear, and the pilots of the hurtling machines kicked rudder to get on target, until the 800-foot-long deck was right below and coming up fast. Lieutenant-Commander Bill Burch leading *Yorktown*'s Scouting 5 was the first American pilot in the Pacific war to attack a Japanese fleet carrier, and his own plane and all six others were hit by flak or shell splinters on their long flight down. But the radiomen/rear-gunners were also hitting the Zeros as the stubby little fighters, wings and nose sparkling with cannon and machine-gun fire, twisted and weaved on the dive-bombers' tails. These first Dauntlesses claimed four Zeros destroyed but at the cost of failing to get a hit on the *Shokaku*, now thrashing about evasively like a great frenzied fish.

Bombing 5 which followed had an easier time of it as most of the twenty-four Zeros were occupied below. But the first pilot to make a hit was, rightly, the man who had done so much towards improving the confidence and skill of the *Yorktown*'s air crews, and had made a public promise the evening before – Jo-Jo Powers himself. Several aviators saw their hero zooming down, in and out of cloud and gunsmoke. A layman might think a near-vertical dive is like any other near-vertical dive, but the real professional looks that much faster, that much more vertical, and shows a distinctive style hard to define. The enemy appeared to have recognized this too, and were concentrating on this one machine, knocking it off its line with near-misses with heavy shells and setting it on fire.

There was a brief radio call, just a few words, like 'We're both hit....' Then the Brooklyn boxer managed to get his doomed machine on to line again, and at 1,000 feet he was right over the centre of the *Shokaku*'s flight deck. The Dauntless was a racing torch when Powers somehow released the bomb at little more than 200 feet. The flames were extinguished and the agony ended only when the bomber hit the sea alongside the carrier. But Powers had laid his 'bomb right on her flight deck', a straight right hook as he might have recounted if he had lived, knocking the *Shokaku* out of the battle.

Other dive-bombers from the *Yorktown* got near-misses, and one more hit to confirm the squadron commander's. Later a *Lexington* dive-bomber got a third hit. The total of a ton and a half of high explosive was not enough to send the carrier to the bottom but she was no more than a crippled and blazing liability to the Japanese task force, incapable of launching or landing planes now, and for a long time to come.

It had not been a well co-ordinated attack: many of the *Lexington*'s planes never even found their target, the torpedo-bombers had been thwarted and in later attacks had suffered heavy losses. The *Zuikaku*, cowering beneath heavy cloud, remained unscathed. But as the squadrons, some scattered, made their way back again, through intermittent squalls of rain and clear patches, they felt exhilarated and confident that they could 'scratch another flat-top'.

Sixty-nine hostile aircraft look more than twice that number to those manning the guns and awaiting attack, especially when the formations are seen only intermittently as they speed between cloud formations or are lost for

half a minute behind a squall. The Japanese planes sighted by the *Yorktown*
and *Lexington*'s airmen half an hour earlier also looked more than sixty-nine
in number on the *Yorktown*'s radar screen. In charge was Radioman Vane
Bennett, as near a radar veteran as you could be when they had been
introduced into the US Navy barely two years earlier. The tiny radarscope
looked like the first television sets put on the market in Britain back in
1936, but it was giving the vital warning at just 10.55 a.m. with the enemy
at sixty-eight miles range. That was an advantage any number of Japanese
scout planes could never match.

'It was one heck of a pip,' Bennett reported. 'It covered about an inch
of our five-inch scope, so I knew it meant an awful lot of planes, spread
out deep.' [11]

Maybe it was a lot of planes, but at least the warning could be given
well before they were overhead, and the pathetically inadequate total of
fifteen Wildcat fighters, including those on standing patrol, were prepared.
A handful of Dauntlesses – all that were left – were also hastily launched
to act the role of fighter, for which they were ill equipped.

It was evident to Admiral Fletcher and his staff that they would have
to rely chiefly on the ships' guns, and their powers of evasion, for their
defence. Every gun had been manned for some time in expectation of this
attack – the .5s, 1.1-inch and heavy 5s. 'Well,' Fletcher was heard to say,
'we've done all we can. I guess the only thing left to do is put on this
tin hat.' [12]

At 11.06 a.m. Radioman Bennett, his screen half-filled with blips, reported
the nearest enemy planes at twenty miles. Five minutes later look-outs were
getting the first sightings. 'Air department take cover. Gunnery department
take over,' came the command on the carriers' loudspeakers. Both carriers,
escort tight around them, were heading south-east, speed 30 knots.

The Japanese Vals, Kates and Zeros were being guided on to their target
by the reconnaissance plane which had earlier spotted the American force
and now was returning to ensure there could be no navigational error,
even though the pilot knew he had not enough fuel to get him back to
his ship.

The duel began at 11.18 a.m., the first shots from the heavy gunfire blasting
out from the ships, while the Wildcats clawed up towards the Vals, still
at 17,000 feet, before they could turn over into their dive. The noise
increased to a crescendo as the Kates came in fast and low – almost twice
as fast as the American Devastators – downwind, from the north-east,
fanning out, first concentrating on both bows of the fatter target, 'Lady Lex'.

Seconds later the *Yorktown* was getting the same treatment, but she had
been designed from the keel up for this sort of occasion and answered
the helm almost like a destroyer, combing the torpedoes' tracks. She evaded
all the tin fish but, like the *Lexington*, at the cost of losing formation with
the five cruisers and seven destroyers, whose firepower would be missed
when the Vals came down; which they did when the Kates were clear.

The *Lexington* had managed to avoid most of the torpedoes, but not all. The two strikes on her port side sent a shudder through the ship and her speed began to fall off as three of her sixteen boiler-rooms had to be shut down. When the Vals reached the limit of their dives, they got three hits on the carrier, too. While there were many casualties and the ship assumed a list of 7 degrees, the structural damage was not too serious, and with some repairs it was judged that she could still take an active part in operations.

When the next wave of bombers came down, the sky was already studded with a thousand black spots, as if someone had thrown a giant paint brush, and the criss-cross of light tracer formed an anarchic, ever-changing pattern. It did not seem as if any aircraft could penetrate such a lethal screen, but this was a lesson soon to be learned in carrier warfare, for they almost all did. It was the fighters, even the Dauntlesses, that were doing the damage rather than the ships' guns as the Kates and Vals concentrated on their targets, or on getting away again. Among the twenty-six which fell to the fighters was Commander Takahashi's, as great a loss to the Japanese air arm as Jo-Jo Powers to the Americans.

It says much for the American carriers' defences, and the strength of the ships, that no more serious damage resulted from this mid-morning mass assault. The *Yorktown* took an 800-pound bomb, which created some internal damage and caused a number of casualties. But this carrier, too, remained serviceable for flying operations.

Again the number of near-misses and the turmoil and tumult of the ship–aircraft battle left a very different impression of the results on the minds of the Japanese air crew. They reported on return that one carrier was sinking and that the second was badly damaged by three torpedo hits and eight direct bomb hits. They needed something to cheer after their savage losses.

Both Admirals were suffering under a delusion, brought about by the highly exaggerated claims of their pilots. For Coral Sea was not only the first fleet action since Jutland in 1916; it was also the first fleet action in which officers in command had perforce to rely upon the observations of a handful of combat-dazed airmen rather than what they themselves could see from the bridge or conning tower of their ship.

In the event, the *Shokaku* was so badly damaged, with internal fires still blazing, that she was incapable of landing back her own planes, and the *Zuikaku* proved incapable of taking them, either, due to slow handling and stowing of the returning aircraft and flight-deck confusion. This led to a number of aircraft having to be tipped overboard to make room for returning *Shokaku* aircraft and others 'splashing' fuelless into the sea. This resulted in an overall Japanese loss of forty-five aircraft out of seventy-two operational at the outset of the battle on 7 May.

The Japanese carrier task force was thus incapable of further operations and retired, the *Shokaku* beginning a long and painful voyage back to Japan, her condition deteriorating with every day, mainly as a result of the many near-misses which had bent and distorted her hull plates, letting in so much water that at one point she almost capsized.

All the same, the American high command was puzzled to know why the Port Moresby invasion did not take place after the withdrawal of the American carrier force. The answer to this lay – and here was a turning of the tables! – in the threat of land-based American bombers in north Australia and Port Moresby and the loss of the *Shoho* with the Zeros that were intended to provide air cover for the transports. For the first time since early December, Japan had lost the initiative, lost control of the sea in a vital area and been frustrated in her ambitions by loss of control of the air, too.

But Coral Sea was not an American tactical or statistical victory, either. 'We thought we had won until "Lady Lex" blew up,' recalled one officer. The catastrophe began at 12.47 p.m. The *Lexington*'s fires were by then under control; she was able to steam 25 knots in spite of a list of 7 degrees and, while her lifts were inoperable, recovered aircraft were parked on her ample flight deck. Commander R.H. Healy, damage-control officer, was confident that the ship could make it to Pearl Harbor for repairs, and had even joked to his captain that if they were going to be torpedoed again, would he please try to arrange for the hits to be on the starboard side.

But below decks the fumes from several fuel pipes and fractured tanks had been steadily building up towards the point where the smallest spark would suffice to ignite them. This was the Achilles' heel of all carriers, leading to other tragedies and much loss of life until the problem was mastered. A sparking commutator in a motor generator room provided this ignition. The explosion sent flames high into the air followed by black smoke. Anyone who had seen the *Hood* blow up the previous May would have expected the same consequences. But in the perverse and unpredictable way of fire, this one died down and was eventually brought under control. Then more explosions followed the first, and stage by stage, as if she were the target of intermittent shellfire, the *Lexington* lost her capacity to survive.

At 5.07 p.m. the order was given to abandon ship. The Captain remained on board a while longer, until a huge explosion burst through the flight deck, hurling all her aircraft into the air, killing many men, including Healy. It was the planes' last flight, just as it was the *Lexington*'s last hour. The Captain left his sinking ship with the carrier looking like a Pacific atoll overwhelmed by a sudden volcano, black smoke billowing high into the sky.

The destroyer *Phelps*, which had enjoyed the distinction of shooting down one of Admiral Nagumo's bombers over Pearl Harbor back in December, now filled the wreck of the great carrier with torpedos in case the Japanese attempted to salvage her. At about 8.00 p.m., according to

Sam Morison, 'the battered amazon gave up her ghost with one final and awful detonation as, head up, she slipped into a 2,400-fathom deep'.

'I couldn't watch her go,' one eyewitness said, according to Morison, 'and men who had been with her since she was commissioned in '27 stood with tears streaming.' And another sailor said, 'All the fellows were crying and weeping like young girls, so was I.' [13]

Over 2,700 men were rescued from the carrier, and only some 200 were killed by the Japanese – a mercifully small toll under the circumstances. The *Lexington* also took down with her thirty-six of her planes, making a heavy toll of sixty-nine for the day.

The strategic American victory at Coral Sea, and the halt to Japanese southern conquests, had a profound political consequence, too, especially for Australia and New Zealand. The Australasian people, who had contributed so many young men and so much of the nations' resources in the First World War, especially at Gallipoli, had been willing to make a similar sacrifice twenty-five years later. By 1941 Australian and New Zealand sailors, soldiers and airmen were serving on every battle front. Then, with the entry of Japan into the World War, Australia and New Zealand suddenly felt as threatened as Britain by Germany. Historically dependent upon the mother country for their protection, the two Commonwealth nations watched with growing fears the loss of British naval and military power in the Far East bastions of Imperial strength, Hong Kong and Singapore.

And now, it was not Britain that lifted the threat of conquest by Japan but the mighty military power of the United States. From May 1942 the people of New Zealand and Australia have looked east to North America 6,000 miles distant for security from military threat, be it Japanese or Russian, rather than to a post-Imperial and gravely weakened Britain on the other side of the world. The presence of thousands of American servicemen and women, of General Douglas MacArthur himself and his Staff, of hundreds of American warplanes and many American naval vessels, represented more than the convenience of bases for the eventual counter-attack and assault against the Japanese Empire. It represented a massive shift of a continent's allegiance and dependency in the free world.

CHAPTER NINE

Midway: The Invisible Enemy

At 7.06 a.m. on 4 June 1942 Lieutenant-Commander Clarence Wade McClusky, strapped into the cockpit of his Dauntless dive-bomber, signalled 'Chocks away' and eased the throttle wide open through its quadrant. It was many years since the veteran McClusky had made his first carrier take-off, with deck crewmen watching the rookie with keen critical eyes. Another pilot had once remarked that it was like going on stage for your first audition. Confidence and rank, and several hundred previous take-offs, had changed all that. Now he was the lead star stepping forth into the footlights, while high above as if from the royal box the admiral, the ship's captain and their staffs on the bridge peered down to admire the opening of the first act.

McClusky's Dauntless, powered by a 1,000-horsepower radial engine, pounded down the deck, tail wheel up, into the light south-easterly breeze, augmented by the 25 knots of the carrier. He left cleanly, without a bounce, taking into the air, besides the SBD itself and its crew, a bomb load of one 500-pounder beneath the belly and a 100-pounder under each wing. Undercarriage up, flaps up, ease back the mixture control, prop pitch from full fine, throttle back as secure height is gained – all this was routine to the commander of the *Enterprise*'s Carrier Group Six (CVG-6). Non-routine was the stark fact that this stage appearance was no rehearsal – not this time. McClusky's Group, already assembling about him, would soon be heading south-west on its first-ever wartime mission against enemy carriers. And what a mighty group he would be heading – twenty-seven Wildcat fighters under Lieutenant James S. Gray, thirty-eight Dauntlesses of VF-6 and VB-6, and fourteen Devastators with their torpedoes under the command of Lieutenant-Commander Eugene F. Lindsay.

A short distance away the second carrier of Task Force 16, the *Hornet* (also back from the Doolittle Tokyo raid), was launching the same number of aircraft. And that was not all. Out of sight over the horizon that blooded carrier of the Coral Sea battle, the *Yorktown*, would soon be launching her attack. The American high command knew the approximate strength and position of the enemy; while, just twenty minutes after McClusky took to the air and waited circling for the Group to form up about him, one of those ubiquitous Japanese scout seaplanes had been spotted hovering like some dark bird of doom on the southern horizon, reporting all that her crew observed.

So this fair June day in the central Pacific seemed certain to witness a battle and a decision that could change the course of history.

'Midway Island acts as a sentry for Hawaii,' declared Admiral Nagumo, which was the primary reason for the presence of four of his most powerful carriers, and a veritable armada of other warships, a short distance north-west of the island on this morning. It was also the reason for the blistering bombing attack he had already delivered before McClusky or any of his pilots had strapped on their parachutes on that early morning. Midway is a typical Pacific atoll of volcanic origin, six miles in diameter, the coral barrier reef like a platinum ring set with two diamonds, in reality islets averaging a mile and a half long. They carry the unimaginative names of Sand Island and Eastern Island. Midway was claimed by the United States in 1867 as part of the Hawaiian chain, which indeed it is, though 1,135 miles distant from Oahu and Pearl Harbor. And, until recently, no one after that had taken much interest in it.

In 1903, according to Admiral Morison,[1] the US Navy took over responsibility for the atoll when it became a station on the cable laid between Oahu and Manila in the Philippines. It is said that a US Navy officer, Hugh Rodman (later the Rear-Admiral commanding the American Squadron serving with the British Grand Fleet in the First World War), chased off a party of Japanese feather hunters to underline the American claim. Forty years later the Japanese returned with more weighty purpose.

Closer naval attention was paid to Midway after Roosevelt, that arch-navalist, became President. Facilities for seaplanes and then the big Catalina flying boats were put in hand from 1935, when Pan American Airways also took a commercial interest in the place as a staging-post for its trans-Pacific clipper flying boats. A 5,300-foot airstrip was built, and construction contracts totalling some $250 million were in hand at the time of Pearl Harbor.

From December 1941, when there could no longer be any doubt of the island's vital importance as a 'midway' base between Pearl Harbor and Tokyo Bay, the build-up of offensive and defensive material was rapid, and there were over 100 aircraft there in December 1941, including four-engine B-17 Flying Fortress bombers.

In mid-May 1942 Admiral Nagumo and his superior, Admiral Yamamoto – and the whole Japanese naval high command for that matter – were still well pleased with themselves. They had every reason to believe that, sooner or later, Port Moresby would drop like a ripe cherry into their hands. The Battle of Coral Sea had, in their estimate, revealed the weakness and inferiority of the American naval air arm, which had lost one, and probably two, of its scarce fleet carriers. The British Eastern Fleet was, thanks to Nagumo's Easter raid, not a force to bother about.

Midway, and the western Aleutian Islands far to the north, were the obvious next targets on the all-conquering naval advance east towards Hawaii. The need to capture Midway was intensified by the Doolittle raid, which had so thoroughly upset the *amour propre* of the Japanese high command. Not only would a further movement east make such raids virtually impossible, but there were some authorities in Tokyo who believed that the Mitchells had in fact flown from Midway and not from a carrier at all.

On 5 May 1942, therefore, Imperial Headquarters issued the order: 'Commander-in-Chief Combined Fleet will, in co-operation with the Army, invade and occupy strategic points in the Western Aleutians and Midway Island.' It was this message and subsequent events which had led to Lieutenant-Commander McClusky's taking off from the Enterprise just one month later, with three bombs secured beneath his aircraft. But so confident were the Japanese of achieving their targets that all preparations for the next stage of advance – Samoa, Fiji and New Caledonia – were already well in hand.

It is easy enough to understand the Japanese belief in their superiority and their conviction that little stood between them and American–Australasian surrender in the Pacific. Except briefly and not seriously in the Coral Sea, they had triumphed everywhere. They had ten carriers to America's one or perhaps two – or so they believed. They had twelve battleships, including the world's mightiest, and most of the rest were superior to their American counterparts – those few that had survived Pearl Harbor. Their heavy cruisers were more powerful, their light cruisers swifter, their destroyers more than a match for modern American destroyers. Their submarines were first class, their long lance torpedoes ten times more lethal than the crank, unreliable American torpedoes. And as for their planes, it is necessary only to contrast the Kate torpedo-bomber with the American Devastator torpedo-bomber:

Kate	Devastator
Speed (loaded): 220 mph	Speed (loaded): 115 mph
Range: 1,220 miles	Range: 455 miles
Armament: 4 machine-guns	Armament: 2 machine-guns
Load: 1 18-inch 1,764-pound torpedo	Load: 1 18-inch 1,300-pound torpedo

The IJN also enjoyed the advantage of longer experience in naval aviation. Even before the Washington Naval Treaty of 1921–2 had restricted Japanese battleship strength to two-thirds of American strength, the Japanese had recognized that air power could compensate for their own inferiority in numbers. By the early 1930s Japan had the most advanced naval air arm in the world. Throughout the IJN there was a confidence and pride in it with none of the doubts and even hostility some senior American and British officers felt towards aviation. In the RN and the USN it was the gunnery officer who was still held in greatest esteem and – especially in the British Navy – pilots were regarded in some quarters rather as hell-for-leather playboys.

In May 1942 there was nothing wrong with the IJN's morale or material. It remained what it had shown itself to be over the past six months: the most determined, professional and effective navy in the world. At every level of rank and trade it was efficient and fearless, except at the top. Here there was a fault so grave that it cancelled out many of the advantages so painstakingly built up since the legendary Admiral Togo had defeated the Russian Fleet in 1905. Togo had shown a marked aptitude for strategy; he would have been in despair had he been alive to witness the follies of his successors.

It is not easy for the Western mind to understand the Japanese urge to weave and then embroider a pattern of strategic complexity, coloured by surprise, spotted with devious traps and curlicues that were feints or counter-feints. Togo and his commanders had learnt their naval strategy in the British school of Nelsonian simplicity based on straightforward offensive and the principle of never dividing your forces, and of such instructions to his captains as 'they might adopt whatever [tactics] they thought best, provided it led them quickly and closely alongside the enemy'. Since Togo's time, and the Battle of Tsu-Shima in 1905 – a Nelsonian Trafalgar-like victory if ever there was one – strategical and tactical principles alike had become distorted in the Japanese Navy. The broad sweep of strategy as conceived long before Pearl Harbor was copybook: a smashing surprise blow, rapidly followed up with widespread attacks to all points of the compass with the enemy still reeling; then consolidation, advance, consolidation, all swiftly carried out with just time for the build-up of supplies and securing of lines of communication before the next push forward.

Then the Coral Sea operations showed for the first time the Japanese weakness for dividing its forces and contriving an over-elaborate strategy which had everyone but the enemy confused. If Yamamoto had despatched the full strength of Nagumo's carrier strike force to the south-west Pacific to support the Port Moresby operation, it is hardly conceivable that there would have been any survivors of Admiral Fletcher's Task Force – with the most baleful consequences for the Americans, Australians and New Zealanders. If the strategic planning for Port Moresby was over-complex, the strategic planning for Midway and the Aleutians was positively tortuous. This was Yamamoto's operation plan:

It would open with a 'Pearl Harbor' on Dutch Harbor, the American base in the Aleutians. This was to be at the same time a feint to confuse Nimitz and an actual preliminary to an invasion of the western Aleutians.

Next, Nagumo's carrier force the following day (4 June) was to bomb the heart out of Midway, prior to an invasion by 5,000 troops. Now Admiral Nimitz would, it was fondly believed, be puzzled to decide whether to go north to counter the Aleutian operation or east to prevent the fall of Midway.

If Nimitz sent all his surviving carriers to Midway, Nagumo would deal with them with his invincible carriers, while Yamamoto himself, flying his flag in the mighty *Yamato* and with a crushing superiority of surface ships, supported by submarines, would carry out the *coup de grâce*.

At dusk on 5 June the troops would go ashore on Midway, and Yamamoto would have a fine air base within bombing distance of Pearl Harbor. Yamamoto would then detach four of his seven battleships, supported by cruisers, to a position half way between the two widely separated operations in order to cover any counter-attack by Nimitz's now much-depleted forces.

This whole vast operation, covering millions of square miles of the central and northern Pacific, had been worked out and discussed exhaustively in the course of numerous war games and exercises before the war as if it were championship chess. All the preliminary permutations, and the solution itself, depended on one presupposition: surprise, that priceless ingredient which governed all Japanese strategical considerations. Surprise, throughout the history of warfare, has always depended on intelligence superior to the enemy's. Once again the Japanese commanders were not so privileged. And the American commanders were.

Even before the Coral Sea action the first indications of a major offensive in the central Pacific were being interpreted by American intelligence at Pearl Harbor. Here the cryptographers were 'reading' Japanese signals referring repeatedly to 'scheduled operations' and the 'imminent campaign'. There were references to expediting supplies and refuelling at sea, and later in the month to a demand for 'delivery during May of the replacement planes for use in the second phase'. More specifically, on 24 May the code-breakers read of deliveries of Zeros to Nagumo's crack carriers, *Akagi*, *Hiryu*, *Kaga* and *Soryu*. What could be the final destination of the military equipment, including shells, torpedoes and bombs, ordered to be delivered to the island of Truk 'during the forthcoming campaign'?

By the middle of May Nimitz was convinced that a major operation was imminent in the mid-Pacific. If he knew precisely where, he could take appropriate steps to counter it and dispose his inadequate forces accordingly. At Pearl Harbor two intelligence officers, Lieutenant-Commanders Edwin T. Layton and Joseph J. Rochefort, proposed to 'plant' some information on their enemy opposite numbers in the hope of acquiring this much-needed information.

This idea of 'planting' was not new. The British had used it in the First World War, and again more recently. The procedure was to carry out a minor offensive operation in the certain knowledge that it would be reported by the enemy in a low-grade code which was already being read, and in the hope that it would later be passed on in a higher-grade code which the British were seeking to break. It was like a back-door entry and depended primarily, like all code-breaking, on assumption.

For Pearl Harbor intelligence, the agreed premise was that the Japanese target was Midway. One of the difficulties of Midway as a base, which would be known to the Japanese, was that it had no fresh water and was dependent on a water distillation system. Midway was therefore instructed *by cable* to broadcast *en clair* that the water distillation apparatus had broken down, a drastic state of affairs. This message was certain to be monitored by the Japanese. What was uncertain was whether the listener would then re-transmit the information to higher authority in a code which the Americans had already broken. But it was all right; he did, using the letters A and F as a geographical code locator. Pearl Harbor then signalled *en clair* that a repair party would soon be on the way.

AF? Could that mean Midway? There was no way of telling; or there was not until someone remembered that those location letters were used at the time of an abortive seaplane attack on Pearl Harbor two months earlier. These planes had had to refuel from a submarine located at French Frigate Shoals near Midway and then had signalled that they had passed near AF *en route*. There was only one island on that line of flight: Midway.

The next thing the cryptographers picked up was an enemy signal ordering a water ship to be included in the forthcoming operation. *Quod erat demonstrandum.*

And so it came about that two American carrier Task Forces were in precisely the right place at the right time to challenge the gigantic double offensive operation set in train by Admiral Yamamoto, in the almost certain knowledge of the time and weight of the attack on Midway. And Admiral Yamamoto had no means of knowing the Americans were there. The code-breakers had helped to get the Americans to the right place at the right time, but other factors were involved and other difficulties had to be overcome – by admirals and riveters, airmen and storemen, engineers and signal officers. And some of the difficulties had at one time appeared insuperable.

Admiral Nelson had once declared that when he died, there would be engraved upon his heart the single word 'frigate'. Never in all his campaigns did he have enough frigates, and this scarcity was a constant anxiety for him. Admiral Chester W. Nimitz in 1942 might have made the same declaration in terms of the aircraft carrier. After the Doolittle raid he had not been able to get the *Enterprise* and *Hornet* back in time to support the *Lexington* and *Yorktown* in the Coral Sea. After that engagement he could scratch together for operations over the entire Pacific Ocean – one-third of the globe's surface – just two carriers, the *Enterprise* and *Hornet*. The *Lexington* was lost, her sister ship still recovering from being torpedoed and working up her air group off the west coast of America. The *Yorktown*, though afloat and mobile, was non-operational from her injuries at Coral

Sea, and it would take three months to repair and refit her. The need for a third carrier was desperate.

It was at this point that Admiral King in Washington swallowed his pride and against all the instincts of his deep Anglophobia asked for the support of a British carrier from the Far East Fleet. Pride also prohibited him from divulging to the British Admiralty the extent of the American losses at Coral Sea, including the sinking of the *Lexington*. Dudley Pound was under the impression that the battle had been an overwhelming American victory. King was therefore a victim of his own vaingloriousness and American propaganda, but he did not see it like this.

This is how Admiral King saw things: one American carrier was in the Mediterranean and another in the Atlantic, fighting in a war which King persisted in judging to be of secondary importance, and he therefore reasoned that it was the least the Royal Navy could do to spare one of its fast armoured carriers for the Pacific. What King did not know was that, without reference to Washington, General Douglas MacArthur in Australia had already made a request direct to Churchill for a British carrier only a month earlier and, after Churchill complained to Roosevelt at this short-circuiting of communications, had been turned down, as had a similar request direct to Washington. MacArthur was told to address such future requests properly through the United States Chiefs of Staff in Washington. Roosevelt excused the *gaffe* by telling Churchill (30 April 1942) that 'the command set-up in Australia is complex and understandings in certain details are reached only as they arise'. Just so.

With no possibility of carrier reinforcement from outside, Nimitz just had to make do with what he had: the *Enterprise* with experienced air crews and high morale; the *Hornet* with green air crews which had yet to see action; and the crippled *Yorktown*. As three carriers were the rock-bottom minimum to face the massive Midway assault, two to attack, one in reserve, the only solution was to do a rapid job on the *Yorktown* to make her fit for action.

The battered carrier limped into Pearl Harbor at 2.10 p.m. on 27 May; she needed to be in position off Midway, with her consorts, at latest by dawn on 4 June, the predicted D-Day for Nagumo's assault. Like termites 1,400 dockies descended on her – welders, electricians, riveters, shipwrights and all the other tradesmen. They were given two days and two nights to restore in a makeshift manner the structural strength of the big ship. Walter Lord graphically recounts what followed:

There was no time for plans or sketches. The men worked directly with the steel beams and bars brought on the ship. Coming to a damaged frame, burners would take out the worst of it: fitters would line up a new section, cut it to match the contour of the damage; riggers and welders would move in, 'tacking' the new piece in place.... And it was hell down there besides – 120° temperature, little light, lots of smoke. When a man looked really ready to drop, Bennett ['the burly supervisor'] would send him topside for a sandwich and a breath of air. He himself

Two of the greatest British fighting admirals of the war: Andrew Cunningham, who kept hopes alive and sea lanes open in the darkest days of the Mediterranean operations; and James Somerville, whose theatres of command ranged from the North Atlantic, through the western Mediterranean, to the Indian Ocean and Far East, finally to head the British Admiralty Mission in Washington.

Below: Malta convoy: a Fleet Air Arm Hurricane prepares to take off from the *Victorious*, while a Fairey Albacore becomes airborne from the *Indomitable*. The third carrier is the *Eagle*, shortly to be sunk.

The ubiquitous 'Stringbag': she may have looked like a First World War bomber, and against a strong headwind some Italian warships could outpace her, but the Swordfish's successes included putting the *Bismarck* out of action and knocking out half the Italian battle fleet at Taranto.

The battleship *Warspite*, severely damaged at Jutland in 1916, did noble service in the Mediterranean as Admiral Cunningham's flagship.

HMS *Renown* being bombed while on convoy escort, with Admiral Somerville's flagship *Malaya* in foreground.

The battered but life-sustaining tanker *Ohio* is nursed into Grand Harbour, Malta, 15 August 1942, after her heroic voyage.

German and Italian aircrew were accustomed to the fire from 2-pounder 8-barrel pom-poms, but suffered an unpleasant surprise when the battleship *Nelson* opened up with her 16-inch main armament during 'Operation Pedestal', August 1942.

The troopship *Aquitania*, part of a 1942 convoy to Freetown, passes ahead of her temporarily broken-down guard, HMS *Nelson*.

Bari, 2 December 1943. 'Four German bombers suddenly appeared out of nowhere, dropped their loads, and were gone. The damage was awful.' One of the sixteen ships lost was an ammunition ship, another an American freighter loaded with mustard gas (lighter colour) seen here escaping into the murk of the great fires.

Arctic warfare in the Barents Sea: the fatally damaged cruiser HMS *Edinburgh*, loaded with Russian gold, receives the *coup de grâce* from the last torpedo of HMS *Foresight*, Commander J.S.C.Salter RN, 08.30 hrs, 2 May 1942.

To keep flying in the Arctic, the crews of carriers, like HMS *Fencer*, fought a non-stop battle against the elements as well as the enemy.

The Royal Navy's Fleet Air Arm at last has a truly formidable fighter-bomber, in the American Chance Vought Corsair. At first thought unsuitable for carrier operation by the US Navy, the British showed the way and used it with tremendous effect. Aircrews here prepare for a sortie from HMS *Formidable*.

The surrender of the Italian Navy, September 1943. The giant battleship *Italia* under the guns of Malta, a destroyer in the background.

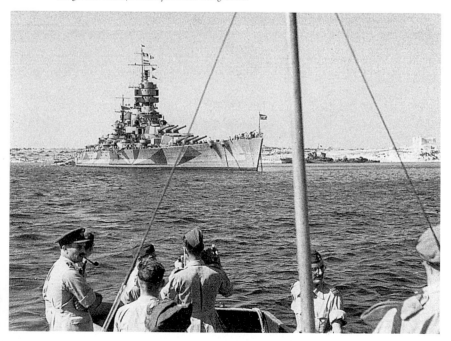

Converted trawlers played a big part in American east coast convoys. This is HMS *Northern Dawn*, under repair from ice damage, Nova Scotia 1942. She was one of a number of trawlers built in Germany before the war for Unilever's fishing fleet, and was the first to fit radar – abaft the funnel.

These 18-inch torpedoes are destined for a Swordfish operation; 8-gun Fairey Fulmars in the background.

never bothered with any of that. Occasionally sucking an orange, he worked for 48 hours straight.[2]

At night, with a million sparks flying, the blue welders' flames and arc lights illuminating the scene, it was like the bowels of hell. The citizens of Honolulu, though they did not know it, contributed passively, too, for such was the demand for electricity from the *Yorktown*'s drydock that areas of the city were successively blacked out. The *Yorktown* was out of her dock at 11.00 a.m. on 29 May; refuelled and replenished, she headed for the open sea on 30 May and began flying on her air group: twenty-seven new Mark 3 Wildcat fighters, fourteen Devastators and thirty-seven Dauntlesses.

As the flagship of Task Force 17 the *Yorktown* had as escort two heavy cruisers, the *Astoria* and *Portland*, and five destroyers. Task Force 16, comprising the *Enterprise* and *Hornet* with their escort and tankers, had already left. The two forces were to rendezvous at a position north-east of Midway. It was code-named 'Point Luck', and it was generally agreed that they would need it. Nimitz had told them that they could expect to face two to four fast battleships, four or five carriers, eight or nine heavy cruisers, four to five light cruisers, sixteen to twenty-four destroyers and about twenty-five submarines. Against them the US Navy could deploy three carriers, one without battle experience and one sketchily repaired, seven heavy cruisers, fourteen destroyers and nineteen submarines. In command of the American task forces was one admiral who had never commanded a carrier group before, and another who, in the opinion of Admiral King, was unfit for his task.

Admiral King, like some reincarnated member of the British Admiralty Staff of 1914, had delusions that he could run the war at sea from Washington. This 'Father knows best' policy had led King to signal Fletcher critically in the Coral Sea when he quite mistakenly believed that this Admiral was flinching from facing the enemy and using refuelling as an excuse. 'The situation in the area where you are now operating requires constant activity of a task force like yours to keep enemy occupied,' King had signalled rebukingly. He had in fact got wrong both Fletcher's position and his intentions. But King's pride never allowed him to accept this, nor to alter his judgement of Fletcher for the rest of the war.

Nimitz, a much bigger man than King in every particular, accepted fully Fletcher's explanation of his action, and then found himself having to defend his subordinate to his superior – pretty acrimoniously at that. He got his way, but it all left a sour taste. It was particularly important that his opinion should prevail because Halsey had suddenly become unfit for command. The stress of the past months, culminating in the risky Doolittle raid, had caused the Admiral to break out into a form of dermatitis, so bad and so irritating that he had to be admitted to hospital. He recommended that his cruiser commander, Rear-Admiral Raymond A. Spruance, should take his place as Commander of Task Force 16.

Spruance, with no experience of commanding anything bigger than a cruiser division, and with no aviation experience, turned out to be a brilliant choice. Many people commented later – and it is said that Fletcher was one – that it was a great blessing for the US Navy and for America when Halsey was struck down. Immensely popular, especially with the lower deck, and a fine seaman though he was, Halsey was the Admiral Beatty of the Second World War – flamboyant and stylish, immensely brave and aggressive but also inclined to be impulsive. He certainly did not possess the brain of his successor and subordinate, and when the odds are stacked against you, careful calculation is an asset.

Spruance was junior to Fletcher, too, so the combined Task Forces were under the command of the Admiral with the single carrier when the two forces rendezvoused at Point Luck. This they did at 3.50 p.m. on 2 June, a murky afternoon with heavy cloud around and occasional rain. It had been the same at Coral Sea. Was this a good or a bad omen?

Seen from a latter-day spacecraft, the central and north Pacific in the last days of May and first days of June 1942 would be scored by the wakes of more than 200 Japanese vessels, forming convoluted patterns from as far towards the Arctic as 53° North and as close to the equator as 13° North. The white trace lines most clearly visible were created by Yamamoto's battleship force and Admiral Nagumo's 30,000-ton carriers; while the presence of Japanese patrol vessels off the Aleutians and minesweepers off Wake Island would scarcely be discernible in this imaginary global view of the build-up before the offensive.

Among the tens of thousands of sailors and aviators manning this immense and widespread armada, two key figures had unfortunately been struck down. Like Napoleon before Waterloo, Yamamoto was in considerable pain, in his case from his stomach rather than his piles; while Commander Mitsuo Fuchida, commander of the *Akagi*'s air group, who had led the Pearl Harbor attack, was down with appendicitis and was distraught that he could not repeat that triumph.

But everything was running according to plan, and Yamamoto could flatter himself that he was one up on the enemy in the intelligence in his possession. For the IJN also had its secret sources of information on the American Navy. Radio traffic picked up by Japanese intelligence suggested unusual activity at Pearl Harbor. Much of it recently – some 40 per cent – was of a high-priority nature, which suggested that something big was afoot. Later, it had become clear that a carrier force was at sea. But where? And in what strength?

Far away in the south-west Pacific two American cruisers were playing at being carriers, pretending to launch and land aircraft with all the accompanying signals. These were transmitted on a waveband known to be listened to by Japanese intelligence. If there were two carriers as distant as these, and a maximum of three in the Pacific altogether (as was the new Japanese estimate), then the carrier off Pearl Harbor must be working alone, surmised Japanese intelligence. That was the reasoning in Tokyo anyway. Yamamoto was not so sure. But, despite his stomach pain, he experienced no loss of confidence in the effectiveness of the overall plan, nor in Admiral Nagumo's ability to deal with any opposition put up by the Americans. And, as far as intelligence on Midway itself was concerned, he had a submarine watching every event and every move on the island, like a spectator in a front stall seat in a darkened auditorium.

I-168's commander, Yahachi Tenabe, spent three days watching the island at close range through his periscope and three nights on the surface ranging over the atoll with his powerful night glasses. The scale of activity could only be described as frenzied, with defences and buildings going up by the glare of arc lights, and never a moment when an aircraft – a Buffalo fighter, a four-engine B-17 bomber, a Catalina – was not approaching to land or taking off down the long runway. Tenabe observed these long-range Catalinas going out in the morning on a westerly course and returning at dusk, certain evidence of very long-range reconnaissance.

All this intelligence, and more, was despatched in a constant stream to Japanese headquarters, and to Yamamoto and Nagumo as they approached the island for the first assault. But if any officer interpreted it as evidence that Operation MI(dway) had been rumbled, no report was presented. Perhaps the intelligence officers did not want to believe it, or perhaps they did not want to make their conclusion known for fear of attracting wrath or being proved wrong. Perhaps it would have been futile to do so, high command having made up its mind that the operation must go ahead anyway. Or, most likely, Yamamoto and Nagumo thought that the Americans knew that they were coming and welcomed the inevitable battle that must ensue, confident in their own superior strength and skill.

The Battle of Midway opened with a muffled overture, far to the north, when aircraft from two Japanese carriers bombed the American base at Dutch Harbor. It was not a very serious or successful business. The weather was terrible, the target hard to locate, the damage committed, including that to a hospital and a Russian orthodox church, not serious. For the Americans, with a notional list of events in sequence, this was the number-one item, and it was ticked off with increased confidence that the order would now conform all the way to the last and biggest item, the outcome of which still had a bold question mark against it.

On that same morning of 3 June at 8.43 a.m. in the central Pacific west of Midway a Catalina crew sighted a suspicious unidentified small ship. It was a moment to compare with the opening of the previous greatest naval contest of the twentieth century, when a British scouting cruiser had sighted an unidentified little steamer in the North Sea, a seemingly unimportant preliminary to the discovery in turn of ever-bigger men o'war and

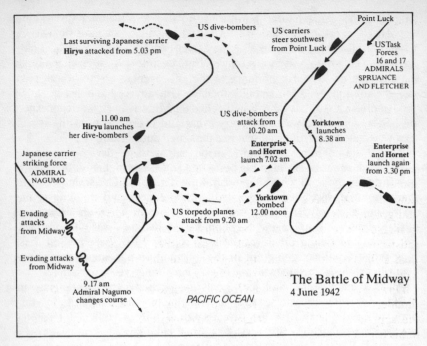

Point Luck

US dive-bombers

US carriers
steer southwest
from Point Luck

US Task
Forces
16 and 17
ADMIRALS
SPRUANCE
AND FLETCHER

Last surviving Japanese carrier
Hiryu attacked from 5.03 pm

US dive-bombers
attack from
10.20 am

Yorktown
launches
8.38 am

Enterprise
and **Hornet**
launch again
from 3.30 pm

11.00 am
Hiryu launches
her dive-bombers

Enterprise
and **Hornet**
launch 7.02 am

Japanese carrier
striking force
ADMIRAL
NAGUMO

Evading
attacks
from Midway

Yorktown
bombed
12.00 noon

US torpedo planes
attack from 9.20 am

Evading attacks
from Midway

9.17 am
Admiral Nagumo
changes course

PACIFIC OCEAN

The Battle of Midway
4 June 1942

finally of the German High Seas Fleet itself.

Ensign Jewell H. Reid, the Catalina's skipper, next reported more ships, which turned out to be units from the Japanese minesweeping group *en route* from Wake Island to Midway. As Reid continued his patrol he reported more and more vessels, at one time misidentifying them as 'the main body'. In fact he had chanced on the transports carrying the invasion groups, and the first positive military move in the battle was the despatch from Midway of a squadron of B-17 Flying Fortresses, each armed with four 600-pound bombs. The transports were duly found just before 4.30 p.m. and bombed from 8,000 feet, the bombers claiming hits on six ships, two battleships, two cruisers and two transports. In fact every bomb missed and the group continued on its course towards Midway, happy with this evidence of American inaccuracy.

Just as it was a Catalina that made the first sighting, by an odd stroke of fate it was another of these PBYs that committed the first damage to the enemy. Guided by new airborne radar, Lieutenant Charles Hibberd found the transports again in bright moonlight, and at very short range succeeded in putting a torpedo into the bow of a tanker: a Japanese torpedo would have blown her to bits. Nevertheless, the Lieutenant flew back to

Midway highly pleased with himself.

Unaware of this little skirmish, Admiral Nagumo prepared to strike at Midway, increasing the speed of his carriers to 25 knots until he was in a position 250 miles to the north-west of the island. He intended to commit only half his air strength on the Midway attack, reserving a second strike either to finish off the island's defences or, in the unlikely event of the intervention of an American carrier, to deal with her promptly. For this reason the reserve Kates in the *Kaga* and *Akagi* were armed with torpedoes instead of bombs.

Shortly after dawn on 4 June Nagumo began launching the attack that was intended to cripple the defences of Midway and allow the invading forces to march ashore. One after another, Zeros, Vals and Kates roared down the flight decks of the four big carriers in a garish display of red and green navigation lights, signalling lights and deck lights, 108 aircraft in all. Not a fault, not a mishap. Nagumo watched the scene with professional satisfaction, his mind going back to that earlier dawn launch little more than a thousand miles away to the east. But this time it was more than a raid: it was a raid followed by an invasion.

Down in the sick bay of the *Hiryu* Commander Fuchida listened to the thunder of the engines and reflected on the ill fortune that had led to the appendectomy from which he was recovering, and the good fortune of his friend Lieutenant Joichi Tomonaga who had taken his place as leader of the attack. For some of the 108 pilots this was their first operation; they had listened time and again to the accounts of Pearl Harbor, Darwin and Colombo from the veterans who made up the majority of the air crews now heading south-east on the two-hour flight.

'What was Midway like that morning of June the 4th? I'll tell you what it was like. It was like Little Bighorn in '76 waiting for the Sioux to come. Except we did better than General Custer.' Never was any fort more prepared for an assault. The heavy guns were manned, the marines in their recently dug defences, firefighters at the ready, everything covered that could be covered. There were bunkers to store bombs, gas, fuses and water, bunkers even for aircraft that could not be got into the air. Besides the usual weaponry – and there was plenty of that thanks to the last-minute build-up – there were a lot of makeshift weapons around like Molotov cocktails from the stacks of empty whisky bottles, and man-killing mines offshore made from gelatin rammed into lengths of piping.

As for the air defence, the Catalinas were ordered off and to keep well clear until the attack was over, along with a heterogenous collection of old planes. The remainder were briefed to carry out an attack on the Japanese carriers, the fighters to deal as well as they could with the Japanese attacking planes. The raw pilots who had recently arrived, many just out of school, were given the worst and oldest planes, the Vindicator dive-bombers from way back and the Buffalo fighters, always guaranteed to make a nice *hors d'oeuvre* for any Zero. It had been the same in the RFC on the Western Front in 1917; the same in the Battle of Britain two years ago. The Dauntlesses were assigned to veterans and semi-veterans; the Wildcats – the only fighter that could tangle with a Zero – to any fighter pilot who could show 500 hours in his log-book. Some of these pilots were sent up on standing patrol, others kept at instant readiness, strapped in their cockpits, at the end of the runway.

'We were told not to expect any help from Navy carriers. They were away defending Pearl. We were on our own. That somehow made things simpler.' *J'y suis, j'y reste*. There was no alternative anyway.

The island's radar picked up fat blips in the west at a ninety-three-mile range at 5.53 a.m. The alarm sirens screamed, loudly enough to half-deafen those close to, but not loud enough for pilots warming up their engines. A truck thundered down the runway, the driver shouting the news, with bearing and range of the enemy, and by 6.00 a.m. the fighters began taking off, twenty-six of them against more than 100 Japanese planes. But there had been worse odds for defending fighters over Pearl Harbor and over the *Scharnhorst* and *Gneisenau* belting up-Channel in February, for example.

Then the torpedo-bombers were away, the venerable Vindicators, four army B-26 bombers rigged at the last minute to carry torpedoes, their newly arrived crews bemused by the whole business, scarcely knowing where they were, what they were supposed to do and how to *torpedo* a ship.

Lieutenant Tomonaga never expected to be jumped far out at sea, and many of his pilots got the surprise of their lives as snub-nosed Buffaloes and Wildcats came roaring down at them from 17,000 feet, sending some of the *Hiryu*'s bombers down in flames. It was a good start for the Americans. But in less than a minute the Zeros joined the party, cutting to pieces the American fighters with their 20-mm cannon. When was the navy going to get cannon in their fighters? Not for a while yet.

The air fighting, mostly fighter to fighter, continued until the bombers arrived over Midway, where the sky was black-spotted with anti-aircraft bursts. Mostly badly damaged already, the Buffaloes and Wildcats continued the fight over the island, even when the bombers turned back for the carriers. But there were not many left by then. Outgunned, outmanoeuvred, outpaced, the American fighters stood little chance of survival, and few of them did. One Wildcat and one Buffalo landed undamaged, and ten more shot up – most of them unfit to fly again. Twelve out of twenty-three: that figure represented not only the inferiority of the American aircraft but also the grit of the pilots, many inexperienced, who had never before fought together. How many Japanese planes they accounted for will never be known, but most post mortems agree it was around a dozen. Nor will anyone ever know how many bombs would have fallen more accurately if it had not been for this spirited defence.

And what of Midway after the last Val climbed away from its lethal dive? What of America's fourth aircraft carrier, an unsinkable carrier which the

Japanese thought they were about to board, like a pirate crew of the 1700s, with carbines for cutlasses and 635-pound bombs for cannon balls?

Among all those lying in slit trenches and shelters as well as those who were exposed at gun emplacements, as silence descended upon the two islets it seemed that every building had been levelled to the ground and that no facilities could be functioning. But in fact the damage was not too bad. The worst was to the obvious targets like the seaplane hangar and the fuel tanks, which were sending up so much black smoke that from a distance the island looked like an erupting volcano. The fuel lines' destruction was bad, too. But only one plane had been destroyed, an antediluvian biplane, plus a dummy which had attracted a great quantity of 20-mm shells and machine-gun bullets. And returning planes would have no trouble in landing back on the airstrip. The Japanese had still to learn the lesson, long since accepted by their allies, the Germans, that airfields are very difficult to knock out. Best of all, there were only eleven dead on Midway after this tremendous pounding and strafing.

Commander Tenabe, who had watched the whole show through his periscope, thought the island had been destroyed as a base. So did many of the Japanese air crew. Lieutenant Tomonaga knew better. Apart from the fighters which had attacked them, where were all the American aircraft, especially those B-17 four-engine bombers reported to be operating from Midway? As he flew back towards his carrier, Tomonaga radioed, 'There is need for a second attack.'

The Japanese carriers were being attacked at around this time but only by bombers and torpedo-bombers from Midway, not from a carrier: Nagumo was confident of this, which also accounted for Tomonaga's failure to catch the planes on the Midway airstrip. The attacks by a mixed bag of Dauntlesses, modern TBFs, aged Vindicators, B-17s (bombing from 20,000 feet this time) and B-26s, bore all the hallmarks of a hastily prepared makeshift operation by mainly unskilled pilots. The Dauntlesses, for example, resorted to the curious tactic of glide-bombing, which gave the Zeros plenty of opportunity for getting and keeping their sights on the machines during their run-in. Eight out of sixteen splashed into the sea, including the Marine Corps leader, Major Loften R. Henderson, who had resorted to this method because he judged his pilots were too unpractised to carry out an orthodox 70-degree dive-bombing attack.

The period between 7.00 a.m. and 8.30 a.m. was the most eventful and critical ninety minutes in the short, glorious history of Admiral Nagumo's carrier force. In those ninety minutes the fierce but ineffectual air attacks from Midway were beaten off. However unco-ordinated the attacks from the Midway-based planes had been, it had been an anxious period with a number of near misses, and full marks were earned by the carrier commanders for evading the launched American torpedoes, by the anti-aircraft gunners and by the Zero pilots.

At the same time, amidst the clatter of anti-aircraft fire and the crash of bombs, Nagumo had to react to the report that a second strike against Midway was required. That would have been bad news had there been an American carrier to contend with. Instead he was able to give the order: 'Planes in second attack wave stand by to carry out attack today. Re-equip yourselves with bombs.'

Onboard the *Kaga* and *Akagi*, the torpedo-equipped Kates were immediately struck below for the laborious business of discarding the torpedoes and rearming the planes with heavy bombs, while all the carriers cleared their decks to fly on the returning Midway planes. With the need so urgent, the operation of switching torpedoes to bombs could be completed in under one hour, but not many minutes less; and it would take another half-hour or so to wheel the heavy planes back on to the lifts and strike them on the flight deck for take-off. Certainly eighty minutes in all.

The armourers had never worked with greater speed and concentration with their own special equipment understood only by themselves – trolleys and fuses, jacks and firing pins, dangerous work at any time, more than ever hazardous under this pressure and in mid-Pacific summer heat.

They had been at work for perhaps thirty minutes and were making marvellous progress when the order came to halt.

Shortly before 7.30 a.m. Admiral Nagumo had been thrown into a dilemma. Long before sunrise he had prudently ordered seven float planes to be catapulted from his cruisers to fly a series of search patterns in order to ensure that the seas about Midway were clear of American ships. For more than two hours nothing was reported and, like a set of balancing scales, with every passing minute the relief among Nagumo and his staff increased. By 7.20 a.m., with the first air strike returning and the second preparing for take-off in about two hours' time, Operation MI appeared to be a certain success.

A scout seaplane from the cruiser *Tone* was late taking off, was not in the air until 5.00 a.m., and therefore reached the limit point of her 300-mile search half an hour later than the others. Then the seaplane turned north on her next sixty-mile leg before heading back to her cruiser. Like a change of bowler in a cricket match, or a pitcher in baseball, this alteration of course produced an immediate result. Almost dead ahead there were ships – many ships. The radio operator at once began tapping out his message: 'Sight what appears to be ten enemy surface ships bearing 010° 240 miles from Midway Course 150° Speed over 20 knots.'

Rapid calculations revealed that if there were no carriers it would be six hours before they would be within gun range, but if there was a carrier then they were already within range of its aircraft. Then again, if the enemy had a carrier, some of Nagumo's planes ought to be armed with torpedoes; if not a carrier they would need only bombs for the second strike on Midway. It was as simple, and as complicated, as that.

This was the point when Nagumo ordered all work on the Kates to cease. Two minutes later he ordered the seaplane crew to 'Ascertain ship types and maintain contact'. All he received in reply to this was the news that the enemy ships had changed course to 80 degrees and still maintained 20 knots. Not very helpful. 'Advise ship types,' Nagumo signalled peremptorily.

The raid from Midway was in noisy progress, flaming planes and bombs falling out of the sky, when the seaplane transmitted the reassuring details Nagumo had been awaiting: 'Enemy is composed of five cruisers and five destroyers.' The time was 8.09 a.m. The Midway attack was petering out.

Nagumo's relief was short-lived. At 8.20 a.m. the seaplane's operator transmitted the dread word 'carrier': 'The enemy is accompanied by what appears to be a carrier.' Inadequate identification maybe, but sufficient to present the Japanese Admiral with an entirely fresh and exceedingly hazardous situation. Torpedoes, after all, were needed!

I will tell you how bad it was [one surviving Japanese officer has declared]. We had about one hundred Zeros, Vals and Kates in the air, low on fuel, the Zeros out of ammunition, too, some of them damaged. They all had to be recovered and serviced. That would take one hour. And we could not launch an attack meanwhile. The Zeros which had not gone to Midway were out of ammunition and half out of fuel as a result of defending our carriers. Some of our bombers were armed with bombs, some with torpedoes, some unarmed. It was not a good situation – not good at all.

Admiral Tamon Yamaguchi, Nagumo's second-in-command and flying his flag in the *Hiryu*, favoured an immediate strike at the American force, which was now presumed to include a carrier. 'Consider it advisable to launch attack force immediately,' he signalled his superior, breaching IJN etiquette; but then Yamaguchi had never been orthodox and always impulsive.

To launch an immediate attack must lead to the loss of a number of Tomonaga's returning aircraft, many of which had been airborne for five hours, and an immediate attack would perforce be virtually without fighter escort. And the consequences of attacking carriers unescorted had been witnessed all too clearly over the past hour, when 40 per cent of the Midway bombers had been destroyed and none had made a hit.

The only rational solution was to recover Tomonaga's planes, refuel and rearm them, switch the Kates' armament back to torpedoes, and then launch an all-out attack on the American force. At 9.17 a.m. the last of the Zeros, most of them with an American plane to their credit, entered the final approach to the *Akagi*'s flight deck, canopy thrown back, undercarriage and flaps lowered. It had been a good start to the day for these pilots and every one of them relished the thought of getting into the air again 'and knocking more Yankees out of the sky'.

Nagumo was signalling all ships by lamp: 'After completing landing operations proceed north. We plan to contact and destroy the enemy task force.'

Then the entire First Carrier Striking Force, four carriers and their accompanying cruisers and destroyers, turned on to a northerly heading, speed 30 knots, in order to distance themselves from the enemy before turning back to attack. All the ships had lost station during the rapid manoeuvring of the past hour and the subsequent recovery of the carriers' planes. Now they attempted to tighten up the formation so that they could concentrate their anti-aircraft fire. The condition of the carriers' decks varied from clear to chaotic. Some returned planes were being refuelled from bowsers or rearmed with long clips of machine-gun ammunition. On the hangar decks below refuelling hoses snaked like giant cobras, oil was being hand-pumped into engine sumps, bombs and torpedoes lay everywhere – no time to return unwanted 550-pound bombs to the ships' magazines – or were being jacked and clipped into position, the smaller bombs by hand with the usual accompanying grunting and heaving.

There was a lot of noise, especially in the *Kaga* and *Akagi* where the struggle to complete the second change of armament for the Kates was in full swing. The sweet smell of sweat was in the air; it was not so strong as the sharp smell of fuel.

No ships' crews could have laboured with such pace and dedication. Down through every rank, from admiral to armourer, the need for speed was fully appreciated. Yet some of the delicate work required careful and measured manipulations and the supervising petty officers had to shout words of caution, too. But every crew member was a veteran in his trade, and never before had Zeros been serviced so rapidly: rearmed with 500 rounds of 7.7-mm machine-gun ammunition, sixty 20-mm cannon shells, seventy gallons of fuel – oil checked, controls checked for possible damaged cables, screen and canopy wiped clear of insects and oil flecks.

As Walter Lord has written, 'There was no reason to panic. They had plenty of strength: all they really needed was a little time....'[3] And above all they had plenty of experience of winning and none of failure, and that is a battle-winning factor whatever the circumstances.

At five minutes to nine the distant seaplane, which had first raised the alarm and was now on the way back to the *Tone*, sent one more signal: 'Ten enemy torpedo-planes heading towards you.' Nagumo glanced at the message but did not react. He had many other things on his mind and as they had successfully dealt with half a dozen or more attacks already there was no reason to believe they could not deal with this one from Midway. From what he had seen of American torpedoes – slow and unreliable – he reckoned there was little to fear.

If it was inexcusable earlier for the seaplane's skipper to misidentify a carrier for a cruiser, he can scarcely be blamed for failing to identify the formation of Devastators which had crossed his path as carrier-borne. If any of Nagumo's staff suggested to their Admiral that these planes might not have taken off from Midway, there is no record of it, and there was certainly no reaction from Nagumo, whose mind was concentrated on getting his own attack launched.

And what an attack it would be – one that could not fail to send perhaps the last of America's carriers to the bottom: eighteen torpedo Kates from his flagship, twenty-seven from the *Kaga*, thirty-six Vals from the *Hiryu* and *Soryu*, and a dozen Zeros to cover them. But hurry!

It was just before 9.20 a.m. when the first flags fluttered at the yardarm of ships of the starboard screen, a destroyer first, the cruiser *Tone*, another destroyer, the cruiser *Chikuma*. The signal was a simple one, recognized by everyone: 'Planes in sight.' They were still almost twenty miles away, fifteen tight-packed dots, but the ships of the outer screen already began making smoke. The heavy anti-aircraft gunlayers began to take readings; on the bridge of all twenty-one ships of the fleet the order was rung down for maximum speed.

Wade McClusky was at 20,000 feet steering west with mixture at full lean, prop at full coarse for economy, his eyes ranging to and fro across the scarcely rippled blue sheet of ocean, using his binoculars to double check the remotest distances. Behind and on each side were his thirty Dauntlesses, rising and falling gently formation, the two figures in each slightly hunched behind the long ribbed Plexiglass canopy, the face of one or other of his pilots turned towards him from time to time to check position. Twelve-plus tons of high explosive, sixty-two navy airmen, twelve miles above the Pacific Ocean.

They should be dropping their bombs by now. At 9.20 a.m., 155 miles from the *Enterprise*, they should be right above the Japanese flat-tops. But there was nothing to be seen from horizon to horizon except the little white cotton wads of cumulus and the dark shadows of these clouds on the ocean.

Because every pilot but the Group leader had to make minute throttle adjustments to keep formation, McClusky knew he had marginally more fuel in his tanks than anyone else; and his fuel situation, while not yet critical, was not very happy either, thanks to the forty minutes of futile circling over the *Enterprise* before the Admiral had sent them on their way without escort.

McClusky hand-signalled a left turn and steadied on a south-west heading. He held his squadrons on this course for thirty-five miles, then turned north-west. Just before 10.00 a.m. a few minutes before he would have to head back home if he were to land his machines on a steel deck instead of the Pacific, he saw his first ship since leaving Task Force 16. All ships are small from 20,000 feet; this ship was very small, a slip of a thing and going fast: he could tell that from her long white wake and the twin tiny bow waves. He had never before seen any vessel playing so convincingly the part of a ship trying to catch up.

The destroyer *Arashi*, 1,500 tons, six 5-inch, eight 21-inch torpedo tubes, 34 knots, guided him like the proverbial arrow, north-east, beyond the Dauntless's point of no return. Pertinacity at last rewarded at 10.05 a.m., the *Arashi* presented them with a distant view of the Japanese First Carrier Striking Force in all its majesty.

Still McClusky maintained radio silence, and at least one of his pilots thought thankfully that the skipper had brought them back to Task Force 16. And just in the nick of time, too, because the fuel gauge needle was nudging the empty pin. Ensign Tony Schneider heard his engine hesitate, then cut out. His Dauntless dropped out of formation and he headed down, aiming to ditch alongside a destroyer if he could not make a carrier. Then he spotted the fat shape of a battleship far below, two heavy gun turrets forward and two more abaft the midships superstructure. That was not right at all: there were no American battleships in the central Pacific. Experiencing a sudden *frisson*, Ensign Schneider released his bomb to stretch his glide and headed south, preparing to splash.

Wade McClusky now broke radio silence, giving his carrier their position and giving his two squadrons their targets. There were four carriers, as expected. Unexpected were their wild evolutions marked by the sinuous pattern of white wakes etched on the sea, as if they were already taking evasive action. Then it occurred to him that *Enterprise*'s torpedo-bombers had got there first and were attacking right now. That would account, too, for the absence of Zeros up here; the absence of anti-aircraft fire, too.

They would never get back to the *Enterprise* anyway, even if they survived this attack; but at least he had brought his squadrons to the right spot at the right time. McClusky patted the back of his head – the sign to go down – and did so himself, very steeply, dive brakes open, his eye on the three-power telescopic sight.

By the time Wade McClusky had located the Japanese carriers and led the Devastators down in their bombing attack twenty of his shipmates in Torpedo 6 were already dead, their planes ravaged, burnt wrecks at the bottom of the Pacific Ocean. Many of the torpedoes had never even been launched; none had struck a ship.

To Japanese eyes the approach of the torpedo-planes through the smoke made by the *Chikuma* and *Tone* and several destroyers looked like some religious act of self-immolation: no attempt at dividing the labouring Devastators or taking evasive action, the fifteen planes with their prominent 'pickles' slung below their bellies came straight in, heading like migrant birds on their set flight pattern.

One after another the planes were torn to pieces by the waiting Zeros or by the screen of anti-aircraft fire hosing out from every ship in the Carrier Force. Some caught fire and dropped straight in, others cartwheeled in a cloud of spray or lost a wing and hovered as if abstracted for a surprising length of time before dropping the last fifty feet.

One Devastator piloted by George Gay did try an original trick, attempting a dummy starboard approach, switching to an attempted port approach.

He released his torpedo at the *Soryu* at close range before he was shot down. *Soryu* evaded but Gay survived – the only survivor – to be picked up the next day by a Catalina.

VT-6, arriving a few minutes later, suffered almost as badly, although four Devastators contrived to escape from the holocaust. Finally, the *Yorktown*'s Devastators came ambling in for their ordeal like doomed men walking to the executioner's block. VT-3 was the most experienced torpedo squadron of the two American Task Forces and had the special advantage of an escort of half a dozen Wildcats. But the Zero pilots had got their eye in, intercepted the Devastators eighteen miles out, and by sheer weight of numbers neutralized the fighters by occupying them while others tackled the torpedo-bombers. Only two escaped the axe. No hits.

It was the gyrations of the carriers evading this last attack that McClusky and his pilots had witnessed. Until this moment, everything, it seemed, that could go wrong had gone wrong. The earlier Devastators on the scene should have enjoyed fighter protection, and the bombing and torpedo attacks should have been closely co-ordinated. Instead, the *Hornet*'s dive-bombers never did find the enemy carriers, and the Devastators had been almost annihilated.

Admiral Nagumo had every reason to be satisfied with the situation as the barrels of the guns began to cool and his invincible, indestructible Zeros swooped about his Carrier Force joyously, their appetite for enemy aircraft unsatiated. Now he could complete preparations for his own all-out attack, and the *Akagi*, *Kaga* and *Soryu* began their turns into wind for launching. There must be more than one American carrier, he now surmised. If there were two, both would be at the bottom of the Pacific before nightfall: that was his certain conviction.

In a naval gun duel in the days of sail there was little opportunity for surprise. Two days elapsed between the sighting of the Spanish Armada off the Lizard and the first exchange of shots off Eddystone. Long after they had met one another, the *Constitution* and *Guerrière* were still manoeuvring before firing their first broadside. Even at Jutland the battle-cruisers were in sight of one another for thirty-two minutes before opening fire, and after that the shells still took more than half a minute to arrive.

Admiral Nagumo was granted no more than five minutes, and probably less, to relish the defeat of the last of the American torpedo-bombers before he heard the cry of one of the *Akagi*'s look-outs – 'Dive-bombers!' There was no time to do anything, no time to pray let alone give an order, scarcely time to look up, or duck. Those who did look up – Commander Fuchida was one and Teiichi Makishima, a news cameraman, another – caught a glimpse of three planes pulling out of a steep dive directly above the carrier, dark objects falling from each.

The three explosions were not quite simultaneous. Survivors told of the first bomb landing very close to the port side, shaking the great ship like a beaten dog. The sea towered up higher than the mainmast and tumbled like water from a broken dam on to the bridge, soaking, without respect for rank, assistant signalmen and admirals. But by then the first killer had struck, dead centre in the flight deck by the bridge, through the midships elevator, exploding on the hangar deck below.

The ingredients for incendiary catastrophe were all still present in abundance: armed planes, refuelled planes, high-octane avgas in tanks and lines, 7.7-mm and 20-mm cannon ammunition, quarter-ton and half-ton bombs, 1,700-pound torpedoes. The explosion tore the heart out of the 30,000-ton ship, destroying everything and everyone there. Debris, evil black smoke, fragments of planes and sailors, chunks of steel decking and bulkheads, rose up out of the ship with staggering force, tossing aside like autumn leaves the Zeros and Kates and Vals spotted on the flight deck.

The third of this first batch of bombs struck the flagship right aft, where the planes were parked like cars at a supermarket. The last flight of some of them, considering their unairworthy condition, lasted longer than some eyewitnesses expected. But not much longer. The fact that the ship's rudders were jammed by the explosion, too, seemed of trivial importance. The *Akagi* could steam straight ahead, or to port or starboard, for all that it mattered by now. In fact the rudders were jammed 20 degrees to port, and by some freak of chance the 131,000-horsepower engines were still running although every man was dead down there in the starboard engine-room, suffocated by the fire drawn down through the air shaft.

For those on the bridge there was suddenly nothing to do. Everything was dripping wet, stunned and helpless – no signals to hoist to a non-existent yardarm, with no radio, no rudder, no helm to control, no one to respond to instructions in the engine-room, and certainly no aircraft to order off. By another freak chance a Zero, still almost looking like a Zero, thrown hard against the island, suddenly burst into flames which rapidly licked up the steel plating to the top of the bridge.

Admiral Ryunosuke Kusaka, Nagumo's tubby Chief of Staff, told his chief that it was time to shift his flag.

'No, it's not time yet,' the C-in-C replied. Nagumo was standing, half in a trance, by the compass platform. The ship's Captain was equally unsuccessful. 'I will look after the *Akagi*, sir. It is time for you to go.' Admiral Kusaka tried again:

Admiral Nagumo thought the situation was under control and refused to come down from the bridge, but the captain of the ship advised him that the ship was out of control and that it should be abandoned, and wanted him to abandon ship, but he refused; Admiral Nagumo was an extremely hot-tempered person, and consequently insisted on remaining on the bridge. I myself as chief of staff tried to convince him that it was his duty as C-in-C to abandon ship and transfer to some other ship where he could control the actions of the fleet, because it was no longer possible to communicate with other ships by wireless from *Akagi*, and the signal flags and semaphore weren't sufficient to direct the battle. Although Admiral

Nagumo refused to come down, I finally had the others drag him by the hand and talk him into leaving the ship, but couldn't find a way down, everything was so covered with smoke and flame; there was no way of getting down from the bridge except by a rope which we hung from the bridge.... When I got down, the deck was on fire and anti-aircraft and machine-guns were firing automatically, having been set off by the fire aboard ship. Bodies were all over the place, and it wasn't possible to tell what would be shot up next.... I had my hands and feet burned – a pretty serious burn on one foot. That is eventually the way we abandoned the *Akagi* – helter-skelter, no order of any kind.[4]

By 11.30 a.m. the *Akagi* was still blazing and firing off exploding ammunition as if in mid-battle. Admiral Nagumo had hoisted his flag in the light cruiser *Nagara*. And it was from her bridge that he could survey and comprehend for the first time the true extent of the catastrophe which had struck his fleet.

The *Kaga*'s condition was no worse, no better, than the *Akagi*'s: both were doomed, both were blazing infernos, defying all the rules of buoyancy. The first three bombs had missed; then four in quick succession sealed the carrier's fate as swiftly as the *Bismarck*'s shells had settled for the *Hood* a year and two weeks before. The first, a 1,000-pounder, landed on the starboard side of the flight deck where the Kates, torpedoes secured, were lined up for take-off. The next two were close to the bridge and killed the captain and everyone else. Thereafter it did not matter where the bombs landed, or what their size. No one counted them. The internal explosions were so fearful that they could have been bombs from Dauntlesses or the carrier's magazines. As for the flames:

The fire raced along rivulets of gasoline, spreading disaster below decks. Men trapped behind blistering bulkheads were roasted alive. Hoses rolled out in a frantic effort to hold back the flames caught fire. Some officers and men, their uniforms smouldering and their faces blackened by smoke, were driven back to the edge of the flight deck and from there they leaped into the sea. Then the fire travelled to the bomb storage lockers. Suddenly there was a thunderous detonation, and sheets of glowing steel were ripped like so much tin foil from the bowels of the ship. The hangar deck was a purgatory within a few minutes, and great clouds of black smoke rose from the *Kaga*, carrying with them the smell of burning gasoline, paint, wood, rubber and human flesh.[5]

As for the *Soryu*, her condition was just as clearly terminal as the bigger carriers'. Three bomb hits sealed her fate as decisively as her consorts'. 'The entire ship burst into flames,' Morison recorded, 'and within twenty minutes the crew were ordered to abandon by Captain [Ryusaku] Yanagimoto, whom they last saw bellowing "Banzai!" on the bridge.'[6]

Only the *Hiryu*, ten miles to the north of this area of carnage, escaped the attention of the American flyers, anyway for the time being. Upon her rested the responsibility for striking back at the enemy, and this the dispossessed Admiral Nagumo now ordered her to do.

Perhaps it was as well that, in the heat and excitement of the American dive-bomber attack, it was impossible to credit accurately which squadron attacked which carrier, and which Dauntless had made a hit and which had failed to place his bomb on the deck of a flat-top. As a commanding officer who is awarded a Victoria Cross for bravery in action accepts the honour on behalf of every member of his ship's company, so the stunning success of four dive-bomber squadrons who destroyed three carriers in ten minutes was a team operation. Anyone who dropped out of the sky on that June morning in 1942 deserved equal credit and honour. Nor would one of those air crew wish the sacrifice of the torpedo-bomber crews before them to be forgotten, for it was the unfortunate old Devastators which distracted the attention of the ships' gunners and kept the Zero pilots down low. Then just as they were counting their score, the Dauntlesses came in vertically instead of horizontally.

Only four dive-bomber crews knew for sure that they had not made a hit. Lieutenant-Commander Maxwell Leslie, CO of the *Yorktown*'s Bombing 3, had had the wretched misfortune, shared with three more of his pilots, of suffering from wiring failure in the fusing of his bomb. Instead of fusing it, the circuit released it, high above the sea, far from the Japanese carriers. But he continued to lead his squadron, determined it should not be demoralized by this accident and calculating that if there were any Japanese anti-aircraft fire around, he should take his share.

Picking the most easterly of the Japanese carriers, Leslie led down his squadron at exactly 10.25 a.m. from 14,500 feet, the bitter irony of his mishap leading him to dive steeper and better than he could remember ever before achieving. Bombing 3's accuracy was sublime. With Leslie using his .5 machine guns on the carrier's gunners, the first pilots made so many hits that the last four veered off to other targets – a destroyer and a battleship.

There was no doubt about which squadron hit the *Soryu*, but as for the *Kaga* and *Akagi*, who hit what and where has ever since led to unacrimonious debate amongst surviving air crew and historians alike.

For Wade McClusky the eventfulness of his morning did not cease, as it really deserved to do, with his squadron's destruction of a carrier – no matter which.

Admiral Morison writes:

As McClusky pulled away from the burning *Akagi* his plane was pursued by two Zeros for about 35 miles. He kept his SBD skimming the water, only 20 feet above the surface, which baffled the Zeros. They used 7.7-mm tracers to get his range, and then opened up with their 20-mm, but fortunately had only a small supply of this caliber. At that they put 55 small and three big holes in the plane – one of them through No. 9 cylinder, which continued nevertheless to function – besides peppering the pilot's left shoulder with fragments. As McClusky wove the plane this way and that, his radio mechanic W.G.Chochalousek did wonders with a .30-caliber Browning; he shot down one Zero and discouraged the other so that it pulled away.[7]

Even that was not the end of it for the Air Group leader. The *Enterprise* was not where she ought to have been, and he almost put down on the *Yorktown* in error. When he did find his carrier he had about five gallons of fuel left. He was stiff from the long flight but hurried straight to Admiral Spruance and reported three carriers burning, the fourth untouched. He had not noticed, nor had the Admiral, that there was blood running down his sleeve. It was the carrier's executive officer who exclaimed, 'My God, Mac, you've been shot!' In the sick bay they found five wounds in his left arm and shoulder.

Of the *Enterprise*'s other thirty-one bombers which had begun launching just after 7.00 a.m. only eighteen had returned by midday. And that was all. The Zeros had got some of them, so had the ships' guns. But the sea claimed the majority, the pilots stalling in with empty tanks and full flaps, into a trough across the line of the waves if they could, hand on the straps' release. With Mae Wests and dinghies, the sea warm and calm, most survived, to be picked up by Catalinas or destroyers later that day or the next.

But the American carriers' plane losses had been fearful, seventy-two in all. A number of the air crews survived to fight again, others too badly wounded were taken off flying or discharged from the navy. The torpedo-bomber crews suffered worst in numbers, and in their manner of dying, many of them burning to death in their cockpit. Then, worst of all perhaps, were the Americans fished out of the water by the Japanese. None survived. The fate of two will never be known, but can be surmised. The third, one of the *Yorktown*'s torpedo-bomber pilots, was tortured until he gave all the information that could be torn from him, then hacked to death. The Americans were learning that in the Pacific they were fighting an enemy who had no consideration for the accepted tenets of human behaviour, even in total war. Roosevelt privately code-named them simply 'the barbarians'.

Admiral Nagumo from his new flagship was in no position to control the tactical nature of the final phase of the battle. This he transferred temporarily to Rear-Admiral Hiroaki Abe commanding the Carrier Striking Force's screen of two battleships, three cruisers and a dozen destroyers, and would now include the single surviving carrier, the *Hiryu*. Admiral Yamamoto, as a result of the multi-option strategy he had devised, was still far away to the north-west with his battleships and carrier, and their tremendous anti-aircraft-gun capacity. He was still hopeful of salvaging something from the ruins of the morning. The information extracted from the unfortunate American pilot had not reached his lofty eminence, and he still believed that the massed assaults on his carrier force came from one enemy carrier and Midway, or two carriers at the most. This appeared to be confirmed when a scout seaplane signalled to Admiral Abe, and thence to Yamamoto, 'Sighted enemy composed of one carrier, five cruisers and six destroyers at position bearing 10° 240 miles from Midway.' So it had been only one.

Abe ordered an immediate all-out attack. The fiery Yamaguchi had pre-empted him: 'All our planes are taking off now.'

They were, in fact, launching in two groups of eighteen dive-bombers (Vals), ten torpedo-bombers (Kates) and a dozen Zeros.

Lieutenant Rikivini, a Zero pilot, recalled:

We felt better once we were in the air. The day had started well for us but the sight of the three burning pyres of the *Kaga*, *Akagi* and *Soryu* and the sounds of the battle to the south had badly affected our shipmates – we saw that when we had landed. But now we saw our chance to avenge this Yankee blow. And, remember, we still had superior strength in all types of ships and we knew that before long we should be reinforced. Meanwhile my group followed a seaplane which knew just where the enemy carrier was and we knew that it would soon be destroyed.[8]

Rikivini was quite right on both counts. But at this stage he did not know that Yamamoto had already ordered down from the north the two carriers which had been engaged on the futile Dutch Harbor expedition, one of them the brand-new 24,000-ton *Junyo* – and would not she have been of priceless value that morning at Midway? Yamamoto had also ordered a rendezvous with the Aleutians' screening force and his own battleship at 9.00 a.m. in preparation for a fleet action against the American naval forces. By no means was everything lost; on the contrary everything could still be gained.

Like the Midway defenders earlier, the *Yorktown* defenders enjoyed a mile by mile, minute by minute, commentary on the weight and range of their approaching assailants. Pale electronic smudges on glass screens were trans-lated into the reality of dots on the horizon, then the distinguishable details of planes. Everyone on carriers did some aircraft recognition. With the aid of binoculars the experts could make out the fixed undercarriages of the Vals, the sleeker configuration of the Kates that came in later.

As a bizarre preliminary to the proceedings Max Leslie's Dauntlesses beat the Vals to the *Yorktown*. Their last sight of a carrier had been of flames and smoke and great explosions; now, weary, triumphant, all that these Americans wanted was to put down, get out, stretch their legs and light a Camel. But Max Leslie was signalled away on his final approach, and was not best pleased. Next in line, Lieutenant Paul Holmberg prepared to touch down, and then suddenly at the last minute was waved off. Walter Lord completes the poignant anecdote:

He was just opposite the after gun gallery when the four 5-inchers opened up. Smoke, fire, blast scared him half out of the cockpit. Thoroughly frightened, he darted away from the ship and joined up with Leslie. The *Yorktown*'s radio crackled a belated warning: 'Get clear – we are being attacked.'[9]

The Vals had been bounced by the *Yorktown*'s patrolling Wildcats long before they got over their targets. The dive-bombers did not stand a chance, and in less than a minute six of them were spiralling down, riddled with .5-inch machine-gun bullets. Then the outlying destroyers opened up on the surviving dozen Vals, soon joined by the heavier guns from the cruisers and the *Yorktown* herself. There were seven left, in ragged formation, when they turned over and began to come straight down. Now the automatic light gunfire filled the air, and everyone not behind the sights believed that nothing could get through this screen of flying metal.

This seemed to be confirmed when the lead plane fell to pieces like a duck caught at the same time by three 12-bores. But its bomb fell, too, released at the last split-second by a dead pilot who had known how to aim. It landed on the flight deck aft of the island. The second bomb to hit went deeper before exploding in the funnel uptake. A third hit the forward elevator and went down fifty feet into the ship's bowels before exploding.

It was the second hit that did the worst damage, dropping the *Yorktown*'s speed from 30 to 6 knots, and causing a vast black cloud of smoke to rise up into the sky – a warning signal to the *Enterprise* and *Hornet* away on the horizon that their consort was in real trouble.

But not fatal. Unlike the Japanese carriers, the *Yorktown*'s fire precautions were elaborate and efficient. Damage control flooded the ship's magazines, elaborate sprinkler systems doused fires that would otherwise soon have been out of control, the fuel lines full of high-octane avgas had been drained and the fuel itself isolated under carbon dioxide at high pressure. Unlike Nagumo's fire-fighting crews, the *Yorktown*'s had pushed overboard a fuel bowser on the flight deck containing 800 gallons. Soon the *Yorktown* was stationary, the power for every facility gone, a derelict wreck incapable of flying operations; but she floated, and on an even keel, and by any judgement appeared recoverable.

Five dive-bombers and one Zero escaped from that murderous shell screen and the wheeling Wildcats. But just one was enough to report their success back to Admiral Abe: 'Carrier burning!' It did not delay for one second the readying of the Kates, now lined up on the *Hiryu*'s flight deck, Lieutenant Tomonaga in command. The carrier they eventually located bore no resemblance to the condition described by the surviving Val crews. This carrier was speeding at 20 knots and had already launched eight of her Wildcats.

What had brought about this metamorphosis? Simply valiant, sustained work by the damage-control crews, and brilliant work in the engine-rooms an boiler-rooms, regardless of the corpses of their shipmates about them. The *Yorktown* was, amazingly, in business again. So were her defences. With her cruiser screen adding to the tumult and cacophony, they cut down Kate after Kate, and the carrier's captain dodged a number of torpedoes. But not all. Admiral Nagumo was not to be denied his one success on this bloody day. Two torpedoes struck the much-battered *Yorktown*, jamming her rudder, breaking the fuel tanks on her port side, and sending her into a 17-degree, then a 26-degree, list.

It was heartbreaking after all the repair work, but by 3.00 p.m. the carrier was clearly doomed and the abandon-ship order was given. The gallant old lady did not pass away easily. Her tenacity for life lasted until 6.00 a.m. on 7 June, and even then it was only because a Japanese submarine found her and gave her the *coup de grâce* with two torpedoes.

Lieutenant Tomonaga's attack with his torpedo-bombers did not end the round of tit-for-tats on this June day. Admiral Fletcher had despatched a search mission from his carrier before the first *Hiryu* attack, and one of these planes found her at 2.45 p.m., along with two battleships, three cruisers and four destroyers. Forty-five minutes later Admiral Spruance launched no fewer than twenty-four dive-bombers, every pilot blooded in the morning massacre and hellbent for more destruction. At a cost of three Dauntlesses, these carrier planes repeated, in fire and explosion and mighty mountains of smoke, the violent end of the *Kaga*, *Akagi* and *Soryu*.

It was the dive-bombers' day, and no mistake. Four of their bombs were again enough. Hundreds died in the holocaust, including Admiral Yamaguchi. And now the Kates returning from their own mission of destruction of the *Yorktown* had nowhere to land: no Midway, no carrier, only the sea.

While three of Admiral Nagumo's four fleet carriers had been destroyed in six minutes, Operation MI lasted for another 100 hours, until midday, 8 June 1942, when Admiral Yamamoto finally turned for home. The carriers themselves took many hours to sink, their fires blazing away into the night like four funeral pyres, dousing the reflected moonlight on the sea's surface.

Appropriately, the flagship led the way down to the ocean bed at 4.50 a.m., with 221 dead. *Soryu* survived until the dawn of 5 June, sinking at 7.13 a.m. with over 700 of her company. The *Kaga* disappeared eight minutes later with some 800 sailors and airmen. The *Hiryu* was still afloat and smoking at 9.00 a.m., but was sunk a few minutes later by a Japanese destroyer's torpedoes, 416 of her company with her. Planes could be built more speedily than sailors could be trained, but the loss of 250 carrier aircraft was a serious blow.

The night after battle is a time of confusion and trial, when weary men, admirals and gun crews as much as fliers and engine-room artificers, cry out for sleep but know only that they must not, or cannot for the tautness of their nerves and the images of pace and violence housed starkly in the retina of their eyes. What should be a time of rest becomes a time of anxious reliving of experiences.

For Admiral Spruance, now effectively in command of both Task Forces, the critical decision had to be taken: to pursue or to withdraw. Spruance did not doubt that his fliers had hit and set burning the four enemy carriers, but none had seen them sink, and he had witnessed the remarkable recovery of the *Yorktown* after her assailants must, too, have reported her knocked out and blazing. The Admiral had little knowledge of the quality of Japanese carrier fire control. A B-17 bomber from Midway following up the attack on the *Hiryu* had reported Zeros in the sky. They could have flown off a repaired carrier, off a fifth carrier speeding from a support force, or they could have been simply flying around using up their fuel before ditching. There was no way of telling. What Spruance did know for sure was that he had lost many planes, had many more under repair and that his flight crews and deck crews were exhausted; that the enemy had more carriers available, whereabouts unknown, at least half a dozen battleships and a powerful cruiser and submarine force; that he was responsible for the only two American carriers in the central Pacific that night, and that his primary task was to guard Midway against renewed attack.

He made the right decision. He took his force east, out of harm's way, for the night, determining to return. As he wrote in his report:

I did not feel justified in risking a night encounter with possibly superior enemy forces, but on the other hand I did not want to be too far away from Midway the next morning. I wished to have a position from which either to follow up retreating enemy forces or to break up a landing attack on Midway.

It is likely that the Battle of Midway would have been turned from an American triumph to a Japanese victory and the capture of Midway if Spruance had done anything else. Admiral Morison[10] calculated that if Spruance *had* followed up 'retreating enemy forces' he would have run into a light carrier, the fleet carrier *Jintsu*, two battleships, numerous heavy cruisers and destroyers *in addition to* Yamamoto's flagship *Yamato* and the rest of his and Nagumo's forces: nine battleships in all. A clash would have been certain; the outcome catastrophic for the Americans with the loss of new-found confidence as well as carriers and crews.

American offensive action on the following day, 5 June, came at first from Midway bombers which found two heavy cruisers at about the time Nagumo's carriers were at last expiring. Earlier in the night the two heavy cruisers had collided while taking counter-action against an American submarine. The bombers added to the self-inflicted damage already suffered. But once again it was the carrier-borne dive-bombers that were most deadly. Around midday on 6 June Spruance's fliers made a crushing attack on the two big ships, sinking the *Mikuma* and ripping apart her sister ship, the *Mogami*, which managed to struggle, crippled, to Truk. These big Japanese cruisers had earlier sunk the *Perth* and *Houston* at Java Sea, so there was some element of justice in this secondary victory. More important, this setback contributed to Yamamoto's decision to call off his final attempt to settle the score with the *Enterprise* and *Hornet*. He spent the next day, 8 June, refuelling, and then, as the cricket definition has it, he 'retired hurt'.

The Battle of Midway was over. Japanese naval-air supremacy was broken; after six months the tides of fortune and conclusion had turned; and the people of America and her allies – especially those of Australia and New Zealand – cheered with relief. On hearing the final outcome Churchill at once signalled Roosevelt. 'This is the moment for me to send you my heartiest congratulations on the grand American victories in the Pacific which have very decidedly altered the balance of the Naval war.'

No decisive battle, at sea or on land, had been marked by so many minor occurrences which governed the final outcome. Perhaps the most critical of all was the delay of thirty minutes in the cruiser *Tone*'s catapulting of one of her scouting seaplanes. If that number four plane had been launched at 4.30 a.m. instead of 5.00 a.m. the crew would have found the American Task Force half an hour earlier – perhaps even sooner – and reported its presence before Lieutenant Tomonaga had called for a second strike against Midway; and certainly by 7.00 a.m. The Vals with their bombs and the Kates of the *Akagi*, already equipped with their 1,760-pound torpedoes, would have been launched and on their way to the American carriers, guided by the seaplane, while the American planes from the *Enterprise* and *Hornet* were on an opposite course *en route* to Nagumo's carriers: those who found them. Judged by what a handful of Vals and Kates did to the *Yorktown* later, the chances are that Task Force 16's planes would have lost their carriers after completing their strike; nor would the American strike have found the Japanese carriers in the desperately vulnerable state of which they took full advantage.

Then there is the curious case of the American submarine *Nautilus*, Lieutenant-Commander W.A.Brockman Jr. She had picked up the American sighting report on the position of Nagumo's carriers and had sought them out, with almost too much success. The submarine came up to periscope depth slap in the middle of Nagumo's force. 'Ships were on all sides....' Brockman, the object of immediate and intensive shelling, launched a single torpedo at a battleship, and dived fast.

Nagumo ordered a destroyer to remain and persevere with a series of depth-charge attacks. It was this destroyer which in attempting to catch up and resume station guided Wade McClusky to his target as he was on the point of heading back to his carrier. Instead his dive-bombers sank a carrier.

The ubiquitous *Nautilus* later came across the damaged carrier *Soryu* and put three torpedoes into her at short range, speeding her end. Her performance was in marked contrast with that of the Japanese submarines at Midway, which were so late on their patrol line that they missed the passage of Task Forces 16 and 17 from Pearl Harbor to Midway, a failure with mammoth consequences.

Chance and mischance. A temporarily unserviceable cruiser catapult, a lucky sighting, a lucky hit, an electrician's crossing of fusing and releasing wires – like a single dart of flame licking at a carrier's magazine, all these minor occurrences combined and led to permutations that resolved the control of the central Pacific Ocean.

A dozen pilots, boring down steeply from a great height, eye concentrated through bomb sight on to a rectangle 100-feet wide, changed the course of naval history and ensured the eventual crushing of Japanese tyranny and cruelty. From start to finish no surface warship had even sighted an enemy surface warship, let alone opened fire: the enemy had remained invisible. The events of the morning of 4 June 1942 suggest that Neptune had determined to show the world in a shuddering few minutes that new weaponry had taken over control of the seas from the big gun.

CHAPTER TEN

The Long Struggle for the Midland Sea

The Battle of the Mediterranean lasted for three years, from the entry into the war of Italy in June 1940 until the Italians and Germans laid down their arms in North Africa on 12 May 1943, continuing after that only along German-occupied coasts. The whole long campaign, in all its features and swings of fortune, can be seen in terms of the basic definition of sea power. It was concerned with amphibious warfare, with the four navies, British–British Commonwealth, American, Italian and German, landing and supporting and supplying military forces from the Aegean to the Straits of Gibraltar. Control of the sea spelt success; loss of that control led inevitably to failure.

Sea power was born in the Mediterranean, the Midland Sea as the Romans called it, some 5,000 years ago. Over the centuries since the Egyptians fought the 'Northmen of the Mediterranean', Phoenicians, Greeks, Minoans, Corinthians, Macedonians, Carthaginians, Romans and Trojans had fought one another in their swift and manoeuvrable galleys in support of their land campaigns. Christian fought infidel, the Venetians fought for their Levantine trading rights and fought their rival Italians, the Genoese. Turks and Greeks, Americans and Barbary pirates, French, Austrians, Italians and British, all exercised their sea power in the Mediterranean, an ocean which was also witness to the development of new types of ship, tactics and weaponry, right down to the all-big-gun battleship – the Dreadnought – conceived by the Italians in the nineteenth and early twentieth centuries.

Anyone still unconvinced that the nature of sea power had been radically altered by the German control of the air off Norway in April 1940 was now forced to yield to reality when the German Stuka dive-bombers, like the Vals over Pearl Harbor, screamed out of the sky with their lethal loads. But this was only a matter of weaponry. The full exercise of sea power still depended in the end on the surface ship, whether it was carrying troops and guns, transport and ammunition, tanks and fuel; or whether its holds were loaded with goods of trade and food supplies for a civil population.

The Mediterranean is studded with thousands of islands and dozens of fine harbours. But in the 1940–43 campaign the key island was Malta, set approximately half way between the British bases at Alexandria in the east and Gibraltar in the west. While Malta remained in Allied hands, the enemy could never claim complete control of the Mediterranean. Malta was the Britain of southern Europe, an island set in disputed seas, bombed, threatened with starvation and invasion, and after the fall of France the only central base for counter-operations against the besiegers. As convoys sailed east across the Atlantic, threatened all the way by the enemy, to bring succour and arms to beleaguered Britain, so merchantmen loaded to the gunwales with arms and food sailed east and west across the Mediterranean to dock in Valetta harbour.

In June 1940 British and Commonwealth forces in the eastern Mediterranean were concerned with the protection of the oil wealth of the Middle East and the Imperial arteries of trade and transport to British India, the Far East and Australasia. Ironically, the Prime Minister who came to power that early summer had presided over the conversion of the Royal Navy from home-produced coal to foreign oil in 1912–14. While this decision was inevitable, his chickens had indeed come home to roost thirty years later when oil supplies were of such critical concern to him.

In North Africa in 1940 empire nudged empire on the frontiers of Egypt and Italian-controlled Libya, and Sudan and Italian Eritrea. Here the powerful Italian Army threatened Cairo, the Suez Canal and the Red Sea, just as the Italian Navy threatened the already hard-pressed Royal Navy. With the evacuations from Norway and France, and no possibility of a counter-invasion for many years – East and North Africa were the only places where British and Commonwealth forces could fight the enemy. They were soon to do so, with mixed results.

Meanwhile, with the fall of France, the British Mediterranean Fleet based on Alexandria faced the Italian Navy alone. Admiral Sir Andrew Cunningham flew his flag in the battleship *Warspite*, one of the first big oil-fired warships in 1914 but modernized comprehensively and still capable of her original speed of 24 knots, like her sister ship *Malaya*. He also had two more unmodernized battleships dating from the First World War, an equally aged carrier, the *Eagle*, just three obsolete biplane fighters and seventeen Swordfish spotter-torpedo-planes. As the First Sea Lord bleakly accepted, 'I am afraid you are terribly short of "air"....' Cunningham could also muster a few cruisers, destroyers and minelayers, but not much else.

The Italian Fleet had its shortcomings, chiefly in the senior officer class which lacked aggressive bite, but the gunnery and equipment generally were first class. The ships might have been designed by a Renaissance artist. They were certainly the most beautiful and also the fastest in the world. It was said that the evident caution exercised by ships' commanders stemmed from concern that anything of such beauty as their ship should on no account be *damaged*, let alone sunk. This anxiety for preservation of the individual ships was compounded by the determination of the high command in Rome to 'keep the fleet in being' like the High Seas Fleet in the First World War.

THE ENGLISH CHANNEL
AND MEDITERRANEAN

SWEDEN

NORTH
SEA

DENMARK

BALTIC SEA

EIRE

GREAT
BRITAIN

HOLLAND

GERMANY

Dover

Dunkirk
Ostend

BELGIUM

CZECHO

ENGLISH CHANNEL

Boulogne

Cherbourg

LUXEMBOURG

Brest

AUSTRIA

Normandy landings

FRANCE

SWITZERLAND

Bay of
Biscay

ADRIATIC SEA

Gulf of
Genoa

PORTUGAL

CORSICA

ITALY

SPAIN

La
Maddalena

Naples

Tarant

BALEARIC IS.

SARDINA

TYRRHENIAN
SEA

Decimomannu

Messina
Catania

Cagliari

Palermo

MEDITERRANEAN SEA

SKERKI
BANK

Trapani

SICILY

Reggio
Calabri

TANGIER

Gibraltar

Bizerta

THE NARROW

Syracuse

SP MOROCCO

Oran

Algiers

Bône

Tunis

Pantellaria

Comisa

Casablanca

MALTA

Sfax

Lampedusa

MOROCCO

ALGERIA

TUNISIA

Kerkenah Is.

Tripoli

Buerat

TRIPOLITANIA

0   100   500 miles

The two new 15-inch-gun battleships *Vittorio Veneto* and *Littorio*, soon to be joined by a third, the *Roma*, reflected the Italian style and talent for design as clearly as the *Bismarck* was heavily Teutonic, and also stronger. In fact all the Italian classes of ships were relatively lightly armoured, much being sacrificed for speed. The navy relied on the army for its bombing force on the principle that the distances involved in Mediterranean operations did not justify the use of carriers.

Admiral Cunningham had an early taste of what it would be like fighting the Italian Navy early in June 1940. A large Italian convoy *en route* to Libya from Naples was spotted by a British submarine, the *Phoenix*, and by a flying boat operating from Malta. The convoy was escorted by two battleships and no fewer than sixteen cruisers and a strong force of destroyers.

Cunningham luckily was already at sea in order to provide cover for two convoys due to leave Malta for Alexandria. The Italians were equally aware of Cunningham's position and with great skill and promptitude laid on a massive bombing attack by high-level bombers. The bombs fell, visible almost all the way down, in dauntingly accurate sticks from the tight-packed formations, the pilots seemingly unconcerned at the heavy anti-aircraft fire put up by Cunningham's ships. At first it seemed that none could miss. But so small is the target for bomb-aimers at a high altitude that however accurately the bombs are dropped it was at that time statistically very difficult to make a hit, as the American B-17 bomber crews were to discover in the Pacific. Only the cruiser *Gloucester* took a hit in this the first of many attacks the Mediterranean Fleet was to suffer in the months ahead. The rest of the ships steamed safely through the forest of tall splashes.

When Cunningham later learned that the Italian Fleet had altered course on to an easterly heading he rightly concluded that the convoy was destined for Benghazi, and steamed at full speed to place himself between the Italians and their base at Taranto.

The results were not so dramatic as at Jutland but by the afternoon of 9 July the cruisers on both sides were in visual contact. The more heavily gunned Italian cruisers were the first to open fire and Vice-Admiral John Tovey, commanding the British cruisers, was subjected to some very accurate 8-inch fire before Cunningham came up at full speed in his flagship – at least 4 knots faster than his other two battleships – and gave him the support of his 15-inch guns.

The old *Warspite*, which was to see more action in its lifetime than any other battleship this century, caused the Italian cruisers to make off rapidly under cover of a smokescreen. But a few minutes later the Italian battleships came into view and the *Warspite* opened fire again at extreme range of fifteen miles. The shooting was superb and she scored a seriously damaging hit on the *Cesare*, which was forced to reduce speed and fall out of line. More smoke concealed the Italian heavy ships, and the brush with the enemy – and it was never more than that – continued intermittently as the great clouds of smoke permitted. No more hits were made on either side and the action was broken off by 5.00 p.m., with the Italians scuttling away at speeds up to 40 knots towards the Messina Straits. Here the Italian Air Force, the *Regia Aeronautica*, interceded, but on the wrong side, and British disappointment was somewhat alleviated by the overheard frantic and furious radio signals exchanged between ships and bombers.

A cheer went up the next day, too, among the *Eagle*'s pilots when they returned from a raid on enemy shipping and reported a destroyer sunk. The Australian cruiser *Sydney*, Captain John Collins RAN, chanced upon some of the survivors in the water and began to take them onboard. The rescue operation was interrupted by a peremptory order from Tovey, 'Rejoin forthwith.' 'So we left them a cutter and a signalling lamp and told them the course to steer,' Collins recalled. 'Many years later on a NATO exercise when I found myself with a group of Italian naval officers, one of them suddenly remarked, "We love the Australian Navy. When they had to steam away, they gave us a boat and we got back to Italy."'[1]

Calabria, as this skirmish was to be named, marked a good start for Andrew Cunningham, who never lost an opportunity for attacking the enemy and successfully revived the spirit of the Royal Navy of the Napoleonic Wars. And, like the Battle of Heligoland Bight at the outset of the First World War, it led to the enemy henceforth pursuing an even more cautious strategy.

Captain Collins figured in a more productive engagement a few days later, which served to confirm the Italian Navy high command in its policy of ultra caution. 'At Alexandria A.B.C.[Cunningham] said to me, "I want you to go to the Aegean to look for Italian shipping passing to or from the Dodecanese. Follow up behind Nicolson. He'll have four destroyers and keep one with you."'

Commander H.St L.Nicolson was in the *Hyperion* and the five destroyers were drawn from the 2nd Flotilla. Cunningham himself picks up the story:

At daylight next morning, when Commander Nicolson's destroyers were somewhere off the north-western end of Crete, they sighted two Italian cruisers coming in from the westward. Quite rightly they turned and ran for it, and were very soon under fire with the enemy in full pursuit. The *Sydney* about forty-five miles to the northward, received the *Hyperion*'s report of two enemy cruisers, and at once turned south and went on to full speed.[2]

The cruisers were of the *Condottieri* class and faster than any British destroyer, while their total gunpower was twice that of the *Sydney*. The outlook appeared highly speculative to Admiral Cunningham listening in to the distant signals. Two hours passed 'and I was on tenterhooks'. Then came the signal that the *Sydney* had hit and stopped one of the cruisers and was pursuing, and hitting, the second ship. Thanks to her 37 knots she got away, badly damaged, but with the help of Nicolson's destroyers the *Bartolomeo Colleoni* was sent to the bottom.

Again Collins was interrupted while picking up survivors, this time by

Italian aircraft which bombed them – to the disgust of the 545 Italians –
while they were stationary and for most of the way back to Alexandria.
Nicolson was given a bar to his DSO and Collins was awarded the CB
for this forceful action.

This was all very encouraging but Cunningham realized that fortune
might not always be so kind to him, and knew that the Italian Fleet had
taken delivery of more ships. Should the battle fleet choose to challenge
him to a fleet action, the odds would be overwhelmingly against him, especially as it would almost certainly take place within range of land-based
bombers from Italy, Sicily or North Africa. The Admiralty had already
responded by creating Force H, based on Gibraltar, which would help
to look after things in the western Mediterranean, under the exceptionally
able Admiral Somerville – whose distasteful task it was to bombard the
French Fleet at Oran. Now, on 1 September 1940, Cunningham received
reinforcements in the shape of the modern armoured fleet carrier *Illustrious*
with Fulmar fighters, the battleship *Valiant* which had been modernized
up to the *Warspite*'s standards, and two anti-aircraft cruisers.

This new strength arrived in time for the opening of the Italian offensive
towards Egypt and the declaration of war against Greece on the north
side of the Mediterranean.

From the naval point of view [Admiral Cunningham wrote] this news was good
and bad. It meant that we could now use Suda Bay in Crete as an advanced base
for our operations in the Central Mediterranean.... On the other hand, with Greece
in the war, it was quite certain that we should presently have to send her troops
and quantities of war material. This would mean a steady stream of convoys to
and fro across the Eastern Mediterranean and the Aegean, all liable to attack by
submarines and within easy each of the Italian airfields in the Dodecanese. This
in turn would entail an additional strain upon our already overworked destroyers
and escort forces.[3]

One naval officer has commented:

What was very important for us at this time was somehow to neutralize the Italian
battle fleet. It was clear that they were no more likely than their allies the Germans
in the First World War to face a fleet action. They had every opportunity of giving
us an almighty blow on September the first before we met the reinforcements from
Gib., with the *Illustrious* a sitting duck. But they scuttled off home as usual.

The operation to bring about this neutralization had been among Admiral
Cunningham's plans for months, and the arrival of the modern *Illustrious*,
with the aggressive and able Rear-Admiral Lumley Lyster, made it practicable. Cunningham's thinking was unknowingly in parallel with Admiral
Yamamoto's, if on a much-reduced scale, while the British C-in-C experienced the same doubtful initial response from the Admiralty as Yamamoto
received for the proposed Pearl Harbor venture on the other side of the
world.

With the most careful planning, Lyster and Cunningham believed that it was possible to strike a decisive air blow at the Italian Fleet at anchor in Taranto harbour. It would not be an easy task. Taranto was protected by twenty-one batteries of 4-inch anti-aircraft guns and countless light guns and by balloons, underwater nets and searchlights, as well as the gun protection of the ships themselves. Everything would have to favour the attack if it were to succeed.

The final planning was greatly helped by the arrival in Malta of modern American reconnaissance aircraft. Just as the useful very long-range American Catalina, newly arrived in Britain, was to make it possible to relocate the fleeing *Bismarck* in the Atlantic, so the newly arrived Martin Maryland was able to fly high and fast (280 mph) over Italian bases to bring back to Malta photographs of the current situation. There were only three of them, but they made all the difference. Shortly before the planned date for the attack, which was to be carried out in moonlight, one of the Marylands brought back photographs showing five of six Italian battleships tucked neatly at anchor in the circular Mar Grande, the outer Taranto harbour. One last reconnaissance photograph showed the sixth heading for the slaughter yard. The air crews could hardly ask for more.

At 6.00 p.m. on 11 November 1940 Cunningham detached the *Illustrious* to the north-west. 'Proceed in execution of previous orders for "Operation Judgement",' the C-in-C signalled. Then, less formally, 'Good luck then to your lads in their enterprise. Their success may well have a most important bearing on the course of the war in the Mediterranean.'

The air crews, numbering no more than forty-two in all, were imbued with excited optimism. By any rational judgement twenty-one Swordfish bombers and torpedo-bombers, looking like the second stage of development after the Wright Brothers' machine, appeared pathetically inadequate for the task of taking on six battleships ('3 Stringbags per Dreadnought'). But there were factors on their side: a number of the balloons had been recently blown free in a gale; surprise would be complete; and they had new torpedoes fitted with a magnetic device which would allow the projectile to be set deep enough to travel beneath the defensive nets and yet explode *under* the target ship if it did not directly strike it.

At 8.35 p.m. Lieutenant-Commander Kenneth Williamson led off the first wave of planes from the *Illustrious*'s flight deck. Lieutenant M.R.Maund, an 18-inch torpedo under the belly of his Stringbag, prepared to follow:

Parachute secured and Sutton harness pinned, the fitter bends over me, shouts 'Good luck, sir' into my speaking-tube, and is gone. I call up Bull in the back to check intercom – he tells me the rear cockpit lighting has fused – then look around the orange-lighted cockpit; gas and oil pressures OK, full tank, selector-switches on, camber-gear set, and other such precautions; run up and test switches, tail incidence set, and I jerk my thumb up to a shadow near the port wheel. Now comes the longest wait of all. 4F rocks in the slip-stream of aircraft ahead of her as other engines run up, and a feeling of desolation is upon me, unrelieved by the company of ten other aircraft crews, who, though no doubt entertaining similar thoughts, seem merged each into his own aircraft to become part of a machine without personality; only the quiet figures on the chocks seem human, and they are miles away.

The funnel smoke, a jet-black plume against the bright-starred sky, bespeaks of an increase in speed for the take-off; the fairy lights flick on, and with a gentle shudder the ship turns into wind, whirling the plan of stars about the foretop.

A green light waves away our chocks, orders us to taxi forward; the wings are spread with a slam, and as I test the aileron controls, green waves again. We are off, gently climbing away on the port bow where the first flame-float already burns, where the letter 'K' is being flashed in black space.

At 4,000 feet we pass through a hole in scattered cloud – dark smudges above us at one moment, and the next stray fleece beneath airwheels filled with the light of a full moon.

Six thousand feet. God, how cold it is here! The sort of cold that fills you until all else is drowned save perhaps fear and loneliness. Suspended between heaven and earth in a sort of no-man's land – to be sure, no man was ever meant to be here – in the abyss which men of old feared to meet if they ventured to the ends of the earth.... We turn towards the coast and drop away into line astern, engines throttled back. For ages we seem to hover without any apparent alteration; then red, white and green flaming onions come streaming in our direction, the high explosive shell bursts get closer, and looking down to starboard I see the vague smudge of a shape I now know as well as my own hand. We are in attacking position. The next ahead disappears as I am looking for my line of approach, so down we go in a gentle pause, glide towards the north-western corner of the harbour. The master-switch is made, a notch or two back on the incidence wheel, and my fear is gone, leaving a mind as clear and unfettered as it has ever been in my life. The hail of tracer at 6,000 feet is behind now, and there is nothing here to dodge; then I see that I am wrong, it is not behind any more. They have shifted target; for now, away below to starboard, a hail of red, white and green balls cover the harbour to a height of 2,000 feet. This thing is beyond a joke.

A burst of brilliance on the north-eastern shore, then another and another as the flare-dropper releases his load, until the harbour shows clear in the light he has made. Not too bright to dull the arc of raining colour over the harbour where tracer flies, allowing, it seems, no room to escape unscathed....

And so we jink and swerve, an instinct of living guiding my legs and right arm; two large clear shapes on our starboard side are monstrous in the background of flares. We turn until the right-hand battleship is between the bars of the torpedo-sight, dropping down as we do so. The water is close beneath our wheels, so close I'm wondering which is to happen first – the torpedo going or our hitting the sea – then we level out, and almost without thought the button is pressed and a jerk tells me the 'fish' is gone....

Turning to look back at last, my nearly hysterical mind is amazed. 'Bull! Just look at that bloody awful mess – look at it! Just look at it!' and more of that tempo. A huge weeping willow of coloured fire showers over the harbour area; above it still the bursting high explosive shells and sprays of tadpole-like fire, whilst every now and then a brilliant flame bursts in the sky and drifts lazily down.

At last we are free to climb. At 3,000 feet it is cool and peaceful, a few shining clouds casting their dark shadows on the sea, the warm orange cockpit light showing up the instruments that tell me all is well. All we have to do now is to get back and land on, thoughts that worry me not at all.[4]

Williamson was shot down and he and his observer were taken prisoner. Another Swordfish had crashed, killing the crew. Those were the casualties. Lieutenant Maund and the others had flown back, some with planes riddled by splinters and bullets, and by 2.50 a.m. all were safely onboard the *Illustrious*. And the score: three of the six battleships had been hit and sunk at their moorings: the *Littorio*, the *Duilio* and the *Cavour*, the last fatally while the other two would be out of action for months. With the *Doria* unserviceable anyway, the Italian Navy was reduced to two battleships. At the cost of two lives and two planes, the balance of power of the battle fleets in the Mediterranean had swung strongly to the Royal Navy. Maybe the Italian battleships would never have fought anyway, but while they remained a fleet in being they were a constant threat. In addition the seaplane base had been destroyed and bomb hits scored on several cruisers and destroyers.

The Italians were stunned by this bolt from the blue. Captain M.A. Bragadin was on duty at the Ministry of Marine, and wrote later:

From Taranto telephone messages began to come in, each one more serious than the last and quite unexpected; alarm-flares over the zone – attack by bombers – almost simultaneously aircraft torpedo attack launched at the ships in the teeth of intense gunfire – *Littorio* struck by three torpedoes – *Duilio* by one – *Cavour* by one – a medium-sized bomb pierces the decks of the *Trento* but does not explode – *Libeccio* hit by an unexploded bomb – at least three aircraft shot down, one strikes the bow of a destroyer and breaks itself up – *Littorio* remains afloat – also *Duilio* – *Cavour* is sinking; by dawn she had sunk, resting on the bottom with upper deck under water – news follows news.... It was as if we had lost a great naval battle, and could not foresee being able to recover from the consequences.[5]

For a few weeks after Taranto the tide flowed strongly in favour of the Royal Navy in the Mediterranean. The support to the army in North Africa, the escorting of convoys to Malta, the shelling of Italian and Italian-held ports, the bombing by the *Illustrious*'s aircraft of Italian airfields – all these operations were pursued with few losses while any intervention by the Italian Navy was brief, timid and ineffectual.

But in mid-winter 1940–41, like the onset of a cold wind from the north, the *Luftwaffe* began to make its presence known.

Fliegerkorps X, which had been operating from Norway, was withdrawn and flown south to put some spine into the Axis campaign in the Mediterranean, to deal with the British Fleet and neutralize Malta. It was a crack force of some 300 aircraft, Stuka dive-bombers, Junkers 88 bombers, twin-engine fighter-bomber Me 110s and single-engine Me 109s. The Royal Navy had had painful evidence of the efficiency of this corps during the disastrous Norwegian campaign.

The new German presence made its debut in the course of the passage of the most important Mediterranean convoy since the Italian entry into the war. The movement consisted of five ships for Malta and four for Greece sailing from Gibraltar, and two supply ships from Alexandria for Malta and two empty ships from Malta to Alexandria.

Admiral Cunningham with two battleships and the *Illustrious*, with supporting craft, placed himself in the Sicilian channel in order to be able to support all these convoys. His cruisers played the role of close escort between Malta and Alexandria; while Admiral Somerville's Force H would be responsible for the dangerous run from Gibraltar to Malta. It was an amazingly complicated as well as important movement of ships which required the closest co-ordination. This was wrecked, along with one of the ships intended for Greece, before the operation had even begun. The German heavy cruiser *Hipper* was enjoying one of her few raids into the Atlantic, which led to the scattering of the convoy even before it reached Gibraltar. Somerville sallied forth to greet his guests and round them up, and for thanks met a full winter gale which badly damaged his flagship.

Signals flashed from London and from end to end of the Mediterranean rescheduling the various stages, so that at last on the evening of 6 January 1941 the four surviving merchantmen with a vital mixed load of ammunition, crated Hurricane fighters and seed potatoes, cleared Gibraltar and set course on an easterly heading. The German bomber crews waited restlessly on their new Sicilian airfields.

But it was the British bombers on Malta that sprang first into action, bombing the much-reduced Italian battle fleet in Naples harbour. Of the two Taranto survivors one was damaged too badly to put to sea, and the flagship, the mighty *Vittorio Veneto*, retreated to Genoa. Then it was the turn of the Italian bombers, Savoia 79s, in customary parade-ground formation, which came out to meet the Gibraltar convoy. Up came the *Ark Royal*'s fighters to break the tidy pattern and shoot down two of the Savoias, none of which made a hit. Another Italian attack, this time ordered to bomb Cunningham's force to the east, never even found its target and jettisoned its bombs into the sea. So far so good, until the afternoon of 10 January:

Then things started to go wrong [reported Admiral Cunningham]. I was watching the destroyer screen taking up their new stations ... when I suddenly saw a heavy explosion under the *Gallant*'s bows. She had been mined, and in water through which the battle-fleet had passed only a short time before. Her bow was blown clean away and she was left helpless. . . .

In the meantime the fleet steamed south-east after the [Gibraltar] convoy, presently to be located and reported by enemy aircraft. . . . Just before 12.30 p.m. we were attacked by two Italian torpedo-bombers, which came in low. Their torpedoes passed astern of the *Valiant*. This incident had the unfortunate but natural result of bringing the fighters down from where they were patrolling high over the fleet.

It was like a preview of the American attack at Midway eighteen months later when the Devastator torpedo-bombers drew down the Zeros to give the dive-bombers a clear run.

Almost immediately large formations of aircraft were sighted to the northward, and were very soon overhead. They were recognized as German, three squadrons of Stukas. The *Illustrious* flew off more fighters; but neither they nor the patrol already in the air could gain sufficient height to do anything. We opened up with every A.A. gun we had as one by one the Stukas peeled off into their dives, concentrating almost the whole venom of their attack upon the *Illustrious*. At times she became almost hidden in a forest of great bomb splashes.[6]

The carrier received six direct hits by 1,000-pound bombs and a great number of near misses which buckled her plating and did internal damage. It was all over in ten minutes, leaving her burning and without being able to steer. But by 3.30 p.m. her fire and repair crews had things under control, and the carrier was able to head for Malta at 17 knots, a credit to the strength of her construction and the wisdom of providing all British fleet carriers with an armoured flight deck. It was also a great credit mark to her ship's company when she was the target again for twenty more Stukas. 'My heart sank as I watched her,' Cunningham recalled, 'wondering how with all her heavy damage, she would stand up to it. I need not have worried. As the attacks developed I saw every gun in the *Illustrious* flash into action, a grand and inspiring sight.'[7]

Fliegerkorps X had not finished with her within what had once been the security of Valetta harbour. She was too valuable a prey to be allowed to escape after all the attention they had given her. Sixty Stukas made her their target a few days later, but now she was better protected, by Malta's guns and patrolling fighters, and they scored only one minor hit. In spite of another ferocious dive-bomber assault, the *Illustrious*, patched up, slipped out of the harbour during darkness, *en route* to Norfolk, Virginia, where the Americans had agreed to repair her.

The *Illustrious* survived to fight again, but *Fliegerkorps X* had made an explosive mark on the strategy of naval warfare in the Mediterranean. The advantage of the land-based bomber over the carrier-based plane had been exposed starkly during those ten minutes of assault, confirming the wisdom of the Italian naval authorities' decision not to build carriers for the Mediterranean, even if (like the British) they had not foreseen the lethal nature of the dive-bombers and had opted for the far less effective high-level bomber.

Like Midway in the Pacific, there was only one safe aircraft carrier in the Mediterranean, and that was an island. From now on the vital importance of Malta was enhanced. The Allies knew it, and the Axis powers knew it, concentrating all their strength on neutralizing it, dropping on it thousands of tons of bombs, mining its waters, even stealing into its forbidden waters with miniature submarines – a skill which the Italians practised with relish and with successful results. The siege of Malta had begun.

*　　*　　*

Later in 1941 German U-boats penetrated the Mediterranean and began to make their mark as swiftly and destructively as the *Luftwaffe*. The Italian Navy had the use of some 100 operational submarines when they joined the war, twice as many as the German Navy. They were, statistically, a major item in Admiral Cunningham's considerations, but they turned out to be a damp squib. It was a different story when Hitler ordered six U-boats into the Mediterranean in September 1941 and four more in December.

The role of the carrier in the western Mediterranean was extended at this time to the delivery of fighters to Malta, the machines being flown off at maximum range from the island, when the carrier turned and hurried back to Gibraltar. The *Ark Royal* was returning from one of these successful missions on 13 November 1941. Her value was at this time especially high as British fleet carriers had been suffering from grave misfortunes for some time. As well as the *Illustrious*, still under repair in America, the *Formidable* sent to replace her in the eastern Mediterranean had suffered a similar fate at the hands of Stukas and was now undergoing a similar cure. The *Indomitable* was the victim of careless handling and had damaged herself running aground. Friedrich Guggenberger, a veteran U-boat commander of the Battle of the Atlantic, had the good fortune to intercept the *Ark Royal*, heavily escorted, off Gibraltar, stalked her skilfully and torpedoed her amidships. She sank before she could be towed the last thirty miles to her base.

Twelve days later Hans-Dietrich von Tiesenhausen, operating at the other end of the Mediterranean, penetrated Cunningham's screen and put three torpedoes into the battleship *Barham*. It was too much for the one-time flagship of the 5th Battle Squadron at Jutland. She took on a steep list and then exploded, taking down almost her entire company. Then, on the night of 14–15 December *U-557* caught the cruiser *Galatea* off Alexandria and sent her to the bottom, too. Later, the cruiser *Hermione* succumbed under similar circumstances.

This handful of U-boats had many more successes over the following months, among them the *Medway*. This ship had been built as a submarine depot vessel, and the British submarine offensive in the Mediterranean largely depended on her for maintenance and supplies. When she was sunk by *U-372* on 30 June 1942 she took with her ninety torpedoes, whose loss paralysed operations for many weeks.

The enormous influence of the torpedo as well as the bomb upon events and the tide of naval warfare in the Mediterranean was demonstrated by the British submarine force, too, in spite of the loss of the *Medway*. In the summer of 1940 British submarine successes against Italian merchantmen – some 45,000 tons – were bought at a high price of ten losses. This was no reflection on the quality of the commanders, rather because large, old and unsuitable boats had been sent to the Mediterranean. The Admiralty responded by sending a force of smaller, newer boats designed to work in inshore waters, which eventually formed the 10th Flotilla, whose exploits became 'an inspiration to submariners everywhere'. The exploits of commanders like Malcolm Wanklyn, E.D.Norman, R.D.Cayley and Alastair Mars made marvellous reading in Britain at a low period of the war, and they became household names.

For many months, from January 1941, the 10th Flotilla operating from Malta provided the most effective means of destruction of Axis supply ships to North Africa. The early catastrophic defeats of the Italian Army in Cyrenaica had been balanced by the arrival of the German Afrika Korps under General Erwin Rommel, just as the U-boats and the bombers of *Fliegerkorps X* had put steel into the other two services. Malcolm Wanklyn, a tall, bearded Scot, was perhaps the most skilful of all these young submariners who operated so effectively with their new U-class boats. On his first operation Wanklyn naturally had much to learn. He was off Cape Bon on the North African coast in the *Upholder* when two big Italian troopships, escorted by an Italian auxiliary, came into view shortly before midnight. He manoeuvred his boat close to the big German ship *Duisburg*, but not close enough. His two torpedoes were spotted in time to evade them. Wanklyn set off in pursuit but was forced to dive with the onset of daylight. A Sunderland flying boat from Malta took over as scout, keeping the valuable convoy in distant sight until torpedo-carrying Swordfish, also from Malta, could form up to attack. They made short work of one Italian ship, the *Iago*.

Wanklyn kept station with the remaining two ships all through the following night, and soon after 5.30 a.m. put two torpedoes into the *Duisburg*, which was already crowded with survivors from the *Iago*. The crippled ship could not be claimed by Wanklyn as she was eventually towed into Tripoli and salvaged.

Wanklyn made no mistakes on a patrol in April. He knew now that the chances of success increased in ratio with the shortness of the range. On 25 April 1941 he found the big Italian transport *Antoinetta Laura* and worked his way so close to her that he was able to save the last two torpedoes of four because the first had already sealed the fate of his victim before he could fire the last of the salvo. Next Wanklyn finished off a transport, packed with vehicles for Rommel, which had already been damaged by surface ships operating from Malta.

Now bursting with self-confidence and with a crew who were relishing their skill and success, Wanklyn picked up a convoy of five heavily escorted transports. He fired at two of them at point-blank range in rapid succession, and then went down deep to avoid the worst of the inevitable counter-attack by depth-charges. His boat was badly knocked about but when things died down he went up to periscope depth and saw that he had sunk one of his targets, while the other ship was under tow from a destroyer. Two more torpedoes finished her off.

Wanklyn's most successful and dangerous patrol of all led to Admiral Cunningham recommending him for the VC. The C-in-C describes briefly the latter part of his top submariner's patrol off Sicily in May 1941. The

Upholder had already been severely damaged by depth-charges after sinking a big tanker.

The *Upholder's* listening gear was out of action and the light was falling but sighting a south-bound troop convoy heavily escorted by destroyers he went in to attack. After nearly being rammed by a destroyer he fired torpedoes which sank the 18,000-ton liner *Conte Rosso*, crammed with troops. Thirty-seven depth-charges were dropped in the subsequent counter-attack.[8]

Lieutenant-Commander Wanklyn VC, DSO survived another eleven months of this wickedly dangerous work. His score was ten large merchant-men including three liners of around 20,000 tons, a destroyer and two U-boats, and he also damaged a cruiser and three more merchantmen.

As one distinguished and much-decorated British naval officer has noted:

The nervous strain on the crews mounted with each patrol. The supreme quality of submarine captains such as Wanklyn lay, as much as anything, in their ability to exude calm confidence during the nerve-racking counter-attacks when there was nothing to be done but wait passively as the depth-charges sank down through the water to explode with hull-hammering violence. Even so, in the *Upholder*, after the attack on the *Conte Rosso*, a signalman was so deranged temporarily as to try to open the conning tower hatch while the submarine was at a depth of 150 feet. It was in the *Urge*, where another outstanding officer, Lieutenant E.P.Tomkinson, commanded that a Leading Stoker would walk up and down loudly reciting the Lord's Prayer during depth-charge attacks.[9]

For a time, when the *Fliegerkorps X* bombing offensive against Malta was at its height, the harbour was virtually unusable and the airfields so pock-marked with craters and destroyed hangars that the submarines pro-vided the only form of attack against the German–Italian convoys. For a short period even the submarine flotilla had to be withdrawn.

At other times during the siege of Malta surface raiders were able to operate, and the pickings were as rich as the dangers were high. For a time, from April 1941, Captain Philip Mack with the destroyer *Jervis* and three more destroyers of the 14th Flotilla conducted a series of night sorties, the only way of circumventing the enemy's dominance of the air.

The night of 15–16 April 1941 was one of the bloodiest and most destructive for Mack and his men. A convoy of five fat transports escorted by three destroyers was known to be making its way along the Tunisian coast to Tripoli. Mack's destroyers should have been spotted against the moonlight when he unknowingly passed the convoy on an opposite course. Soon after reversing course, however, the relative position of hunter and hunted was reversed, and at 2.20 a.m. the *Jervis* spotted one of the Italian destroyers silhouetted against the moonlight and opened fire. The gun crews of the *Lampo* responded with commendable speed but they could get off only three salvos before their destroyer was overwhelmed.

The British destroyer *Nubian* dealt as swiftly and roughly with the *Baleno*, the first salvo hitting the bridge and killing all on it. In less than a minute the destroyer was smashed to a wreck of twisted steel, too.

'A night battle between light forces is the most terrifying experience I have ever faced,' an officer who had been in many of them has said. 'You're never quite certain you're not firing at each other instead of the enemy, and the confusion, cacophonous row and the dazzle of tracer, exploding shells, fire and searchlights all send the mind reeling.'

The inferno on that night was increased in volume of sound and intensity of light when Mack's destroyers set about the five ships, and reached a climax when the Italian ship *Sabaudia*, packed with ammunition, blew up. And the four German transports, loaded with troop reinforcements, supplies and vehicles for Rommel's army were all lost in 'Mack's night out'.

Mack himself did not get away unscathed, though. The escort commander, Commander Pietro de Cristoforo in the destroyer *Tarigo*, attempted to intervene between Mack and his charges. The first salvo mortally wounded him, but as he died he managed to regain control of his ship and launched three torpedoes, two of which struck and sank the *Mohawk*. Forty-one of her crew went down with her, but the *Tarigo* paid the full price too.

Mack's destroyers were later replaced briefly by Captain Lord Louis Mountbatten's flotilla which was despatched almost at once to the eastern Mediterranean where they were needed for the evacuation of Greece by the Allied army. It was not until 21 October 1941 – suitably, Trafalgar Day – that a striking force of surface ships again began to operate from Malta.

There were times when the German High Command became exasperated with the performance of their allies in the Mediterranean theatre, by land, by sea and in the air. In the early weeks of 1941 even Italy's best friends could not pretend that her campaign in Greece was prospering, and the Germans became increasingly aware that they would have to intervene and settle that matter before proceeding with their mightiest campaign of all, Operation Barbarossa, the invasion of Russia. Meanwhile supplies were pouring in to Greece from Egypt and the Italian Navy appeared to be doing nothing about it.

The Italian Naval Command had long since decided upon a waiting game and was strongly averse to sweeps against this well-defended traffic across the Aegean. Besides, oil fuel was short. However, early in March Admiral Angelo Iachino was prevailed upon to plan a sweep into the eastern Mediterranean. He assembled a very considerable fleet consisting of the *Vittorio Veneto* (flag), six heavy cruisers, two light cruisers and thirteen destroyers – all modern, fast ships which could choose their range and attack or retreat as they chose. What the Admiral lacked, and had been deficient in since the outbreak of war, was efficient air reconnaissance; but he had been reassured that the *Luftwaffe* would provide that.

Iachino sailed from Naples at 9.00 p.m. on 26 March 1941, intending to rendezvous with his cruisers from Brindisi and Taranto the following morning. This was accomplished successfully, but not without part of his force being spotted by a Sunderland flying boat from Malta. He altered course as if heading for North Africa, but after hearing that the decoded message back to base by the Sunderland (the Italians were sharp on code-breaking) had referred to only four ships, he resumed his course east, intending to sweep through the convoy route to Greece from Alexandria and return at high speed.

As Iachino had feared, he got none of the promised reconnaissance help from the *Luftwaffe*, and was reduced to launching his own inadequate spotter planes at first light on 28 March. He was in luck. At 6.43 a.m. one of them sighted British light cruisers and destroyers to the south-east, indicating a convoy.

At this time the Italian Fleet was in three groups shaped like a reverse arrow on a course 130°, the two forces of heavy cruisers ten and twenty miles respectively ahead of the flagship. An hour after the air sighting, the *Trieste* observed smoke and identified light cruisers heading for Alexandria at high speed. The *Trieste*, *Trento* and *Bolzano*, with their three destroyers, set off in confident pursuit. They were all faster than any British light cruiser and their broadside weight was double that of the fleeing enemy.

The big Italian ships opened fire at extreme range of over fourteen miles, at which the British cruisers could not reply, and the gap between the two protagonists was swiftly and uncomfortably narrowing.

These unfortunate British cruisers were commanded by Vice-Admiral H.D.Pridham-Wippell. His Staff Officer (Operations), Commander R.L.Fisher, recalled the day's proceedings so far:

I was on the bridge and we were off Gavdo [island] and we saw a small aircraft of a type which somebody said could only have come from an Italian cruiser. Pretty soon after that we saw the *Trento* lot and ran away for all we were worth, our four cruisers in line abreast zig-zagging and making smoke.... We were shot at for quite a long time and lots of salvos came close – close enough for us to get some splashes on deck – but nobody hit.[10]

Soon the Italians were within range of the British cruisers' 6-inch guns, and a spotter plane was launched to assist the gunlayers with reports on the fall of shot. The observer could see little for the smoke but was just able to make out four more Italian cruisers pounding down fast from the north-east. 'It began to look as if we were going to be trapped between the devil and the deep blue sea. . . .'

Then, in the mysterious way that the Italian Navy had, fire suddenly ceased and the ocean was clear to every horizon.

At this time – shortly after 9.00 a.m. – the position between the two forces was closely parallel to the preliminary moves at Jutland, the scouting forces of both sides being unaware that the enemy was operating battleships, and that, moreover, they were steering towards the same spot. Admiral Cunningham had taken his fleet to sea at dusk on the strength of the Sunderland flying boat's report. His force consisted of his flagship *Warspite*, the *Barham* and *Valiant*, the newly arrived carrier *Formidable* and nine destroyers, a daunting force with the advantage of a modern carrier and the disadvantage of much slower speed than the Italians.

At first light the *Formidable* flung out search aircraft, and Cunningham began to build up a picture from their sightings and the reports from Pridham-Wippell. At 9.56 a.m. he was able to reassure his cruiser commander that torpedo aircraft with a pair of fighters were on their way to give support. Pridham-Wippell's retort did not express gratitude.

On reaching the target area [one of the pilots recalled] we passed four British cruisers steaming in line ahead. In spite of our repeated attempts to identify ourselves to them they kept up a steady barrage of A.A. fire at us until we eventually passed out of range.[11]

Disappointed that they had failed to shoot down any of the 'enemy' planes, the light cruisers continued their westerly course, hoping to re-sight the enemy heavy cruisers in order to 'draw' Cunningham's battleships on to them. They were in for their second surprise of the morning. Commander Fisher continues his account:

We now steamed westward again, feeling braver and braver as we recovered from our first plastering. It was sunny and the sea void of the enemy; the turret crews were sitting on the roofs of their turrets, and action bully beef sandwiches arrived on the bridge. The commander came on the bridge and, with his mouth full of sandwich, nudged me and said, 'What battleship is that over on the starboard beam? I thought ours were miles to the east of us.' As I took my binoculars to examine a vessel hull down to the northward there was a whistling noise and the first salvo of 15-inch from the *Vittorio Veneto* landed somewhere around.[12]

The fire rapidly became intense and accurate. The light cruisers turned south and made smoke but the *Orion* received a near miss which did some damage before the screen obscured her from the enemy battleship.

The next phase of the action is best seen from the air where for a while there was a lot of activity. The Albacore pilots could see the *Vittorio Veneto* firing at a range of fourteen miles at Pridham-Wippell's fleeing cruisers.

Since the battleship was steaming at 30 knots, it was clear that our cruisers were in for trouble [reported one of the pilots], and they could expect no help from the main fleet which was more than eighty miles away.[13]

The survival of Pridham-Wippell's scouting squadron appeared to depend on the six pilots of the Albacores, and all of them were aware of their heavy responsibility: six old biplanes against a modern 35,000-ton battleship and its escort. Moreover, its escort had suddenly been reinforced by German fighter-bombers. *Fliegerkorps X* had made a belated appearance in the form of two Ju88s, armed with cannon and machine-guns. The two British fighters went at them. 'It was a head-on attack we made and we did not see him hit the sea, but Pinky Haworth did,'[14] reported one of the fighter pilots. They also, rather surprisingly, drove off the other Junkers.

The problem still remained of mounting a torpedo attack on the Italian battleship. And that could not be solved until they caught up with her. With the battleship still doing 30 knots and a 30-knot headwind when they could do only 90 knots, progress was sluggish. Meanwhile, the *Vittorio Veneto* slammed away at Pridham-Wippell, with ninety-four heavy shells in all, getting a number of straddles but mercifully without scoring a hit.

Then at last, down went the Albacores, the wind whistling through the bracing wires. The battleship had plenty of time to manoeuvre and made the attack difficult for the pilots. But they all dropped their 'tin fish' through a ferocious stream of light and heavy anti-aircraft fire, and got away without loss while confident that they had made at least one hit.

They had not done so. But they had saved the light cruisers which, not so long before, had also been trying to shoot them down. Admiral Iachino broke off the action and headed for home at best speed with all his cruisers.

It looked like one more abortive effort to force the Italians to do battle. Cunningham was now forty-five miles south-east of the Italian fleet and knew that his only chance was to slow down the enemy with more torpedo attacks. These were mounted, one in the afternoon and a second one at dusk. At the cost of his life the squadron leader, Lieutenant-Commander J.Dalyell-Stead, scored a hit on the stern of the *Vittorio Veneto* by taking his machine in to point-blank range before dropping. It slowed the battleship down to 17 knots. Hopes rose in the *Warspite* that the enemy flagship might be caught during darkness, a favourable time for the British with the inestimable advantage of radar. But by strenuous endeavours the Italians succeeded in repairing some of the damage and raising the battleship's speed. The final strike by the torpedo-bombers failed again to hit her.

It was not entirely a wasted strike. Seeing that he could not manoeuvre to get at the main target, one pilot aimed at the heavy cruiser *Pola*. The torpedo caught her amidships and brought her to a complete standstill. The Italian Admiral did not pause in his headlong retreat, sensibly leaving the *Pola* to her fate. Aware how close the end was, the crew got out of hand and broached the wine casks with the intention of going down drunk and happy. They calculated that they had about two hours before the British caught them up, enough for a litre or two of chianti each.

The sun had set, it was a warm, clear, moonless but starlit Mediterranean night. Admiral Cunningham still nursed some hope of catching up with the damaged *Vittorio Veneto*. Shortly after 10.00 p.m. radar revealed the blip from a large vessel, and it did not appear to be moving. A few minutes later a keen-eyed officer on the *Warspite*'s bridge picked out two large cruisers and one smaller one crossing the bows of the battle fleet from starboard to port. 'I looked through my glasses', recalled Cunningham, 'and there they were.' Not just one stationary ship but several more, steaming fast. . . .'

Admiral Iachino had changed his mind about leaving the *Pola* to her inevitable fate – whether prompted by compassion or guilt, or persuaded by his Staff, will never be known. But in despatching the heavy cruisers *Zara* and *Fiume* and four destroyers to the *Pola*'s rescue, he sealed the fate of some of his best ships, and the lives of hundreds of his officers and men. The rescue party arrived at almost the same time as Admiral Cunningham, who manoeuvred his battleships unseen by the Italians so that almost every one of his 15-inch guns – twenty-four in all – could bear on the hapless enemy at a range of a mile and a half.

There then ensued the most terrible massacre of the Mediterranean war. Cunningham later wrote:

One heard the 'ting-ting-ting' of the firing gongs. Then came the great orange flash and the violent shudder as the six big guns (Y turret was not bearing at this moment) were fired simultaneously. At the very same instant the destroyer *Greyhound*, on the screen, switched her searchlight on to one of the enemy cruisers, showing her momentarily up as a silvery-blue shape in the darkness. Our search-lights shone out with the first salvo, and provided full illumination for what was a ghastly sight. Full in the beam I saw our six great projectiles flying through the air. Five out of the six hit a few feet below the level of the cruiser's upper deck and burst with splashes of brilliant flame. The Italians were quite unprepared. Their guns were trained fore and aft. They were helplessly shattered before they could put up any resistance. In the midst of all this there was one milder diversion. Captain Douglas Fisher, the captain of the *Warspite*, was a gunnery officer of note. When he saw the first salvo hit he was heard to say in a voice of wondering surprise: 'Good Lord! We've hit her!'[15]

There is no need to linger on the events of the next minutes. One by one the big Italian ships were torn apart by salvo after salvo of heavy shellfire, setting them on fire. The *Pola* herself missed the first phase of the massacre but was dealt with by destroyers later, as were two of the enemy destroyers.

It was indeed a terrible night of fire and sudden death, costing the lives of almost 2,500 Italians, as many as the Germans lost at Jutland. The Battle of Cape Matapan was Cunningham's greatest victory. What was left of Italian fighting will after Taranto four months earlier disappeared in the flames and smoke and tortured steel of five fine fighting ships on that March night.

There is no better example of the effectiveness of close integration between the fighting forces in the Mediterranean than the 'Tiger' operations of May 1941. The skill with which the three services operated together shows the remarkable advance gained after almost two years of war at the cost of the lessons of the Norwegian campaign, the withdrawal from Dunkirk, Dakar and other operations.

This was the position in North Africa around the middle of April: General Archibald Wavell, C-in-C 8th Army, was successfully holding off the fierce offensive of General Rommel, whose seasoned and highly skilful troops had brought an entirely new element into the enemy's struggle to gain control of Egypt. Wavell was in the middle of dictating a telegram to Churchill on 20 April, describing his weakness in tanks and referring anxiously to Rommel's 150 tanks when he himself received a message which told him that an armoured division of German tanks had just arrived safely at Tripoli. As an armoured division would contain about 400 tanks, this was a devastating blow, and would almost certainly lead to Wavell's defeat and a German advance to the Nile.

Churchill responded with characteristic speed and firmness, issuing instructions to strip the home forces to the bone of tanks, embark them on transports and rush them through the Mediterranean. The Cape route was far too slow for the need, and the Admiralty was ordered to organize a super-swift convoy through the western Mediterranean. In a directive issued on the same date as Wavell's telegram, Churchill wrote:

The only way in which this great purpose can be achieved is by sending the fast mechanical ships of the fast section of [Convoy] WS7 *through the Mediterranean*. General Wavell's telegram shows that machines, not men, are needed. The risk of losing the vehicles, or part of them, must be accepted. Even if half get through the situation would be restored. Speed is vital. Every day's delay must be avoided. Let me have a time-table of what is possible, observing that at 16 knots the distance is only about eight days.... This would give General Wavell effective support during the first week in May.[16]

Of the many dangers to be faced by this fast convoy from U-boats, mine-fields, surface fleets, torpedo-boats and torpedo-bombers and bombing, the most lethal were the *Luftwaffe* dive-bombers, operating from airfields in Sicily, which had succeeded in bolting the door to the central Mediterranean from Gibraltar. Admiral Cunningham, far from flinching from this task, characteristically decided to exploit it and increase the chances of its successful conclusion by despatching a convoy of tankers and supply ships from Egypt, which he would escort, also using the occasion to bombard enemy-held Benghazi on the way out and on the way home again.

Similarly, Admiral Somerville at Gibraltar used the occasion to add to his force a battleship and two cruisers due to reinforce Cunningham. Besides the air cover provided by fighters from the *Ark Royal*, newly arrived long-range twin-engine Beaufighters, with the crushing armament of four 20-mm cannon and seven .303 machine-guns, would operate from Malta.

Under the utmost secrecy the tank-carrying transports were detached from the Cape-bound convoy WS7 in the Atlantic and steamed fast for Gibraltar. There Somerville picked them up, and the armada, with its light umbrella of Fulmer fighters, sped east. Tiger had reached a point south of Sardinia before being spotted by the enemy. Air attacks followed, but they were hampered by the poor weather which providentially set in to play a major role in the success of the operation. Only enemy mines took their toll, sinking one of the transports and damaging, not fatally, a second. By the afternoon of 9 May Wavell's tanks were in the custody of the Mediterranean Fleet after a massive rendezvous south of Malta.

So far Cunningham's end of the operation had prospered. His cruisers intercepted and sank two ammunition ships just outside Benghazi. This, coincidentally, was immediately followed by a lone low-level bombing attack on Tripoli harbour. The pilot's daring brought rich reward. He, too, hit an ammunition ship, the mighty explosion also wrecking the only quay capable of unloading tanks and transport.

With the aid of his fighters Cunningham managed to beat off all attempts by the *Luftwaffe* to hit his ships, his carrier and the precious tank transports alike. On 12 May 1941, scarcely three weeks since Wavell had appealed for tanks, the navy delivered 238 of them, with a bonus of forty-three crated Hurricane fighters, safely into his eager arms.

The British triumph of Matapan and the success of Operation Tiger was followed by the tragedies of April and May, conforming to the pattern, now almost predictable, of success and failure in this long-drawn-out campaign. German intervention in Greece had now become inevitable. On 6 April German troops of the 12th Army crossed the frontier and, in a mere three weeks, finished the job so unsuccessfully started by the Italians. Once again overwhelming air power, provided by *Fliegerkorps VIII* and part of *Fliegerkorps XI*, provided the main punch, while ground troops swarmed over the difficult Greek terrain, driving the Greek, British, Commonwealth and Polish troops before them. Suddenly it became clear that there would have to be another Dunkirk, and that this time, because of the *Luftwaffe*, the evacuation of over 50,000 troops would have to be conducted at night.

Admiral Pridham-Wippell, fresh from his part at Matapan, was placed in command of the evacuation at this headquarters at Suda Bay, Crete. It was like Norway all over again, with the men struggling to board boats off open beaches in many cases, then the rough and dangerous passage to the troopship, clambering on board, the call for speed and more speed, and the race to get well clear of the coast before the inevitable arrival of the *Luftwaffe*. The sailors were as weary and in many cases as hungry as the soldiers they were rescuing, and over all the proceedings there lay the grey, baleful mantle of defeat. One troopship, the *Slamat*, was found by Stukas at first light and sent to the bottom with heavy loss of life. Two destroyers dashed to the scene, rescued 700 men in another hailstorm of Stuka bombs, and raced for Crete. They never completed their mission. The Stukas, like schoolboy bullies, seemed to tease the destroyers with near misses before pouncing. Fewer than forty men survived the onslaught.

With the involvement of almost the entire Mediterranean Fleet some 34,000 troops were brought safely back to Egypt, while 16,000 less fortunate men were diverted to Crete to form a garrison in the event of a German attempt at invasion.

As night follows day, that invasion began on 4 May 1941. It is difficult to judge which was the greater folly, the British decision to defend Crete or the German decision to seize the island. General Kurt Student, the German paratroop and airborne specialist, was the inspiration behind the operation. Hitler gave him his support, without reference to his General Staff. The island, it was agreed, would be taken initially by glider-borne troops and paratroopers, landing under a thick umbrella of over 700 aircraft. There was not a solitary plane to support the Allied ground forces.

The naval part in the ferocious battle for the island which began on the morning of 20 May was to bar the passage and landing of reinforcements and armour to support the airborne troops, and where practicable to bombard enemy positions. In this they were completely successful. Among those taking part was Captain (D) Lord Louis Mountbatten, whose 5th Flotilla was newly arrived from Malta. He described one night's operations:

After pouring a barrage of 4.7-inch shells on to German-held positions, we turned our guns on to some Greek fishing vessels packed solid with supplies and German troops, striking two of them. It was an absolute massacre. None of that group of vessels survived, and not one German soldier arrived by sea of the thousands who embarked from the Greek mainland.[17]

But the greater the losses of German troops in attempting to land on Crete, the greater and more effective the revenge meted out by the *Luftwaffe*. For days on end Admiral Cunningham's cruisers and destroyers fought off bombing attacks by dive-bombers, high-level bombers and fighter-bombers, using up vast quantities of anti-aircraft ammunition, a factor which led to a number of ships returning prematurely from attacks on German convoys of troop transports. Their own casualties were terrible, in ships and men. The daily toll of destruction made savage reading for the C-in-C: cruisers *Fiji*, *Gloucester*, *Orion* and *Dido*, Mountbatten's *Kelly* and the *Kashmir*, the *Hereward* and *Greyhound* – the *Warspite* herself – all sunk or severely damaged.

One by one the battered men o'war, with their gallant crews almost at the limit of human endurance, crept back to Alexandria, many with rescued comrades from other ships. The destroyer *Juno* took a direct hit from a heavy bomb which penetrated to her magazine, blowing her to pieces. Cunningham's only carrier, the *Formidable*, was knocked out of action. Captain Back of the *Orion* was not the only ship's commander killed by machine-gun fire while on his bridge. And 260 more were killed below decks when a heavy bomb penetrated deep into the cruiser.

On the island, as more German troops were landed by air, the stubborn defence by the Australian, New Zealand, Polish and British troops slowly cracked, and on 27 May 1941 the navy was called upon to carry out an evacuation. Cunningham issued a rallying signal: 'We must not let them down. It takes the Navy three years to build a ship. It would take three hundred to rebuild a tradition.'

And so, once again, over three dreadful nights, some 12,000 troops were saved from certain death or capture by the overwhelmingly powerful airborne forces. The cost to the navy was many more lives, severe damage to a cruiser and two destroyers and the loss of an anti-aircraft cruiser. But neither the navy nor the army cracked under the stress of the German onslaught, nor in the face of such severe losses.

As for the Germans, so near had they been to defeat during those early days after the invasion, and so appalling were their losses, that while General Guderian had proved his point, airborne troops were never again to be used in the role for which they had been trained. Six thousand casualties had broken the back of Germany's airborne army. *Fliegerkorps XI* never recovered, unlike the Mediterranean Fleet, which was to regain ascendancy as German airpower was drawn east for Hitler's invasion of Russia.

So, by July 1941 the tide had turned once again, and over the following months British submarines and bombers obtained and held a tight stranglehold on Axis supply lines across the Mediterranean. By November it had become possible to operate an offensive surface force, known as Force X, the successor to Captain Mack's destroyer force. Under the command of Captain William Agnew, later to earn two DSOs and be knighted, with the 6-inch-gunned cruisers *Aurora* and *Penelope* and a couple of destroyers, Force X was soon busy creating mayhem among the Africa-bound convoys.

Captain Agnew's most productive operation was on the night of 8–9 November 1941. One of Malta's valuable Marylands reported a convoy leaving the Straits of Messina in the afternoon, its importance marked by its escort of seven destroyers and close support of the crack heavy cruisers *Trieste* and *Trento* and four more destroyers, plus eight aircraft.

The seven transports should have been safe enough with this protection which had been carefully planned in the knowledge of Agnew's arrival at Malta. What had not been taken into account was that, after almost eighteen months of naval operations in the Mediterranean, the Italian Navy had still not undergone any night battle training.

Agnew's ships stalked this quarry like a pack of hungry wolves. Every man under his command was a seasoned campaigner by now, and though completely outgunned and outnumbered they had the advantage of radar, and the additional surprise this gave them. The moon was in the east, outlining all seven ships and their escort.

In a sudden blaze of 6-inch gunfire Agnew and his men sank every merchantman in the convoy, and confused the defences so comprehensively that the escort commander thought they were being attacked by aircraft, ordered a smokescreen, and then, realizing his mistake, formed up his surviving warships and set off north in what he later claimed was an attempt to intercept the enemy on its way back to base. Malta was to the south-west. As a final insult, Wanklyn surfaced his submarine among the racing Italians at dawn, sank another destroyer and disappeared again in his own mysterious way.

Captain Agnew repeated this treatment and sank both ships carrying fuel, ammunition and transport to Rommel in a convoy on 24 November 1941. Axis losses in transports to and from North Africa rose to 63 per cent that month, and like the Allied convoys to Russia the following year, had to be halted. As a direct result of their local loss of control of the sea, Rommel suffered an unpleasant defeat on land in November, too.

The last weeks of 1941, like the last weeks of 1940, reflected a great upsurge in Allied fortunes in the Mediterranean. Malta was operating submarines, Force X and aircraft, and as a result Rommel had been informed that he could expect no more than a trickle of supplies and reinforcements. Short of fuel, transport, ammunition and aircraft, he was forced to retreat clean out of Cyrenaica and to postpone all plans for another offensive.

One officer who saw much service in the Mediterranean during 1941 and 1942 comments on the strain suffered as a result of the frequent, unpredictable and violent changes of fortune:

One day we thought we had at last got the upper hand and we could cut off Rommel from all his supplies – starve him to death, never mind his tanks and transport and ammo. Then something like Crete comes along and we lose half our ships in a few days, our only carrier and our base at Suda Bay. The same eight months later. We thought we had just about wrapped things up by December '41. It was pretty different after Christmas, I can tell you.

The Allied ability to wage war in North Africa and ensure the safety of the Middle East oilfields depended in the final count on the movements and activities of the *Luftwaffe*. When its planes came, as in January 1941, they saw and they conquered. When they departed, as they did for Russia at the conclusion of the Greek–Crete operations, the waters of the Mediterranean returned to a state of relative serenity.

By December 1941 Hitler was at last able to turn his previously fixed attention from his armies in Russia to the Mediterranean and North Africa, where Rommel – not ordinarily a complainer – was in low spirits, to match his supplies. Hitler's directive of 2 December was intended to give cheer to his Afrika Korps commander and his men. *Fliegerkorps II* was to be transferred from the Russian front to Sicily and combine with *Fliegerkorps X* in one massive *Luftflotte 2* under the command of Field Marshal Albrecht Kesselring. Their brief?

(a) to achieve air and sea mastery in the area between southern Italy and North Africa and thus ensure safe lines of communication with Libya and Cyrenaica. The suppression of Malta is particularly important in this connection;

(b) to paralyse enemy traffic through the Mediterranean and to stop British supplies reaching Tobruk and Malta.

Paradoxically the first serious blow to the Mediterranean Fleet was brought about by the Italian Navy and not the *Luftwaffe*. The Italians, like the Japanese and the British later, had been experimenting for some time with miniature submarines for penetrating enemy bases. The Italians had concentrated on what they called Slow Speed Torpedoes, or 'pigs', submersibles upon which the crew of two, in breathing apparatus, rode astride. On reaching their target the pig riders detached a time-fused charge and clamped it to the bottom of the target. Delivered to the doorstep of Alexandria harbour by a submarine, three of these pigs succeeded in slipping into the harbour when the boom defences were open to admit a ship, and clamped charges to the bottom of the battleships *Queen Elizabeth* and *Valiant*. Both were seriously damaged and were out of service for months, an appropriate tit-for-tat for Taranto.

This blow, inflicted by six brave Italians (all escaped death but not capture), left Cunningham virtually without a battle fleet. But that was far less important than the activities of the *Luftwaffe* pilots, thankful to be away from the Russian front in winter, who now set about the task of suppressing Malta with relish. They also took their part in covering a massive convoy to Tripoli on 5 January 1942 which got through unscathed. This so powerfully reinforced Rommel that he was able to counter-attack for the first time for months and deliver a savage blow to the Eighth Army, which was forced to yield much recently recovered ground and the valuable port of Benghazi.

The isolation of Malta as a prelude to the dark days of her worst ordeal in early 1942 was signalled by the failure to pass through a convoy of desperately needed supplies and ammunition in February. Even the superb skill and courage of Philip Vian could not prevail against the *Luftwaffe*'s onslaught. One by one the four fast freighters in his charge were sunk, the last just outside the range of Malta's few fighters.

Cunningham was left with no alternative but to try again. If Malta fell now Axis control of the Mediterranean, would be total, and there would be no limit to the increase in Rommel's strength, with the catastrophe which must inevitably follow. On 20 March 1942 three fast freighters and the Special Supply Ship *Breconshire*, a Mediterranean convoy survivor if ever there was one, steamed out of Alexandria harbour and headed west. No one could claim that their chances of survival were high; but, thanks to Vian, spirits were buoyant and everyone was imbued with a sense of gritty determination.

There could be no concealing the intended destination, no possibility that they would not be attacked with all the numerous weapons the enemy could bring to bear. Even Admiral Iachino prepared to take part in the massacre, with the *Vittorio Veneto*'s sister ship *Littorio* (repaired after Taranto), three cruisers and four destroyers.

All that Vian had were four light cruisers and sixteen destroyers, and from 22 March no air cover at all. The Italians were first into the attack, with torpedo-bombers, which were kept at a distance by anti-aircraft fire, as were high-level bombers later. Next came an attack by German bombers. Again no hits. At 1.30 p.m. on that busy day Captain Eric Bush (DSO and two bars, and a DSC earned during the war) of the cruiser *Euryalus*, who flattered himself that he had unusually powerful eyesight, proved his claim.

'Quick, Jones,' I called to the Chief Yeoman. 'Make to the flagship: "Smoke on the horizon bearing 350 degrees."' The time was 2.10 p.m. The sea was reasonably calm with visibility maximum, but the wind was freshening.

Spotting ships hull down is not an easy matter. I swept the horizon again and again with my binoculars and found nothing beyond the smoke; then suddenly objects appeared.

'Three ships bearing 359 degrees,' I almost shouted in my excitement. Up went the signal flags, closely followed by a similar message from the destroyer *Legion*, but we were definitely the first. The time was 2.17 p.m.

'Captain speaking. The Italian Fleet is in sight. Masts and funnels of three big ships are clearly visible from here. Good luck, everyone!' The reaction to this broadcast, I was told afterwards, was encouraging in the extreme. Here was the Cockney at his best. 'Let 'em all come!' they said.[18]

And come they all did! Ten-thousand-ton, 8-inch-gun Italian heavy cruisers and 6-inch light cruisers, pitted against the light cruisers of Vian's 15th Cruiser Squadron, unarmoured 5,500-ton ships armed with 5.25-inch popguns, as Bush called them. There was only one way to meet this threat and that was to go out and meet the approaching Italian ships, making smoke to conceal the convoy, which was left in the care of destroyers and an anti-aircraft cruiser.

The Italians opened fire at a range of over fifteen miles, well beyond the range of 5.25s, while high-level Italian aircraft chipped in with a mass bombing raid. Neither the shooting nor bombing was up to the usually high Italian standard, partly because of the smoke and the high-speed manoeuvring of Vian's ships. Once again Admiral Iachino was not prepared to let his cruisers pierce the smokescreen for fear of what they would find on the other side, and the Italian force withdrew, leaving Vian to return to his escorting duties. The convoy had meanwhile been heavily dive-bombed by Junkers which, unusually, were deterred by the fierce anti-aircraft fire of the destroyers and cruisers.

Captain Bush almost at once heard that the Italian force had been sighted and was returning to the attack.

'Stand by again,' I said into the loudspeaker. 'There's more to come!'

Admiral Vian led us out as before, first to the north to clear the convoy, then to the east to lay another smoke screen, and then back to the west again, while the convoy with heavy heart turned south and increased to its maximum speed.

The enemy, as we know now, was in two groups at this stage, the nearer, about nine miles away, consisting of the two 8-inch and one 6-inch cruisers and four destroyers we had met before, and the second group, at a distance of 15 miles, comprising the modern battleship *Littorio* and four destroyers. We were in for something now all right! I knew that Admiral Vian would never leave the convoy to its fate, so if needs be we would be fighting to the end.[19]

The action was a graphic illustration of how a much inferior force can defy an enemy by employing all the skills of naval tactics combined with uncompromising aggression. At one time it fell on four British destroyers alone to hold off a battleship with cruiser and destroyer support by playing on the enemy's fear of a massed torpedo attack and dodging in and out of smoke.

At another time the *Littorio* had Bush's *Euryalus* clearly in the sights of her 15-inch guns. 'An age seemed to pass before her shells arrived with a deafening crash as they plunged into the water all round us, engulfing the ship in columns of water masthead-high. We'd been straddled.'

At last, at 6.45 p.m., more than four hours after the first salvo had been fired, another destroyer charge broke Iachino's nerve and he withdrew his force.

The Second Battle of Sirte* was a bloodless victory of moral superiority, one Italian and one British ship being hit; although, as salt in Iachino's wounds, two of his destroyers foundered in heavy weather while returning to base. But Sirte could also be called a hollow victory. The diversion from their course forced upon the transports prevented their entering Valetta harbour that night, and in the morning dive-bombers picked them off – all but one – in spite of the efforts of Vian and his men. Only 5,000 tons of 26,000 tons of sorely needed supplies reached the beleaguered island.

The Second Battle of Sirte also marked the opening of Malta's worst ordeal, with the *Luftwaffe* combining with the Italian Air Force to destroy the offensive and defensive power of the island and starve out the civil population. In the last two weeks of April 1942 there were no fewer than 115 air raids, making life hell for the citizens of Valetta and wherever there were military facilities. All the services suffered. It became impossible to operate the submarine flotilla, and the boats were withdrawn, some of them badly damaged. Wanklyn's was not among them for the *Upholder* had been lost with all hands on her twenty-fifth patrol.

Anti-aircraft ammunition ran low, the barrels of the guns began to wear out, it became more and more difficult to operate the few remaining fighters from the airfields, pock-marked like a First World War battlefield. A measure of survival was provided by deliveries of fighters flown off the American carrier *Wasp*, some fifty at a time. After her second delivery Churchill signalled her captain characteristically, 'Who said a wasp couldn't sting twice!' But the arrival of these Spitfires was as closely observed as everything else that happened on the island. The pilots were barely out of their cockpits

---

*Named after the Libyan gulf Khalij Surt to the south of the scene of operations. The First Battle of Sirte was a minor skirmish during the previous December.

before the Junkers came down. Of the second batch only three remained in flying condition after three days.

Beneath the ocean, too, the struggle continued relentlessly, month by month. While German U-boats and Allied submarines continued to take their toll, the British boats were frequently used for bringing urgently needed supplies to the island, including aviation fuel – not a sought-after cargo – ten tons at a time. Minelaying and minesweeping were constant activities on both sides. The entrance to Malta harbour was one obvious rich area for reaping a good crop from the black metal pods. As soon as one group of mines was cleared another took its place, often dropped at night from the air.

The minesweeping service was not the navy's most popular. 'Like a bloody bomb-disposal job after a raid on London,' one rating described it. 'Except we never stopped and we had the sea to fall into. And a good many Jerries strafing and bombing away. . . .'

Many minesweepers were without radar to give warning of imminent air attack. A Lieutenant RNVR, J.B.Clegg, HMS *Espiegle*, told of the unique warning system employed in his minesweeper:

We found 'Charlie the Gander' aboard after some servicing at a local port. Very quickly Charlie learnt to differentiate between the engine sounds of friendly and enemy planes. Indeed, he heard them at distances when we could not even see the planes, when he set up an incessant cackle and spread himself flat on the bridge deck with outstretched wings, just as we were trained to do to avoid scattering shrapnel. Charlie gave us good notice and enabled us to warn our sister ships of the 12th Minesweeping Flotilla.

Charlie was so concerned for our protection that he later learned to lie outstretched on one of us on the bridge deck. Despite efforts by destroyers and cruisers to secure a transfer of his services, he stuck faithfully to *Espiegle* during his wartime service.[20]

*   *   *

Malta's ordeal continued through the summer months, the civil population hungry, nerves in tatters. This was the period that earned the island the George Cross, and led to numerous military decorations as well as deaths. By August the Combined Chiefs of Staff decided that an all-out effort must be made to get a convoy through from Gibraltar, or the island would be forced to capitulate. Operation Pedestal, the despatch of fourteen merchantmen to Malta, marked the turning-point in the siege of Malta and the war in the Mediterranean.

The merchantmen were new, fast vessels, in the hands of experienced masters who had long since recognized at first hand the dangers and depredations of Mediterranean convoys. Among the ships was the tanker *Ohio* with 11,000 tons of fuel on board, the most valuable and most vulnerable of all the vessels, and the obvious first target for the convoy's attackers.

As far as the Sicilian Narrows, the convoy was to have the protection of a massive armada comprising two 16-inch-gun battleships, four carriers, including one loaded with Spitfires for Malta, three cruisers, four anti-aircraft cruisers and two dozen destroyers. Any attempt at concealment was useless, and the Axis powers had all the time to prepare their attacking forces. And what forces they were! U-boats, motor-torpedo boats, the entire Italian Fleet and *Reggia Aeronautica*, the *Luftwaffe* in Sardinia and Sicily, including planes carrying target-seeking torpedoes, and radio-guided unmanned bombers.

A U-boat made the first 'kill', *U-73* putting four torpedoes into the carrier *Eagle*. Sitting in his Hurricane's cockpit waiting to be launched from another carrier, the *Indomitable*, the pilot, Hugh Popham, witnessed the catastrophe:

The wind was chancy, and we were to be boosted off. I was in position on the catapult, engine running. The flight-deck engineer waggled the ailerons to draw my attention to something or other, and I looked out over the port side to see what he wanted. And, as I did so, I stared in shocked surprise beyond him to where *Eagle* was steaming level with us, half a mile away. For as I turned smoke and steam suddenly poured from her, she took on a heavy list to port, and the air shook with a series of muffled explosions.

Over the sound of the engine, I yelled: '*Eagle*'s been hit!'

Listing to port, she swung outwards in a slow, agonized circle, and in seven minutes turned abruptly over. For a few seconds longer her bottom remained visible; and then the trapped air in her hull escaped, and with a last gust of steam and bubbles she vanished. All that remained was the troubled water, a spreading stain of oil, and the clustered black dots of her ship's company.

Popham was launched from his catapult a few minutes later, 'my mind still numbed by what I had seen'. In the evening of the same day Popham was airborne again when aircraft were spotted on the radar screens. He and the three other pilots in his flight found Ju88s at 20,000 feet:

One after another we peeled off and went down after them. They broke formation as they saw us coming, and Brian and I picked one and went after him. He turned and dived away, and we stuffed the nose down, full bore, willing our aircraft to make up on him. At extreme range we gave him a long burst; bits came off and smoke poured out of one engine, and then he vanished into the thickening twilight. We hadn't a hope of catching him and making sure; already he had led us away from the convoy, and so, cursing our lack of speed, we re-formed, joined up with Steve and Paddy, the other members of the flight, and started to climb back to base.

The sight we saw took our breath away. The light was slowly dying, and the ships were no more than a pattern on the grey steel plate of the sea; but where we had left them sailing peaceably through the sunset, now they were enclosed in a sparkling net of tracer and bursting shells, a mesh of fire. Every gun in fleet and convoy was firing, and the darkling air was laced with threads and beads of flame.[21]

The *Furious* had successfully flown off her Spitfires at their maximum range from Malta on 11 August. On the following day the air attacks built up to a ferocious climax, and the *Indomitable* was hit so badly that she could no longer launch or collect her aircraft. The *Victorious*, too, had been hit but, mercifully, not so badly that she could not operate her own and the *Indomitable*'s planes. So far, not too bad. One of the merchantmen had been hit, and an Italian submarine had been rammed and sunk.

But the Italian Navy struck back the next day when the submarine *Axum* torpedoed in turn the cruiser *Nigeria* and the anti-aircraft cruiser *Cairo*, sinking the latter, while another Italian submarine torpedoed the cruiser *Kenya*. It was time for the big ships to return to Gibraltar. That night, 12–13 August, the convoy, now without battleships or carriers, crept south hugging the Tunisian coast from Cape Bon. It was the German E-boats' turn. Swarming at high speed in and out of the light escort, they sank four of the merchantmen in short order, and then, in a final parting shot, the cruiser *Manchester*.

Like Kipling's dawn, it came up like thunder, the German bombers arriving to take over the next shift from the E-boats. By breakfast they had sunk one merchantman and damaged three others. The *Ohio* was hit for the first time. She was hit twice more before sundown, destroyers fussing round her giving moral and practical support.

Commander Anthony Kimmins was a witness to the *Ohio*'s torture:

She was forced to stop, and later, as we went up alongside in the *Ashanti*, another merchantman was blazing not far off. It was that night when things weren't looking too good. Admiral Burrough hailed her from the bridge. 'I've got to go on with the rest of the convoy. Make the shore route if you can and slip across to Malta. They need you badly.' The reply was instantaneous. 'Don't worry, sir, we'll do our best. Good luck.'

By next morning, by some superhuman effort, they had got the engines going and had caught us up in spite of having lost their compass and having to steer from aft. She then took station on our quarter and *Ohio*'s next bit of trouble was when a Stuka attacking us was hit fair and square and crashed right into her.

For the rest of the forenoon she was always picked out for special attention, and time and time again she completely disappeared amongst the clouds of water from bursting bombs. But again and again she came through. Then at last one hit her. She was set on fire, but after a terrific fight they managed to get the flames under control. Her engines had been partly wrecked, but she just managed to make two knots and plodded on. Destroyers were left to look after her, but later she was hit again and her engines finally put out of action. They took her in tow, but the tow parted. During the night with the help of a minesweeper from Malta they got her a further twenty miles. All next day she was again continuously bombed and towing became impossible.[22]

She was dragged along like a crippled soldier from the battlefield, a twenty-foot hole in her side, her forecastle awash, fires breaking out intermittently and terrifyingly close to her lethal cargo and the destroyers lashed close to her on either beam.

She made a brave and terrible sight as she was inched into Valetta harbour, her cargo of fuel, like liquid gold, miraculously still intact. Her crew and her escorts' crew were almost dead with fatigue, along with the *Ohio*'s Master, Captain D.W.Mason, soon to be awarded the George Cross, the civilian equivalent of the VC.

Malta was, quite simply, saved by the arrival of the *Ohio* and four more of the convoy. Operation Pedestal was expensive, but as the First Sea Lord signalled Admiral Cunningham, 'Personally I think we got out of it lightly considering the risks we had to run.'

Operation Pedestal did not raise the siege of Malta. Rather, it marked a pause in the downward trend of Allied fortunes as Coral Sea stemmed the dismal tide in the Pacific. Things were never to be so bad again, but participants in the siege noted only a touch less desperation in the conduct of daily life on the island. The easing of the supply situation was only nominal in its effect: gunners received two slices of bully beef accompanying the slice of bread for the main meal of the day, instead of one.

During the late summer of 1942 conditions remained rough, life on the island still hazardous. Early in October Kesselring was personally ordered by Hitler once and for all to destroy Malta's defences. Again the bombers came over in great numbers. But the 'Happy Days' for the *Luftwaffe* and *Reggia Aeronautica* were past. The guns had been augmented, there was plenty of ammunition, and there were over 100 modern Spitfires and a squadron of Beaufighters in the splinter-proof bays on the airfields, ready to scramble when the new far-seeking radar picked up the first blips. Bomber losses increased alarmingly, forcing the enemy to fly a ten-to-one fighter-to-bomber ratio in most raids. So serious were the German losses of twin-engine bombers that Kesselring withdrew them from the battle altogether. It was all very different from the days when a couple of Hurricanes and a biplane Gladiator might take off between the bomb craters to oppose 100 well-escorted bombers in a single raid; and by the end of the month the German Field-Marshal was forced to accept defeat. Grandly named Operation Hercules, the destruction of Malta's defences, followed by the island's occupation, was cancelled.

During all this summer and early autumn period Allied air-sea power based on Alexandria and Malta was slowly intensifying its squeeze on Rommel's jugular vein. Convoys to North Africa were suffering the same ratio of casualties as convoys to Malta had once suffered – 60 per cent, sometimes higher. In October torpedo-bombers, bombers and mainly light naval forces sank some 50,000 tons of shipping *en route* to the Afrika Korps. Sixty-five per cent of the German cargo was fuel for Rommel's 470 tanks, countless trucks and 700 aircraft. The effect was devastating. When General Montgomery struck at El Alamein on 23 October 1942, Air Marshal Sir Arthur Tedder enjoyed the kind of air superiority the German armies had been accustomed to deploy.

The turn of events was startlingly swift to the veteran participants, to the gun crews at their posts on Malta, and to the RAF fighter ground crews who for months had been the hardest worked tradesmen in any sphere of operations. Between 10 and 30 November 1942 just four ships reached Tripoli with supplies for the retreating German and Italian forces, while 60,000 tons were at the bottom of the sea. 'The Tripoli route', the Italian Naval Staff announced on 3 December, 'is now exposed to such peril from Malta-based naval forces and aircraft that there is little point in continuing with our convoys. Only the Air Force can alter the situation.'

But it was quite incapable of doing so. Rommel was now in full retreat, and on 8 November 1942 Operation Torch, the Allied landings in French North Africa, marked the beginning of the end for enemy forces in North Africa. No event could more clearly signify Allied domination at sea than this successful invasion with scarcely any losses. Soon the Mediterranean was no longer 'the disputed lake', the siege of Malta really was lifted at last, and the way was open for the invasion of Sicily, the island which had been the enemy's main base during Malta's long ordeal.

Then, on 3 September 1943, the Eighth Army was carried across the Messina Straits from Sicily in over 300 landing-craft, and set foot on Italian soil. Five days later the Italian Government accepted the Allied terms for an armistice. These terms provided for the immediate surrender of the Italian Fleet. In the early hours of 9 September 1943 the three modern 15-inch-gun battleships and six cruisers, accompanied by a strong force of destroyers, left Spezia. They were met by those Mediterranean veterans, *Warspite* and *Valiant*, which conducted them to Malta.

The other survivors of two years and three months of war, three older Italian battleships, with accompanying cruisers, departed from Taranto, were also met at sea and brought to Malta. There had been nothing like it since the surrender of the German High Seas Fleet, equally unwilling to fight, on 21 November 1918.

'Be pleased to inform Their Lordships', signalled Admiral Cunningham, 'that the Italian battle fleet now lies under the guns of the fortress of Malta.'

But as a sharp reminder that the war was not yet over, that the Royal Navy and the United States Navy still faced dangers in the Mediterranean, the *Luftwaffe* launched radio-controlled bombs at the Italian battleships *en route* to their point of surrender. One struck the recently completed *Roma* (35,000 tons) and blew it to pieces with the loss of almost everyone on board. It was a characteristic and salutary gesture of defiance and contempt. But it failed to delay by one day the final despatch by Allied naval forces of German land, sea and air forces from the Mediterranean.

CHAPTER ELEVEN

Guadalcanal

The determination to take the offensive in the midst of disaster was as strong in Washington as in London. Within days of the fall of France, Churchill and the Combined Chiefs of Staff had considered short- and long-term plans for counter-attacking the enemy. Similarly, four days after the fall of Singapore, Admiral King handed to General George Marshall, Chief of Staff of the American Army, a memorandum outlining the plan for America's first major offensive operation in the Pacific.

The Solomon Islands operations of the second half of 1942 were one of the longest and fiercest sea struggles of the Second World War; they were also critical to the future of Australia and New Zealand, which came close to abandonment by the United States in early March 1942. Then in a much-publicized statement of solidarity, Admiral King declared to President Roosevelt: 'We cannot in honor let Australia and New Zealand down. They are our brothers, and we must not allow them to be overrun by Japan.' He also had in mind naval priorities between the Atlantic and the Pacific.

To prevent this catastrophe the American Joint Chiefs of Staff calculated that 416,000 troops would be required, and it was expected that the US Navy would deploy in the Pacific by the end of 1942 ten battleships, six fleet carriers, four escort carriers, twenty-six cruisers, and around one hundred destroyers and submarines: quite a fleet, twelve months after the Japanese were supposed to have written off the US Navy. Meanwhile, in preparation for these first offensive operations, the Pacific was divided into three Command areas.

1. South-West Pacific, including the Philippines, New Guinea, Bismarck and Solomon Islands and Australia. General Douglas MacArthur Supreme Commander.

2. Pacific Ocean Area, which meant the rest of the Pacific, excluding the south-east, divided into North, Central and South, all under the supreme command of Admiral Nimitz.

3. South-East Pacific, a subsidiary area containing a token force of old fighting ships.

After the defeats and humiliations of the past months it was with considerable relish that the offensive plans were formulated. The Solomon Islands form a 700-mile-long, much-broken volcanic archipelago running south-east from Bougainville to San Cristobal, the islands running in parallel for much of the way, the narrows between them being known colloquially as the Slot. The first target was to occupy the Santa Cruz Islands and establish a base there and on the island of Tulagi in order to begin the 'rolling back process' against the enemy, ejecting him from New Ireland and New Britain, and then from eastern New Guinea.

It was an ambitious enterprise against an enemy who had so far proved himself as tough as he was well equipped. But even while the plans were being formulated, news arrived of the success at Midway, which put new heart into everyone and ensured that a substantial carrier presence could be made available for the Solomon Islands operations. Vice-Admiral Richard Ghormley, recently in London, had meanwhile been placed in command of the South Pacific Area, under Nimitz. On passing through Washington *en route* to his base headquarters at Auckland, New Zealand, King had told him, 'You have a large and important area and a most difficult task. I do not have the tools to give you to carry out that task as it should be done ...' – which cannot be described as the most heart-lifting cheer for anyone taking over a new command at the outset of a long war.

Actually, Ghormley did not turn out to be as ill equipped as all that, and when the expedition was ready at the end of July 1942, it comprised:

1. An Expeditionary Force under Rear-Admiral Frank Fletcher of Midway fame. Fletcher himself and Rear-Admiral Thomas C. Kinkaid and Rear-Admiral L. Noyes commanded the three carrier units, comprising the *Saratoga* (at last repaired and war-ready), *Enterprise* and *Wasp* (just back from delivering Spitfires to Malta). For escort, the carriers had the new battleship *North Carolina*,* five heavy cruisers, plus an anti-aircraft cruiser and a powerful destroyer screen.

2. South Pacific Amphibious Force commanded by Rear-Admiral Richmond K. Turner, with twenty-two transports (19,000 officers and men of the Marine Corps) and as solid evidence of Australian participation, two Australian heavy cruisers and a light cruiser, as well as an American heavy cruiser, as escort under the command of Rear-Admiral V. A. C. Crutchley RN, who had won the Victoria Cross at Zeebrugge in 1918; known popularly as V. C. Crutchley VC, and living in his Dorset manor house until his death just before this book went to press.

In addition there was made available a Submarine Force South-West Pacific with six boats under Rear-Admiral Charles A. Lockwood based at Brisbane, Australia, and MacArthur also made available as support some bombing and reconnaissance planes.

D-Day for 'the occupation of Tulagi, the Santa Cruz Islands and adjacent positions' was set for 1 August 1942. As if the rush were not enough to

---

* Nicknamed 'USS Showboat' for the fuss that was made of her during her trials. Commissioned New York 9 April 1941. Entered Pacific 10 June 1942 to begin her eventful war career there.

tax everyone concerned in the preparation and organization, aerial photos of the target area revealed that the Japanese were one step ahead. It was known that their seaplane base at Tulagi was still operational in spite of the earlier bombing before the Coral Sea battle. There was no concern about Allied ability to eject the small Japanese force there; but now, on the south side of the Slot and the north coast of Guadalcanal itself, there was clear evidence that not only were the Japanese building an airfield on about the only stretch of land on that marsh-ridden, mountainous jungle-strewn island where it was possible to construct one, but that it was nearly completed.

Urgency became more intense than ever, but this dire intelligence also required large changes in plans, plans which were not yet fully formulated anyway. D-Day was put back to 7 August 1942. The whole vast armada assembled at a point south of Fiji on 26 July – carriers, battleship, cruisers, destroyers, and the key to the whole enterprise, the transports, packed with the marines, their arms and equipment.

It all looked very impressive, and there was a heartening note of optimism in the air. But the truth was that the Allied force was a mixed bag varying from the veterans of the *Enterprise* to the raw marines, with a British admiral commanding American and Australian ships under an American admiral. The marines were given brief practice at landing on some local islands during the last days of the month; then they were all on their way.

The first amazing thing about Operation Watchtower was that it took the canny Japanese command by surprise. Even 350 years earlier, the English knew every move of the Spanish Armada from the day it left, without the aid of seaplanes, submarines and radio interception. And what could be a more obvious target for a counter-offensive after Midway than the Solomon Islands? Admittedly the weather was not very good, but it was good enough for air reconnaissance. Instead, the first knowledge of what was going on was not transmitted to Vice-Admiral Gunichi Mikawa, Commander at Rabaul, until 7.25 a.m. when the US Marines were already wading ashore on Guadalcanal.

Once informed of the serious situation that threatened all Japanese Guadalcanal plans, Mikawa acted fast, scrambling an air strike of twin-engine bombers and escorting super-long-range Zeros from Rabaul, 560 nautical miles distant. While they were flying south-east the American Marines occupied the airfield from which, within a few more days, the Japanese would have been operating. It was as close as that. In view of what this famous Corps was to face later on this same island, the marines had a soft time of it, having to deal with no more than a Japanese labour force. It was different at Tulagi. Here the garrison gave a preview of what the American Marines and Army were going to have to face in displacing the enemy from countless Pacific islands. Outnumbered ten to one, the fanatical Japanese fought to the end, causing the marines some 300 casualties.

The first day of the Guadalcanal campaign was a satisfactory one in the air, too, because the American–Australian force was kept as well-informed about the progress of the threatened air strike as the Japanese had been kept in ignorance of the invasion. Nowhere did the coastwatchers have greater opportunities than in the Solomons. They had mostly been in the service of the Australian Government as planters and civil administrators who knew the terrain well and had been formed into small groups with radio transmitters, living off the land and with the help of friendly natives. One of them was Paul Mason, a bespectacled planter. He had been waiting for months for this chance. His first 'action' was to note the passage overhead of the Japanese fighters and bombers early on that morning. It was all tapped out in Morse: so many twin-engined bombers, so many fighters.

High in the mountains Mason watched the Japanese planes flash by in the sunlight, then keyed a radio message to Malaita, 400 miles away, near Guadalcanal. 'From STO. Twenty-four torpedo-bombers headed yours.' The STO was a code to establish the authenticity of the message. It was the first three letters of the surname of Mason's sister, Mrs John Stokie. Malaita received the warning clearly, relayed it to Mackenzie, who passed it back to the fleet at Guadalcanal. On HMAS *Canberra*, the bosun piped: 'The ship will be attacked at noon by twenty-four torpedo-bombers. All hands will pipe to dinner at eleven o'clock.'[1]

Radar took over at a range of around sixty miles so the Japanese pilots ran straight into a stirred-up wasps' nest of Wildcats, sixty in all, flown off the carriers in plenty of time.

It was very different from the *Prince of Wales* and *Repulse* business, or the attack on Darwin or Ceylon. In the course of a brisk dogfight the Zeros could not protect the bombers completely. Fourteen of the bombers and two Zeros (Japanese figures) were shot down by the Wildcats and anti-aircraft fire, for the loss of eleven carrier planes (American figures), some of the pilots being recovered. One of the Bettys set alight a transport by crashing on it in flames, and the ship had later to be sunk. The destroyer *Javelin* was hit too, losing all its communications and much else.

The first night ashore on Guadalcanal passed without any alarming incident. The marines were firmly in command of the airfield and had worked some way inland. There was still some sporadic fighting at Tulagi, but the last resistance was stamped out the next day. It was a highly unpleasant place for campaigning, steamy hot and marshy with relentless malarial and other insects that made life miserable. But they now experienced the satisfaction of all soldiers and sailors who had feared the worst and now enjoyed the relief of anti-climax.

The satisfaction of Admirals Turner and Crutchley that they had gained their first objectives with only nominal loss did not lull them into the belief that they, too, were safe from surprise, in spite of the long notice they enjoyed of the first air attack. The position on the evening of 8 August, with the transports requiring one more full day to complete their unloading, was that they were shielded on both sides in the Slot, a Southern Group of two Australian and one American heavy cruisers operating between Guadalcanal and Savo Island in mid-channel, and three more patrolling heavy cruisers with destroyers responsible for the area east and north of Savo Island. On a patrol line to the east were two more cruisers, light ones with 6-inch guns, one American and one Australian. Farther up the Slot two radar-equipped destroyers had orders to patrol through the night to give advance warning in the highly unlikely event of a night attack by surface ships.

During daylight on 8 August reports had come in from both submarines and aircraft, especially from long-range B-17 patrols, based on Espiritu Santo in the New Hebrides, that there was some enemy activity. One belated report referred to three cruisers, three destroyers and two seaplane tenders, which Admiral Turner interpreted as an enemy intention to set up a seaplane base, a very sensible thing to do under the circumstances.

There is no doubt that everyone was tired after a long and, for a time, alarming day, in tropical heat of a peculiarly enervating nature. There was also a certain degree of unjustified confidence in the new radar with which they were equipped, and in the *idée fixe* that because the US Navy was not trained in night fighting, neither was the IJN. All the evidence pointed to the Japanese, noted for their myopia, being poorly endowed for fighting a naval action at night. What about those outsize Zeiss binoculars they had been seen resorting to in peacetime?

In fact the Japanese had for years been very highly trained in night action and, on characteristically ruthless and risky exercises with a casualty level no other navy would countenance, had perfected their skills in close-range gunnery. Taking the enemy by surprise was a highly regarded tactical principle, which was the reason why Vice-Admiral Mikawa, also fresh from Midway, was stung into such an instant determination for revenge.

Immediately after ordering off the Bettys and Zeros, Mikawa called back to Rabaul the five heavy cruisers of his command, which were at the northern end of New Ireland. He also ordered the reinforcement of the Guadalcanal garrison, embarking troops on six transports with an escorting destroyer; the biggest of these was sunk *en route* by the US submarine *S-38*, Lieutenant-Commander H.G.Munson, with such heavy loss of life that Mikawa recalled the others, an astonishing act of defeatism after the operation he personally conducted to the Solomons.

Mikawa left Rabaul flying his flag in the light cruiser *Chokai* with two more light cruisers and the five formidable heavy cruisers which had hastened back to their base. From the beginning everything went right for him. The following morning he catapulted his seaplane scouts in accordance with consistent Japanese practice, and their keen-eyed observers fed him back all he needed to know; fifteen transports off Guadalcanal, one of them conveniently blazing, three off Tulagi, six supporting cruisers, numerous destroyers – and one battleship. But no carriers. All absolutely correct, for Fletcher, fearing attack by land-based torpedo-planes, had insisted on withdrawing his carriers.

All the way, at 24 knots, Mikawa expected to be spotted and attacked. He was in fact seen early on by Commander Munson who crash-dived just before they passed over him. The squadron was so close that he felt the thrust of their wash. Then he surfaced and reported destroyers 'and three larger vessels'.

During daylight hours on 8 August Mikawa lay low to the east of Bougainville and briefed his commanders. What we are going to do, he told them in effect, is to carry out a high-speed dash down the Slot, keep south of Savo Island on the way in, head for the Guadalcanal transports, open fire at the last moment, dealing with any opposition at the same time. Then we'll swing across the Slot, destroy the transports off Tulagi and make a high-speed escape north-west to be out of carrier-plane range by daylight, passing on the other side of Savo Island this time. Three cruisers will launch seaplanes before the opening of the attack at 1.38 a.m. and drop flares. That is all.

It was not quite all, for Mikawa at 6.40 p.m. semaphored his ships: 'Let us attack with certain victory in the traditional night attack* of the Imperial Navy. May each one calmly do his utmost.'

During the first hour of 9 August this formidable Japanese force was dashing down the Slot, guns and torpedo tubes manned, everyone nerve-tight alert. The night was black, the calm waters scarred by the ships' wakes by which they guided each other – all but the *Chokai* in the van, whose look-outs had night glasses clamped to their eyes. At just 12.54 a.m., one of these look-outs sighted a ship on the starboard bow, moving south-westerly. It was the destroyer *Blue*, on her correct patrol line, unaware that, seconds later, thirty-four 8-inch, ten 5.5-inch and twenty-seven 5-inch and 4.7-inch guns were trained on her – never mind sixty-two torpedo tubes: unaware, in spite of their silhouette, their smoke, their bow waves and wakes, of the squadron flashing past. Was her radar faulty? If it was no one knew it, and if there were look-outs they were looking the wrong way.

Mikawa sped on, scarcely able to believe his luck. Half an hour later the *Chokai* identified another enemy destroyer. This time it was the damaged *Javelin*, and whatever she saw she could not communicate. Then they were on top of the transports, the look-outs calling one sighting report after another.

Suddenly, right on time, flares from above turned the darkest night into the brightest day, and the execution began.

Above the sounds of a warship at sea, the hum of turbines, the deeper note of ventilating fans, the grind of rotating radar aerials, a number of

* He was referring to the surprise night attack by torpedo-boats on Port Arthur which signalled the opening of the Russo–Japanese War 1904–5.

men of the middle watch on the American and Australian cruisers and destroyers heard the sound of aircraft overhead. They must, of course, be friendly. But the commander of the destroyer *Ralph Talbot*, on picket duty north of Savo Island, decided a report was called for. 'Warning, warning. Plane over Savo headed east,' he called on the R/T. Several look-outs saw it, too. It was not difficult: it was burning navigation lights. The senior officer of the Northern Group of cruisers, Captain Frederick Riefkohl of the *Vincennes*, agreed that there was no cause for alarm, even when a second plane was heard. He was very tired and turned in. Up and down patrolled the cruisers of both groups at a soporific 12 knots, and to and fro droned the planes. It was like a Turkish bath on the bridge.

Two hours passed. The planes were still there. The reason for their presence at last became clear, at 1.43 a.m., along with much else. The destroyer *Patterson* was the first to get off a warning, though no one heard it: 'Strange ships entering harbour.' At the same moment flares spread out precisely over the two groups of transports, illuminating them and – such was their range of light – the bigger, more appetizing targets: the slab side of the flush-decked *Canberra*, the twin-funnel *Chicago* with the big hangar amidships, the daintier silhouettes of destroyers; and the Northern Group cruisers, too, distant to the north-east but clearly etched against the flares over Tulagi.

The long lance 24-inch torpedoes were already hissing towards their targets at 49 knots. But the 8-inch shells arrived first, on a flat trajectory. The first to suffer was the *Canberra*, proudly admired at every Australian port over the peacetime years, and now with alarm bells clanging, men running on hot decks, guns still trained fore and aft.

This was what the Italians had experienced in their heavy cruisers at Matapan the year before, in the dark, with heavy shells cutting brutally into the ship's side and upper works before a roused man could reach his action station. In two minutes the *Canberra* was a blazing wreck, her captain dead on the bridge amongst many other bodies and a handful of wounded. So he never felt the shock or heard the deep roar of two torpedo hits on his cruiser's starboard side.

The *Chicago* was probably hit by the same spread. It was certainly at the same time. Captain H.D.Bode, heavy with sleep, succeeded in combing the tracks of several torpedoes, but not all. At 1.47 a.m. a long lance caught the *Chicago* forward and took away part of the bow. The explosion and dousing of the ship back as far as the forward funnel added to the gun crews' confusion. Fear was predictable, but blindness was paralysing. Several of the 5-inch guns got off rounds of starshell. Every one was a dud; but not the Japanese shell which hit the *Chicago*'s foremast. Captain Bode ordered the searchlights to be switched on to bring some sense to the crazy situation, but they picked up nothing.

In fact, like a blind man groping in a crowd for space, the *Chicago* had found clear water. The firing had drifted off in one direction, the *Chicago* in the other direction, towards the west and Cape Esperance, the northern tip of Guadalcanal. Her captain could not be accused of running away, but he can be blamed for failing to warn the Northern Group, and everyone else for that matter.

Admiral Mikawa's cruisers had made some involuntary evolutions, too, leading to their division, which worked out very satisfactorily. The *Vincennes*, *Quincy* and *Astoria*, all American 8-inch-gun cruisers, all fine modern ships each with a complement of more than 600, were turning on to the north-west leg of their box patrol when they observed firing to the south and were illuminated from above. Captain Riefkohl, told nothing, ordered an increase in speed while he tried to comprehend what was happening. Whatever it was, it was too fast-moving for him; at least until a searchlight beam shot out blindingly from the darkness, followed by accurate shellfire. All three cruisers were illuminated now, and the firing was from port and starboard simultaneously, if possible adding further to the confusion.

The *Astoria*'s gunnery officer was the most alert and aware of what was happening. He commendably got off a salvo of six 8-inch shells and was about to fire another when his half-asleep captain groping his way to his bridge ordered the cease fire. He was convinced a tragedy was unfolding with American ships firing on one another.

Japanese shells were making near misses before the pleading gunnery officer got his way, and the enemy were making hits before he could reply. One of the American 8-inch shells did hit the Japanese flagship, narrowly missing Admiral Mikawa and killing thirty officers and men. But that was all. Eight-inch and 6-inch shells from both quarters now tore the 10,000-ton *Astoria* apart from end to end like giant hammer blows. Ablaze and with hundreds of dead and wounded, she was pulverized to a standstill.

Among the lessons of warfare being learned by every navy was the danger posed by ship-borne aircraft. Out in the open or in unarmoured hangars and with tanks full, they were often the first to blaze up, a hazard to the ship and a sure guide to enemy gunlayers. The Japanese, aware of imminent action, had sensibly launched theirs. For the Americans these fires were one more item on the price-list of being caught by surprise.

Japanese searchlights could be switched off when the *Vincennes*' plane provided a blazing beacon. But like the *Astoria*'s captain, Captain Riefkohl still believed that it was the Southern Group's cruisers firing at them. It was just like Pearl Harbor: no one seemed able to believe a real enemy was firing real shells, intent on blowing them to pieces. In a desperate attempt to convince his assailants of his identity, Riefkohl ordered an outsize ensign hoisted at the foremast. Believing that they were hitting an American admiral's flagship, the Japanese replied by intensifying their fire.

The poor *Vincennes* was left sinking, but remained in agony for another forty-five minutes, when she rolled over in the night on her beam ends, extinguishing her own fires, and went down with 332 dead, leaving over 250 more wounded to be picked from the water.

The *Quincy*'s suffering was no less dreadful. With her sick bay packed to capacity, it was suddenly no longer there: pulverized to nothing. The engine-rooms were sealed death traps. Her captain, too, could not believe that this was the enemy's doing and flashed recognition lights. As the Japanese cruisers closed, almost every shell fired was a direct hit. 'On anti-aircraft batteries, guns and men were flattened down,' Admiral Morison has written, 'chopped up and blown to bits. At No. 4 five-inch gun a shell neatly removed the bases from several cartridge cases and ignited them, "causing them to burn like a Roman candle and killing all hands on the left side of the gun".'

Lieutenant-Commander J.D.Andrew, sent to the bridge by his superior officer to ask for instructions because all communication was lost, described the scene that met him:

When I reached the bridge level, I found it a shambles of dead bodies with only three or four people still standing. In the pilothouse itself the only person standing was the signalman at the wheel, who was vainly endeavouring to check the ship's swing to starboard and to bring her to port. On questioning him I found out that the Captain, who was at that time lying near the wheel, had instructed him to beach the ship and he was trying to head the ship for Savo Island, distant some four miles on the port quarter. I stepped to the port side of the pilothouse, looking out to find the island and noted that the ship was heeling rapidly to port, sinking by the bow. At that instant the Captain straightened up and fell back, apparently dead, without having uttered any sound other than a moan.[2]

Like men groping their way from an orgy, the Japanese cruiser captains were as stunned by their success as the Americans who surveyed the reality of this sudden catastrophe. The Japanese ships were scattered, their torpedoes exhausted. Admiral Mikawa considered with satisfaction the extent of his victory, and considered with growing anxiety the completion of his task: the destruction of the American transports, always his first target. It was 2.20 a.m. It would take at least an hour to gather together his force and set about the ships off Guadalcanal and Tulagi. And he would still be in the Slot, within easy range, he calculated, of the American carrier aircraft at first light. The memory of Midway, those dive-bombers hurling down to destroy the cream of the Empire's Task Forces, was still vivid in all its awfulness. He had been lucky. Four American shells in all had hit his ships. Should he push his luck further?

Unaware that the American carriers had withdrawn for fear of the same enemy as the Japanese Commander feared; unaware that there was almost nothing left to protect the half-unladen transports, Admiral Mikawa chose the safe course and withdrew at top speed.

As they sped toward the regrouping rendezvous north-west of Savo, their wakes washed over a thousand oil-covered American seamen clinging desperately to empty shell cases, life rafts, orange crates – to any piece of flotsam or jetsam that might keep them afloat. Marine Corporal George Chamberlin, wounded five times by shrapnel, was saved when a sailor named Carryl Clement swam to his side, removing

Chamberlin's shoelaces and tying the wounded man's wrists to ammunition drums. Other wounded were not so fortunate, for Savo's shores abounded in sharks. Blood attracted them. Throughout the night men vanished with horrible swiftness. At dawn rescue operations would begin and sailors and Marines would stand on the decks of rescue craft to shoot sharks while others hauled 700 survivors aboard, blanching, sometimes, to see men with streamers of tattered flesh flopping on the decks like octopus or others so badly burned that corpsmen could find no place to insert hypodermic needles. Gunichi Mikawa's guns had taken the lives of 1,270 men and wounded 709 others.[3]

So, four Allied heavy cruisers, the prime strength of the Guadalcanal Escort Group, were sunk, lying in what was now grimly named Ironbottom Sound, and only the *Australia*, *San Juan*, the badly battered *Astoria* and the light cruiser *Hobart* and a few scattered destroyers remained to guard the marines and secure their supplies. The *Australia* would almost certainly have been a further victim if Admiral Crutchley had not been summoned to a conference with Admiral Turner at 8.30 p.m. the previous evening. Could it have been worse? he was to be asked. Yes, much worse. Admiral Mikawa had come for the transports, the fat cattle; and all he had got were the cowboys, and there would soon be plenty more of those back in town.

The Battle of Savo Island was a grisly, demoralizing Allied defeat, there can be no doubt of that. It touched with uncertainty the buoyant optimism which had coloured the outset of the first great counter-attack by the Allies in the Pacific. From being all over in weeks, Guadalcanal was to grind on for bloody months.

One short footnote to the Savo Island report could be read with consoling satisfaction by the American–Australian commanders: at 9.00 a.m. on 10 August Lieutenant-Commander John R.Moore USN, of *S-44*, by chance found himself amongst the rapidly withdrawing Japanese cruisers, and put a salvo of four torpedoes smack into the *Kako* at 700 yards. She went down within minutes.

*   *   *

It has been said that the first year of war in the Pacific was, for the American Navy, an amateur versus a professional football team. This is a strong over-simplification. The US peacetime navy was a highly professional body, lacking neither in skill nor resolution. But its warmest admirers had to admit that there were some yawning gaps which had to be painfully filled after Pearl Harbor. The lack of experience in night fighting and night flying were two; a third was poor material, especially in torpedoes; and a fourth was poor communications.

In many respects the position of the US Navy in 1941 was analogous to that of the Royal Navy in 1914, when the British ruled out fighting at night through lack of training and experience, suffered from poor mines and torpedoes by comparison with the Germans, and committed a series of signal *gaffes* right up to and including Jutland in 1916.

Radar had proved to be a most timely advantage at Midway, but over-reliance upon this new wizardry had directly led to the cruiser catastrophe off Savo Island. Compounding this belief in the infallibility of radar, a demand for a reduction in the discomforts of destroyer service, which included glass-enclosed bridges, led to a commander's reliance on lookouts on the bridge wings for enemy sightings rather than his own, more experienced eyes.

The US Navy also had the most sophisticated communication system of any navy. 'TBS' (Talk between Ships) was just that: you lifted a telephone and talked. Simple. But like the telephone at home, it also led to over-use; and, again, over-reliance upon it led to a loss of efficiency in the operation of the traditional flags, Morse and lamp.

But no, it was not amateurs against professionals; it was at first an 'away' match for the Americans, and the home side had some skills and tricks which her opponents had failed to rumble. In the first twelve months after Pearl Harbor the US Navy had perforce to learn a lot of lessons. As in her competitive industry, her marketing and much else, the Americans learned with astonishing speed. If Ironbottom Sound off Guadalcanal was well named, a lot of prejudices, misconceptions and bad American practices were also sunk in those waters. Guadalcanal cost the Americans dear, in the lives of American marines, soldiers, sailors, aviators and ships, but victory on this unsavoury island of swamps and disease, and the waters about it, must lead to eventual overall victory. Admiral Nimitz knew it, and Admiral Yamamoto knew it. And this was why the struggle was so cruel and relentless.

The scale of the fighting on Guadalcanal, geographically and in terms of numbers, was minuscule within the 163 million square kilometres of the Pacific Ocean. But the fate of Greece had once hinged upon the twenty-five-foot-wide pass of Thermopylae, and the Ypres Salient once held the key to the Western Front and the fate of Europe in the First World War. On the few miles of swamp coast and hinterland of northern Guadalcanal American marine fought Japanese soldier at the same close range as Wildcat pilot had fought Zero pilot above the waters of Midway. Both were engaged in blocking operations.

'The way we saw it,' one American junior officer put it, 'the Jap had been rolling us up since Pearl and we had to stop him somewhere. It's not easy standing in front of a rolling truck, and the gradient was on his side and the driver knew where he was going. We chose the beaches of Guadalcanal,' he added with a knowing look, remembering the mud and the jungle and the swampy estuaries. 'There were worse places to get him bogged down.'

As in any land campaign, whether in Greece or North Africa, Norway or the Philippines, the outcome depended upon a chain of interdependent links. First, as always, was the soldier on the ground in Guadalcanal, huddled in his foxhole or racing forward between shattered stumps of palm trees, bayonet fixed, mortars pounding, and machine-guns rattling. He had been brought to this God-forsaken terrain by the navy, was supplied and kept alive by the navy, and the navy could sustain his supplies and reinforcements only if it controlled the waters *and* the air above.

There were exceptions to this rule of control and chain of responsibility. For most of the campaign, thanks largely to the early American coup of seizing Henderson Field, the air was American during daylight although – at prodigious cost – the Japanese continued to bomb. But the Japanese extemporized a swift destroyer service down the Slot almost every night (known locally as the 'Tokyo Express') under the intrepid command of Rear-Admiral Raizo Tanaka. These vessels had to be beyond American air range by daylight. They were not always, and then nemesis was swift.

Fifty years before Guadalcanal an American admiral, Alfred Thayer Mahan, had written of the Fleet bearing the responsibility (as always) for preserving Britain's liberty: 'Those far distant, storm-beaten ships, upon which the Grand Army never looked, stood between it and the dominion of the world.' He might have been writing of Admirals Turner and Fletcher in 1942. The British admirals of the eighteenth century may have been hundreds of miles from the homeland they were protecting, the American admirals thousands of miles, but it was the same ageless story. The US Navy's equivalents to the Battles of The Saints, Glorious First of June and Cape St Vincent were reflected through time to another Fleet as the Battles of Cape Esperance, the Eastern Solomons and Guadalcanal.

The nature of sea warfare had changed quite a bit, too, but the ultimate aim, to sink or capture the enemy, had changed not at all; and, paradoxically, in at least two respects sea fighting in the Pacific in the 1940s had more in common with sea fighting in European waters a century and a half earlier than with the long-range gunnery duels of the First World War. Both the dive-bomber and the torpedo-bomber delivered their missiles at a cannon's range; and wind direction and force had suddenly become an important factor again because it governed the direction of the carrier for launching its aircraft. At Midway the *Yorktown* had been obliged to steer *away* from the enemy at high speed while launching her strike, giving her pilots a longer flight to their target with the risk of running out of fuel. This restriction was soon to be demonstrated again.

Admiral Yamamoto now personally re-entered the scene of operations, his presence meaning that the south-west Pacific had become once more the centre of fleet operations. The importance which the Japanese high command attached to Guadalcanal was borne out by this Japanese admiral's arrival at Truk with his Combined Fleet: and, Midway notwithstanding, what a Fleet Yamamoto could still put together!

The C-in-C flew his flag, as always, in the giant *Yamato*, with a Supporting Force under Admiral Kondo comprising the 16-inch-gun battleship *Mutsu*, five cruisers and a powerful seaplane contingent for reconnaissance.

The Carrier Group included the two big fleet carriers *Shokaku* and *Zuikaku* with two fast accompanying battleships, *Hiei* and *Kirishima*, and a powerful force of destroyers and cruisers; while from Rabaul came Admiral Mikawa's four surviving cruisers from the Savo Island battle and a Reinforcement Group of the light cruiser *Jintsu*, five destroyers and other small craft.

Finally, Yamamoto had a similar 'bait' force as at Coral Sea, an expendable Group to lure the enemy, comprising the light carrier *Ryujo* (thirty-seven aircraft), a cruiser and a couple of destroyers.

The first task of this formidable force was to cover the landing of reinforcements for Guadalcanal numbering some 1,500 men from four old destroyers and a converted light cruiser. But it was not in that passive role that Yamamoto saw himself. He and his subordinate and ace carrier commander, Vice-Admiral Chuichi Nagumo, were set once more on a final showdown with the American carriers before they inevitably grew into an overwhelmingly omnipotent force in the months ahead as the numerous carriers fitting out in American yards joined the fleet.

Japanese dispositions for the Battle of the Eastern Solomons were very much 'the mixture as before', revealing a poverty of tactical inspiration in the IJN's high command. The reason for this, by comparison with American flexibility and adaptability, was that the Japanese had so intensively and for so long prepared for their naval war that they considered that they had brought their tactical theories to perfection under almost 'real war' conditions, while the US Navy after the first almost fatal hammer blows was forced to extemporize.

This was how Yamamoto sailed into his set-piece battle: far ahead a scouting line of submarines; another scouting force under Admiral Kondo flying his flag in the heavy cruiser *Atago* with the seaplane carrier *Chitose*; then a Vanguard Group of two battleships and three heavy cruisers for a good old-fashioned gunnery duel if opportunity occurred; then Nagumo with his two big carriers and over 130 aircraft; and finally at the rear, Tanaka and his destroyers as direct escort to the destroyer-transports and cruiser-transport. As for Yamamoto himself, he remained in his flagship, his floating bastion of 18-inch armour plate and 18-inch guns, to bring himself to the scene of battle if required, perhaps to deliver the *coup de grâce* before bringing home his triumphant fleet.

For Admiral Fletcher, the situation was almost a repeat performance of those stirring days before Coral Sea back in May. This time his flag flew in the *Saratoga*, the late-*Lexington*'s sister ship, and he had three instead of two fleet carriers, as well as a modern battleship, the *North Carolina*, to help offset the disparity with Nagumo's big-gun power. And the two carriers he was to face were the same as at that earlier meeting. But in the three months since Coral Sea he had learned almost a lifetime of tactical and material experience, like holding back adequate fighter defence during an offensive strike, while the poor old Devastator had been pensioned off to be replaced by the new Avenger torpedo-bomber. (American war production was already beginning to tell at the front line; in fact it reached its peak the following month.)

On 23 August 1942 Fletcher was at the eastern approaches to the Coral Sea, with air reconnaissance beginning to send him back news of the strength of the enemy and where he was north of the Solomons. Unsurprisingly, it was Yamamoto's submarines that were the first to be spotted, cruising on the surface at high speed, as clearly betokening a fleet as the first gusts augur a typhoon. Soon after, the destroyer-transports were picked up, and for Fletcher that was enough. He launched a mixed strike of dive- and torpedo-bombers at 2.45 p.m., while Admiral John McCain, commanding the mixed marine and navy air force on Henderson Field, scrambled dive-bombers. They found nothing. Not only was the weather terrible but there was nothing to find, as yet. Tanaka had wisely reversed course when he knew he had been spotted.

Had it all been a false alarm? Rear-Admiral Noyes's carrier, *Wasp*, needed refuelling so Fletcher sent him away to top up. It was a bad time to be without a third of his carrier strength, for at 10.00 a.m. the next day Fletcher learned that an enemy carrier group had been sighted, and that it was heading their way. He hastened north, the wind behind him, so that he had to reverse his course every time he wanted to launch his reconnaissance planes and Wildcats to shoot down Japanese seaplanes which were smudging the radar screens from time to time.

This was carrier war at its most testing. Fletcher had many options, as always: he chose the despatch of an armed reconnaissance by twenty-nine mixed bombers from the *Enterprise*. While they were on their way radar revealed an apparently heavy force of aircraft passing from the direction of the enemy carriers towards Guadalcanal. Fletcher sent up prayers that they would have no flight deck to return to: a repeat of Midway.

Fletcher did not yet know it, but the enemy aircraft were from the light carrier, the live bait *Ryujo*, and they were heading for Henderson Field, there to rendezvous with land-based Japanese bombers from Rabaul. Their efforts were not well rewarded. They had a rough reception from Henderson's Wildcats, losing twenty-one of their aircraft, leaving only a few carrier planes to return to the *Ryujo* if she did survive.

She did not. Fletcher despatched another strike of thirty-eight bombers, this time from the *Saratoga*, which he hoped would find the two big carriers. Instead they pounced on the *Ryujo*, dive-bombing from 14,000 feet and scoring enough hits to leave her looking like the *Hiryu* at the end of Midway. The six Avengers with the strike also showed what an American torpedo-bomber pilot could do if he had something better than the hopelessly antique Devastator, and scored at least one hit. And that was that.

The *Enterprise* boys did not have the same luck. The ether that morning was a shambles of mixed messages overlapping one another and in any case barely audible due to static interference caused by the thundery conditions. One or two Dauntlesses found the *Shokaku* and dive-bombed her at 3.15 p.m., but only got a near miss.

Nagumo took the news of the *Ryujo*'s end with equanimity. She was the sacrificial pig, after all; and meanwhile, six minutes after the abortive American attack on the *Shokaku*, she and the *Zuikaku* sent off a strong strike force, heavily escorted by Zeros. Thanks to the survival of one of his seaplanes long enough to get off a sighting report before a Wildcat shot it down, Nagumo knew the exact position of Fletcher's carriers while Fletcher had hardly a notion of Nagumo's whereabouts. The need to avenge Midway burned as deeply in the hearts of his fliers, and they had the means to do so. The prognostications could not be better, the weather firmly on their side, as Admiral Morison richly describes.

Poseidon and Aeolus had arranged a striking setting for this battle. Towering cumulus clouds, constantly rearranged by the 16-knot SE tradewind in a series of snowy castles and ramparts, blocked off nearly half the depthless dome. The ocean, two miles deep at this point, was topped with merry whitecaps dancing to a clear horizon, such as navigators love. The scene, with dark shadows turning some ships purple and sun illuminating others in sharp detail, a graceful curl of foam at the bow of each flattop, *North Carolina*'s long bow churning spray, *Atlanta* bristling like a porcupine with anti-aircraft guns, heavy cruisers stolid and businesslike and the destroyers thrusting, lunging and throwing spray, was one for a great marine artist to depict. To practical carrier seamen, however, the setup was far from perfect. Those handsome clouds could hide a hundred vengeful aircraft; that high equatorial sun could provide a concealed path for pouncing dive-bombers; that reflected glare of blue, white and gold bothered and even blinded the lookouts and made aircraft identification doubtful. Altogether it was the kind of weather a flattop sailor wants the gods to spread over his enemy's task force, not his own.[4]

But this was to be no surprise assault. Fletcher knew just what was coming and his officers and men went through the drill of preparation as a knight once readied his men with their weapons on his castle's ramparts.

We were battened down, ready for anything that came, knowing it was not going to be the greatest fun of all time [a lieutenant j.g. reported]. Avgas drained from the fuel lines, inert gas pumped in. Tanks isolated, every gun manned. For the first-time men like me it was an experience I'd remember to my grave. For the vets. who'd seen it all before it was just as testing. They'd mostly seen death once, felt they'd cheated it and couldn't be so lucky again. In some ways it was worst for the men manning the guns, because they felt most exposed, but they also had something positive to do when the time came, and a lot of others like the medics' teams and repair parties just had to sit it out until they were needed – and when that happened it meant not good news. But at least this time we had real fighter defence. More than fifty Wildcats were up there at different altitudes and ranges when radar picked up the bogies at 4 p.m.[5]

The two carriers operated in two groups ten miles apart, encircled by their protectors at a mile range, the *Enterprise* additionally supported by the *North Carolina*'s tremendous anti-aircraft firepower, while the fighter-director officers struggled to bring some order into their charges. The trouble was that 'there were too Goddamn many planes in the sky', as one witness remarked. Apart from the Japanese strike advancing in two waves, there were search planes, anti-submarine patrols and the returning aircraft of both the *Enterprise*'s and *Saratoga*'s earlier strikes, with fuel low and anxiety to land correspondingly high.

IFF (Identification Friend or Foe) was as new as the radar with which it worked in harness. Introduced by the RAF in good time for the Battle of Britain in order to discriminate the blip of a 'bogey' from a friend, it was still not wholly reliable, and with the screen smudged with blips like a winter snowstorm, the radar operators were having as hard a time as the fighter-director officers, who seemed quite incapable of silencing the R/T exclamations, injunctions and cries of the fliers – both returning bombers and waiting fighters, who were all on the same channel.

In spite of the vocal bedlam, the Wildcats were having the greatest party of their lives. The Kate torpedo-bombers, though faster than the high-flying Vals, made the easier target and the fighter pilots, aided from time to time by returning Dauntlesses, knocked them out of the sky with consummate ease and so comprehensively that there was not a single certain report of the sighting of even one of them by any of the ships throughout the action.

It was different for the Vals, flying at 18,000 feet, underside camouflage making them virtually invisible at deck level when they did emerge from the packed cumulus, and heavily escorted by Zeros. A few Wildcats got up above to bounce them. Warrant Machinist Donald E.Ryan got among them before they reached their target and knocked down three Vals, using incendiary bullets, and two Zeros supposed to be protecting them. But some thirty Vals still got through, to turn over above the tiny toy rectangle three and a half miles below, and start their long near-vertical journey.

No one on the *Enterprise*'s deck saw the Vals until they were committed to their dive. The 5-inch opened up at once, quick fire, dozens of them, staining the sky with their black cotton-waste puffs with angry red hearts; then the 1.1s, many of them 16-barrel jobs, and the 20-mm and finally the .5s.

The *Enterprise* was making 27 knots, soon to increase to a snaking, heeling 30, the sky about her suddenly blackened as if a tropical storm rather than a rain of 1,000-pounders was about to descend upon her. When the Vals were hit their bomb nearly always exploded, but one or two with dead pilots just came on down, and down, until in one heart-rending split second, the little streaking single-engine machine plunged explosively into the sea.

A battery officer spotted a single Val and ordered his 20-mms to designate the target with a stream of tracer bullets. That thin thread of golden tracers was the baton for a cacophony of 5-inch, 1.1-inch and 20-mm gunfire from all ten ships, converging on the tiny silhouette of the Japanese plane leader. *Enterprise* put her rudder over in a series of violent turns, weaving and twisting to dodge the enemy bombs. She was in a tough spot.

In the carrier's gun sponsons and on her island superstructure, men watched with indrawn breath. Sky lookouts and gun pointers craned their necks backward to follow the long lines of darting tracers to the point where they met on the target. Huge blobs of black fragment-filled smoke materialized from 5-inch shell bursts. On and on came the flying Nip. Behind him in a long spiraling column were his fellows, tangling with a few angry American pilots who chanced the anti-aircraft fire for the sake of destroying one more assailant. The leading dive-bomber filled more and more of the gun-sight field. 'Val's' distinctive landing-gear 'pants' and the dark carcass of the bomb tucked under his fuselage were now plainly visible. Then plane and bomb separated....[6]

For a few breathtaking seconds Fletcher and his staff thought they might get away with it, as the helm was flung over from port to starboard and the 30,000-ton carrier heeled over as if in a force 10 gale. Then one, two and later a third bomb struck the *Enterprise*'s flight deck. The first penetrated the after flight deck lift and reached the third deck compartment before exploding, killing more than thirty men and piercing the ship's side, which let in water. The second struck close to the first, opening the wound wider and igniting an ammunition locker. Thirty-eight more men, a 5-inch-gun crew, were blown to pieces, and flames shot up into the sky.

The last bomb struck just abaft the island structure and would likely have killed Fletcher and most of those exposed on the bridge if it had fully detonated. It was the beginning of 'the Big E's' amazing run of good luck. On this occasion the *Saratoga* (*not* a lucky ship) got away scot free, and the *North Carolina* was the only other ship to be 'Val-ed'. She made the biggest target of all; she also sported the greatest anti-aircraft batteries and – by far – the greatest strength and thickest armour plate. Two groups of ten and six dive-bombers gave her exclusive attention. They all missed; some were shot down, one or two got near misses which the huge battleship shrugged off like a rhino disregarding an air-pistol slug.

Meanwhile the *Enterprise*'s medical teams and damage-control parties were working like men possessed to save lives and save the ship. Their prodigious efforts paid off. Within sixty minutes of taking that last bomb, the 'Big E' was steaming 24 knots into wind and recovering her aircraft. It was just before 6 p.m., and it had been a hectic day.

The fleet action which had promised such decisive results for both sides faded away like retreating Vals, without resolution. Admiral Fletcher had reason to feel he should have done better, and regretted his decision to dispense with the *Hornet* at such a critical time. Admiral Nagumo, deceived by his optimistic pilots into believing he had seriously damaged if not sunk two American carriers, was less dissatisfied, although he dearly wished he had firm evidence of a really overwhelming victory to report to the Emperor.

Eastern Solomons was, without doubt, a modest American success, a smaller step than Midway in the process of the piecemeal destruction of the IJN. But the Dauntless dive-bomber, expertly and bravely handled by navy and Marine Corps pilots, and the equally skilful Wildcat pilots, had between them sunk a carrier and destroyed a large number of carrier planes and pilots, which the Japanese could less afford to lose than the Americans.

And worse was to come. Spirited Rear-Admiral Tanaka with his force (the *raison d'être* of the clash) pressed on in spite of Nagumo's withdrawal of his carrier support. Admiral Kondo with his big guns had gone north, too, after making a futile run south in search of 'two crippled carriers'. So Raizo Tanaka was on his own in his flagship *Jintsu*, eight destroyers, cruiser-transport and the four old destroyer-transports. He was 120 miles north of Henderson Field when Marine Corps dive-bombers from the strip, searching for Nagumo's carriers, chanced on this mini-invasion fleet.

None of the distracting fire that made dive-bombing carriers so dangerous and difficult came up at the Dauntlesses. On the other hand the targets were small, and it says much for Second-Lieutenant Lawrence Baldinus's accuracy that he placed his bomb smack on the *Jintsu*'s forecastle between the two forward turrets. It made a thorough mess of the flagship cruiser, with fires and many dead, forcing Tanaka to shift his flag to a destroyer. Another direct hit on the cruiser-transport caused worse loss of life, and when another destroyer came alongside the 9,000-ton ship, by unhappy chance for Tanaka, a formation of eight B-17s from their New Hebrides base cruised by and sank the destroyer with a rare (for high-level bombing) direct hit. The hard-pressed Tanaka was forced to withdraw, and was later content to send in the surviving reinforcement troops piecemeal on the Tokyo Express. So they got there in the end.

The mark of Midway is clearly seen in the tactics of both Nagumo and Fletcher at the Eastern Solomons battle. The strong element of aggression to the point of rashness in that June battle, which had resulted in the overall loss of five fleet carriers, had very strongly conditioned Admiral Nagumo's thinking, and Admiral Fletcher's only a little less. Fletcher had failed effectively to attack either of the enemy's two big carriers, which in turn resulted from a failure of scouting and communication. Nagumo did find one of the American carriers but failed to sink it, and never scratched the *Saratoga*. Then both Admirals quit the scene, Nagumo more thankfully than Frank Fletcher.

It was in their individual skill and courage that the Americans had reason for satisfaction, rather than in overall tactical professionalism. But then the war was still young and there was much to learn. And the unread Japanese accolade to the Americans, inscribed in the diary of a Japanese officer, provided a succinct summary: 'Our plan to capture Guadalcanal came unavoidably to a standstill, owing to the appearance of the enemy striking force.'[7]

Then, in the see-saw of fortunes which swung as violently in the south-west Pacific as in the Mediterranean, fate struck twice at the American carrier force which had fought so valiantly and at such small cost through three major battles in four months. Again in parallel with the Mediterranean, it was the submarine that, striking swiftly and unseen, altered the balance of power.

Japanese submarines had not made a notable contribution to the war in the Pacific so far. Their record at Pearl Harbor was a fiasco, and they were late on station at Midway when they could at least have given Nagumo priceless information even if they had failed to hit any of the American carriers. Their torpedoes were many times more efficient than the American counterparts but the American submarine service was already well in to its crushing campaign against Japanese shipping.

On 31 August and 15 September 1942 the Japanese submarine service redeemed itself. *I-26* stalked the *Saratoga* on patrol some 250 miles south-east of Guadalcanal in the early hours of the last day of August, a week after Eastern Solomons. On the carrier's bow, *I-26* launched a spread of six torpedoes, a repeat of *I-16*'s successful attack on the *Saratoga* off the Hawaiian Islands on 11 January 1942. An American destroyer was, it was claimed, only 30 feet from the submarine when she fired, and actually grazed her hull. This destroyer had got a sonar contact but only seconds earlier – why not sooner? it was asked.

The destroyer gave belated warning, the big carrier began to turn to comb the tracks of the torpedoes, but was too slow to respond to the helm and caught one of them on the starboard side abreast the island. *Saratoga* was lucky not to catch more. But the 'Sara' had to be withdrawn from operations for almost three months, while her planes were flown off, to be warmly welcomed at Henderson Field, where they could be more usefully employed.

Worse was to come. Equally slack destroyer work led to *I-19* putting three torpedoes into the carrier *Wasp*. The Task Force of *Wasp*, *Hornet* with *North Carolina*'s guns and numerous destroyers, was first attacked by a submarine six days after the *Saratoga* was hit. Undismayed, Admiral Noyes remained in the same area south-east of Guadalcanal where the *Saratoga*, too, had nearly 'bought it'.

Four days later, on 15 September 1942, two enemy submarines worked around the Task Force with impunity. *Wasp* had six destroyers close about her, but none of them picked up either of these assailants. The carrier had just completed one leg of a zig-zag when look-outs saw the unmistakable trace of four torpedoes, running with typical Japanese speed and precision. And the exceptional explosive power of Japanese warheads was confirmed with awful reality seconds later.

Two racing warheads struck deep, forward on the starboard side; a third broached, then dove under to hit the hull about fifty feet forward of the bridge; a fourth missed ahead and ran harmlessly under destroyer *Lansdowne*.

The ferocity of the explosions buffeted men and gear like a Kansas twister. Planes on flight and hangar decks took the air vertically only to fall back and smash their landing gears. Planes suspended from the hangar deck overhead ripped loose to fall on other planes and on men. An engine-room switchboard tumbled over; generators were pulled from their foundations. Fire broke out, spreading to ready-ammunition and to airplanes full of fuel and bombs. Oil and gasoline – the gasoline pumping system was in use – spread the scurrying tongues of fire. The writhing of the ship's hull broke all forward water mains, which boded ill for fire fighting. Decks canted crazily as the ship took a heavy starboard list.[8]

I-19's consort, *I-15*, also made an unheralded attack on the *Hornet*, but she missed and by chance, such was the close-packed formation of the force, one torpedo caught the *North Carolina* and another the destroyer *O'Brien*. The battleship took it like a flyweight's punch to Carnera; *O'Brien* sank later on her way to the repair yard.

The *Wasp* was clearly doomed. None of the precautions applied before an air attack had been taken, and the flames were all-consuming, punctuated with the inevitable awful explosions of fuel tanks and ammunition. Abandon ship was called at 3.20 p.m., and the carrier which had done such fine service in the Atlantic and Mediterranean sank in another ocean on the other side of the world at 9.00 p.m. on 15 September. As a sorry reflection on the continuing inferior quality of American torpedoes, two of the five torpedoes fired for the *coup de grâce* failed to explode.

Admiral Nimitz was not pleased:

The torpedoing by submarines of four warships, with the loss of two of them, was a serious blow that might possibly have been avoided. Carrier task forces are not to remain in submarine waters for long periods, should shift operating areas frequently and radically, must maintain higher speed and must in other ways improve their tactics against submarine attack.[9]

*   *   *

Two new figures now took the centre of the stage in the long-drawn-out drama of Guadalcanal: Rear-Admiral Norman Scott and the curiously Italian-sounding Japanese Rear-Admiral, Aritome Goto; both of them cruiser men, neither of them in the first rank of Pacific commanders. They were destined to meet and fight on the night of 11–12 October 1942.

The struggle on Guadalcanal remained the same in October as it had been in September, and in the bloody months ahead the fighting at sea and in the air was concerned, as before, exclusively with the reinforcement of the fighting men on land and their supplies. For the Japanese, the Tokyo Express was all very well but the need for a really substantial reinforcement was becoming desperate in the face of increasing American Marine Corps advances. The only way of accomplishing this was by means of a smaller but similarly desperate Operation Pedestal-like convoy, such as the British had resorted to in the Mediterranean.

The packed transports would run the gauntlet of daylight air and sea attack, race down the Slot in darkness and just run themselves aground off Japanese-held Guadalcanal beaches, while Admiral Goto with his powerful cruiser-destroyer squadron would cover this convoy down the

Slot and, as soon as the landings were completed, treat Henderson Field to a heavy bombardment.

The engagement which came to be known as the Battle of Cape Esperance (the northern tip of Guadalcanal) began when American scout planes spotted the advancing armada and then followed the progress of Goto down the Slot. When darkness fell Scott in his flagship *Salt Lake City* was off the western end of Guadalcanal, racing north at 29 knots, the cruiser *Helena*'s new surface radar probing ahead.

In a complete reversal of the Savo Island engagement, the Japanese force this time raced down the Slot in complete ignorance of the American force hurrying to meet it. After months of mainly uninterrupted use, the Tokyo Express route was regarded as exclusively Japanese and all that Goto looked forward to was a bombard-and-run operation after ensuring that all the transports arrived safely. He was to pay for his overconfidence.

Like Admiral Togo at Tsu-Shima, Admiral Scott had brought his ships in to the perfect position to 'cross the T' of the enemy, so that all his guns could be brought to bear on the leading Japanese ships, which could answer only with their forward-firing guns. Alas, American signalling and co-ordination once again let down the side, and the advantage of superior equipment was lost by mishandling.

Helena picked up the Japanese cruisers at 11.25 p.m. at a range of fourteen nautical miles, but failed to pass the news to the flagship for fifteen precious minutes; by this time Admiral Scott, in single line ahead, was beginning to reverse course at the end of his patrol line, much of his tactical advantage dissipated.

The turn was not carried out very successfully and when the Admiral knew roughly where the enemy was, his own destroyers were unfortunately on the same bearing, with all the risk of mis-identification that meant. The confusion was compounded when his cruiser *Boise* also gained radar contact and, rather than merely delaying her signal as the *Helena* had done, instead sent the wrong one, indicating the sighting of aircraft rather than surface ships.

By now the *Helena* could clearly see the enemy at 5,000 yards and asked permission to open fire. The signal (why not just open fire anyway?) was either despatched incorrectly or received incorrectly, and made no sense to Admiral Scott. So the *Helena* at length did open fire. Scott, convinced that she was firing at his own destroyers, ordered him to quit. Then, at last, the spirit of Nelson intervened. The *Helena*'s fifteen extremely rapid-firing 6-inch guns pumped shells into Goto's flagship *Aoba*; and then, with the other American cruisers all joining the party, along with the destroyers, the *Furutaka* (8-inch-gun heavy cruiser) was set ablaze, a destroyer sunk and two more destroyers also set on fire.

Admiral Scott remained uncertain that his ships had not been firing on one another, and when the firing fizzled out asked the destroyer commander anxiously, 'Are you OK?' Yes, he was told, we're OK. It was like a street greeting, until Scott enlarged on the subject and asked more specifically if his cruisers had been firing at the destroyers. 'I don't know who you were firing at.' Impasse.

At 11.51 p.m. Scott ordered firing to be resumed, and set off in pursuit of the fleeing Japanese, while the rearmost enemy cruiser accompanied by a destroyer dodged aside, only to chance upon the stray American destroyer, *Duncan*. They opened fire on the unfortunate vessel, and shells began to hit her from another direction, too. Now Scott really was firing on his own side, and it was American shells as well as Japanese salvos that set the *Duncan* on fire, killing almost half her crew. And that was not all: 6-inch American shells also hit time and again the friendly destroyer *Farenholt*.

Once again the American Admiral ordered the cease fire, while continuing the pursuit. The enemy answered by re-opening fire, so accurately that the American gun crews could not be restrained, while the helmsmen did their best to comb the tracks of fast-running torpedoes; and there were some horribly near misses.

The captain of the cruiser *Boise* chose this moment to confirm visually a radar sighting by switching on her searchlights. Two enemy cruisers seized this golden opportunity and almost blasted the *Boise* out of the water, killing more than 100 of her crew.

As a final act of gallantry in this tragedy of errors the American flagship interposed herself between the blazing *Boise* and the enemy, driving them off – up the Slot and back to their base on Shortland Island, leaving behind a cruiser and a destroyer but bringing home safely the gravely damaged *Aoba*.

Statistically, the Americans had the better of this confused mêlée, with damage to the *Boise* and *Farenholt*, and the *Duncan* adding another carcass to Ironbottom Sound. But through muddle and confusion Admiral Scott had lost a wonderful opportunity of annihilating the enemy; and above all, he had not been able to prevent the convoy of transports from getting through with troops and heavy artillery. No wonder relations between the marines' commander on shore, Major-General Alexander Vandegrift, and the US Navy were becoming strained. The more the disease-ridden, gallant and hard-pressed marines fought the ever-growing enemy, the more the navy failed to interrupt the enemy's supplies and reinforcements; so it seemed to the ground troops clinging precariously to their one priceless asset – the fixed aircraft carrier, Henderson Field.

Admiral Scott put a brave face on the business by claiming four Japanese cruisers and four destroyers sunk. He was hailed as a great hero back home. The boost to the navy's morale was fine, but by 'defeating' the Japanese at night for the first time, the tactics he employed – single line ahead with his destroyers – was now regarded, quite incorrectly, as the right formula. All in all, it was a sorry affair.

The Battle of Cape Esperance on the night of 11–12 October 1942 was followed by a ferocious night bombardment of the airfield by two Japanese battleships, whose 14-inch shells tore up the strip, destroyed more than half the aircraft and most of their fuel, too. Then came two air raids and a further bombardment on the night of 14–15 October by 750 8-inch shells from heavy cruisers, which finally and conclusively made Henderson non-operational. By dawn on 15 October another 4,500 Japanese reinforcements with supplies and ammunition had been landed. That night again, two different heavy cruisers – 'I guess the Navy counted wrong!' – opened fire and this time poured 1,500 shells on to the airfield and its perimeter.

When Admiral Nimitz heard this news at Pearl Harbor he had to accept that the navy had failed and that 'we are unable to control the sea in the Guadalcanal area'. It suddenly seemed a long time since the euphoria of June, and the memory of those four Japanese fleet carriers burning off Midway before going down. Morale ashore and at sea and inter-command relations could scarcely sink lower. Only the obstinacy and grit of 'the 23,000 fever-ridden, battle-weary Americans' sustained this toehold on the island they hated almost as much as the enemy.

New American disasters in the south-west Pacific could only be avoided by a new overall commander, who would also have to conduct the new offensive that must follow. Time and again in war, when all has seemed lost, the finger of fate has swung and settled on a commander whose sudden injection of inspiration has converted men from abject misery and pessimism to the heights of aggressive zeal. This was what was needed at Guadalcanal.

'The critical situation', declared Nimitz simply, 'requires a more aggressive commander.' Admiral Ghormley's qualities and capabilities had been seen at their best behind a desk in London and Washington. A meticulous, careful, shrewd and altogether likeable officer, he had shown himself less at ease in the front-line decision-making required of an amphibious operation aimed at driving out the ferocious and tenacious Japanese from a volcanic island of swamp and forest.

Several senior naval officers had expressed relief that, in the short term, Bill Halsey had been unavailable for command of the Task Forces sent to defend Midway, where the impetuosity and swashbuckling style of this charismatic Admiral might have led to disaster. But 'Bill was just the man for this job. He liked all that fighting room on the other side of the enemy,' as one officer close to him once remarked.

William Halsey Jr came from a naval and sea-going family. There were privateering, whaling and other rough pursuits back in his family history, and his father had been a captain USN. His first command, the destroyer *Charles W. Flusser* in 1910, led later to his close association with the Assistant Secretary of the Navy, Franklin D. Roosevelt, who remained a friend for life. Halsey earned the Navy Cross in the First World War for his work in little ships in the first Battle of the Atlantic. Ten years later he experienced a metamorphosis in his naval career.

With a far-sightedness not shared by all his contemporaries he recognized the paramount importance of aviation and the carrier in any future war at sea.

From 1927, like Yamamoto in Japan, Halsey worked for the cause of the Navy's air arm, eating, drinking and breathing aviation, as he himself put it. He tried to take a course in flying, was turned down for inadequate eyesight, then paradoxically was appointed commander of a carrier on condition he took a flying course as an observer. Somehow this was converted into a pilot's course, with Captain Halsey wearing special goggles. At the age of fifty-one he earned his golden wings.[10]

And so it came about that by 1938 Halsey was appointed to command Carrier Division 2 with the navy's two new carriers, *Enterprise* and *Yorktown*. To many of his admirers he *was* naval aviation, its most popular admiral, loved for his straight, fruity talk, his aggressive no-nonsense style. And he was a good hater. 'Before we're through with 'em,' he would exclaim, 'the Japanese language will be spoken only in hell.'

By October 1942 Admiral Halsey had sufficiently recovered his health to renew his active service, and it was in the course of an inspection tour of south Pacific bases, preparatory to taking over a new carrier task force, that he received a sealed order from Pearl Harbor. Admiral Nimitz's order was to the point: 'You will take command of the South Pacific Area and South Pacific Forces immediately.'

It was hard on Admiral Ghormley at the conclusion of his appointment to see many of the reinforcements, for which he had been begging for weeks, pouring in for his successor. But this is a common fate for displaced commanders, and there were never any hard feelings between the two men, who were old friends. To reinforce the marines on Guadalcanal (when they could be landed), an infantry division was despatched from Oahu and a surface Task Force of a modern battleship and cruiser was rushed to Nouméa, Halsey's headquarters. But for the time being the carrier cupboard was bare, and the new C-in-C had to be content with the *Hornet*, to be joined by the *Enterprise* when her latest injuries had been dealt with.

The reinforced Japanese on Guadalcanal, well supported by artillery and reserves, now planned to overcome the last American resistance round Henderson Field. To synchronize with this attack Admiral Yamamoto once again brought a massive fleet to bear, with the intention of launching fighters and bombers from his carriers to land at the airfield the moment last resistance was overcome. In all there were no fewer than four battleships, four carriers, fourteen cruisers and some thirty destroyers, under the overall command of Admiral Kondo. D-Day was 22 October 1942.

This day and the next passed without the expected signal from the island being received. The answer was in the desperate defence put up by General Vandegrift's men. They had not yet heard Halsey's simple slogan now going round the Fleet: 'Kill Japs. Kill Japs. Kill more Japs!' But they were certainly conforming to it. Every day was a miniature of the First Day of the Somme in 1916, when the British suffered over 57,000 casualties, with Japanese infantrymen charging machine-gun posts regardless of certain death.

On the following day, 24 October, the two American carrier Task Forces 16 and 17, imbued with Halsey's new spirit of aggression, rendezvoused and prepared to intercept Admiral Kondo's much more powerful fleet. With the precedent of Midway always before him, Tom Kinkaid knew what a handful of American dive-bombers could accomplish, and he could also count on the added advantage of new Avenger torpedo-bombers and the experience of all the carrier clashes of the year to draw upon.

In the early hours of 26 October Kinkaid received the first news of his foe's whereabouts – 300 miles to his north-west – but he wanted a full picture of his dispositions before mounting an attack. At first light, therefore, he launched eight pairs of Dauntlesses armed with 500-pounders from the *Enterprise*. With them went a cryptic message from Admiral Halsey: 'Attack! Repeat, attack!' That was their intention. By 6.50 a.m. Kinkaid knew that two big Japanese carriers were just 200 miles to the north-west, and he hastily mounted an attack in two waves.

Soon after 7.00 a.m. two Dauntless pilots did Halsey's bidding and dropped unseen out of the sky, their sights set on the carrier *Zuiho*, a big, fast, converted tanker, easily recognizable by its long, completely flush deck. Their dives were uninterrupted: not a puff of anti-aircraft fire, not a Zero in sight – except those Zeros lined up on the deck towards which two bombs were soon heading. The lieutenant-commander and ensign responsible must have been in very tight formation for the two 500-pounders landed together, making an enormous joint hole near the stern, setting her ablaze and putting the *Zuiho* out of action.

The opening blow went to the Americans, but it was to be a day-long struggle, following the pattern of all the carrier clashes of 1942. In addition to the *Zuiho*, which burned throughout the action, the big *Shokaku* took four 1,000-pounders in quick succession, crippling her, too. On the American side, the 'Big-E' was lucky again, finding a convenient rain squall as the biggest Japanese attack forged in against the lethal opposition of Wildcats and the most intensive fire any of the pilots had seen.

The *Hornet* became the only target, a rich prize to be sure, but a dangerous one – the hornet's sting being notoriously sharp. At one moment there were fifteen Vals falling out of the sky on her from 17,000 feet. The next minute there were only three. But three were enough with pilots as dedicated as these young aviators. The squadron commander was either dead or a pioneer *kamikaze*, steering straight at the carrier's bridge while two of his bombs exploded in the heart of the ship. Three more bombs and two torpedoes added to the *Hornet*'s agony. Within ten minutes she was reduced to a burning shambles, her surviving crew struggling to control her countless blazes.

Later in the day the *Enterprise*'s luck ran out too, and she took a couple of bombs. Then, unseen, a Japanese submarine entered the combat. She should never have got through the powerful destroyer screen, but she did and at 10.00 a.m. blew a destroyer to pieces. Late-morning second-wave attacks led to the *South Dakota* taking a 500-pound bomb plumb on one of her forward turrets, but it scarcely dented her 18-inch hardened steel armour plate.

Until the late afternoon the sky over the Pacific thundered to the sound of many aero engines at heights from 20 to 20,000 feet, the notes rising and falling in tune with the violent evolutions of combat and destruction. Time and again the sky was scored with the thin white trail of a burning plane, the more distant victims heard screaming seconds after the splash of impact; while the sound of an exploding plane, scarlet and black against white cumulus, was only heard when the fragments had fallen into the water. From high above, the evolutions of the ships appeared equally desperate to the aviators, their twisting wakes like marine contrails.

Over all that stretch of sea close to the Santa Cruz Islands no fires were more stubborn and more spectacular than the *Hornet*'s, drawing assailants like moths to a flame. Kates came weaving down at 3.15 p.m., little disturbed by gunfire and not at all by fighters.

The ship's engineer officer, below decks, felt the strike of a torpedo:

A sickly green flash momentarily lighted the scullery compartment and seemed to run both forward toward Repair Station 5 and aft into the scullery compartment for a distance of about 50 feet. This was preceded by a thud so deceptive as to almost make one believe that the torpedo had struck the port side. Immediately following the flash a hissing sound as of escaping air was heard followed by a dull rumbling noise. The deck on the port side seemed to crack open and a geyser of fuel oil which quickly reached a depth of two feet swept all personnel at Repair 5 off their feet and flung them headlong down the sloping decks of the compartment to the starboard side. Floundering around in the fuel oil, all somehow regained their feet and a hand chain was formed to the two-way ladder and escape scuttle leading from the third deck to the second deck.... All managed to escape in some fashion through this scuttle ... and presented a sorry appearance upon reaching the hangar deck.[11]

When at last the skeleton crew left aboard were evacuated, still the carrier refused to sink. Sixteen torpedoes (typically, only eight ran correctly) were fired at her, then 400 rounds of 5-inch shell – to ensure she should not fall into the hands of the enemy. Darkness closed about the suffering, blazing husk, and it became too dangerous for the Americans to hang around. When they had left, the Japanese crowded round the dying *Hornet*, like criminals returning to the scene of their crime. She succumbed at last to the explosions of four long lance torpedoes.

Tactically, the Japanese won the day, leaving the US Navy with just one damaged carrier in the south Pacific, while Admiral Nagumo left the scene of the battle with two repairable and two undamaged carriers. But, paradoxically, he lost so many planes in the day's fighting that he did not have enough left to half fill his hangar space: only enough to operate two light carriers. Nor, yet again, would he find it easy to replace nearly 250 lost air crew.

Both sides therefore retired chastened from the scene. Admiral Kinkaid had failed to gain another Midway, but he had severely mauled the Japanese air arm; while on land the seemingly impregnable Henderson Field continued to assert local air control with its fixed-base fighters and bombers. As the Japanese prepared another great reinforcement convoy, Admiral Turner's Amphibious Force, in the teeth of Japanese air attack, brought in massive supplies and reinforcements to the deep-dug-in marines and infantry.

By the second week in November, with the struggle on land still unresolved, the naval situation was approaching its climax off Guadalcanal as a powerful surface fleet was reported approaching under the command of Vice-Admiral Hiroaki Abe, flying his flag in the battleship *Hiei*. He had in all two battleships, a cruiser and fourteen destroyers, five of which were positioned on the flanks to deal with the increasingly determined American motor-torpedo-boats (PT boats).

To oppose this threat Admiral Daniel Callaghan could muster only two heavy and three light cruisers and eight destroyers. It was like starting a game of chess without the queen. The once-again-repaired *Enterprise* with the modern 16-inch-gun battleships *Washington* and *South Dakota* had just left Nouméa but, even at best speed, could not hope to be in the area until the following day.

Callaghan departed boldly to meet the enemy with his force in single line ahead, a formation to which, quite wrongly, Admiral Scott's supposed success in an earlier night engagement had been attributed. On this night of 12–13 November it proved to be as disastrous as before. The American commanders, still untrained in night fighting, still over-dependent upon their somewhat sketchy and unreliable radar, still misusing their voice radio, had far less idea than the radarless but highly trained Japanese of what was going on when the two sides met in the same old Ironbottom Sound in pitch darkness. Americans fired on Americans, causing terrible damage and casualties, as well as on Japanese battleships, cruisers and destroyers. One of the American ships to suffer worst was Admiral Scott's new flagship, the anti-aircraft cruiser *Atlanta*, one shell (American or Japanese?) killing Scott and those about him. Then the battleship *Kirishima* illuminated Callaghan's flagship *San Francisco*, which was still busily engaged in trying to sink the *Atlanta*, and pulverized her with 14-inch shells, killing the Admiral and all his staff.

Even more damage was done by the streaking long lance torpedoes, while American torpedoes still lived up to their reputation for unreliability. American destroyers, too, sank one by one on that terrible night, and on the following morning Japanese submarines did awful execution among the American cruisers and destroyers retiring damaged. One torpedo caused the *Juneau* to blow up and vanish entirely within seconds: only ten of her entire ship's company survived for long enough to be picked up by flying boats the next day.

All in all the American force accounted for two Japanese destroyers. But the heavy cruisers did catch the battleship *Hiei* at a vulnerable moment. No doubt impelled by anger at their own sufferings, the cruiser gun crews pumped a great number of 8-inch shells into her substantial hull and upperworks. The *Hiei* slunk away to safety north of Savo Island, where at daylight she became the target for numerous American air attacks. Two of the many torpedoes launched at her actually ran true, bringing the giant to a halt. At this, her crew gave up the struggle, abandoned and scuttled her. She was the first Japanese battleship to be sunk in the Pacific war; and that was a considerable satisfaction to the American survivors after the worst night in American naval history.

The scene of the battle the next morning caused many tough sailors to weep. Burnt survivors, men with shattered limbs, untended wounds, drifted in the water, hundreds of them, many to be finished off by sharks. Others lay on driftwood and makeshift rafts under the tropical sun awaiting rescue. The *Atlanta*, shattered by American and Japanese shells and with her dead admiral lying with his dead staff amongst the twisted steelwork of her bridge, struggled for life. At 9.40 a.m. on the morning of 13 November she was taken in tow by a tug from Guadalcanal. Half her crew were dead and never knew how hard their shipmates struggled to keep the flagship afloat. But they lost the battle in the end, and the *Atlanta* had to be scuttled.

In the long-drawn-out Guadalcanal campaign, the morale of the naval forces operating off the island had never been so low. But in the midst of their misery and knowledge of defeat that swept through the battered and decimated force, they knew that Bill Halsey would not let them down. Help was, indeed, close at hand. Even as the Japanese prepared new attacks, new bombardments and the delivery of yet more reinforcements, Admiral Kinkaid was racing up from the south like Marshal Blücher coming to Wellington's rescue at Waterloo.

The *Enterprise*'s planes arrived first, in vengeful frame of mind, tearing apart Tanaka's latest and largest convoy of transports, aided and abetted by B-17 heavy bombers from Espiritu Santo. Then came Rear-Admiral Willis Lee's battleships to exact revenge for the sufferings of American cruisers and destroyers.

The second night naval Battle of Guadalcanal revealed all the same weaknesses and inexperience as the first. The *Washington* and *South Dakota* were equipped with the very latest radar, and relied upon it as heavily as the cruisers before them. And it was no help at all when the *South Dakota* developed an electrical fault which made her set inoperable and left the great battleship blundering about helplessly in the darkness.

At one point in the engagement the *South Dakota* was suddenly illuminated by Japanese searchlights. Every Japanese sailor had been trained again and again for this moment: an American battleship caught unawares at point-blank range in a night action. Fourteen-inch and 8-inch shells began to smother her. A less stoutly protected battleship would soon have succumbed, but she lasted long enough for the *Washington* to come to her rescue in the nick of time. At last radar, properly handled, showed what it could accomplish. At a range of five miles she poured in salvo after salvo of 16-inch shells at the *Kirishima*, which in turn had been taken completely by surprise from an unexpected quarter. Nine 16-inch and some forty 5-inch hits finished off the big battleship, leaving her with raging fires, rudderless and stationary in the water.

It had taken the *Washington* just seven minutes to knock the *Kirishima* out of the battle on that night of 14–15 November 1942. It was the last time that the destruction of one battleship by another decided a campaign. Despised, redundant, obsolete, wasteful – all these epithets had been hurled at the battleship, for so long queen of the waves as a line-of-battleship, an ironclad, a Dreadnought; but on that night these epithets were no more than buckshot against the *Washington*'s armour plate. In spite of all the losses of ships and tragic deaths of brave sailors over two November nights in Ironbottom Sound, the loss of two battleships proved decisive in causing a weakening of resolve in the Japanese high command.

The following day tough, tenacious Tanaka lost the last of his transports, eleven in all. Just 2,000 men struggled ashore plus a few cases of ammunition and 1,500 bags of rice. Fighters and bombers swarmed over the wrecks driven ashore on Guadalcanal killing Japs, killing Japs and killing more Japs, as Halsey had ordered. Outnumbered, outmatched, stricken with disease, the Japanese still fought on for a further six weeks, so fanatical they might have been automatons rather than soldiers.

More American marines were to die on that dreadful island, too, and in a later night action the US Navy suffered further losses at Tassafaronga on 30 November.

The Americans may not yet have learned the special skills of night fighting, but their unquenchable spirit came as a rude shock to the enemy, whom they had eventually out-fought on land, at sea and in the air. And let a tribute be paid, all these years later, to the hard core of American professionals and the far greater number of recent recruits from civvy street who were learning as fast as the US Navy was growing, and became professionals themselves. They were fighting the toughest full-time veteran professionals in the world, and defeating them.

As for the Imperial Japanese Navy, the sinking of two old battleships was not the real loss at Guadalcanal, fatefully symbolic though it might be. The real loss was the aircraft, more than 500 over Guadalcanal and its waters, and the men who flew them. Already a fall in the quality of fighter pilots was noted, and young rookie American pilots in the cockpits of Wildcats were knocking superior Zeros out of the sky. Since early in

1942 juke boxes all over America were playing a song called 'Johnny Got a Zero Today'. As late as June not many fighter pilots were getting Zeros, and the song had a cruel edge for those who watched the Wildcats being outfought and shot down. But by November 'Johnny' was getting his Zeros in droves; the Wildcat, and its successor the Hellcat, were leaving the production line like Model-T Fords in the 1920s, and at many times the rate of Zeros. And the flying training-schools in the USA were turning out pilots who were as capable of dealing with German fighter pilots over Europe as with Japanese fighter pilots over the Pacific.

On 9 February 1943 General Alexander M. Patch, new Commander of Ground Forces on Guadalcanal, sent a message to Admiral Halsey: 'Total and complete defeat of Japanese forces on Guadalcanal effected 1625 today. ... Am happy to report this kind of compliance with your orders.... "Tokyo Express" no longer has terminus on Guadalcanal.' It had been 'the nearest run thing you ever saw in your life' but sea power once again had made it possible for the foot soldier to conquer the enemy.

CHAPTER TWELVE

The War of the Boats

Success against the common enemies by the Allied powers in the south Pacific was matched in the Mediterranean and North Africa during the closing weeks of 1942. It had been a terrible year for those fighting on the long Russian front and for those fighting to deliver to the Russians supplies by way of the Arctic; it had been a terrible year for the American marines fighting on Guadalcanal, for the Australian–American troops fighting the ever-determined Japanese attempting to assault Port Moresby by land, and for 'the forgotten army' defending the Indian borders from the Japanese advancing through Burma.

Many well-informed people in the West in 1942 had held out little hope that a complete victory could ever be achieved by the Allies, and pessimism abounded. Even Churchill was briefly reduced to a state of acute pessimism, writing to Roosevelt (5 March 1942): 'When I reflect how I have longed and prayed for the entry of the United States into the war, I find it difficult to realize how gravely our British affairs have deteriorated by what has happened since December seven [Pearl Harbor].'

Then in quick succession, like the settling of searchlight beams, new pinpoints of brightness appeared about the war-torn world: in Egypt where General Bernard Montgomery broke through Rommel's lines, and this time continued the Eighth Army's steady advance across North Africa; at the other northern corner of the African continent where Allied landings were almost unopposed; as far to the south on the other side of the world, at Guadalcanal, and on the little known Allied battle line 8,500 feet up in the Owen Stanley Mountains in New Guinea.

In the battle for Stalingrad, which made the struggle for Port Moresby look like a platoon-strength skirmish, General Paulus's army was encircled and facing imminent annihilation in the greatest defeat of German arms since 1918.

Only in the North Atlantic was the situation as bad at the end of 1942 as at the beginning of the year. Unless the U-boat could be overcome the invasion of mainland Europe could never take place. And unless the German armies could be driven from the lands they had conquered between 1939 and 1941, Hitler could not be defeated in the West and the Russians must be starved of the vital supplies sent by their Allies.

So the Battle of the Atlantic remained the most critical battle of all. There had been the usual easing of losses during the wild autumn weather of 1942, but as nature's effective but violent protection diminished with the early spring weather, losses rose in proportion to the old sickening figures: 203,000 tons in January, 359,000 in February, 627,000 in March. This was close to twice the rate of new merchant-ship construction, in spite of the remarkable speed of American Liberty Ship building; while the U-boat losses were half the number of new boats coming into service: forty a month.

While a Convoy Conference was sitting in Washington in that terrible month of March 1943, two convoys sailed from Halifax, one slow, the other faster, seventy-seven ships in all. No fewer than twenty U-boats concentrated on this double target in brilliantly co-ordinated attacks. For the loss of one of their number, the packs sent to the bottom twenty-one ships totalling 141,000 tons.

There is no better example of the impunity with which the U-boat packs were roaming about the Allied convoys in early 1943 than the experience of Captain R. Coates, master of the freighter *Kingswood*. In the dead of night, with a gale raging, Coates spotted from his bridge a particularly prominent white splash among the breaking waves. 'It's a torpedo,' he shouted to his mate, but then at once corrected himself. For it was, in fact, a U-boat running fast on the surface like a great whale:

Collision seemed inevitable. About this time I heard the U-boat's engine and a voice in the distance. I was sort of hanging on waiting for the crash when I saw the submarine's wake curling round – the voice I had heard must have been the U-boat's commander shouting, 'Hard a port' in German. The submarine's wake curled right under my stem – how its tail missed us I still do not know.[1]

The U-boat slipped away into the night on its mission of destruction. Thirteen ships were lost from that convoy. Commander Peter Gretton, who was in the thick of this fighting with his brilliantly handled escort group, recalled the agony of the victims, and the agony of a different kind experienced by those who witnessed the suffering:

The unfortunate ship which had been hit was loaded with iron ore and sank within two minutes. Searching for the U-boat, we passed survivors who were scattered in the icy water, each with his red light burning. Some were on rafts, some were alone, but no boats had survived. It is my most painful memory of the war that we had to shout encouragement, knowing well that it was unlikely that they would ever be picked up.

It was an appalling decision to have to make, to stop or go on: but by leaving her place in the search, the ship would leave a gap through which more attacks could be made and more men drowned. We had to go on. After a search plan had been completed I sent back the *Pink* to look for survivors but she failed to find them and after four hours' search I had to recall her to her station....

I could not stop thinking of the men in the water astern and only after the report of the next attack had come in was I able to achieve proper concentration again.[2]

An official report declared that 'We are consuming 3/4 million tons more than we are importing. In *two months*, we could not meet our requirements if this continued.'[3] Later, the official naval historian wrote, 'No one can look back on that month without feeling something approaching horror at the losses suffered ... [and] what made the losses even more serious than the bare figures indicate was that nearly two-thirds of the ships sunk during the month were sunk in convoy.'[4]

The weapon battle between U-boat and aircraft was as intense and sometimes in parallel with the search for ever more sophisticated and deadly weapons of Allied surface ships and the German submarines. Twenty-mm cannon replaced the .303 machine-gun, a 'Leigh-Light' searchlight was employed at night, and in conjunction with new ultra-short-wave radar proved devastatingly destructive.

In the early days the airborne 1.5-metre radar proved useful but was later answered by German detectors. Then, early in 1943, a number of U-boats travelling on the surface on a pitch-black night perhaps 800 miles out into the Atlantic found themselves suddenly illuminated at close range – a mere few hundred feet in some cases – by a blinding light, and then blown apart by a stick of bombs. In the Bay of Biscay alone between May and July 1943 twenty-six U-boats were sunk and seventeen damaged by aircraft employing a new form of short-wave radar which was undetectable. In fact, the German 'boffins' were already at work unravelling its secrets.

As one German U-boat ace has written:

A British Stirling bomber was shot down by a night fighter near Rotterdam. From the wreckage, experts from the *Luftwaffe* and electrical manufacturers discovered that its direction-finding set worked on a wavelength of 9.7 centimetres, something we had never thought possible. It was given the name 'Rotterdam apparatus' and was one of the great surprises of the Second World War.[5]

Heavier depth-charges were thrown into the struggle, and the ahead-firing 'squid' was a revolutionary and highly effective weapon. This enabled sonar to maintain contact throughout an attack. In the traditional method of releasing depth-charges by dropping them over the stern, sonar contact was perforce lost when the attacking vessel passed over the U-boat. 'Squid' cut out that blind period and enabled sonar to retain contact. Then there was 'hedgehog', a 24-barrelled mortar mounted on the forecastle which fired its small charges calibrated to cover a set area. The charges had no depth setting and exploded on impact against a U-boat's hull. Just one did the trick.

In Germany, besides the design of new, faster U-boats, *Schnorkel* breathing tubes (late 1943) and a search receiver to warn of radar signals, an acoustic torpedo which homed on to its target, were perfected to add to the perils of the escorts as much as the merchantmen themselves.

The first trouble for the Allies, however, lay less in new German weaponry than in the allocation of their own priorities. Operation Torch (the invasion of French North Africa) had drawn away escorts from the North Atlantic convoys, so had the American need for the new coastal convoys off the eastern seaboard, and for the Pacific war – devilry stemming from Admiral King in this case. But the worst misallocation of weaponry was in long-range patrolling aircraft.

The most wanted big aircraft in the world in March 1943 was the Very Long Range (VLR) four-engine Liberator. It was built only in the United States, and its allocation was, strictly speaking, in the hands of the lower echelons of the Combined Chiefs of Staff. But there were short cuts through as well as ways around the priority jungle, and no one was better able or better placed to suit these to his advantage than Admiral King. 'His' war was still the Pacific war, and the great majority of the US Navy's 112 VLR Liberators were in the Pacific. None was based in Canada, Newfoundland or Iceland where they could have covered the western end of the Atlantic convoy routes; nor had the Canadians themselves received a single VLR.

The American Army had had two anti-submarine squadrons of this aircraft working the Bay of Biscay, but these had all been transferred to North Africa to cover the convoy routes for the newly landed American forces. That left for the North Atlantic convoys the eighteen VLRs operating with RAF Coastal Command. No wonder those two Halifax convoys had been attacked so soon after departure! One or two Liberators covering them for the first few days must certainly have located and driven off the wolf packs.

The other commander most responsible for depriving the North Atlantic convoys of long-range aircraft was Air Marshal 'Bert' Harris, C-in-C RAF Bomber Command, who, since his accession to power in February 1942, had fought tenaciously against any diversion of his aircraft from the bombing of German cities. He was not interested in dropping bombs on U-boat bases, and even less interested in his precious aircraft ranging about the North Atlantic. Above all, he was averse to giving up even one of his ASV III centimetric radar sets.

When Harris was pressed to deploy a proportion of his strength to Coastal Command he replied to 'The Prime Minister's Anti-U-boat Committee' on 29 March 1943:

In view of the very large number of U-boats which the enemy will operate in the coming months, the proportion of his successes which would be eliminated by accepting the Admiralty proposals [to release more Liberators to Coastal Command and to bomb the U-boat bases in the Bay of Biscay] seems to be so small as to be negligible. The effect of them on the Bomber Offensive would certainly be catastrophic....

In the present case it is inevitable that at no distant date the Admiralty will recognize that U-boats can effectively be dealt with only by attacking the sources of their manufacture.... It cannot be pointed out too strongly that in the Bomber Offensive lies the only hope of giving really substantial help to Russia this year or in the foreseeable future; that its effect can be substantiated by incontrovertible evidence; and that if it is reduced to lesser proportions by further diversions of large numbers of bomber aircraft for seagoing defensive duties, it will fail in its object and the failure may well extend to the whole of the Russian campaign. This in my opinion would be a far greater disaster than the sinking of a few extra merchant ships each week....

I feel, however, that too much emphasis is being given to the possibility of locating U-boats by means of ASV (radar) and too little to the difficulty of attacking them successfully when they are located. Our experience, which is considerable, is that even expert crews find it no easy matter to attack with accuracy even a city by means of H2S. I am therefore rather sceptical of the prospects of inexperienced crews with ASV. Indeed I feel that the provision of aircraft equipped with this apparatus will mark the beginning rather than the end of the difficulties involved in sinking U-boats....

*   *   *

It was a great mercy that Franklin D. Roosevelt was not only a great President of the United States but also a life-long navalist, who had effectively run the US Navy from 1913 until 1921 as Assistant Secretary. He was fully aware that only air power could tip the scales in the Battle of the Atlantic. On 18 March 1943 he asked where all the VLR Liberators were; and no one was prepared to fudge the figures for *him*. Sittings of the Atlantic Convoy Conference led to the transfer of, for a start, one of the American Army (Antisubmarine) Squadrons to Newfoundland. It became operational on 19 April. Before this, RAF Coastal Command VLRs had begun a shuttle service from Iceland to Newfoundland. Forty-one VLRs were operating in the North Atlantic by mid-April 1943. The 'Air Gap' which had permitted the U-boat crews to work so freely in mid-Atlantic had been closed.

Roosevelt's mid-March enquiry was, in its own different way, as decisive in its consequences as the sinking of the battleship *Kirishima* by the battleship *Washington* off Savo Island far away in the south Pacific. Neither appeared decisive at the time, but the consequences that flowed from these two events, one passive and the other most violent, were profound indeed.

History being a notoriously untidy business, it is necessary to qualify the importance of the VLR Liberator in the Atlantic, but not by much. Other types of aircraft, notably from escort carriers, helped to tip the scales; so did Enigma; so did the tightly integrated escort groups and the brilliant leadership of Admiral Noble who was finally responsible for their introduction. And then there was the human factor. It was heartening that the spirit of the merchant seamen and the sailors and airmen of the escorts of all nationalities had not succumbed to the unremitting strain for almost four years. Now, with the first gleams of hope that the U-boat might at last be mastered, everyone concerned redoubled their efforts.

Early in May an outward-bound convoy was scattered by ferocious weather south-west of Greenland, and a pack of twelve U-boats descended upon the ships like eagles among spring lambs. Nine ships were sunk for the loss of only one U-boat. Then two support groups arrived on the scene and in short order nine U-boats were sent to the bottom – by ramming, depth-charging and air attack. Later in the month two convoys got through without a single loss while six U-boats were destroyed. It took just five weeks to achieve one of the great naval victories of all time. Look at these comparative figures of respective losses of U-boats and tons of shipping for the early summer of 1943:

	April	May	June
Shipping losses in tons	245,000	165,000	18,000
U-boats sunk	15	40	17

In the submarine war [wrote Admiral Doenitz] there had been plenty of setbacks and crises. Such things are unavoidable in any form of warfare. But we had always overcome them because the fighting efficiency of the U-boat arm had remained steady. Now, however, the situation had changed. Radar, and particularly radar location by aircraft, had to all practical purposes robbed the U-boats of their power to fight on the surface. Wolf-pack operations against convoys in the North Atlantic, the main theatre of operations and at the same time the theatre in which air cover was strongest, were no longer possible. They could only be resumed if we succeeded in radically increasing the fighting power of the U-boats.

This was the logical conclusion to which I came, and I accordingly withdrew the boats from the North Atlantic. On May 24 I ordered them to proceed, using the utmost caution, to the area south-west of the Azores.

We had lost the Battle of the Atlantic.[6]

The speed of this unexpected defeat had an appalling effect on Doenitz's crews. The *esprit de corps* of this German service had remained remarkably high. The C-in-C sustained morale by a blend of concerned paternalism and encouragement, despatching messages of congratulations to U-boat captains many miles and many weeks from home base in France. At Brest he would mix democratically with officers and men like some football coach, and saw to it that his 'team' lacked for none of the pleasures and rewards when they were resting between operations.

But in May 1943 life at sea was becoming almost unbearably arduous and dangerous, as exemplified by the diary entries of Herbert Werner over three days and nights:

23 May. U-230 crossed the 15th Longitude West, the door to Biscay Bay – and purgatory. We intercepted more bad news. A signal from *U-91* told us that they had seen *U-752* attacked and destroyed by aircraft; there were no survivors. At 1040 we crash-dived before a Sunderland airplane. No radar impulses. Quite obviously it must have attacked on sight. It announced the start of a six-day nightmare.

Under cover of darkness, *U-230* made her dash at a pitiful top speed of only 12 knots. We crash-dived seven times and shook off 28 attacks by bombs or depth-charges. By sunrise, we were stunned, deaf, and exhausted. We disappeared in the floods for the rest of the day.

24 May. Apparently the British were aware that two U-boats were running for port; their aircraft seemed to be looking for us, including the land-based four-engined bombers. During that night we crash-dived nine times and survived a total of 36 bombing runs.

25 May. Three hours after daybreak we floated into the deadly range of a hunter-killer group. Running submerged in absolute silence, we managed to slip by the endless, cruel, ravenous pings. One hour before midnight, we surfaced into the inevitable air assaults. On the first attack, four ferocious detonations rocked the boat as she surged into the deep. Suddenly there was a flash in the rear of the control room. A stream of sparks shot across the narrow space and enveloped us in choking smoke. The boat was afire. It seemed impossible to bring her to surface before we died. The round doors of the two bulkheads were slammed shut, the compartments sealed. Several men fought the fire with extinguishers. *U-230* rose sharply toward the surface where only seconds before the aircraft had dropped its diabolic calling card. Thick fumes choked us. Fire leaped from wall to wall. I pressed my handkerchief against mouth and nose and followed the Captain into the tower. The boat levelled off, she had surfaced. We hastened to the bridge. Somebody threw ammunition magazines on deck. The port diesel began to mutter. Red light and fumes escaped the hatch. We drove like a torch through the blackest night until the men below managed to kill the fire.[7]

It would have been understandable if the U-boat service had never regained its old cheerful optimism and determination of 1942 when a boat might come back from the area around the Azores, the Caribbean, the Cape or even the Indian Ocean with a score of half a dozen merchantmen, and the North Atlantic was still, relatively, 'a happy hunting ground'. Their total monthly score only once rose above 100,000 tons after July 1943, and often fell to near zero, while their own losses continued at a steady rate. Certainly the *Schnorkel* proved an increasing boon as the months passed, and hope was sustained by the promise of a totally new design of a super-fast, super-U-boat. Mercifully for the Allies, although Doenitz was promised as many as 350, only 120 were completed. Allied minelaying in the Baltic greatly restricted the training of the crews and there were mechanical problems to cope with as well. Only two became operational and one of these broke down. The log of the single survivor showed she had a British cruiser in her periscope sights at the moment the surrender order came through. However, by a near miracle of production, more standard U-boats were completed in November 1944 than in any other month of the war. And when Doenitz at length ordered his U-boats to surrender, forty-nine were still at sea, many more than in 1939.

In all 500 of 632 U-boats completed were sunk; and 32,000 of 39,000 officers and men were lost: chilling statistics indeed. One of the most successful 'hunter-killers', Peter Gretton, visited two of the biggest U-boat bases after the surrender and was impressed by the excellent state of the boats and the high morale of the crews.

The spirit of comradeship and loyalty among shipmates tends to increase in inverse ratio with the size of the ship, always assuming that the captain has the right qualifications and characteristics of leadership. Certainly this was borne out by the experience not only of the U-boat crews but amongst all the little ships of all nations, from American PT boats in the Pacific to the 'cockleshell heroes' of the Royal Navy, the men of the Special Boat Service who operated in canoes.

The exploits of the British submarine service have tended to be overshadowed by the devastation caused by Doenitz's U-boats. But from the outset of war in 1939 the British Home Fleet's submarines were on patrol off German bases, with strict instructions to attack shipping only within the terms of international law. HMS *Salmon* made a good start when her captain, Lieutenant-Commander Bickford, sank a U-boat and torpedoed two German cruisers, the *Leipzig* and *Nürnberg*. The operation was neatly rounded off when his fellow Lieutenant-Commander Phillips in the *Ursula* sank one of the destroyers escorting home the crippled *Leipzig*.

Then, as an indication that life was as precarious for British as for German submariners, in January 1940 three craft were lost in the dangerous, mine-strewn waters of Heligoland Bight. A mine caught the *Seal*, a big minelaying submarine, in April 1940. She was forced to the surface and, in spite of every effort of her crew, was captured – almost the only RN ship to fall into the hands of the enemy, and this was only because she was not fitted with a scuttling charge.

After their early trials and tribulations in the Mediterranean theatre the famous 10th Flotilla based on Malta, the 1st Flotilla at Alexandria and the 8th Flotilla at Gibraltar marked up an impressive score of transport successes – 286 in all between June 1940 and the end of 1944, amounting to over a million tons. They also showed unusual skill in disposing of boats of their own kind: sixteen Italian submarines and five U-boats in all. And, for even better measure, their score-sheet also included four cruisers and seventeen destroyers and torpedo-boats. But besides the great aces like Wanklyn and Mars, many more captains and their crews died in this most lethal form of naval warfare – forty-five British boats in the Mediterranean theatre alone.

In home waters the restrictions on German merchantmen attacks were lifted after a year of unrestricted U-boat warfare and from 1940 until early May 1945 RN submarines played a great part in the destruction of the German Merchant Navy, which ceased to exist by the end of the war.

GERMAN MERCHANT NAVY LOSSES

By mines:	600,000 tons
Submarines:	318,000 tons
Surface warships:	303,000 tons

The total figure equals only three or four bad months of Allied losses in the Atlantic, but the tonnage of German merchant ships at sea at any given time was only a fraction of British and Allied tonnage, and in northern waters the only significant trade was with the Scandinavian countries, excluding shipping along the coasts of France, Belgium and Holland.

Traditionally submariners have the reputation, dating back to the pioneer days before the First World War, of being independent, unorthodox and modest: at least, they have written less about themselves and their experiences than seamen of other branches. Chief Petty Officer Charles Anscomb was an exception. He was serving as coxswain in the submarine *Tempest* when, on a minelaying mission in the Gulf of Taranto in February 1942, they were spotted by an Italian destroyer, which attempted to ram.

After crash-diving and just escaping the stem of the Italian boat, the *Tempest* was subjected to a prolonged and devastating depth-charge attack. At the end of the first attack:

My stomach settled down and we carried on as if all this were just a practice run. There were no more explosions for the moment. The moments lengthened and still we went free. After a little while the cook made some tea and cocoa, and this hot brew, with biscuits, was passed round the boat. It made us all feel a lot better, even though we could hear that destroyer's engines as he passed and re-passed above us, stalking us still, hour after hour.

But they dropped no more depth-charges. In fact by 7 a.m. we were beginning to have hopes that they had really lost us when we heard engines very close overhead once more and then another series of shattering crashes as a pattern went off right alongside us. After that they came again and again, dropping pattern on pattern and all of them so close you could smell them. Dazed and shaken and scared, we hung on and hoped against hope. You couldn't tell where he was coming from until you actually heard him.

The master gyroscope was smashed and we had to rely on our magnetic compass. One oil-fuel bulkhead connection in the control-room was damaged, and oil fuel poured into the boat. The chief stoker, George Spowart, and his men got to it quickly and soon stopped the flood. The electrical artificer, John Winrow, slaved to put the gyro right, but it was past all hope of repair and we had to give it up. The fore hydroplanes were out of action and the boat was being controlled for depth by the after planes.

We were at the mercy of that destroyer. At regular intervals we heard her rumble over us. We could hear her Asdic 'pinging' us, the sound wave stinging our quivering steel flanks like an invisible whiplash, but never knew exactly where she was. Each time she turned and came back to try again. Each run did more damage than the last.[8]

But the Italians had still not finished with them. Two attacks later, when they thought they might survive and silence had returned, a member of the crew knocked over a bucket. The row echoed through the boat and was at once picked up above. The next attack proved too much. Water began to mix with the acid in the batteries, the resulting fumes of sulphuric acid being the most dreaded killer for all submariners.

The boat started to fill with it. One whole battery was flooded now. We had reached the end. The boat was just a pitch-dark, gas-filled shambles, flooding at the after end, with no instrument working except 'faithful Freddie' the magnetic compass. What use was a compass now? *Tempest* had nowhere to go any more, except to the bottom. At last, to save us from going with her, the captain decided to abandon ship.

Quietly the ship's company were told to put on the Davis escape gear. Without any fuss everybody buckled the gear on. Then the order was passed for everyone except men at key positions needed to maintain the trim of the boat to muster in the control-room.

Then the captain gave the order 'Abandon ship'.[9]

Twenty-three survivors of the *Tempest*'s complement of sixty-two were saved and made prisoners by the Italians.

Another notable submariner, the first RNVR officer to command a submarine, who wrote so well of the life and dangers of the service, was Edward Young. Before the war as an artist, he had designed the original penguin for Penguin Books. 'Teddy' Young had a notable war record, earning a DSO and a DSC. In 1943 Young took his brand-new submarine *Storm* on an Arctic patrol off North Cape, and then by way of contrast sailed her out to the Far East where he went hunting Japanese transports off the Andaman Islands. On 14 April 1944 the *Storm* made its first 'kill', at once being heavily counter-attacked. Young's log for the following day describes another attack in these dangerous waters:

0810. Sighted merchant ship steering eastward from Port Blair, escorted by same 'screen' as for previous day's target, namely one destroyer, one submarine-chaser and one other A/S vessel rather like a river gunboat. At first I thought, pessimistically, that the target *was* the ship I had attacked yesterday, but on closer examination she was seen to be larger, about 4,000 tons, with a large derrick for'ard which the other ship did not have. Moreover, asdic counted 95 revs with *reciprocating* H.E., and the smoke was coming out of the funnel in typical coal-burning fashion.

·I ran in at speed for as long as I dared. Even then the range was large on firing. I had only two torpedoes remaining in my bow tubes, and the stern torpedo. I considered firing the two bow tubes, and then turning quickly to complete a salvo of three with the stern tube. However, by the time I could have turned and steadied for the stern shot, the first two torpedoes would be well on their way to the target, and before the other could be of any use the first two would either have hit or been sighted, resulting in either case in an alteration of course on the part of the target. I therefore decided to fire the two bow tubes only, and reserve the stern tube for a possible *coup de grâce* if I managed to damage her.

0837. Fired two torpedoes. Range on firing 5,000 yards. Three and a half minutes later there were two sharp explosions. The periscope was dipped at the time of the bangs, but a moment later this is what I saw:

Target turning hard-a-port just past the line of fire, half hidden by a veil of thin smoke; the destroyer, this side of the target, also just past the line of fire with a column of what looked like spray or white smoke just astern of him. I thought at first that this must have been the aftermath of a shallow depth-charge, until I looked at him again two minutes later and saw black smoke and orange flame pouring out of his stern. He was obviously hit. It looked very much as though the target had been hit too; she seemed to be making more smoke than usual,

Above: HMS *Beverly*, one of the ex-American flush-deckers bartered for British bases in 1940, picks up (see below no. 1 funnel) some of the crew of *U-187* which she, with the *Vimy* (Lieutenant-Commander R.B.Stannard VC), has just sunk, 4 February 1943.

Left: And these are some that got away. Surrendered U-boats at Lishally, Londonderry, May 1945.

Left: Admiral Raymond Spruance, the cool, calculating victor at Midway.

Above: Admiral Ernest J. King, C-in-C United States Fleet, flanked (*left*) by Admirals Chester Nimitz and William Halsey.

Below: An American-built Hellcat on the final approach to land on HMS *Formidable*.

Dauntless SBD, the bomber that turned the tide in the Pacific War at Coral Sea and Midway.

The Wildcat was no match for a Japanese Zero in experienced hands.

The advent of the later Hellcat coincided with the steep decline in Japanese pilot quality, and swept the skies. (Long-range tank was dropped before action.)

Above: Pearl Harbor from a Japanese high-level bomber after the torpedo-bombers have opened the attack on 'battleship row'. Note oil gushes from hits on the *Oklahoma* and *West Virginia* and the shock waves from bomb bursts, one hitting the *Arizona* on the right. *Below:* And more destruction at Coral Sea, this time a very much more valuable ship, the carrier, *Lexington*.

Besides the four fleet carriers, the Japanese lost the 14,000-ton heavy cruiser *Mikuma* at Midway, here shown devastated by bombs. Primitive radar tower abaft the bridge superstructure.

20 October 1944, 2½ years after Midway, and the Americans are assaulting Leyte in the central Philippines. B.25 Mitchell bombers dealt roughly with this destroyer carrying reinforcements for the hard-pressed Japanese garrison.

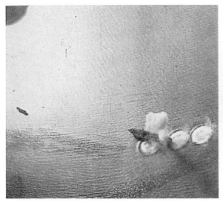 

Above left: Avengers from the carrier *Formidable* dive-bombing a Japanese ship in the closing stages of the Pacific War.

Above right: With her sister ship *Yamato*, *Musashi* was the biggest battleship ever built, with the biggest calibre guns. On 26 October 1944 she was found in the Sulu Sea and sunk by Liberator bombers, General 'Billy' Mitchell's forecast of the early 1920s realized.

Below: The day before the *Yamato* went down, the fast ex-depot ship *Zuiho*, converted into a carrier, was sunk at Cape Engaño by bombs and torpedoes – the first torpedo has just struck her amidships on the starboard side.

Captured German F-lighter, a formidable river barge-type coastal vessel, much used in the Adriatic and bristling with guns up to 88 mm.

63-foot 'MASBY' (Motor Anti-Submarine Boat) capable of 40 knots and armed with an Oerlikon 20 mm, two .5-inch, and gas-operated Vickers .303s.

Top: D-Day, 6 June 1944: landing-craft passing the assault anchorage position fifteen minutes before opening fire.

Left: Monitor HMS *Roberts* bombarding beach defences, a *Hawkins*-class cruiser in the background.

Below: 'Off go the good old 49th!'

began to pursue a very erratic course, and finally almost stopped, pretty well beam on. Seeing this I began to manoeuvre to attack her with my stern torpedo.

Two muffled depth-charges were heard shortly after the first two explosions, but the hit on the destroyer seemed to have demoralized the screen, as no further attempt at a counter-attack was made. I was able to watch the whole affair quite happily from a range of two miles or so, and Petty Officer E.R.Evans, the TGM, was able to have a look at his victim burning furiously.

The target was now at a range of three miles, zig-zagging wildly in all directions at a plotted speed of five knots. (Asdic counted 65 revs.) From her reduction in speed I felt certain she must be damaged. However, in spite of speeding up I could not get near enough to shoot with any chance of success.

In the meantime a submarine-chaser had come out from the shore and taken off the destroyer survivors, all of whom had been waiting disconsolately on the forecastle. An aircraft had also arrived and was performing inefficient aerobatics over the scene of confusion (all of which, incidentally, was well within sight of the staff office on Ross Island).

At 0952 the destroyer emitted a huge sheet of flame and a pall of thick black smoke and slowly sank. The submarine chaser returned to harbour with the survivors, and the remaining two escorts caught up with the merchant ship and made off towards the ESE. I decided to follow submerged, and surface for a chase when sufficiently far from Port Blair.[10]

If Nazi Germany failed by a whisker to win the Battle of the Atlantic with its U-boats, the American submarine was the most decisive war-winning weapon of the Pacific campaign. No single class of warship did as much as the submarine to defeat the Japanese at sea. In August 1945 the Japanese Merchant Navy had ceased to exist: 63 per cent of it had been sent to the bottom by American submarines, and more than one-third of Japanese warships were disposed of by American submarines. Yet the American people knew little about the work of the US submarine service at the time, and even today after close on fifty years their war-winning contribution is not widely appreciated.

There are three reasons for this. Firstly, by the very nature of the beast, its unexciting configuration, its secretive, underwater, almost underhand method of fighting does not make the submarine as immediately attractive a man o'war as, say, the mighty battleship, or the lean, swift destroyer. Like a nuclear missile, there is not much beauty or romance in the sight of a submarine: its powers of destruction are implied rather than stated. Secondly, while Germany was being pilloried for its unrestricted warfare against merchantmen in the Atlantic, a similar campaign pursued with equal ruthlessness in the Pacific did not call for propaganda exploitation. Thirdly, the United States did not think it was in its interests to reveal its secrets and its successes to the enemy.

More than this, the United States wanted its chief ally to turn down the volume of propaganda proclaiming success in the Atlantic against German U-boats in case Japan picked up any useful tips.

On 10 November 1944, for instance, Roosevelt wrote to Churchill:

I realize that it is very trying for many people that we should continue to prevent information from leaking out about anti-submarine methods, but our own submarine campaign in the Pacific is playing such an important role that the Barbarian will seize desperately upon any information that will help him in anti-submarine measures. I do hope, therefore, that we may continue to do all that we can to keep anyone from talking too much....

Churchill, always tightly security-conscious, did what he could to prevent this from happening, but it was not always possible to keep good news about the long-drawn-out Battle of the Atlantic out of the newspapers when it was so ardently wished for by the British public.

The submarine Battle of the Pacific, then, was fought silently, as befitted a service which relied upon stealth and upon self-imposed silence when under attack from above. 'As the "silent service" operated under conditions of highest secrecy,' Admiral Morison has written, 'few stories of its exploits were given out and no correspondent was taken to sea before 1945.' [11]

The US Navy's submarine service, which failed to sink a single ship in the First World War, looked at one time as if it might not do any better in the Second World War. The nation which had built the first serviceable submarine, the Holland-type, the father of every boat since, showed about as much interest in this type of vessel as the American Army had shown in the Wright Brothers' flying machine. The near-total success of the U-boat in 1917 changed all that, but not for long. In the isolationist, pacifist years that followed, reflected in international treaties outlawing submarine attacks on merchantmen 'without having first placed passengers, crew and ship's papers in a place of safety', the American service went into decline.

Originally the submarine was regarded as a possibly useful weapon of sea warfare for defending harbours and anchorages, a poor nation's coastal defence vessel because that was all it could afford. This doctrine was revived in the 1930s, in spite of the terrible lesson of the First World War. Later, it was allowed that the submarine might be used to attack warships if the occasion arose. 'The primary task of the submarine is to attack enemy heavy ships. A heavy ship is defined as a battleship, a battle-cruiser, or an aircraft carrier. On occasions, the primary task may, by special order, be made to include heavy cruisers, light cruisers or other types of ship.' [12]

After Pearl Harbor no one, from Admiral Nimitz down, visualized the role of the American submarine as a weapon in the *guerre de course*, in spite of what Germany had twice demonstrated to the world. The navy had a total of 111 boats, seventy-three of them in the Pacific, a high proportion of them old and with cramped accommodation. They lacked radar and (as they were soon bitterly to discover) their torpedoes' magnetic pistols were dreadfully unreliable. American fleet submarines had a complement of seven officers and seventy or so men, had a speed of 19 knots on the surface and 9 knots submerged, and carried twenty-five to thirty torpedoes. Their gun armament was limited to a single 3-inch and a couple of .5 machine-guns.

If Japan had declared war in the generally accepted custom of the time, the American submariner would certainly for a while have been further disadvantaged by being as fastidious as the British in 1939. But Pearl Harbor was regarded as such an outrage that all the customs and rules of war were blown sky-high, too, and the order that went to Rear-Admiral Charles A.Lockwood, Commander Submarines, Pacific, based at Pearl Harbor, was 'Execute unrestricted submarine warfare against Japan.'

But for many early months of the war most of the navy's submarines were involved in what had once been called 'work with the Fleet', operating offensively and defensively in conjunction with the Task Forces which were to form the spearhead of Pacific naval offensive operations. They acted as scouts and were used for minelaying and for intercepting enemy forces. These 'special missions', as they were now called, were the alternative to patrols in search of enemy shipping. Patrols lasted around forty-five to fifty days, some twenty days of which would be taken up in reaching and returning from the patrol area. Contact was maintained by radio with Pearl Harbor, but the submarines rarely acknowledged signals or reported for fear of being located by the enemy.

Without experience or training in attacking merchantmen at sea, early results from patrols were disappointing. It was not until the later stages of the Guadalcanal operations, when some submarines were equipped with radar and the Japanese concentration of shipping was temptingly rich, that major successes came the submariners' way. On 1 October 1942 an 8,000-ton Japanese aircraft ferry fell victim to the *Sturgeon* which hit with three of four torpedoes in a spread. With Nimitz's son as one of her officers, the *Sturgeon* had already had a number of eventful patrols, and earlier had been responsible for evacuating members of the Asiatic Fleet Submarine Force Staff from Java and taking them safely to Fremantle in Australia. Later in the month the *Gudgeon* and *Sculpin* between them sank three merchantmen totalling 13,500 tons in the same area. By November 1942 there were twenty-four submarines deployed in the Solomons area. Their success rate would have been a great deal higher if they had not still been dogged by unreliable torpedoes.

In the early months of 1943 the destruction of enemy shipping began to accelerate and become a serious problem for the Japanese. Radar was now fitted to all boats, and though unreliable at first, the sets were steadily improved. The same can be said of the torpedoes. The scandal of the early models was recognized and corrected, and submarines working out of Fremantle in Western Australia, Brisbane in Queensland, from Pearl Harbor and later from the advance base at Tulagi, began building useful scores, haunting the Japanese convoy lanes and learning the tricks of the trade which had long been familiar to the great U-boat commanders in the North Atlantic. Officers like Walter G.Ebert, Bernard F.McMahon and Richard C.Lake became the Pacific counterparts of Otto Kretschmer, Günther Prien and Joachim Schepke: but, thank goodness, the casualty rate among American submarine commanders never approached that of the U-boat fleet.

Typical of a wartime submariner captain's experiences and record is that of Commander James W.Davis in the Bismarck archipelago campaign at the turn of the years 1943–4. US submarines were just getting into their stride, and Davis's *Raton* (SS-270) was typical of the many wartime-built subs that poured from the shipyards – in this case the Manitoe Shipbuilding Co. of Wisconsin. Of just over 1,500 tons, the *Raton* could just about manage 21 knots on the surface, 7 knots submerged, and was armed with a single 3-inch gun and machine-guns. But American submarines rarely followed the practice of U-boat commanders by sinking ships by gunfire when it was safe and practicable to do so. And the *Raton*, like all her sister ships, was fitted with ten torpedo tubes.

Davis commissioned the *Raton* on 13 July 1943 and after training on Lake Michigan sailed her to Brisbane, where she arrived on 16 October. Almost at once Davis was sent out to patrol the Palau–Rabaul convoy route. She soon found rich game in the form of two big freighters on 26 November. Because of their exceptionally heavy air and surface escort, indicating their importance, Davis was precluded from making an attack until after dark. Shortly before sunset, after trailing the convoy at maximum submerged speed, *Raton* was brought to the surface to take bearings, dived again, and shortly before midnight made a radar attack on one of the freighters. Three out of the spread of five torpedoes sank the *Onoe Maru*.

A day later the *Raton* sighted another and larger convoy. She attacked submerged this time. 'We planned to get off six at the big one and four at one of the others,' declared Davis later, 'but a radical change of course, just when we were ready to fire, made the range to the large one too great. However, the zig [of the zig-zag] brought the remaining merchantman into an overlapping line of bearing.' In this way Davis contrived to make five hits on two freighters, sending them both to the bottom – 12,000 tons in all. And it seemed safe enough to do the right thing for the crew's morale, so they came up in relays to view the damage and remark upon the two square miles of debris.

Contrary to British and German practice, American submarine policy was to be lavish in the consumption of torpedoes. Who could tell then – or now – whether it was a policy that paid dividends, whether many hundreds of Japanese ships that went down were 'overkilled' with torpedoes? And how many more might have been destroyed had subs not been returning to base empty of ammunition? But a modest-sized freighter struck by a spread of six torpedoes certainly made an encouraging spectacle.

Working out of New Guinea, Fremantle, Pearl Harbor and other bases, the *Raton* continued her patrols in the Pacific *guerre de course* until the end of the year, frequently pounded by depth-charges, and sinking warships as well as 'Marus'. On her sixth patrol she badly damaged one of the few remaining Japanese heavy cruisers, and on her seventh patrol sank a large transport, a large freighter and a tanker. By now the war was almost over and there were few targets left. The *Raton* arrived at San Francisco in mid-September 1945 and was awarded six battle stars for her contribution to victory.

An even longer-serving US submarine than the *Raton*, her sister boat *Trigger*, served first north-east of Midway when that island was attacked, gained her first victim off the Bungo Strait on 17 October 1942, and from that time began to build up a mammoth total of tonnage, including three out of four freighters in one convoy, totalling over 20,000 tons. Edward L.Beach served in her for most of *Trigger's* life, sharing the crises and moments of triumph and the close camaraderie submariners enjoy. Then he was posted to another new submarine, the *Tirante*, which early in her career and quite by chance was ordered to rendezvous with his old boat in the South China Sea on 28 March 1945.

Beach recalled the attempts over three nights to contact the *Trigger* by radio, his anxiety for his old shipmates increasing with every hour. He later wrote of the agony when he had to accept the fact that *Trigger* had sunk on her twelfth war patrol, and the imagined nightmare, experienced by most submariners, of her final moments.

There never was any answer, and deep in our hearts, after three nights, that was answer enough. With your surface ships there are always survivors, messages, maybe a bit of wreckage.... With submarines there is just the deep, unfathomable silence.

We could visualize the sudden, unexpected catastrophe. Maybe a *kamikaze* plane. Maybe a depth-charge – a bull's-eye, after more than four hundred misses. Maybe a torpedo, or a mine, or even – inconceivably – an operational casualty.

In some compartment they may have had a split second to realize that *Trigger's* stout side has been breached. The siren screech of the collision alarm. Instantly the angry water takes possession. The shock has startled everyone in other compartments, and the worst is instantly obvious.

Almost immediately she up-ends. The air pressure increases unbearably. Everything loose or not tightly secured cascades down to the bottom against what used to be a vertical bulkhead. Some men have hung on where they were, but most are struggling around in indescribable confusion at the bottom of the compartment. Instinctively all eyes turn to the depth gauges and watch as the needles begin their crazy spin. Slowly at first, then faster and faster, they race around the dials.... Nothing can be heard except the rush of water, the groaning and creaking of *Trigger's* dying body, and the trapped, pounding pulses of the men.

Down, down, down she goes, to who knows what depth, until finally the brave ribs give way.[13]

The Pacific submarine war never reached the same scale of destruction, nor the degree of intensity and critical peaks of the Battle of the Atlantic. The US Navy never committed the resources or number of boats that the German Navy did, nor were the stakes so high for the Americans in their submarine offensive as they were for Britain and her Allies in their defence in the Atlantic and Arctic. But in war-winning terms the victory of the submarine in the Pacific was as important as its defeat in the Atlantic.

'The American submarine campaign against commerce was probably the most important single factor in the defeat of Japan,' stated Admiral Sir Arthur Hezlet, the much-decorated British submariner of Malta's 10th Flotilla, claiming that it 'weakened Japan to an extent which enabled an amphibious drive supported by carrier-borne air power to succeed'. In all, less than half the number of U-boats – 288 US submarines – sank 4,861,000 tons of Japanese shipping, plus a goodly share of the ships sunk by mines laid by submarines as well as by surface vessels and aircraft.

The Japanese counter-measures and escorts never achieved the same skills, nor for that matter ever possessed the same highly sophisticated weapons, as the Allies in the Atlantic battle. But all honour to the officers and men of the *Trigger*, and of the forty-nine more submarines which failed to return during the Pacific war.

'I have noted with admiration the work of the light coastal forces in the North Sea, in the Channel and more recently in the Mediterranean,' wrote Winston Churchill on 30 May 1943. 'Both in offence and defence the fighting zeal and the professional skill of officers and men have maintained the great tradition built up by many generations of British seamen.' [14]

With the fall of France, the control of 'the narrow seas' – the coastal waters stretching east and west of the Straits of Dover – became a reflection in miniature of the struggle for the high seas. In this battle, as prolonged and hard-fought as the Battle of the Atlantic, everything was on a relatively small scale and everything happened at a high speed, always accompanied by a great deal of noise and wind and spray. It was the battle of the little ships, the motor torpedo-boats, the motor gunboats, the motor launches, the super-fast German E-boats, all swiftly manoeuvring, attacking, retreating, evading, ramming sometimes, launching torpedoes amid a hectic pattern of tracer from light gunfire, starshells at night illuminating friend and foe, though which was friend and which foe there was often no time to distinguish.

Just as the U-boat packs stalked the Atlantic and Arctic convoys, the submarines of the US Navy sent the 'Marus' to the depths of the Pacific and the 10th Flotilla out of Malta attempted to sever the enemy lifelines to North Africa, so in the shallow coastal waters of the North Sea and the Channel MTBs and E-boats sought out the little convoys of coastal traffic and launched their torpedoes.

Speed rather than stealth was the first ingredient of success, but the coastal forces attracted the same type of men as the submarine service, the young individualists and adventurers, competitive-minded with fast reactions and a good team spirit. Just as the submarine service had its great figures – its 'aces' – so Coastal Forces developed heroes, some of whom became legends in their time and were much decorated: P.G.C.Dickens,

C.W.S.Dreyer, Robert Hichens,* K.Gemmel, G.D.K.Richards, Jack Lambert, M.Arnold Forster, D.Gould Bradford and Peter Scott.

If the Fleet Air Arm and the submarine service were the twin Cinderellas of the Royal Navy between the wars, Coastal Forces did not even exist. The first MTBs dated back to the same period as the nation's first single-seat fighter monoplanes, the Hurricane and Spitfire, 1935–6, when serious re-armament was being introduced into all the services as a result of German and Italian aggressive expansionism. These first MTBs were 60-foot wooden boats built by the British Power Boat Co., armed with two 18-inch torpedoes, stern launched, several light quick-firing guns and depth-charges for anti-submarine work. Powered by American Packard petrol engines, they could make some 36 knots but were not capable of keeping at sea at mean wind speeds above 18 knots. Nevertheless, as the 1st MTB Flotilla, the first six boats made the passage under their own power to Malta where they were stationed at a time of crisis with Italy.

Two more flotillas joined the fleet by the time war broke out, and the 4th Flotilla was equipped with slightly larger and more seaworthy boats.

We started the war with almost complete lack of experienced MTB officers [ran a post-war account] and there were no senior officers who could train the young ones; there was no considered amalgam of doctrine and experience. The navy generally knew nothing about the boats.[15]

Later development of the MTB led to the Fairmile 'D' class, with a specification similar to the early torpedo boat-catchers of the 1880s: 115 feet long, 120 tons, armed with two 21-inch torpedoes and 2-pounder pom-pom, 20-mm Oerlikons and machine-guns in multiple mounts. Three 1,500-hp supercharged Packard engines gave the 'Dog' boats a top speed of about 28 knots, and the complement consisted of a commanding officer, a first lieutenant, navigating officer and about thirty men.

To operate in unison with the MTBs in their offensive work against enemy shipping, the Motor Gun Boat was developed, originally from the navy's existing Motor Anti-Submarine Boats. In accordance with their title, they were to use their heavier gun armament while the MTBs attacked with their torpedoes. Later, they were equipped to carry torpedoes, too, just as the MTBs carried heavier guns.

Finally, there were the motor launches, MLs, essentially defensive boats, originally intended to guard harbours as HDMLs. They too were adapted to a different role as the need arose, especially in the Adriatic and Aegean, where they assumed a ferocious guise.

There was one main enemy of Coastal Forces, the German E-boat, or *Schnellboote*. This was a contemporary of the early British MTBs, but far

---

* Tragically killed on 12 April 1943. He was awarded the DSO and bar, the DSC and two bars, three times mentioned in despatches. Of him Peter Scott wrote at the time, 'He left a rich legacy... that example of courage that makes people think, as they go into action, "This would have been a mere nothing to Hich."'

from being despised by the hierarchy, and with typical German thoroughness, they got the design right first time. Diesel powered, with a low fire
risk compared with the British Dog boats' 5,000 gallons of 100-octane
petrol, they had a top speed of around 38 knots, were highly manoeuvrable
and 'dry', although they were not such steady gun platforms as the British
boats. In all, however, most MTB commanders would have gladly
exchanged boats with the enemy.

Some of the MLs developed later in the war had a ferocious battery
of weapons. Lieutenant Walter Blount DSC, RNVSR, recalled his ML
577 in June 1943:

Starting off with a 3-pounder signalling gun, we had a Holman Projector which
chucked out hand grenades for close action, two 21-inch torpedo tubes, a 40-mm
pom-pom two-pounder, four 20-mm Oerlikons, four .5s and four .303s. Those
MLs were about 120 tons, and our four Packard-Merlins [12-cylinder aero engines
such as powered the Spitfire, Mustang, etc.] gave us a top speed of around 28
knots.

We also had – and this was important – the latest American SO [Surface Operat-
ing] radar, very high voltage so that we had a special generator for it, and it could
pick up a ship at twenty-five miles: a great advantage over the enemy.[16]

In the course of 464 actions in home waters British Coastal Forces were
responsible for the destruction of 269 enemy merchantmen, mostly amid
the shot and shell described above. At the beginning, according to Peter
Scott, they were dubbed ironically 'Costly Farces'. No one spoke of them
in those terms by the time Churchill sent to them that accolade of May
1943.

Coastal Forces did not get into their stride until the summer of 1940,
and some of the early efforts were marked by failures and misunderstandings
inevitable with an untried form of warfare. The first really successful
operation involving MTBs occurred off Ostend on 8 September 1940, at
a time of tense expectation of a German invasion of south-east England
and with the aerial Battle of Britain raging. Three boats were involved,
commanded by Lieutenants R.I.T.Faulkner, E.Hamilton-Hill and
J.A.Eardley-Wilmot. The last of these officers tells the tale laconically in
contemporary slang:

We were sitting on the lawn one afternoon, when a message was sent up for us
to return immediately. At the Base we were told that a convoy of thirty merchant
ships had been sighted by aerial reconnaissance and was now either in or approaching Ostend. When we got over the other side I nearly got lost, as I tried to attack
what I thought was a floating dock, which turned out to be a wreck. I managed
to catch up, and after stooging around for about three hours without seeing anything,
'Pip' Faulkner called us up and told us we would go into the anchorage of Ostend.
Ham-Hill broke down and lost contact with us about fifteen minutes later, but
the two of us went in. The RAF were having a lovely time when we got there
and lots of muck was flying into the air. We found all the ships at anchor and
'Pip' flashed 'Disregard my movements' and went in to attack. I turned off to
the largest thing I could see and fired one fish, with the speed of the current

as deflection. Both he and I hit with one torpedo, then we came round and did another attack individually. Unfortunately there was so much explosive business going on, because of the RAF and also because, we found out later, I had hit an ammunition ship, that it was impossible to see the results. However, on the way out the examination vessel started firing at us. Our organization in those days was that all the stokers were armed with rifle grenades. As we passed about forty yards off (I hadn't seen the blasted thing till the last moment) these boys had a whale of a time, and what with rifle grenades and our Lewis guns we gave them quite a good innings. Next day an aircraft reported three new wrecks in the anchorage, but whether we got all three I do not know.[17]

The terrifyingly close action of these MTB engagements was graphically described by Ian Trelawny DSC, RNVR. It was the night of 10–11 December 1943, and two divisions were despatched to deal with a convoy off the Hook of Holland – a convoy consisting of three large merchantmen with an escort of nine heavily armed trawlers and 'several' E-boats.

We were met with an absolute storm of abuse from the Hun, who appeared to be putting down a barrage at about 1,200 yards range and about 200 yards deep. In that area the surface of the sea was absolutely seething with bullets like a puddle in a hail-storm. It wasn't much fun going through, but once we got there the shower eased off a bit, though it was still hard to pick out the targets in the dazzling tracer. However, there was one really big fellow spitting tracer at us along his entire length, so we closed in and let him have it. As soon as we had fired we turned away, and had a very nasty few minutes getting out of it. They were very angry. The gunfire was so intense that I did not myself see the result of our attack, but when we rejoined the others they said they had observed two definite hits.

Then we went off to harry the Hun again while the other division tried to get in an attack. While we were stooging around inside the convoy, to my amazement I suddenly saw something that looked like a Thames barge under full sail. We went over to have a look and found it was an enormous black bow sticking out of the water, a bow we'd last seen on the front end of our target. Nearby were four trawlers pooping away with their guns at anything and everything they saw. They weren't shooting at any of our people, so we left them to it.[18]

Like the U-boats, the German E-boats in northern coastal waters fought almost to the end of the war, their spirit unconquered, too. The last of these close fights took place in April 1945, by which time the Royal Navy had got the upper hand by reason of greatly superior numbers and a form of close co-operation with defensive patrols and air reconnaissance. And then, on 13 May, the ceremonial surrender took place after the surviving E-boat flotillas put out from Rotterdam and for the last time crossed the North Sea in formation and were met by British MTBs off Felixstowe.

The first serious involvement of Coastal Forces in the Mediterranean was in the hard-fought evacuation from Greece and the struggle for Crete, which decimated the small force of MTBs and HDMLs. By this time – the early summer of 1941 – the value of Coastal Forces in home waters, and their potential value in the Mediterranean, was belatedly recognized by the Admiralty, and strenuous efforts were made to build up a force of light craft based in the eastern Mediterranean.

They came – freighted – from the USA and Canada, as well as from Britain, round the Cape, and a few made the dangerous passage through the Mediterranean. Some were even built in Egypt. Coastal Forces Mediterranean was, therefore, made up of a mixed bag – 70-foot Elcos from the USA, Scott-Paines from Canada as well as home-produced MLs, MGBs and MTBs.

In 1941 this growing force was used for clandestine operations in the Aegean, for running in essential supplies to Tobruk and for attacking German supply craft. The first enemy throughout the Mediterranean campaign was the German F-lighter, an ingenious multi-purpose vessel with very shallow draught which could be used in the role of freighter, troop-carrier or flak ship according to need, or the three roles simultaneously. In its most offensive role it boasted a firepower which no MTB or MGB could hope to match: an 88-mm dual-purpose gun, a 40-mm and multiple 37-mm and 20-mm and bristling machine-guns. Because of their shallow draught they were very difficult to torpedo, and for a while the only method of attack was to get in so close under cover of darkness that their guns could not be sufficiently depressed to make a hit.

One of the Mediterranean MTB pioneers, Lieutenant Dennis Jermain, was also a pioneer in attacking surface vessels with depth-charges, a highly lethal proceeding. He had already had some success in home waters before coming out to the Mediterranean. His first experiment against an F-lighter was on the night of 26–27 May 1942 off Bomba where he was patrolling. At 3.00 a.m. they sighted an F-lighter:

We fired torpedoes at it, but at least two of them ran under because of the vessel's very shallow draught. Then I had another go with depth-charges and managed to explode one right underneath the craft. We were unable to find any trace of it afterwards, except for a lot of bubbles, but could not definitely say it was sunk because while disengaging from the F-lighter's heavy guns we had momentarily lost sight of it.[19]

Working out of Alexandria, the steadily growing Coastal Forces concerned themselves with attacks on Rommel's supplies, and – for a few miserable, hazardous hours – in the evacuation of Tobruk when it was surrounded and falling to the enemy. By October 1942, when General Montgomery was ready to go over to the offensive in Egypt, and began to advance after the victory of El Alamein, Coastal Forces were employed in making fake landings behind the German lines and in ensuring that no supplies got through to Rommel from the sea. By early December 1942 Dennis Jermain was able to take his 10th Flotilla across to Malta to establish a base there while other flotillas moved into the shattered harbour of Benghazi, and later to Bone.

Paradoxically, the real war for Coastal Forces in the Mediterranean began after the Germans and Italians had been swept out of North Africa. For a while the boats were used for minelaying and other subsidiary tasks, but their first function, almost until the end of the war, was to attack enemy shipping off the coasts of Sicily, Italy, Yugoslavia and Greece, although the boats were also employed in other roles, notably in supplying Tito's insurgents and landing what they called 'false nose chaps' for various clandestine activities.

Besides an increasing number of E-boats and the dangerous F-lighters, the MTBs, MGBs and MLs also found themselves up against another ferocious and typically ingenious German man o'war, the Siebel ferry. This, believe it or not, was a vessel like a catamaran made up of two Dutch barges joined by a bridge deck, giving a total beam of 50 feet and powered by two truck engines. The maximum speed was 10 knots or less, depending on its 'cargo'. This could consist of nothing but anti-aircraft guns, when it became a flakship; or 88- and 37-mm guns, when it became a bombardment vessel; or a mixture of the two, when it became the terrifying foe of any MTB within range; or simply a troopship (150 capacity) or cargo vessel.

Nothing could be more unlike the Dutch coast with its ever-shifting sandbanks, shallow waters and treacherous currents than the coastline of Yugoslavia north of Dubrovnik with its deep indentations and countless rocky islets and islands. But, especially in 1944, these two contrasting and widely separated areas were among the busiest hunting grounds for Coastal Forces. In the Adriatic the 'hottest' part was north of Zara, and it was in this area that one of the most interesting actions took place on the night of 11–12 October 1944.

Three MTBs and a gunboat left their base at Komiza to patrol off Zara in the hope of picking up a German convoy. They were under the command of Lieutenant-Commander Tim Bligh, DSO, DSC (MGB 662), a highly successful veteran in this form of warfare. With him he had 634, Lieutenant Walter Blount, DSC; 637, Bob Davidson; and 638, Denis Lummis. Blount went ahead to try to pick up some intelligence on the whereabouts of the enemy (if any), and learned that a convoy of mainly F-lighters might be coming north from Zara before long.

At 8.40 p.m. on 10 October 1944 the unit closed the coast of Vir Island and lay stopped. It was a dark, thundery night with flashes of lightning, which after a while appeared to develop into something more lethal – like the flash of shellfire and starshell. Blount was again detached to find out what was going on and reported by R/T that the local partisans had seen two destroyers. He rejoined the unit which then made an abortive sweep outside the islands, the unit returning to Ist to hole up for the greater part of daylight hours.

A meeting with the partisans seemed to confirm that the convoy was likely to emerge the following night, so the four boats hove to off Vir Island.

More flashes and flares and tracer fire appeared to suggest that there was some kind of action going on of an unfriendly nature. At 10.45 p.m. all four boats started rolling unduly, indicating the passage of some ships nearby.

Walter Blount describes the opening moves:

The visibility was now very low, and I was not prepared for the shock of suddenly seeing enemy ships on the port bow, at about 400 yards' range.

The unit was at once stopped and the boats headed into the shore just north of Vir Light. The targets were four F-lighters, of which one was altering course towards us: he appeared to be higher out of the water than the others and was an escorting flak-lighter closing to drive us off.

MTB 634 was ordered to try and carry out a torpedo attack on this target. *MGB 662* ordered 'Single line ahead, speed 8 knots,' and went ahead in order to engage by gunfire.

The flak-boat opened fire on *MGB 662* at 2306, at once killing one of the pom-pom loading numbers. Fire was returned from all guns, and *MTB 638* illuminated with starshell.

The visibility was such that the leading boat in the line had a completely different picture from the fourth boat, and the slight offshore breeze was blowing smoke from *MGB 662*'s gunfire across the line of sight of our ships and the enemy convoy, which was, of course, much more of an advantage to us than them, as we had the inshore position and knew where to expect them, while the only ship that they could see was *MGB 662*.[20]

It was not easy to make any sense of the mêlée. Bligh noted vast quantities of 88-mm and 20-mm fire and all of it coming at them. Then he noted one enemy boat blow up after being hit by his own 6-pounder, F-lighters being hit by his pom-pom and 20-mm shellfire. One of the British boats set an E-boat on fire, which blew up seconds later; the gunboat's 6-pounder also pumped innumerable shells into an F-lighter and sank another smaller boat. 'Everywhere on the port side there were burning ships and explosions. There were visible many more ships than the original four F-lighters. The sight was fantastic!' exclaimed the commanding officer, who signalled 'Single line ahead, speed 8 knots' and opened fire. The enemy could clearly be seen now – four F-lighters, one of which was closing on them. Blount continued:

I prepared to attack the flak-lighter with torpedoes, but the range had closed to 100 yards, too close, so I opened up with all guns on the flak-lighter firing at *MGB 662*.

As I turned, less than fifty yards from the flak-lighter, *MTB 634* was hit in the port pom-pom ready-use locker, which exploded and went up in flames. The fire was extinguished.

All our guns continued to pour an intense fire into the flak-lighter, which burst into flames from stem to stern. Every detail of her could be discerned. She appeared to have an 88-mm amidships, a quadruple 20-mm aft and many 20-mm in sponsons down the starboard side.[21]

The fight continued intermittently but with the same ferocity until 3.37 a.m. when there was nothing much left for the British Force to sink. The total score by the four Coastal Forces boats was six F-lighters, each a very tough adversary, four smaller Pil-boats and an E-boat, with four more enemy vessels probably sunk or extensively damaged. As Lieutenant-Commander Bligh summed up: 'This was the first really decisive victory of D-boats over the old enemy, F-lighters, and was made possible due to low visibility, land background, uncertainty of identification, absurdly close ranges, excellent gunnery and coolness on the part of the following commanding officers.' The official report from HQ also mentioned the 'brilliant and inspiring leadership'.

F-lighters also made their challenging appearance on the west coast of Italy where the German armies experienced increasingly severe supply problems as the Allies drove them north and air attack destroyed the railway system and fighter bombers attacked road convoys and blew up bridges. As in Yugoslavia the sea remained the last resort for passing supplies to the hard-pressed troops, making use of coastal convoys from French ports, down the Ligurian and Tuscan coasts. The riper targets these convoys became, the more the Germans had to reinforce them with destroyers, E-boats and the F-lighters with which the Adriatic MTBs and MGBs had become familiar. The offensive against these very heavily guarded supply convoys was mounted for a while by US, Royal Navy and Royal Canadian Navy light coastal forces operating in close union and complete harmony. The story of these highly dangerous joint operations, however brief and relatively confined in its scope, marks some of the happiest episodes in Anglo–American naval co-operation.

The American Patrol-Torpedo(PT)-boat had had an even tougher time in becoming accepted by the US naval authorities than the British MTB. There was small-boat experimentation between the wars, notably by the sporting millionaire industrialist Gar Wood, who used 1,000-horsepower Packard aviation engines in his boats to take many international speed trophies. Competition between Gar Wood and the British innovative designer, Hubert Scott-Paine, speeded up the development of highly efficient hydroplanes with speeds of over 100 knots. But this racing and record-breaking attracted even less naval attention in America than in Britain, and it was not until the Roosevelt-inspired reformation and expansion of the US Navy took place in 1936 (like the carrier and battleship programmes) that serious attention was given to the development of a PT-boat force.

In December 1936 the Chief of the Navy's Bureau of Construction and Repair recommended that fast, light patrol craft would be useful for the protection of coastal areas, relieving larger ships of this burden. From this came 'a modest development program'. A specification was later drawn up and competitive tenders invited. The specification called for a 40-knot speed, 550-mile cruising range and an armament of two torpedoes, depth-charges and anti-aircraft guns.

The boat that provided the genesis for all early Elco-built PT-boats was the British Power Boat's Scott-Paine-designed PT-9, which was delivered to New York from its British yard a few days after the European war broke out in September 1939. Other designs put into service included Professor George Crouch's 54-foot award-winning design, later put into production by the Fisher Boat Works of Detroit, Michigan, and the Higgins Company of New Orleans.

There was plenty of progressive experimentation during these early days. Meanwhile, the formation of three squadrons initially had been authorized, the first made up of experimental boats, among which the Elco 70-footers were predominant. Many of these were later turned over to the British Admiralty under lend-lease before Pearl Harbor.

In the Pacific in the early months of the war, the PT squadrons gained fame first in the Solomons where they did sterling service during the Guadalcanal campaign in the infamous Slot, operating from the Tulagi PT base against the Tokyo Express supply and reinforcement ships; aces like Lieutenant Lester Gamble gained honours and fame.

It was not until April 1943 that the first PT-boats appeared in the Mediterranean, a time when they were most wanted for the operations against German coastal convoys off the north-west coast of Italy. Squadron 15, made up of 78-foot Higgins boats, was moulded into Allied Coastal Naval Forces based in Sardinia and under the overall command of Captain J.F.Stevens RN. The American-manned and operated PT-boats provided the radar for scouting, British and Canadian-manned MTBs formed the torpedo spearhead, and MGBs, as befitted their name, provided the gunpower.

This was all very well and looked – and was – formidable enough, but the massive gunpower of the F-lighters which provided the main escort punch was too much, and in early 1944 Commander Robert Allan formed the Coastal Forces Battle Squadron, based on Bastia, Corsica. The lethal heart of this squadron were LCGs (Landing-Craft Guns) armed with two 4.7-inch and two 40-mm quick firers, which were to prove more than a match for the ferocious F-lighters.

One of the most lively actions in which this Battle Squadron participated took place on the night of 24–25 April 1944, involving two LCGs, two MGBs, a pair of MTBs and no fewer than seven PT-boats headed by *PT-218*, Lieutenant (jg) Thaddeus Grundy, in which was embarked Commander Robert Allan RNVR. The Operation SO Bobby Allan's part was to orchestrate the whole operation from the PT's radar screen, his R/T serving as the conductor's baton. The other three American boats would act as scouts, probing ahead with their highly efficient radar.

From Leghorn harbour there emerged at 8.00 p.m. that evening three F-lighters and a tug with supplies for San Stefano. Also at sea that night were three more heavily armed F-lighters and two patrol vessels both towing a barge.

The PT-boats' radar and Allan's radar in *PT-218* picked up two of these targets shortly after 8.00 p.m.

Examination of the plot [Allan reported later] led me to believe that the target off Piombino, which was northbound and opening the coast, formed an escort group which was probably going to rendezvous with the southbound convoy. I decided to attempt to cross the bows of this group, getting between it and the convoy. Course was therefore altered to the northward at 2300.[22]

By 11.00 p.m. the Battle Squadron was heading directly for the German escort group at a range of three miles, while Allan watched it suddenly turn to starboard, which gave him the opportunity of getting at the first target – the convoy – without interference from its escort.

Manoeuvring his force like a fast game of remote-controlled dominoes, Allan had his LCGs 3,000 yards from the convoy on the most favourable bearing soon after midnight. The crack Royal Marine gun crews at the 4.7s opened fire, some of them with starshell to illuminate the target. The illumination was more successful than they could have expected, some of the starshells setting alight the shore tree and shrub line as well, providing perfect silhouette targets at which to aim.

Almost at once the F-lighters began to blow up with spectacular ammunition explosions. Then more F-lighters and a tug were discovered, and attacked with equal ferocity. The PTs, MTBs and MGBs joined the party, the three MGBs closing to pick up survivors, among whom were six unfortunate conscripted Dutch sailors. Five F-lighters and the tug in this convoy were sunk.

Meanwhile, with their tails up, the LCGs went after the escort, which having failed in their task were now beating it northward.

The second action [wrote Allan] commenced by the firing of starshell only. I had assumed that this force was the escort force previously encountered, and before engaging so heavily armed a unit I was anxious that its composition and position should be clearly established.... Immediately our starshell burst the enemy fired a five-red-star recognition and I ordered a cease fire. Two minutes later, having informed the LCGs that the first rounds would count, I ordered them to open fire with all guns.[23]

This time the LCGs, and the other boats, did not have such an easy time and Allan provoked the enemy gunners by ordering Grundy to increase the PT's speed to draw the fire from the LCGs. This resulted in some very near misses on his *PT-218* but also in increasing slaughter as the heavy shells tore into the F-lighters, setting them on fire one after the other.

The German report on this unpleasant stage of the battle ran:

The leading barge, *F610*, was repeatedly hit by large-calibre shells. At the same time *F350* received a direct hit and went up in flames. On *F610* a fire was started and ammunition began to explode, so an order was given to abandon ship. The barge developed a heavy list and finally sank with a loud explosion.

The remaining barge, *F589*, tried to escape behind a smoke-screen, but she was hit and severely damaged and two of her guns put out of action. A fire started in the ammunition, but this was extinguished by the crew. In a panic some of the men had jumped overboard.

Allan then ordered *PT-209* to lead the MTBs in to attack at close range and complete the destruction. PT-boats then participated alone in the third action of the night, this time against another escort group and with torpedoes. Before they could be manoeuvred into a good launching position the enemy spotted them and opened a heavy fire. Things rapidly became extremely uncomfortable for the Americans until a bright officer in *PT-202* remembered that in some locker or other they had a five-red-star recognition cartridge identical to the one earlier fired by the enemy. It worked like a charm; enemy fire instantly ceased, so that DuBose was able to take his boats to within 1,700 yards of the German force to launch their torpedoes. Then they hurriedly left under cover of a smokescreen but pursued by some angry German fire, particularly angry from a hit and sinking German destroyer.

Every boat returned safely from Operation Thrush, without a casualty. It had been a highly successful night for the Anglo–American–Canadian Battle Squadron.

A number of these German coastal convoys did reach their destination safely enough to keep Field-Marshal Kesselring's armies supplied, and by no means all the actions were as free of Allied casualties as Operation Thrush. These night actions were just as much a part of the *guerre de course* as the endless Battle of the Atlantic with as severe effects on German supplies as the U-boat war had on the Allied war effort. Every other night – on average – the Coastal Forces were out on patrol during 1944 off the west coast of Italy, sinking thirty-two F-lighters and forty-four enemy vessels altogether, with another dozen probably destroyed; while about twice that number succumbed to the guns and torpedoes of the Adriatic flotillas.

This was an immensely exciting form of naval warfare, requiring the steady nerves, sharp responses and 'unflappability' of a fighter pilot, and resulting in many well-deserved decorations. Speak to an old PT-boat man or MTB veteran today and they will remember every detail of every action as if it had happened yesterday, illuminated by starshells and searchlights.

CHAPTER THIRTEEN

The Central Thrust: Tarawa

There was abundant heroism on both sides in the long-drawn-out Guadalcanal campaign. The leadership was more patchy. The American command could have benefited more swiftly from the lessons learned so expensively in night fighting, and emulated their professional opponents. The Japanese, too, were slow at learning that the Americans facing them were not the effete, spoilt amateurs they had been told they were: there is no greater let-down at a crisis in a war (and the closing months of 1942 were the ultimate crisis period for the Japanese) than to discover that your opponents are tougher and better equipped than you had been led to believe.

But if there is one great hero of Guadalcanal it is Rear-Admiral Raizo Tanaka. Time and again he showed the quality of his leadership in night fighting, and the way in which he kept the Tokyo Express on the rails elicited the respect of his enemies.

Admiral Tanaka's greatest accomplishment was the negative one of supervising the evacuation of the Japanese forces from around Henderson Field and from Guadalcanal. Over three nights in early February 1943 Tanaka with superlative skill and cunning utilized destroyers racing down the Slot to take off the 12,000 troops facing the American Marines and their auxiliaries. At negligible loss, too. On 4 February, for example, he sent down a cruiser and twenty-two destroyers, which embarked thousands of men under the noses of the Americans and got them out at the cost of two damaged destroyers.

This success was attributable not only to Tanaka's skill but also to the continuing American inability to cope with his high-pace tactics. A few PT-boats, it is true, carried out some determined attacks but without any serious success. On 9 February American forces opened up another offensive, only to find that the last of the birds had flown forty-eight hours earlier. It was a great relief but also a somewhat shaming anti-climax. They would be meeting them again.

Even after Yamamoto's decision to pull out there were more night clashes with the Allied naval forces, which included the New Zealand cruiser *Leander* and small anti-submarine craft. The *Leander* was of an older generation of light cruiser beside the new American cruisers with their fifteen very quick-firing 6-inch guns, but she fought the good fight at their side until knocked out by a long lance torpedo at the Battle of Kolombangara on the night of 12–13 July 1943.

In these night clashes and skirmishes the Japanese continued to show their superiority almost to the end, greatly assisted by their super-torpedoes, which could tear the heart out of a ship from a range of 10,000 yards. Moeover, while rapidly developing and producing their own radar, they already had in use a form of German radar detector, which cancelled out many of the advantages of possessing the real thing.

But the Japanese were not immune to being caught by surprise. On the night of 6–7 August 1943 in the Vella Gulf, Commanders Frederick Mossbrugger and Rodger W.Simpson with six destroyers set out to intercept a Japanese force of four fast, modern destroyers, three of which carried 900 troop reinforcements and supplies for the beleaguered Japanese force on Kolombangara, north-west of Guadalcanal. The destroyer men, who believed passionately that they had been tied too closely to cruisers in all the Solomon Islands actions for too long, relished the chance of operating alone. They had up-to-date radar and full confidence in themselves and their weapons.

The two commanders got everything right. Mossbrugger's radar picked up a blip at almost 20,000 yards, which turned into four individual blips heading south at under 30 knots. They then manoeuvred their divisions to attack the enemy in succession. They had not been seen by the surprisingly unalert Japanese when the American destroyers launched a mighty spread of torpedoes at 6,300 yards. Even the white wakes were not spotted until too late. Helms were put over in a panic. Only the nimbler destroyer *Shigure*, empty of troops and stores, turned in time and got off her own counter-spread.

The other three Japanese destroyers were torn apart by the explosions and then subjected to intense and rapid 5-inch shellfire. The carnage was appalling. After searching for further sign of the enemy, the two Commanders brought their divisions back to the scene to rescue enemy survivors. There were many still in the water. Commander Simpson took his destroyer in among them, listening uneasily to the curious chanting sound, a chorus of grief or pain or defiance – who could tell? There were shrieks, too, and the destroyer's crew stood by with lines. But when threatened with rescue, a whistle was blown, silence descended on those close by in the water, while they swam away desperately to avoid the shame of capture. 'Know thine enemy!' These young Americans were learning fast. And they had participated in the most successful destroyer night torpedo attack of the war so far.

American destroyers scored again, and for the last time in the south-west Pacific, in the early hours of 2 November 1943. The Allies landed on Bougainville at a place called Empress Augusta Bay on 1 November, and Rear-Admiral A.StantonMerrill was ordered out to cover the landing of stores and reinforcements the following day. In the early hours of the morning his new 6-inch-gun cruisers with two destroyer divisions clashed with a superior force of Japanese cruisers and destroyers commanded by Rear-Admiral Sentaro Omori.

Proving that the US Navy had at last got the hang of fighting the Japanese at night, Merrill, handling his destroyers cleverly, committed enough damage on the enemy to cause Omori to break off the action. Omori claimed the usual exaggerated total of losses to the enemy (which were negligible), but Japanese high command was no longer listening and Omori was sacked.

Hellbent on destroying the Allied amphibious force before it could get a grip on Bougainville, Admiral Kurita now came down south from Truk with half a dozen very formidable heavy cruisers. Halsey had no surface forces to oppose the enemy, so, being an aviation man, he sent off forty-five bombers with fifty-two Hellcats from his carriers to deal with them instead. They did so while the cruisers were refuelling and damaged them all more or less badly – badly enough for Kurita to be recalled to Truk, if he could make the voyage. He did. But it was the end of any disturbance to the Allies' sea and air control of the south-west Pacific. The roll-back of the Japanese could now be accelerated, a task that, as we shall now see, was facilitated by the shooting down of a single enemy aircraft, and further eased by shooting down a second.

After the evacuation of Guadalcanal, Admiral Yamamoto decided to make a tour of the upper Solomon Islands to inspect the defences and raise morale by making his presence known and encouraging local commanders. There can be no doubt that this was the right thing to do. Yamamoto was a latter-day Nelson and Togo in the eyes of the IJN, admired and inspiring. He carried out this task in the first half of April 1943, and with his Chief of Staff, Vice-Admiral Ugaki, in a second Betty, took off from Rabaul at 11.00 a.m. on 18 April for Kahili Airport, Buin. To ensure a safe journey, nine Zero pilots had the honour of escorting him.

All this was known to the American code-breakers, down to the hour of departure, so sixteen new army twin-engine Lightning fighters, with cannon armament (at last!) took off from Henderson and were conveniently flying low along the west coast of New Georgia at a time that would permit them comfortably to be over Buin at 11.35 a.m. The Lightnings waited unseen until the Bettys were on their final approach. Yamamoto's plane crashed in the jungle, Ugaki's in the sea – where, in fact, he survived though critically injured. The great Yamamoto, instigator of Pearl Harbor, hero of the Japanese Navy, died at once. The catastrophe, according to one of his fellow admirals, 'dealt an almost unbearable blow to the morale of all the military forces'. Now, it could truly be said, Pearl Harbor had been avenged.

Admiral Yamamoto's deadline for Japanese victory had been exceeded by six months at the time of his death. All that he had predicted was coming to pass, although the extent of the failure of his forces in the Solomons

– especially his naval air forces – was concealed by wildly over-optimistic claims. His airmen would report fifty American planes destroyed when half a dozen had been shot down and the numbers of Japanese losses were divided by four. For example, in early April 1943 hundreds of Japanese aircraft attacked the Allied base at Milne Bay at the eastern end of Papua and other bases in the Solomons and New Guinea. Yamamoto· was told that they had sunk a cruiser, two destroyers and twenty-five transports, and had shot down 175 of the enemy. In fact they sank in all one tanker, one destroyer, a corvette and a freighter, and shot down about twenty-five Allied planes. Yamamoto died believing that his fleets were still capable of regaining total control of the Solomons.

The truth was very different. The truth was that, as Yamamoto had predicted, the battle for the Pacific was already lost by the middle months of 1943 even if it were to take another two years for the Japanese high command to accept the unpalatable truth. If Waterloo was won on the playing fields of Eton, the Pacific was won on the airfields of America where thousands of airmen were being trained for combat, and in the aircraft plants of Lockheed, Douglas, Grumman and Boeing and in the shipyards all over the nation. No fewer than twenty-four fleet carriers *of one class* were under construction or about to be laid down, and many more escort carriers.* Ever more powerful battleships, battle-cruisers and cruisers, destroyers, submarines and many hundreds of landing-craft of all types were being produced in shifts round the clock in an unprecedented total output of war material.

The winning of the war in Europe remained the first priority but the Combined Chiefs of Staff recognized that overall strategy in the Pacific could not be limited simply to holding the Japanese on the line they had reached by May 1942. Moreover, while the invasion and liberation of Europe would require considerable naval forces, thanks to British and Commonwealth output, there would be a massive surplus for the Japanese war.

The Combined Chiefs of Staff also recognized that the rolling-back, island-hopping policy pursued by General MacArthur, against a fanatical foe prepared to die to the last man at every stage, would be too slow and too expensive in human life, an American priority consideration throughout the war. In March 1943, some weeks before the death of Yamamoto, a fresh American policy – the results of which he was never to witness – was already being thrashed out. In essence it called for a deep thrust into the centre of the Japanese defence line from the mid-Pacific through Micronesia, while General MacArthur completed the ejection of Japanese forces from the Solomons and the Bismarck Peninsula and advanced north to liberate the Philippines.

This policy represented a threat to the previous priority given to

---

* Fifty of another class of escort carrier were completed in the Kaiser shipyard alone in the twelve months between June 1943 and June 1944.

MacArthur and the south-west Pacific, and predictably was opposed by him. MacArthur continued to argue in favour of his own strategy, a counter-offensive along the south-west Pacific route from New Guinea to the Philippines, which would deprive Japan of her newly conquered sources of raw materials – rubber, minerals and, above all, oil. This, he claimed, would alleviate Australian anxieties more effectively than the central Pacific thrust, which would be open to attacks on both flanks from the numerous Japanese-occupied islands on which bases had been installed. After much acrimony the central-thrust policy was proceeded with anyway, and the highly complex business of setting it up went ahead.

The organization was not made any easier by the need to settle the claims of four strongly competing services, each with their own strongly competing internal branches. The US Navy, for example, was sub-divided into the carrier men, the 'battlewaggon' men, the independently minded destroyer crowd and the equally independent submariners.

Then there was the US Army with its Air Corps, strongly jealous of its own *esprit de corps*, pride and traditions, yet often dependent upon the navy for transport and for being launched into battle. The Marine Corps, also with its own aviation branch, possessed a pride in traditions and belief in its superiority in inverse ratio to its size.

Somehow all these forces were welded, accompanied by the banging together of a number of quarrelling heads, into a Central Pacific Force, the Fleet under the command of Admiral Spruance, and divided into three Task Forces. It was only a year since Spruance's shining hour at the Battle of Midway, yet already he commanded the most powerful fleet in the world, and one which made Admiral Nagumo's Carrier Striking Force of early 1942 seem relatively puny.

Task Force 50 consisted of eleven carriers, six battleships and the same number of heavy cruisers, together with numerous destroyers, light cruisers and other light craft, all defended by a porcupine-like array of anti-aircraft guns served by vastly enlarged magazines which the screens of exploding steel demanded. Task Force 54 was an Amphibious Assault Force, while Task Force 57 was composed of as many varieties as the products of Heinz: repair and supply ships, tenders, tugs, tankers, combined with operational control of all land-based aircraft.

This Central Pacific Force, later renamed US Fifth Fleet, was the summation of American naval power developed since President Teddy Roosevelt had determined to pursue the precepts of Admiral Mahan and make America into a great naval power. Sucess in naval warfare in the Pacific had for long been seen to depend on mobility and self-sufficiency. Striking out of the blue and backed by amphibious forces, the navy would rip holes in the outer skin of Japanese defences, spreading out within these defences like a dum-dum bullet, before striking at the heart of the enemy. The rise in the power of aviation demanded no alterations to this traditional peacetime strategy; aircraft only speeded up the pace of operations so that the enemy fleet could now be destroyed out of sight and out of range of the fleet's guns.

By the second half of 1943, throughout 1944, and in 1945 until the enemy was crushed, the strategy of American and Allied amphibious operations, requiring no fixed base, preceded by bombardment by sea and by air was practised with ever-growing efficiency, power and pace. It was a spectacular logistical exercise, calling for hundreds of thousands of men, thousands of vessels and aircraft, thousands of tons of high-explosive.

At the Trident Conference in Washington in May 1943 the Joint Chiefs of Staff decided to initiate both the MacArthur and Nimitz operations simultaneously, which would keep the Japanese in a state of uncertainty and oblige them to divide their forces. The two prongs would eventually meet then press forward to link up with Generalissimo Chiang Kai-shek's forces in China for the final stage: the bombardment of Japanese industry from the air and from the sea, and the invasion of mainland Japan. There can be no doubt that political considerations relating to Australia and New Zealand, and personal considerations relating to the intractability of MacArthur, guided the supreme policy-makers.

For better or worse, then, the command structure for the pursuit of this strategy was set up, with MacArthur having strategic responsibility for the New Guinea–Solomons theatre, operating with Admiral Halsey, C-in-C South Pacific, retaining tactical control of naval and amphibious forces, including seven divisions, two of the marine divisions and one New Zealand division. Just to complicate things further, Admiral Nimitz continued to maintain command over Pearl Harbor-based naval forces operating in the MacArthur area.

While all this was being sorted out in May 1943, the American Chiefs of Staff decided to put on a sideshow in the Aleutian Islands, the archipelago that (almost) links Siberia with Alaska. Certain small Japanese successes among these islands at the time of Midway had led to disproportionate anxiety among the American people who disliked having the Japanese sitting on their back doorstep even if they were constantly told that there was no risk whatever of a Japanese invasion from this or any other direction. On 11 May 1943 the US Navy, after a massive bombardment by battleships, landed a force of over 10,000 to deal with a Japanese garrison of 2,500 on the island of Attu. After some tough fighting the Japanese initiated a suicide charge in which all but twenty-six of them were killed in the first mass slaughter of the Pacific war. A Japanese garrison of twice this size was evacuated from the second American target of Kiska. By the middle of July 1943 the Aleutians were cleared of the enemy and considered 'safe'.

Four months later the long pause in operations in the central Pacific came to an end, and Admiral Raymond Spruance's massive force, now more-or-less trained for their task, began to move against the Japanese bases in Micronesia. Spruance would have liked to postpone the proposed major offensive until December when a full moon would give the assault troops a higher tide and thus, for the landing-craft, a greater clearance over the reefs which bounded the islands of Micronesia. But Admiral King would have none of this. Obsessed as always with the perfidious British and with his thwarted wish to reverse the priority between Europe and the Pacific, he insisted on the earlier November D-Day 'so that the British could not back down on their agreements and commitments'. He continued, 'We must be so committed in the Central Pacific that the British cannot hedge on the recall of ships from the Atlantic.'[1]

This was now to be an offensive war, a war of crushing bombardment and invasion in overwhelming numbers, the rapid establishment of American air bases and fortified naval anchorages before sweeping through the Japanese perimeter on to the next shell- and bomb-torn beaches of atolls and islands scattered about the vast wastes of the central Pacific.

The Gilbert Islands operation, code-named Galvanic, was set for the third week in November. On the vast scale to which everything in the Pacific conforms, Micronesia was to Imperial Japan what the Western Front became to the Germans in the First World War. The defence of the *Vaterland* then rested upon needle-small defence points protected by almost impenetrable and concealed gun-positions, approachable only through a web of minefields and barbed-wire defences. The smallest elevation of ground grants the defender an advantage out of all proportion to that suggested by the contour lines.

The islands of Micronesia (the name derived from the Greek 'small island') offered countless strongpoints to the Japanese for the defence of the homeland. Every one selected was made secure by beach defences and minefields, fixed and mobile gun positions and foxholes as deep and elaborate as the trenches of Flanders. The key islets and atolls incorporated an airstrip for one branch of the heavy artillery of the Second World War, the bomber, while more distant were the mobile heavy artillery, the carrier-borne bombers and the big guns of the battleships.

Admiral Nobumasa Suetsugu once boasted that these Micronesian islands were 'made to order for Japan'.[2] But, successfully assaulted, they were as valuable to the victor as they had once been to the defenders. Yet, as an American admiral remarked, 'Every one was a tough nut to crack, some of them peanuts, others old walnuts.'

Of the groups of Melanesia forming Japan's distant defence line, Mariana, Pelew, Caroline, Marshall and Gilbert, the last one was the obvious first choice for an all-out Allied assault. The Gilberts, discovered by 'Foulweather Jack' Byron, the poet's grandfather, in 1765, consist of sixteen main groups of islets. They are named after Captain Gilbert, who with Captain Marshall visited the islands in 1788. They were annexed by Britain fifty years before they were occupied and fortified by the Japanese.

About four out of five of the Americans taking part in this assault had been young civilians in offices, farming or factory employment only months earlier, and the great majority of these had never been to sea before. Their training back in the USA had been efficient but basic. From Marine Corps privates to cooks and gunners, aircraft mechanics and junior officers – US Army, Marine Corps and Navy – engineers and signalmen, for thousands of these specialists this was their first experience of war. They were imbued with a very considerable hatred for the enemy and an enthusiasm to get at him. The Japanese had indeed behaved in the war so far with a primitive barbarism which had shocked the tender susceptibilities of the American people, and this had played into the hands of those engaged in arousing the warlike passions of the millions of new American service recruits.

All through the summer of 1943 the new ships and these new men were put through their paces, learning the technique of shore bombardment, the manipulation of radar sets and how to get ashore alive on a coral beach, how to get a bead on a diving Zero and run out the hoses when a Val made a hit. But the most important skill to be learned was teamwork, in the air, on the ground and at sea; for a nation of individualists brought up to fend for themselves this was the most difficult to acquire.

Most of those serving under the command of Admiral Nimitz had never had such a busy time. Then in September several tip-and-run strikes against enemy targets by carrier task forces gave those taking part a taste of the real thing, a dress rehearsal for D-Day. On 5 and 6 October 1943 a fast carrier force of six flat-tops of the new *Essex* and *Independence* classes struck at Wake Island while battleships and cruisers carried out a bombardment. It was good to have a real target at last; men who wondered how they would feel in action now knew and felt the better for it. More practically, several pilots who were shot down close to enemy territory were picked up by American submarines stationed for just this contingency, and that gave all the aviators greater confidence.

By early November 1943 all was ready for the big occasion, and a glance at the Fast Carrier Force, TF 50, confirms the enormous increase in strength of the US Navy in less than two years since Pearl Harbor: of the eleven carriers, only the *Enterprise* and *Saratoga* were in commission at the outbreak of war. Under the overall command of Rear-Admiral Charles A. Pownall, the Group was subdivided into four Task Groups:

TG 50.1 Carrier Interceptor Group, responsible for bombing Japanese air bases.

TG 50.2 Northern Carrier Group, ordered to bomb the defences of Makin Island preparatory to landings.

TG 50.3 Southern Carrier Group, to bomb Rabaul, destroy long-range enemy aircraft and their airstrips, then bomb the defences of Tarawa prior to the landings there.

TG 50.4 Relief Carrier Group, also to bomb Rabaul and the enemy air base at Nauru, then provide air cover for landing-craft until they reached Makin and Tarawa.

Further air cover and bombing operations, as well as reconnaissance, were to be carried out by TF 57, land-based aircraft – Catalinas, VLR Liberators and Venturas.

The main body of the Northern Attack Force, TF 52, was destined for Makin and commanded by Admiral Turner flying his flag in the old battleship *Pennsylvania* (in drydock at Pearl Harbor and little damaged). It comprised four battleships and four cruisers for bombardment and added protection for the escort carriers which in turn provided air support for the ten large landing-craft, incuding three Landing-Ship Tanks (LSTs) with newly devised amphtracs (LVTs).*

The Southern Attack Force, TF 53, destined for Tarawa, was mounted in New Zealand under the command of Admiral Harry W. Hill, flying his flag in the old battleship *Maryland*, and sailed from Efate in the New Hebrides. The sixteen transports had as protection three battleships, five cruisers, five escort carriers, twenty-one destroyers and a tank landing-ship. It was later joined by light cruisers and LSTs.

Spruance in the *Indianapolis* and Turner left Pearl Harbor on 10 November on the nine-day passage to Butaritari Island in the Makin Atoll while Hill with the Southern Attack Force steered north-east to the rendez-vous just south of the equator on longitude 180, just about the mid-point of the earth between the poles and from Greenwich.

D-Day was 20 November 1943, and at tropical nightfall on the evening before, the great double armada of warships, transports and landing-craft heading north-west for the targets, Admiral Turner issued his rousing prior-to-battle message to all officers and men:

Units attached to this force are honored in having been selected to strike another hard blow against the enemy by capturing the Gilbert Islands. The close co-operation between all arms and services, the spirit of loyalty to each other and the determination to succeed displayed by veteran and untried personnel alike, gives me complete confidence that we will never stop until we have achieved success. I lift my spirit with this unified team of Army, Navy and Marines whether attached to ships, aircraft or ground units, and I say to you that I know God will bless you and give you the strength to win a glorious victory.

For the troops attacking Butaritari Island, Makin, where an air base was to be established as speedily as possible, it was a victory all right but not an especially glorious one, almost 6,000 American assault troops taking three days to take this little atoll from fewer than 800 of the enemy, many of them Korean conscript construction men untrained for combat. The Americans completely dominated the air while battleships and cruisers offered gun support when and where required. There was dilatoriness,

---

*Track-driven amphibious vehicles derived from the 'alligator' used for peacetime rescue work. They made light of reefs and shoals and barbed wire, and were ideal for attacking an atoll. They weighed 23,000 pounds, were 25 feet long, had a capacity of 6,500 pounds or twenty men with a crew of 6 when fitted with machine-guns.

much confusion, congestion on the beaches and a marked lack of enthusiasm to get at the enemy.

Most of the failures could be put down to inexperience and over-reaction to the fanatical defence put up by the few seasoned Japanese troops, who were eventually killed or killed themselves. It was not until 10.30 a.m. on the fourth day that General Ralph Smith, commanding the ground troops, could signal to the Admiral: 'Makin taken.' The little strip of an atoll had cost sixty-four American lives.

At sea it was a different story. Without sufficient carrier support, the powerful Japanese fleet at Truk, including the mighty *Yamoto* and *Musashi*, dared not intervene, but nine submarines were ordered to the area to respond to the surprise American attack. One of these, *I-175*, Lieutenant-Commander Tadashi Tabata, found units of the Southern Attack Force twenty miles south-west of Butaritari on 24 November.

Just before dawn on that day, the submarine had the escort carrier *Liscombe Bay* square in her sights and hit her with a single torpedo amidships.

There was a terrible explosion. A column of bright orange flame rose a thousand feet in the air. Within a few seconds the aircraft bombs stowed in the hold detonated, and with a mighty roar the carrier burst apart as though she were one great bomb, tossing men, planes, deck frames and molten fragments so high that the deck of *New Mexico* 1,500 yards to leeward was showered with fragments of steel, clothing and human flesh.[3]

Almost 650 officers and men died in that split second, including the ship's captain and Rear-Admiral Henry M. Mullinix. The catastrophe evened up the numbers who died in the defence and assault on Makin Atoll, and was a shocking and sobering sight for the many recently enlisted men who witnessed it and had deluded themselves that, with the recent evidence of overwhelming American strength, the Pacific war would be a walk-over. Nor did the sinking improve relations between the army and the navy, the navy pointing out unequivocally that if the assault troops had been quicker about their work, the *Liscombe Bay* would have been withdrawn before the enemy could have brought up their submarines.

There were better, and grimmer, reasons for delay in the conquest of Betio Isle in the Tarawa atoll, 'the walnut' of the Gilbert Islands assaults. Betio was less than three square miles in all but this area included a prized airstrip and defences so formidable that Makin was a seaside picnic in comparison. And here the 1914–18 Western Front analogy bloodily applied. The defences even included 8-inch guns, captured at Singapore, dating back to that earlier war, but no less effective for that.

The defences began outside the beaches with mined concrete obstacles and barbed-wire barricades designed to channel landing craft into routes vulnerable to enfilading fire. On the beaches were high barricades covered by heavy and light machine-guns sited in concrete or armour-plated pillboxes, while larger pillboxes concealed field artillery and heavy and light dual-purpose guns. All this formidable array was supported by immobile tanks well dug in and armed with 37-mm quick-firing guns.

Behind the beach there were numerous bomb-proof shelters protecting headquarters staff, living quarters and ammunition stores reminiscent of the German Western Wall coast defences against the threatened invasion from Britain. 'No military historian who viewed these defenses', claimed one of their number, 'could recall an instance of a small island's having been so well prepared for an attack.'[4] As for the 4,500 men who manned these defences, they were one and all tough, professional and ready and happy, even honoured, to die after killing as many Americans as they could.

In the event they killed 1,000 Americans and wounded another 2,000, figures that caused ignorant outrage back home in the United States, where photos of corpses floating in the lagoon and sprawled on the beaches were printed in every newspaper. Nothing since Pearl Harbor opened the public's eyes wider to the realities of war in the Pacific.

The casualties would have been many fewer if the opinion of Admiral Spruance on the timing had been listened to by Admiral King; or, for that matter, if an old Tarawa hand had been listened to. A Major Holland had been keeping tide records for the British Government for years. When he was wisely called in for consultation before the invasion, the Major pointed out the vagaries of the tides and consequently the depth of water over the reef. 'You won't have three feet!' he told Admiral Hill and his staff. Unwisely, his advice, too, was ignored. Charts showed four and a half feet. Those eighteen inches cost hundreds of lives as landing-craft failed to get over the reef and milled about or stuck on it, equally irresistible targets for the Japanese heavy guns. No fewer than twenty landing-craft stuck on that concealed coral trap 'full of dead and wounded.... One large gun was horribly accurate; several times it dropped a shell right on a landing-craft just as the ramp came down, spreading a pool of blood around the boat.' Many more marines were picked off by rifle and machine-gun fire as they waded the long walk – up to 700 yards – to the shore.

It was a foretaste of Omaha beach on D-Day in France. By the evening 5,000 men had been landed, but they were confined to a beach-head 300 yards deep, and 1,500 of them were dead or wounded. A further marine landing the next morning was equally disastrous. But the survivors, linked with those already dug in, won new glory for the marines in desperate close action. The deadly flame-thrower was one of the weapons which proved decisive in the end. Robert Sherrod, famed newspaper correspondent up in the thick of the fighting, witnessed the taking of a pillbox:

A Marine jumped over the seawall and began throwing blocks of TNT into a coconut-log pillbox.... Two more Marines scaled the seawall, one of them carrying a twin-cylindered tank strapped to his shoulders, the other holding the nozzle of the flame thrower. As another charge of TNT boomed inside the pillbox, causing smoke and dust to billow out, a khaki-clad figure ran out the side entrance. The flame thrower, waiting for him, caught him in its withering stream of intense fire.

As soon as it touched him, the Jap flared up like a piece of celluloid. He was dead instantly but the bullets in his cartridge belt exploded for a full sixty seconds after he had been charred almost to nothingness.[5]

It took three days to clear Betio/Tarawa, too, but the fighting was twenty times as tough and the casualties were twenty times higher than at Makin. It ended with a Japanese suicide charge like an old-time Red Indian assault on a fort. At its conclusion, 325 corpses lay on the ground, some of them close to the perimeter of the American defence.

By 24 November 1943 the Allies had an air base deep in the heart of the Japanese outer perimeter, and the way was open for the next advance, even deeper, to the Marshall Islands. Better still, at relatively small cost, Tarawa had provided experience and lessons for the future which saved many times the number of lives tragically lost in the lagoons and on the shores of Betio Island.

Tarawa was the Dieppe of the Pacific, as dangerous and bloody for the raw marines as that French port had been for the raw Canadians. The navy's lessons could never have been learned in any number of exercises. Only a real heavy-gun bombardment, for example, could show how the dust from a churned-up atoll could drift on to the beaches and obscure the progress of the landing-craft. And henceforth task-force commanders would be provided with special command ships to replace old battleships, whose heavy guns damaged or interfered with delicate communications equipment; while at the other end of the ship scale, future amphtracs would be much faster and much more heavily armed.

Before the Tarawa assault the Japanese admiral commanding the atoll declared that it could never be taken. He had reason to make this claim over and above the need to keep his men in good cheer. An inspection of the defences suggested that even the bravest assault troops would be cut down to a man, or thrown back in panic retreat. Admiral Keiji Shibasaki then required his men 'to defend to the last man all vital areas and destroy the enemy at the water's edge. In a battle where the enemy is superior,' he continued, 'it is necessary to lure him within range of our fixed defense installations and then, using all our strength, destroy him.'[6]

The German defenders of the Normandy beaches were equally confident in their ability to throw back any assault on their shores. They, too, under-rated the stunning and destructive power of bombardment from the air and the sea, and the courage and fortitude of men fighting for a righteous cause. From the siege of Acre to Orleans, from Yorktown to the Hindenburg Line in 1918, indefatigable spirits had shown that no defences are impregnable. The Allies in the Pacific were to prove this historical truism time and again over the following year and a half.

CHAPTER FOURTEEN

Overlord and After

In December 1943 Allied naval forces in the Pacific still had long, costly and fiercely fought campaigns ahead of them with the Imperial Japanese Navy still powerful and capable of severely damaging the American Task Forces. In European waters, with the sinking of the *Scharnhorst* on Boxing Day 1943, there was no fight left in the German surface navy, which had shown little of the spirit of Admiral Alfred von Tirpitz's proud High Seas Fleet of an earlier war. Two days after the *Scharnhorst* went down, a gunnery action in the Bay of Biscay pointed up once again the uncharacteristic German reluctance to fight at sea – Doenitz's U-boats being notable exceptions.

For the greater part of the war Germany had employed blockade-runners – fast, armed merchantmen – which by guile and deception frequently succeeded in breaking through the Allied blockade, early in the war to the USA and latterly to Japan, using French Atlantic ports. Late in 1943 one of these returning blockade-runners was sighted approaching the Bay of Biscay and was promptly sunk by bombers. But the Germans already had at sea a force of ten warships to meet and escort this ship to her home port. To seek out and destroy them the navy sent the 6-inch-gun cruiser *Glasgow* and the old *Enterprise* laid down in the First World War, and now Canadian manned.

The British cruisers sighted the German destroyers soon after noon on 28 December 1943, and in typically dirty 'Bay' weather opened fire. Four of the German ships were new 'Z' class super-destroyers, light cruisers really of 3,650 tons fully loaded and armed with 5.9-inch guns, while the other six were of more orthodox destroyer size, 1,318 tons. Instead of manoeuvring to close the British ships, using their powerful torpedo armament and superior gunpower, the German ships fled south-east with both sides firing in the difficult conditions, both the *Glasgow* and *Enterprise* making several hits.

At length the German commander split his force, four of his ships doubling round to the north-west in the hope of escaping behind the cruisers, which set off in pursuit. Their hits became more and more telling, slowing up and finally sinking one of the big Z-boats and two of the smaller destroyers. The *Glasgow* and *Enterprise* were then subjected to a variety of ferocious air attacks, including radio-controlled glide bombs. They both returned to Plymouth, pleased with themselves and undamaged.

Beyond the confines of the Bay of Biscay the U-boats had now been driven clean out of the Atlantic. In the last three months of 1943 just three merchantmen had been sunk in the North Atlantic where the monthly toll had so recently been around 200,000 tons. In a move bordering on desperation, the U-boats still operating close to the European coast were equipped with more powerful anti-aircraft armament and ordered to fight it out on the surface. The consequence for the Allies was that a bombing or rocket attack became marginally more hazardous, but it also led to a dramatic rise of U-boat sinkings.

Victory against the U-boats was gained in time for the final plans to overthrow Germany from the west to be effected. Without the prodigious build-up of supplies of men and material in Britain invasion could never have been organized; and without naval power to transport the assault forces across the English Channel, the mainland of Europe must have remained in German hands indefinitely.

Through the summer months of 1943 plans were drawn up for Overlord, and the Chiefs of Staff reported their conclusions at the first Plenary Session of the second Quebec Conference on 19 August 1943:

After securing adequate Channel ports, exploitation will be directed towards securing areas that will facilitate both ground and air operations against the enemy. Following the establishment of strong Allied forces in France, operations designed to strike at the heart of Germany and to destroy her military forces will be undertaken.

Landing-craft was the governing requirement, as artillery was the governing requirement for the defeat of Germany in 1918. In spite of the prodigious output in the United States, Canada and Britain, there were never enough. When it was later agreed that the initial landings should be on a broader front than originally planned – five divisions instead of three – the perennial shortage of landing-craft became critical, and in the end they had to be drawn from the Mediterranean and even from the South-East Asia Command where Mountbatten had only just taken delivery of them for his own amphibious plans.

A broader front also required more shipping of all kinds – minesweepers, escorts, bombardment vessels, assault craft, supply ships and numerous auxiliary craft. When other theatres had been stripped and Atlantic convoys denuded there was still a shortfall, and this could be filled only from the Pacific where, thanks to Admiral King, Admiral Nimitz and General MacArthur had no such problems. King, predictably, dug in his heels: nothing could be spared for what he regarded as the European sideshow. A few weeks before the May D-Day he was obliged to relent. His final despatch of more than had been asked for suggested that the sacrifice had not been too painful. But meanwhile, the date of the invasion had to be put back a month in order that four weeks of British construction could help fill the shortfall.

The naval command of Overlord – Operation Neptune's C-in-C – was in the safe hands of Admiral Sir Bertram Ramsay. No other choice was possible, and not merely because as Flag Officer Dover in 1940 he had been in charge of the Dunkirk evacuation, making it only fitting that he should guide the tidal wave back across the Channel. In 1942 this 'organizing genius', as Deputy Naval Commander in the Mediterranean to Admiral Cunningham, had been in charge of the Torch landings in North Africa. His great forté was the management of massive amphibious operations; and Overlord was to be the greatest of them all.

The role of the British, American, Canadian and Allied navies in Overlord was complicated and made more difficult by the decision to effect the landings where the enemy would least expect them. The Germans would naturally presume that any major landing would be made with a view to capturing a port in order to sustain the prodigious supply needs. But at Quebec it was finally decided that the landings would be made on the Normandy beaches east of the Cotentin peninsula, far distant from any major port, and that the navies would build their own harbour – code-named Mulberry. The disastrous Dieppe raid had ruled out the capture of a port as a prelude to invasion.

Sheltered waters were to be provided by blockships which would steam under their own power to their appointed place and scuttle themselves, forming five artificial breakwaters. This part of the operation alone called for fifty-five merchantmen, a couple of cruisers and two old battleships. These breakwaters – Gooseberries – were then extended by sinking 213 prefabricated caissons of concrete and steel. Within the two harbours so formed piers and pierheads were constructed which rose and fell with the tide. In all two million tons of concrete and steel were demanded by this unique and enterprising facility, without which the armies could never have been kept supplied. The whole thing was invented and constructed in Britain, and had to be towed across the Channel to the landing beaches, every pontoon and girder, rivet and caisson: one more naval responsibility.

The Allied navies in the Pacific became involved in amphibious operations on a large scale that called for complex logistics and large numbers of ships of various types. But Neptune was responsible for over 7,000 ships in all, including over 4,000 landing-craft – all to be manned and escorted and brought back for further operations. These included everything from Special Boat Service canoes for last-minute surveys of the beaches, and midget submarines to guide in the first landing-craft to British and American battleships built between 1915 and 1943 to bombard the defences.

Everything about Overlord was immoderate in size and numbers, but the greatest surprise of all was that the location and timings came as a surprise to the enemy. Every security provision had been taken. The camps of the assault troops were isolated from the civil population, which themselves suffered severe restriction of movement. Ships' crews were given no shore leave before sailing. An elaborate feint was engineered to suggest that the landing would be on the Pas de Calais where the Channel crossing was shortest.

The precise timing of the landings was a matter of the utmost nicety. An approach by moonlight was required for the sake both of the airborne troops, the only assault forces not dependent on naval transport and protection, and for the passage of the seaborne assault troops. Then there had to be a brief period before the hour of landing for the sake of accuracy both of the landing itself and the bombardment immediately preceding it. But it must be a brief interval, not long enough to permit the defenders to recover from the bombardment and the shock of the assault.

The approaches to the beaches were even more thoroughly and lethally protected than the most comprehensively defended Pacific atoll. At low tide the assault forces would have to face too long a distance across the exposed beaches, and if too high the mined underwater obstacles would trap and destroy the landing-craft. Three hours before high water was about right; any other time dangerously wrong.

Especially now that the length of the assault had been extended, a further complication was that the time of high tide varied by almost an hour and a half between the beaches at the extreme ends of the assault front.

All these pre-conditions were met on only three days in each lunar month. Now that the month of May had been lost, only the 5th, 6th and 7th of June qualified. Otherwise it would have to be July, with all the loss of material and moral momentum and the almost certain loss of surprise.

On 3 June, as the bombarding force for the American beaches left Belfast and the first assault convoys set out from their West Country ports, the weather became gusty and the sea got up. With low, scudding cloud racing across the sky, it was apparent that the Channel was in for a typical summer storm. General Dwight D. Eisenhower, Supreme Commander, spent anxious hours with his meteorologists and his land, sea and air commanders.

The 4th of June was a Sunday. Eisenhower and Ramsay were told the weather would get worse on the chosen day, the 5th. Eisenhower made the difficult decision, with all its consequences and ramifications, of postponing Overlord by twenty-four hours. Ships already at sea were ordered to reverse course, and the fighting men made the usual observation on the abilities of their superiors: 'Another f—ing cockup!' One convoy of tank landing-craft never picked up the signal and came close to carrying out its own invasion single-handed.

Thankfully, there was a promise of the storms abating, and at 4.30 a.m. on 5 June 1944 General Eisenhower issued the order for the landing to take place little more than twenty-four hours hence. It was a brave decision. The Germans knew that something big was afoot and that it must be the invasion: but where would it strike and when? The German meteorological officers informed the high command that neither the 5th nor the 6th of

June would be possible for a mass invasion.

Churchill referred to the invasion as 'today's stupendous event' to Roosevelt, and later wrote of this climax to more than five years of war, for the armies and air forces as well as the Allied navies:

All day on June 5 the convoys bearing the spearhead of the invasion converged on the rendezvous south of the Isle of Wight. Thence, in an endless stream, led by the minesweepers on a wide front and protected on all sides by the might of the Allied Navies and Air Forces, the greatest armada that ever left our shores set out for the coast of France. The rough conditions at sea were a severe trial to troops on the eve of battle, particularly in the terrible discomfort of the smaller craft. Yet, in spite of all, the vast movement was carried through with almost the precision of a parade, and, although not wholly without loss, such casualties and delays as did occur, mostly to small craft in tow, had no appreciable effect on events.

Round all our coasts the network of defence was keyed to the highest pitch of activity. The Home Fleet was alert against any move by German surface ships, while air patrols watched the enemy coast from Norway to the Channel. Far out at sea, Coastal Command, in great strength, supported by flotillas of destroyers, kept watch for possible enemy reactions. Our intelligence told us that over fifty U-boats were concentrated in the French Biscay ports, ready to intervene when the moment came. The hour was now striking.[1]

An officer who had observed from the Admiralty Intelligence Centre the full cycle of world war, from the preliminaries to this climax, observed later:

Behind all the men, all the ships, and all the aircraft which formed the assault force on this June morning, there lay the long battle of the oceans, whose success alone had made possible the conditions of overall superiority in which they could gather in such huge numbers off the beaches of Normandy. Here was to be seen the climax of all the years of bitter fighting at sea; and here was proof of the ability to transfer the victory won in the oceans into its final decisive phase of a victory won across the land.

Even more extraordinary, perhaps, was the fact that tactical surprise had been achieved.[2]

Until H-Hour itself there were many officers who remained doubtful that the supposedly unassailable Western Wall could be breached, especially older men who had watched so many thousands die in the First World War immolating themselves against heavy shellfire, barbed wire, minefields and Spandau machine-guns. Churchill himself, for one, did not for a time warm to the idea of a direct assault and promoted other and more devious plans to bring about Hitler's downfall. Nor did the final approaches to the beaches take place without casualties – to say nothing of the terrible battle to sustain a toehold on the American Omaha beach.

Plenty of guns remained operational in spite of the massive bombing and bombardment from the sea. Take the experiences of one American

patrol craft leading landing-craft into Utah beach. An hour before H-Hour
the boat was straddled; then:

There was a crash – not terribly loud – a lunge – a crash of glass, a rumble
of gear falling around the decks – an immediate, yes immediate, 50° list to starboard
– all lights darkened and the dawn's early light coming through the pilot house
door which had been blown open. The Executive Officer immediately said: 'That's
it', with finality and threw down his chart pencil. I felt blood covering my face
and a gash over my left eye around the eyebrow.

Lieutenant Halsey Barrett watched the landing-craft pass the upturned
hull of his ship:

A landing-craft LCVP with thirty or so men aboard was blown a hundred feet
in the air in pieces. Shore batteries flashed, splashes appeared sporadically around
the bay. Planes were flying in reasonable formation over the beach. One transpired
into a huge steaming flame and no trace of survivors around it. The USS battleship
Nevada a mile off to the north-west of us was using her 14-inch guns rapidly
and with huge gushes of black smoke and flame extending yards and yards from
her broadside.[3]

Over the following days the Mulberry harbours were constructed from
their prefabricated parts (one of them was destroyed by exceptionally heavy
seas), the navies' guns were trained on specific troublesome targets ashore,
massive supplies were shuttled across the Channel from southern ports,
the remarkable oil pipeline, Pluto, was laid on the ocean bed to keep pace
with the consumption of fuel as the Allied armies broke out of their bridge-
head and began their sweeping advance across France, and troop reinforcements and returning hospital ships were safely escorted across the Channel.
The navies carried out all these tasks with such promptitude and efficiency
that the service began to be taken for granted.

There was German interference, and there were some losses, however.
Mines were the first enemy, next the E-boats, darting in after dark, and
there were new long-range circling torpedoes and explosive motor boats.
But the scale of attack against the Channel shipping was as perfunctory
as the attempts by the *Luftwaffe* to dent the massive shield of air power
that held the skies. The days of Dunkirk, when the retreating and evacuating
soldiers had reason to curse the inadequacy of the support from the other
two services, were long since past.

The Allied navies conformed at sea to the eastern progress of the troops
on land, giving what help they could to winkle out fanatical German pockets
of resistance, clearing the devastated and mined harbours, all the way to
Antwerp and the Scheldt estuary. Here the last amphibious operation of
the European war took place in the cold dark days of November 1944.
It was a trifling affair compared with the Leyte Gulf operations of this
time on the other side of the world in the tropical heat of the Philippines;
but as a textbook example of co-operation and unity of purpose between
the services it could not be bettered. And what a long way amphibious

warfare had come since the Norwegian operations of 1940, while the shambles on the beaches of Gallipoli in 1915 was no more than a half-forgotten nightmare.

The Germans had made a good job of blowing up the dock facilities of the Channel ports as they retreated, which increased many times over the value of Antwerp, the second-largest port in the world before the war. It had fallen to the Allies on 4 September 1944 but the approach up the thirty-five miles of estuary was dominated by German forts on the islands of South Beveland and Walcheren forming the eastern banks. South Beveland was taken against stout resistance late in October by Canadians supported by a British landing. Walcheren remained an even tougher proposition, in spite of the breaching of dykes by bombers, which had flooded much of the island.

The main operation marked one more glorious chapter in the history of the Royal Marine Commandos, supported by the Royal Navy which bombarded the German defences with a battleship and two monitors. Twenty-five landing-craft, converted like German F-lighters into heavily armed shallow-draught fighting ships, escorted the commandos' landing-craft. Their casualties when the well-entrenched German heavy guns opened fire were very severe. Once ashore the commandos were forced to fight for every yard, with house-to-house combat through the streets of villages and the town of Flushing. 'The extreme gallantry of the Royal Marines stands forth,' wrote Churchill of this bloody episode. 'The Commando idea was once again triumphant.'

With the securing of these last German defences, the navy's task was not yet over. For three weeks minesweepers combed the long reach of estuary, which had been in German hands for four and a half years. Then at last, on 28 November 1944, a convoy of no fewer than eighteen Liberty ships sailed up the Scheldt and docked at Antwerp, which now became the first supply base of the Allied armies for the spring offensive, the crossing of the Rhine and the final surrender of Germany.

Appropriately, but only by chance, the battleship which led the bombardment, the last of the war, was none other than the gallant *Warspite*, which had played such a significant part in two world wars, from her commissioning on 8 March 1915: the Battle of Jutland and many North Sea operations; victory at the second Battle of Narvik; then as Admiral Cunningham's flagship in the Mediterranean (badly damaged) to the Eastern Fleet as flagship, back to the Mediterranean where she almost met her end again when hit by the same type of radio-controlled glide-bomb which had sunk the *Roma*; back to her old home at Scapa Flow, and so to the beaches of Normandy. Here she fired so many rounds of 15-inch shells that once again she had to have new guns fitted for her last operation.

When the time came for that last dread voyage of any Dreadnought, to the breakers' yard, in April 1947, she would have none of it, her tow breaking in heavy weather while she drifted ashore, settling her great bulk on to the rocks of a beautiful Cornish cove.

The *Warspite*'s was not quite the final operation of the Second World War. Besides anti-U-boat patrols, the last offensive operation appropriately concerned these pests which had brought the Allies so close to defeat in Europe. On 1 May 1945 two cruisers, three escort carriers and five destroyers made an air attack on German U-boat depot ships known to be at Kilbotn near Narvik. On 5 May Avengers and Wildcats blew up one of the depot ships, sank a tanker and a U-boat. So, just as German airpower had led to the defeat of the Allies in Norway, so Allied air power reasserted itself here five years later. Within a few more days *Luftwaffe* officers surrendered the Norwegian airfields from which the devastating attacks on Arctic convoys had originated. And forty-nine U-boats still at sea on patrol were obliged to sail into British ports and give themselves up.

The condition of the U-boats and the bearing of the German sub-mariners, like the E-boat crews, was in marked contrast to the wretched remnants of the German surface fleet. The hulk of the *Gneisenau* fell into Russian hands at Gdynia, the last two pocket battleships and the cruiser *Köln* had been sunk in harbour by bombers, the *Hipper* and *Emden* had long since been derelict. In Danish ports, more or less undamaged lay three more German cruisers, a few minesweepers and destroyers – and that was about all.

No sight and smell recalls to the mind the base squalor of war more than a derelict and abandoned enemy man o'war: its damage neglected, its filth accumulated, and the rank stench of death rising from its bowels. These remnants of Admiral Doenitz's navy also lay as stark reminders of the rottenness of Nazi tyranny and racial hatred which had taken so long, and at such cost, to destroy.

CHAPTER FIFTEEN

The Pacific: The Curtain Falls

The brief golden era of the Imperial Japanese Navy died with Admiral Isoroku Yamamoto, but not its spirit. Long after any possibility remained that Japanese carriers and their aircraft could regain the ascendancy in the Pacific, the conviction of superiority and eventual victory, so deeply inbued in the officers and men of the IJN, tenaciously persisted, stimulated by highly coloured reports on every operation undertaken. It was not in the nature of these samurai warriors to displease their superiors by reporting failure at the end of a mission. And it was not vaingloriousness that led pilots to make absurd claims of Yankee planes shot down and carriers and battleships sunk; it was for the glory of the Emperor and the Empire – 'Banzai!'

Although forced from islands in the Gilberts and Marshalls, driven back in Bougainville and New Guinea, very few of the surviving warriors believed that they would never come back. Officers with a more sophisticated and realistic view of their situation kept the knowledge severely to themselves, and only wrote of their feelings and the facts later, like Masatake Okumiya:

These successive withdrawals from our air bases could be regarded as nothing less than major disasters. Every base which was abandoned meant another enemy advance toward the heart of Japan, and another key point from which the enemy could dispatch his far-ranging bombers. Each air base lost involved not only ground installations taken over by the Americans, but a never-to-be-regained loss in our ability further to resist the enemy. Furthermore, those ordering the hasty withdrawals from advanced air bases often overlooked and abandoned the numerous maintenance crews. Men whose skills represented the experience of many years were deserted.... We were faced with a vicious circle of attrition for which there appeared to be no solution. The shortage of new fighters meant that we had often to send our best pilots into combat with worn and damaged planes. Their chances of survival against an enemy whose strength was growing daily were thereby greatly lessened.[1]

With the ever-increasing losses of pilots, their replacements were of ever-decreasing quality, leading to a spiral of accelerating deaths. At the training airfields, instructors already short of training planes struggled desperately to inculcate the basic principles of flying into recruits who were mainly quite unfit mentally and physically to handle a modern fighter, notwithstanding their enthusiasm.

I found it hard to believe, when I saw the new trainees staggering along the runway, bumping their way into the air [wrote veteran Zero pilot Saburo Sakai]. The Navy was frantic for pilots, and the school was expanded almost every month, with correspondingly lower entrance requirements. Men who could never have dreamed even of getting near a fighter plane before the war were now thrown into battle.

Everything was urgent! We were told to rush the men through, to forget the fine points, just to teach them how to fly and shoot. One after the other, singly, in twos and threes, the training planes smashed into the ground, skidded wildly through the air. For long and tedious months, I tried to build fighter pilots from the men they thrust at us at Omura. It was a hopeless task. Our facilities were too meagre, the demand too great, the students too many....[2]

In the front line, Japanese Group leaders despaired of the inferiority of the new pilots who would have to fight against odds in numbers and against American pilots whose training had not been skimped in the smallest degree and who were flying machines like the Hellcat and Corsair, no longer inferior to the Zero.

The Zero, with small modifications (see Appendix E) remained the standard Japanese fighter until the end of the war. Prototypes and small production runs of new and (on paper) more formidable machines were produced, but were rarely seen in the Pacific. And in spite of the most frantic efforts, the production figures for the Zero steadily declined when American long-range bombers, notably the Boeing B-29 Superfortress, began to ravage the factories. Unlike German war production which did not get into full stride until late 1943 and early 1944 (which has deceived statisticians and some historians that the bombing of Germany was not cost-effective), Japanese war production was at full pitch from the beginning of the war.

As for replacement warship production, even before the shattering bombing of shipyards output was puny by American standards. Carriers were the most desperately needed class of vessel for the fleet, but while American shipyards could and did produce more than one a week, what were the numbers for Japan? The standard work on aircraft carriers by Roger Chesneau comments:

By 1943 the Japanese carrier force was reduced to two fast attack units, two large but slow fleet carriers adapted from merchant designs, and three light carriers, one of which was held for training: further fleet units were building and several conversions were in hand, but if losses were to continue at the rate sustained during the second half of 1942 it was clear that replacements would be required at a furious rate.[3]

In fact only a few trickled from the shipyards and even fewer of these survived the war. The big fleet carrier *Taiho*, laid down before Pearl Harbor, was sunk within three weeks of joining the fleet. The 12,000-ton *Ibuki*, converted from a cruiser hull, was never completed; and of the six 17,000-ton fleet carriers of the *Unryu* class, only two were completed and these were knocked out before they could go into action.

The *Shinano* suffered the cruellest fate of all. She was to have been another *Yamoto* of 65,000 tons but was converted into the biggest carrier of the war. Heavily armoured and bristling with anti-aircraft guns, she would have been a formidable foe. But she never even got as far as the fitting-out yard to which she was steaming when the submarine *Archerfish* chanced to spot her giant silhouette. Her captain could hardly miss. Four torpedoes were enough to send her to the bottom; her watertight doors had not yet been fitted and flooding immediately got out of control.

And that was about the end of the story, and the end of the great Japanese carrier striking groups which had once ranged the Pacific unopposed.

With the possession of Tarawa and control of the Gilberts, Admiral Nimitz wasted not a moment before implacably advancing further into Japan's defence perimeter. Late in January he ordered the destruction of Japanese island air bases, already damaged by earlier raids, as the first step to taking the Marianas, using land-based bombers from the Ellice Islands and the newly captured Tarawa strip. Rear-Admiral J.H. Hoover's machines dealt with Jaluit and Mili, while three carrier Groups shattered the more distant air bases on Maleoelap, Wotje and Kwajalein. Then, on the night of 29–30 January 1944 16-inch-gun American battleships and 8-inch-gun cruisers pounded Eniwetok.

Nimitz was bent on grabbing this atoll as soon as possible, rightly reasoning that certain enemy trouble spots like Jaluit and Wotje could be by-passed so long as bombing could neutralize the presence of enemy air power on these atolls. Kwajalein was the key island in the whole Marshalls campaign according to Nimitz. Morison described it as 'the hub of the enemy's outer defensive perimeter and the distributing center for his Marshall Islands spider web', and declared that Nimitz's leapfrogging, opposed by Admirals Spruance and Turner, was a bold plan, 'advancing the war by months'.

The Marshalls operation, Flintlock, was a repeat with improvements of Galvanic, with everything bigger and more powerful and destructive in order to conclude the task decisively, swiftly and with the minimum loss of life. The preponderance of power deployed by the Americans in the Pacific from the time of this Marshalls operation led to some mockery by critics, especially British critics, later. But the American Joint Chiefs of Staff rightly reckoned that if a ratio of ten to one in numbers over the enemy saved one life, then that was good policy. It was also good policy to add one extra new 40,000-ton battleship or fleet carrier with 100 planes to any operation if a single Marine Corps private came home uninjured instead of leaving his bones to bleach on some distant shore. It also made good military sense. 'The Americans were absolutely right,' Admiral Mountbatten declared later in justifying his own five to one principle, when he had the means to follow it. 'To economize on manpower and to fail to use all your material resources is sheer madness.' Never in American history had the principle of using a machine instead of a man worked to the greater advantage of Americans.

Figures proved the principle of extravagance right within the first few hours of the assault on Kwajalein, when 53,000 troops were landed on 31 January 1944, and by 4 February had effectively occupied the Marshalls for a toll of just 177 dead. Meanwhile the heart of the southern Japanese naval power at Truk, and the air bases on Ponape, Saipan and Tinian, were the target of devastating American air raids. A Japanese officer describes the appalling impact of just one of these mass raids which ground down the spirit of the defenders as the bombs tore up the runways and made them unusable:

Suddenly the lookout on our tower stiffens behind his binoculars; his voice carries to the ground. We see him pointing to the south. Yes ... there they are! Enemy aircraft, fast approaching the air base. The siren screams its warning and the men on the field dash for cover, never too soon, as the enemy bombers close on the field with great speed.

No one really stays down in the ditches and culverts. Hundreds of men stare at the sky, seeing the bombers and searching for the Zekes which should even now be diving against the enemy planes. Here they come, racing from their greater height to break up the bomber formations. But even before they reach the slower, heavier planes the escorting enemy fighters scream upward to intercept the Zekes. No matter how determined the Zeke attacks, the bombers maintain their formations. Even as the Japanese and American fighters scatter over the sky in swirling dog-fights we can hear the rapidly increasing shriek of the falling bombs. The earth shakes and heaves; great blossoms of fire, steel, smoke, and dirt erupt from the airfield as salvos of bombs 'walk across' the revetments and the runway. Sharp sound cracks against the eardrums, and the concussion is painful. Our own machine-gunners fire in rage at the droning bombers above, even as the explosions come faster and faster. There is the rumble of bomber engines, the rising and falling whine of the fighters, the stutter of machine-guns, and the slower 'chuk-chuk' of cannon-fire. The sky is filled with dust and flame and smoke. Aircraft on the field are burning fiercely, and wreckage is scattered across the runway, which by now is cratered with great holes.

Through the smoke we can see the hurtling fighters diving and climbing in mortal combat. Our men curse or only stare silently as we watch Zekes suddenly flare up in scarlet and orange flame, and then plunge from the sky like bizarre shooting stars, leaving behind them a long trail of angry flame and black, oily smoke. Parachutes can be sighted drifting earthward, clearly silhouetted against the deep blue sky. Then, abruptly, the raid is over. The crashing, earth-heaving thunder of the bombs is gone. As soon as the last bomb has expended its fury, the ground crews clamber from their air-raid shelters and with shovels in their hands race for the runway. They work frantically, sweat pouring from their bodies, ignoring the ever-present mosquitoes and flies, shovelling dirt back into the craters, rushing to patch up the field so that our damaged fighters can land.[4]

To the east of the Philippine Islands was the vast no-man's area of ocean, the Philippine Sea, the vulnerable emptiness in the defence structure of the Japanese Empire. Imagine a vast, roughly circular neutral area – a vacuum really – amongst the elaborate, far-reaching defences of a besieged nation, without barbed wire or minefields, trenches and artillery posts, pill-boxes and batteries of heavy guns and enfilading machine-guns. An enemy who occupies and dominates this zone has seized the key to the heart of the homeland. And this was Japan's desperate situation in 1944. On the east side of the Philippine Sea were the fortified islands of Guam, Saipan and Tinian, three forts guarding the gate. Assaulted and overrun they would provide launching-pads for the new mighty B-29s – combat range 3,250 miles and the speed of a fighter – and as naval bases a mere 1,200 miles from Tokyo.

The Japanese high command could face the loss of the Gilberts and Marshalls. The occupation of the Marianas, however, was intolerable, and only the Mobile Fleet, as it was now renamed, could prevent it. But could it? Against Admiral Spruance's Fifth Fleet?

While Vice-Admiral Turner's Joint Expeditionary Force with 127,000 troops in transports and landing-craft prepared to assault Saipan, evidence began to accumulate that the main Japanese Fleet was preparing to intervene. Nor could it be trifled with. Admiral Koga, like Yamamoto, had been lost in his aeroplane, and Admiral Soemu Toyoda now commanded the Fleet.

This, then, in early June 1944 was the Order of Battle of the IJN upon which the fate of the nation depended:

Overall Commander Admiral Soemu Toyoda directing operations from his flagship *Oyodo* in Hiroshima Bay.

Vice-Admiral Kakuji Kakuda, Commander of the First Air Fleet of land-based aircraft numbering approximately 1,000 fighters and bombers flying from airfields in the Marianas, Carolines, Truk and Iwo Jima.

Vice-Admiral Jisaburo Ozawa, Commander of the First Task Fleet and the Third Fleet, flying his flag in the big new fleet carrier *Taiho*, with the repaired big carriers *Shokaku* and *Zuikaku*, the 24,000-ton carriers *Junyo* and *Hiyo*, and the smaller *Ryujo*, *Chiyoda*, *Chitose* and *Zuiho*. Carrying in all over 450 planes, this was the largest single assembly of Japanese carrier power in the war, and its presence in the Philippine Sea was a great credit to the powers of recovery and organization of the IJN after more than two and a half years at war.

Nor had so powerful a force of battleships been brought together under one command. Besides the 18.1-inch-gun *Yamato* and *Musashi*, there were seven more, all built or modernized between the wars, and two of them recently converted into unique battleship-carriers. The *Hyugo* and *Ise*, for the loss of two of their aft heavy gun turrets, had an extended deck with a hangar for fourteen planes, hermaphrodite predecessors of the 1970s Russian *Kiev* class. In company with the 'battlewaggons' Ozawa could count on nine heavy cruisers and numerous light cruisers and destroyers, a fleet of seventy-three fighting ships in all – but all more or less irrelevant except for their anti-aircraft gunfire.

And what had happened to Admiral Nagumo, the national hero of Pearl

Harbor and so many subsequent victories? Alas, his failure at Midway had not been forgotten and Santa Cruz had brought the Admiral no credit, either. He was now demoted to command of the marines and other naval units ordered to defend the Marianas against amphibious assault. (He eventually shot himself as Japanese defenders yielded before the Americans on Saipan.)

If the Japanese were able, greatly to their credit, to assemble such a formidable armada in spite of heavy earlier losses and shattering defeats, see what the Americans could put together two years after Midway and eighteen months after they had been reduced to one damaged carrier in the south-west Pacific:

United States Navy – Fifth Fleet
Commander-in-Chief, Admiral Raymond A. Spruance

Indianapolis
TASK FORCE 58
Commander, Vice-Admiral M. A. Mitscher, *Lexington*

TASK GROUP 58.1 Rear-Admiral J. J. Clark

Fleet carriers	*Hornet, Yorktown*
Light fleet carriers	*Belleau Wood, Bataan*
Cruisers	*Boston, Baltimore, Canberra*
Light cruisers Anti-Aircraft (AA)	*San Juan, Oakland*
14 destroyers	

TASK GROUP 58.2 Rear-Admiral A. E. Montgomery

Fleet carriers	*Bunker Hill, Wasp*
Light fleet carriers	*Monterey, Cabot*
Light cruisers	*Santa Fe, Mobile, Biloxi*
12 destroyers	

TASK GROUP 58.3 Rear-Admiral J. W. Reeves

Fleet carriers	*Enterprise, Lexington*
Light fleet carriers	*San Jacinto, Princeton*
Cruiser	*Indianapolis*
Light cruisers Anti-Aircraft (AA)	*Reno, Montpelier, Cleveland, Birmingham*
13 destroyers	

TASK GROUP 58.4 Rear-Admiral W. K. Harrill

Fleet carrier	*Essex*
Light fleet carriers	*Langley, Cowpens*
Light cruiser Anti-Aircraft (AA)	*San Diego*
Light cruisers	*Vincennes, Houston, Miami*
14 destroyers	

TASK GROUP 58.7 Vice-Admiral W. A. Lee

Battleships	*Washington, North Carolina, Iowa, New Jersey, South Dakota, Alabama, Indiana*
Cruisers	*Wichita, Minneapolis, New Orleans, San Francisco*

The Battle of the Philippine Sea was no naval battle in the old definition;

it was an air struggle which took place almost entirely over the sea and the ships were significant and relevant only as targets and mobile bases for aircraft. Japan's situation as an imperial island nation with responsibilities far beyond her shores was closely similar to Britain's in 1940, fighting alone against a vastly more powerful enemy, her merchantmen and her sea routes assailed by submarines, her war production and her civilian population threatened with destruction from the air, her navy and her air force the last shields against invasion.

June 1944 was to Japan what June 1940 had been to Britain, and the Battle of the Philippine Sea was her Battle of Britain, fought further from her shores but with the same price for failure, and the same odds against success.

Nimitz and Spruance and their staffs had judged that the first threat to the success of the Marianas operation was the shore-based Japanese aircraft on their unsinkable carriers, Guam, Saipan and Tinian. On 11 June hundreds of Hellcats were launched from Admiral Mitscher's carriers with the single intention of destroying Japanese fighter capability. There had been a time when the earlier Wildcats were happy to avoid a collision with Zeros in superior numbers. There was none of that now; not only was the Hellcat a superior fighting machine, but the pilots themselves were superior. Some of the Japanese pilots had no more than twenty hours in their log-books, like the RFC Scout pilots of 1917 when they were so desperately needed at the Front.

Dogfights broke out above the islands and the sea, with all their spectacular accompaniment of diving, climbing, twisting planes, staccato ripples of gunfire, orange-red bursts followed by ugly black spirals of smoke and circular white shapes of parachutes, as planes and men fell from the sky. The battles were as brief as a cavalry charge, speed of reaction, steadiness of mind and keen eyesight deciding the issue.

Once again Japanese indifference to human life revealed its military weakness. Lack of armour and self-sealing fuel tanks as well as rescue services led to the unnecessary loss of many lives, while half the American pilots who bailed out were picked up later from the warm sea.

Then the American bombers devastated the Japanese airfields while seven carriers were detached 650 miles north to neutralize the more distant Japanese air bases on Iwo Jima and Chichi Jima. It took two days for Spruance to gain local air command and then Vice-Admiral W.A.Lee's battleships bombarded the defences of the target islands. The skies were clear of the enemy, and it might have been target practice.

D-Day for the invasion was 15 June 1944, and the Japanese naval-air reaction was predictable. Within hours the Japanese Fleet, which had been refuelling between the Philippines and Negros and Panay, was under way. So was the American submarine *Flying Fish*, Lieutenant-Commander Robert Risser, which was stationed where she was for just this contingency. It was a moment in his life Risser would never forget; he had never seen so many ships together. When darkness fell he surfaced and got off the message beginning, 'The Japanese Fleet is headed for the Marianas. . . .'

Admiral Toyoda's message to his Fleet was more inspirational than informative, a repeat almost forty years later of Admiral Togo's signal before Tsu-Shima: 'The fate of the Empire rests on this one battle. Every man is expected to do his utmost.'

But this message from Toyoda was matched by Nimitz's from Pearl Harbor: 'On the eve of a possible fleet action, you and the officers and men under your command have the confidence of the naval service and the country. We count on you to make the victory decisive.'

By no means did Admiral Spruance have everything in his favour. One authority sums up his situation as the message from Risser was decoded:

Off Saipan, Admiral Spruance calculated distances and weighed the possibilities. The Northern Attack Force was already fully committed to the assault on Saipan. It would be highly vulnerable to any attack and Spruance dared not move far to the west to challenge Ozawa lest the Japanese should outflank him during darkness and fall on Turner's forces in his rear. In his mind was a recollection of the favourite Japanese gambit of tempting the enemy to expend his attack on a decoy. He would therefore await the enemy's advance. On the other hand the enemy could not reach the area until the 19th. Spruance therefore allowed his two detached task groups to complete their interdiction strikes on Iwo Jima and Chicha Jima and ordered a general rendezvous for the evening of the 18th in a position 180 miles to the west of Tinian. From Turner's command he called eight cruisers and 21 destroyers of the five support groups to join his flag and augment the already vast Task Force 58.[5]

Spruance was disadvantaged in one respect. Spotter seaplanes, once to be seen on their catapults and in hangars onboard most American cruisers and battleships, had been discarded for their fire risk. The Japanese had no such scruples, and from the beginning these seaplanes had proved their worth time and again. The Americans might still have the advantage in radar – many Japanese ships now had it, thanks to help from Germany – but in the lead-up to the Battle of the Philippine Sea Admiral Ozawa was kept far better informed about the position and movements of the enemy than Spruance was. The American Admiral had to rely on his submarines and on long-range Army Air Force planes whose crews were still untrained in naval reconnaissance.

By dusk on 18 June Ozawa was well informed on the position and disposition of the Americans, while Spruance remained in the dark, his own search planes having to return because of their relatively short range. A naval flying boat had picked up a radar fix on a great mass of vessels 600 miles west of Saipan but could not get the message through. The most accurate news that Spruance was given came from Pearl Harbor where reports from direction-finding stations fixed the enemy at 350 miles west-south-west.

Both sides were still groping about like Admirals Villeneuve and Nelson in the West Indies in 1805, in spite of all the sophisticated intelligence available to their descendants in 1944. Ozawa's picture might be more detailed than Spruance's but the Japanese Admiral was much more seriously ignorant of what had been happening to Admiral Kakuda's shore-based air groups. Whether Kakuda was too ashamed or too stunned to pass on the news of the virtual annihilation of his fighters and bombers will never be known. But the consequence was that Ozawa went into battle like a medieval knight who has left his sword behind and *does not know it*.

Just as his submarines had proved to be Spruance's best intelligence friend, a submarine also took on the task of striking the first mighty blow on behalf of the US Navy. The *Albacore*, Commander Theodore Blanchard, was one of four submarines stationed in an area which it had been calculated the Japanese Fleet would pass through. And *Albacore* was the lucky one, soon after 8.00 a.m. sighting a mass of enemy ships including a large carrier steaming on a steady course because she was in the act of launching. The situation was a submariner's dream. At ideal range on an ideal bearing Blanchard launched a spread of six torpedoes. One of them was intercepted in an unusual and gallant manner, the pilot of a recently launched plane spotting it racing towards his ship. He dived accurately and his act of self-immolation led to the destruction of torpedo, himself and his plane. But at least one other of the *Albacore*'s spread struck the carrier amidships. Blanchard was disappointed to observe the carrier steaming on, seemingly little damaged and continuing to launch. But, as in the four carriers at Midway, aviation fuel fumes were going about their incendiary business, stirred by an idiotic order to turn on the fans to disperse them. Later in the day a giant explosion tore the great new flagship apart.

By this time the submarine *Cavalla*, which had earlier reported and tailed Ozawa's fleet through the night, manoeuvred herself into a position to attack the *Shokoku* just as she was recovering the survivors of an air strike. She pumped three torpedoes into the side of the carrier which had so often been damaged before. Now there was no mistaking that her end had come. For three hours her crew fought massive fires before the 26,000-ton carrier, whose planes in happier times for the IJN had sunk the *Lexington* at Coral Sea, blew up with one of those massive fuel and ammunition explosions unique to carrier warfare.

Admiral Ozawa had been so preoccupied with the fight for the survival of his flagship, and with finally transferring his flag to the cruiser *Haguro*, that he had mercifully inadequate knowledge of what had been happening to his Air Groups. Even now the curtain concealed the true state of affairs for his new flagship lacked the communications and signals facilities of the *Taiho*. Late on that black evening, however, he learned part of the truth of what had happened that day.

Just as the Japanese were first to locate and report the enemy fleet, they were also the first to launch bomber attacks. At 8.30 a.m. Ozawa sent off his first strike of forty-five Zero fighter-bombers, eight torpedo-bombers escorted by sixteen Zeros in pure fighter form. The Japanese had belatedly discovered what an effective dive-bomber the Zero made, with a single 550-pound bomb slung under the belly. It was a less lethal load than the Val's and other pure dive-bombers', but the Zero was well nigh impossible to catch in a dive, and on releasing its bomb became an unhandicapped fighter again. The only disadvantage was that the pilot had to pull out at a higher altitude or he would crash into the target, although increasingly this was something he was prepared to do anyway.

The Japanese bombing effectiveness was also greatly increased by the introduction of the Yokosuka D4Y1, or Judy, which had the phenomenal range of over 2,000 miles, a speed of over 300 mph (not far short of the Hellcat's) and still with a bomb load of 1,100 pounds, equal to the Val's.

Judys figured in large numbers in Ozawa's second wave of 128 aircraft launched half an hour after the first. The air crews were imbued with tremendous patriotic fervour and determination to get at the enemy. Two years earlier these first two waves of bombers and fighters would have boded ill for an American Task Force. But conditions of men and material had changed radically since the Guadalcanal days. Lavish with everything for successful carrier warfare, from expenditure of bombs and fuel in practice to the creature comforts that kept American warriors happy, lavish in the use of practice ammunition for the anti-aircraft gunners, and in consumption of oil for exercises, Admiral Spruance's men were indulged by contrast with Admiral Ozawa's. No one much cared when a Hellcat was damaged on deck landing; it was simply hoist overboard, and replaced from seemingly unlimited reserves drawn finally from the Grumman plants working round the clock back home.

The Japanese Navy was short of everything, from planes to train its pilots and fuel to keep them in the air, to ammunition of all kinds due to the convoy assaults by American submarines which had now become murderously successful. For the same reason, in order to save precious oil, Ozawa had delayed his departure from the Philippines until he knew he was committed to battle.

Admiral Spruance, while kept waiting for precise information on the whereabouts of the enemy, when he did attack was now many times more efficient at intercepting air strikes than at Midway. Carefully selected and trained fighter-director and radar officers onboard the American carriers were capable of detecting the enemy air strikes forty-five minutes before they arrived. A Hellcat could climb to 20,000 feet in seven minutes, and once turned into wind Admiral Mitscher could and did launch 300 of these fighters to meet the Japanese in less than thirty minutes.

While fighter-director officers vectored the Hellcats on to the enemy formations far from the carriers, on board Mitscher's flagship Japanese-speaking officers listened in to the intercepted orders of the Japanese officer co-ordinating the attacks. With the much-refined radar with which the carriers were now equipped, it was possible to follow every enemy move and make dispositions accordingly.

The zeal of the Japanese pilots was not matched by their skill and experience. Few of the bombers in the first wave got through the lethal curtains of Hellcats, and these were met with an unprecedented volume of fire from the carriers and their escort. Proximity fuses added greatly to the effectiveness of the heavier shells. Only one insignificant hit was scored on the battleship *South Dakota*. Later attacks, right through until the afternoon, were as severely dealt with. Not a hit was scored, and at negligible cost to the Allies some 275 Japanese planes were shot down in what came to be known grimly as 'the Great Marianas Turkey Shoot'.

Admiral Spruance was content to let the Japanese beat their heads, and break their necks, against his near-impenetrable defences. If he could be certain of locating them before sundown, it would be good to round off the day by 'scratching a few enemy flat-tops', but his first priority was to knock down enemy planes, and in this his pilots were proving themselves successful as never before – about one every two minutes since the first blips had appeared on the radar screens at mid-morning.

As in all the great carrier battles, the wind was playing its part too. It was blowing from the east which obliged Mitscher to turn on to an easterly heading every time his carriers launched or recovered their planes. This ensured that he did not stray too far from the amphibious operations now proceeding, but also took him ever further from Ozawa's carriers, so diminishing the chances of his bombers finding and attacking them.

Admiral Ozawa in his new flagship viewed the day's events bleakly. He had lost some two-thirds of his aircraft, even allowing for some which may have landed on Guam, and two of his biggest carriers, while even the most optimistic and doubtful reports could not claim more than four enemy carriers lost – say one or two, Ozawa would correct realistically. What had the land-based bombers been doing all this time – those crack air groups on Guam and Tinian? He had still not been informed of the catastrophe which had struck them several days earlier. With despair in his heart the Japanese Admiral turned his armada on to a north-west heading, intending to rendezvous with his tankers the next day. He was 400 miles distant from the American Fleet by dawn. Kurita, his battleship admiral, did not think that was far enough and advised total withdrawal to Japan. Ozawa would have been wise to listen.

In the evening of that first day of battle, Spruance signalled Mitscher:

Desire to attack enemy tomorrow if we know his position with sufficient accuracy. If our patrol planes give us required information tonight no searches should be necessary. If not, we must continue searches tomorrow to ensure adequate protection of Saipan.

Task Force 58 turned west, eager to attack now so long as the ground forces advancing off the beaches were not hazarded. No night reconnaissance was planned. The Americans were still not happy flying at night, and few of the Hellcat pilots had received carrier night-flying training. But the first search planes were in the sky soon after 5.30 a.m. on 20 June, probing west high above the still waters of the Philippine Sea. The Japanese, maintaining strict radio silence, were as elusive as ever, and it was a case of 'you shall seek all day ere you find them'. It was not, in fact, until after four in the afternoon, almost twelve hours later, that an Avenger from the *Enterprise* at last signalled the enemy's position, and when he did so, in view of the vast size of the widely dispersed fleet, he could not understand why it had taken so long.

Mitscher's staff did some rapid arithmetic. The Japanese were distant about 275 miles, further by the time Task Force 58 had turned into wind to launch. It took very little figuring to recognize that a strike launched now would entail a night landing. But such an opportunity for an annihilating victory might never occur again; and, like any commander, the gallant and forceful Marc Mitscher took a glance ahead in time and considered what his fellow admirals and history would have to say if he performed negatively at this most critical moment in his career.

The decision was his own. It had to be. And it came quickly. 'Man aircraft!' was ordered throughout his carriers at 4.10 p.m. Within twenty minutes 216 dive-bombers, torpedo-bombers and fighters were in the air, heading east into the early-evening sun. Soon it was setting, a brilliant red super-enlargement of the scarlet circles on the wings of the Zeros that came up to meet them when the main body of American aircraft spotted Ozawa's carriers. From the darkness below the fire came up in a dazzling psychedelic display of vari-coloured tracer.

The Hellcats dealt efficiently with the Zeros but, for the dive-bomber pilots especially, conditions were trying, and weariness from the long day of waiting, the long flight and forebodings about the return, played its part in the strike's effectiveness. The torpedo-bombers did best this time, sinking the big fleet carrier *Hiyo*, while the dive-bombers knocked out the *Zuikaku* and *Chiyoda* and badly damaged the battleship *Haruna* and a cruiser.

Twenty minutes later the pilots, most of them in action for the first time, were returning to their carriers, at once elated and anxious. They were watched with equal anxiety on the ships' radar screens, a straggling mass of blips by contrast with the solid shapes of their outward formation flight. Mitscher broke all the rules for them, lighting the sky with flares and searchlights, flashing identification lights, turning a dark night of low cloud into day. A Japanese admiral would not have done this, nor would have had the same need to do so, but Mitscher saved many planes and some lives.

By 10.52 p.m. all the planes that were going to land, or crash-land as many of them did, had done so. Around eighty, out of fuel or lost or both, were at the bottom of the Philippine Sea. But the air crews were well equipped for survival, again unlike the enemy, and the rescue craft and submarines were out looking for them almost before they ditched.

They picked up all but sixteen pilots and thirty-three air crew and some of those missing had earlier been killed in combat.

With the negligible losses of the day before, Admirals Spruance and Mitscher had taken part in the greatest carrier battle in history and won decisively. The survival of most of Ozawa's carriers was almost an irrelevance. Santa Cruz had shown on a small scale, with the withdrawal of the Japanese carriers for lack of planes, that it was the Zeros and Vals, the Kates and Judys, that were the critical and decisive targets. A carrier without aircraft is only a vulnerable floating hangar and airstrip. The important result of that American evening strike was not the escape of all but one carrier but the loss of a further 100 Zeros, leaving Admiral Ozawa with no more than a handful of operational machines and little chance of replacing them. What else could he do but flee from the Philippine Sea for the relative safety of home, pursued vainly by American battleships? Meanwhile the assaulting American troops continued their successful fight ashore on the vital islands of the Marianas, claiming one more stepping-stone to Japan.

There was disappointment among officers and men of Task Force 58 who had not appreciated the significance of the 'turkey shoot' while pleased at their success and the success of their fighter pilots. 'We wanted sunk Jap ships and dead Japs,' one complained. 'And all we did was splash planes.' Criticism from HQ at Pearl Harbor was less forgivable. The destruction of hundreds of Japanese planes was good news for home, but hardly in the same class as 'Jap Fleet Sunk' on the front page of every newspaper.

The Battle of the Philippine Sea was the most decisive naval battle of modern times. When Admiral Jellicoe chased Admiral Scheer back home after sinking only a few of his ships, he ensured that the Germans would never seriously challenge him again. By destroying the IJN's air arm – its artillery – at Philippine Sea, Spruance and Mitscher were in effect chasing the enemy back home with his guns spiked by remote control, never to fire effectively again. If the Japanese carrier fleet was not quite dead yet, it was terminally sick.

At a cost of about 100 lives the US Navy had made its triumphant mark in naval history. At Midway the US Navy had achieved manhood; at the Philippine Sea it had achieved maturity and become at once the greatest and most victorious navy in the world.

With the capture of Saipan there opened the last phase of the Pacific war and the attack on the Japanese homeland. There had, as expected, been strong and sometimes acrimonious debate about the timing of the two island-studded routes between MacArthur in the south-west pushing north and Nimitz in the centre pushing west. Nimitz believed that it was best to by-pass the complex mare's nest of the Philippine Islands and head straight for Formosa now that the Marianas were tight under his control. It would be understandable if MacArthur's judgement were swayed by an abiding need not only to avenge the personal humiliation of being thrown out of the islands in 1941–2, but to relieve as soon as possible the Philippine people from the cruel burden of Japanese occupation, and to reinstate himself as the patriarchal figure he had struck before the Japanese invasion.

The controversy between the two supremos was settled at the second Quebec Conference in September 1944. MacArthur, rather than continue his laboured advance island by island from New Guinea, was to make one giant leap of 1,500 miles to Leyte, by-passing countless Japanese-held islands and bases, relying entirely on ship-borne air cover; while Nimitz was to continue his drive to the same destination in the Philippines via Pelelieu, Yap and Ulithi.

A further radical step was to alternate command of Nimitz's Fifth Fleet between Spruance and Halsey, one Admiral's staff working at Pearl Harbor on the next stage of the campaign while the other Admiral was in overall command.

When Halsey took over, just to confuse matters, the 5th became the 3rd Fleet, while Marc Mitscher remained in overall command of the carriers. Lee, flying his flag in the *Washington*, retained command of the modern battleships, Task Force 34, while Kinkaid with his flag in the *Mississippi* commanded Task Force 77, the Covering Force, with six old battleships, escort carriers, heavy and light cruisers and a strong element of destroyers.

In a naval war of superlatives these combined American fleets formed an armada the power of which the world had never seen. The German feat in building the High Seas Fleet, second-largest after the British Fleet, in fifteen years between 1899 and 1914 had been regarded as a near-miracle of industrial achievement. But Pearl Harbor was less than three years ago, and besides virtually rebuilding the old battleships which had been there, the great majority of the other ships present had run down the slipways of American yards since then.

The Japanese naval defence of the Philippines by contrast presented a sorry picture. To the north and based on Formosa was Ozawa's carrier force, a mere skeleton of a once all-conquering and proud strike fleet, with the four surviving operational carriers and scarcely enough aircraft to quarter-fill the hangars. Ozawa also had the two battleship-carriers and some light cruisers and destroyers. At Lingga Roads, near Singapore, was all that was left of the Japanese Battle Fleet, a still-powerful force under Kurita, of seven battleships, including the *Yamato* and *Musashi*, twelve heavy cruisers and a substantial force of light cruisers and destroyers – *but not one carrier*.

Admiral Toyoda remained in overall command of what was code-named SHO-1 – the defence of the Philippine Islands. His strategy was as tired and over-played as its failure was foredoomed. As always, there had to be a decoy, and poor, desperate Ozawa with his much-repaired surviving carriers was to act as bait. On the supposition that the assault forces would advance up the Philippine Sea and land on the studded, island-strewn east coast, Toyoda divided his battleship fleet in two: Admiral Nishimura with two battleships passing through the Surigao Strait and Kurita with the rest of the battleships cutting through the islands at San Bernardino Strait farther north to 'crush the invading force between the heads of the pincers'. Meanwhile Ozawa was to come down from the north to lure away the invasion's covering forces.

Three linked but separate battles resulted. Waiting only for confirmation that Leyte was to be the enemy's main objective, Toyoda signalled the executive order for SHO-1 early on 18 October 1944. While American carrier planes fought to clear the air and, with the ships' gunners, fought off desperate Japanese air attacks (one American carrier sunk), the three prongs of Toyoda's Fleet began to close about the Leyte beach-head.

By midnight of 24–25 October Nishimura's southern prong was in the Surigao Strait, the two battleships and heavy cruiser *Mogami* in line ahead, light cruisers and destroyers on the left flank and ahead. He knew that he would be met by six American battleships but derived encouragement from the well-known record of American incompetency in night fighting – remember the Guadalcanal Slot! A few PT-boats teased him on his way up the channel. He brushed them aside. It was a moonless night, the water like a dark mirror. Some destroyers made their presence known next, on either flank. Nishimura's ships fired starshells, opened fire, and the destroyers shot away at 30 knots behind their own smokescreen. Nishimura sailed on, his picked look-outs with the big Zeiss night glasses searching ahead, unaware that his battleship *Fuso* had been hit and had fallen out of line behind him.

Minutes later, again unseen, two more divisions of destroyers, hugging the dark shores, positioned themselves to deliver a second attack. Commanding one division was Commander H.J.Buchanan of the Royal Australian Navy in the *Arunta*. Between them they made two hits on the *Yamashiro* before retiring amidst a hail of gunfire, some of it, alas, from American cruisers ahead, which wrecked the destroyer *Grant*, causing 120 casualties.

Now Nishimura knew the extent of the catastrophe he was facing. The *Fuso* was no longer with him: the battleship's back had broken, and she went down a blazing wreck thirty minutes after being hit. One of his destroyers had blown up, and his own ship had been slowed from 20 to 5 knots. The outcome could only be a massacre. The American battleships, reincarnated from the hell of Pearl Harbor, appeared to wreak revenge with a special savagery. Captain C.A.G.Nichols RAN of the Australian cruiser *Shropshire*, firing alongside American cruisers, reported on the opening of fire:

During the preliminary 'ranging salvos' I saw nothing of the 'fall of shot' when the indicator bell rang behind me on the bridge. The smaller projectiles of the quick firing US cruisers who opened fire just before us did not show at all on our bridge radar screen, but when *Shropshire* started straddling the target in about the 3rd salvo, the 8'' fall of shot bell coincided exactly with a big and seemingly red flash on the radar, for every salvo, but one, until we ceased fire. As it was a big ship target, bows on to us, in perfect weather conditions, I would not have expected less I admit. *Yamashiro* did not fire many salvos though some crossed our line, I believe, early on.

The cruiser's gunnery officer, Lieutenant-Commander W.Bracegirdle RAN, recalled:

The US ships were all using flashless propellant, and when our first 8-inch broadside fired, the flash was terrific. I consider that the Japanese ships fired several salvos in our direction, at our flash, mistaking us for a capital ship.

On the fortieth anniversary of the action, John C.Date RANVR described that October night in 1944:

At the time, I was on the upper deck of *Shropshire* to witness these early salvos from *Yamashiro*'s 14-inch guns, which were to pass over *Shropshire* and which, to me, sounded like controlled thunder, or more specifically – thunder in unison.

Yamashiro was repeatedly hit by the 16-inch shells of the battleship *West Virginia* and the 14-inch shells of the *Tennessee* and *California* all of which, equipped with the latest centimetric fire-control radar, made devastatingly accurate shooting. The *Pennsylvania* did not fire at all, the *Mississippi* only two salvos but the *Maryland* joined in by ranging on the splashes of the *West Virginia*.

To those on above deck action stations, the scene was unforgettable: the magnitude and incredible rate of fire of the Americans, particularly the cruisers with their tracer ammunition – the sight of the battleship *Yamashiro*, flagship of Nishimura, on fire from bow to stern, and the unbelievable use of searchlights by the Japanese, undoubtedly the last occasion in naval history.

With the *Yamashiro* now burning fiercely and shortly after being hit by a further two torpedoes from the destroyer *Newcomb*, at approximately 0419 hours she quickly sank taking with her Nishimura and most of her crew.

The heavy cruiser *Mogami* and the destroyer *Shigure*, both badly damaged, retired down the strait and were the sole remnants of Nishimura's force.[6]

When Vice-Admiral K.Shima's supporting cruiser force arrived at the scene of the massacre he found only blazing wrecks, litter and smoke. After firing a few torpedoes and a few rounds into the darkness, he retired. All he could do was to give aid and succour to the stricken *Mogami*, which appeared to have a charmed life and did not go down until American aircraft found and struck her the following day.

Admiral Kurita's 1st Striking Force of battleships and heavy cruisers, the other head of the pincers, had already suffered heavily before Nishimura had gone down in his flagship. It had arrived at Brunei Bay four days earlier, and began refuelling as the American assault forces landed on Luzon, MacArthur wading ashore while the movie cameras whirred, and declaring, 'People of the Philippines, I have returned.' Kurita's ten heavy cruisers and five battleships were picked up by radar at a range of fifteen sea miles by the US submarine *Darter*, Commander David H.McClintock, just after midnight on 23 October. McClintock got off a message a few minutes later. Once again, American air reconnaissance had proved weak and this was the first news Admiral Halsey had of the whereabouts of the Japanese armoured fleet.

Darter, with her consort *Dace*, stalked the 1st Striking Force through the dark hours. The two American submariners were being treated to an historic spectacle: for the last time in naval history a battle fleet was going in to action without air cover, for all the world like a Dreadnought battle squadron of the First World War. Nor did it even have picket destroyers in the van as an anti-submarine precaution.

McClintock manoeuvred skilfully in order to attack Admiral Kurita's heavy cruiser flagship *Atago*, leading one of the two columns, at first dawn light. At a range of under half a mile the *Darter* launched a spread of six torpedoes from her bow tubes. 'After firing two fish into him and one spread ahead,' the Commander reported, 'target was roaring by so close we couldn't miss, so spread the remainder inside his length.' He then turned his boat hard to port and fired his rear torpedoes at the second in line, the *Takao*.

When McClintock turned his periscope on to his victims in turn, Kurita's flagship was already going down in a mass of black smoke, while the *Takao* was dead in the water. The *Dace* had meanwhile taken the third cruiser in the second column and with four torpedoes blew the *Maya* to pieces. When the two submarines left the scene of slaughter, two of Kurita's heavy cruisers were on the sea bed, and a third out of action, while the Admiral himself was swimming for his life. Admiral M.Ugaki in the *Yamato* took over tactical command 'until Kurita could dry out and pull himself together'.[7]

The Battle of Sibuyan Sea, one of the four major actions making up the Battle of Leyte Gulf, began with a major carrier-plane attack on Kurita's battle fleet on the morning of 24 October. At last, after almost three years of war, American pilots were granted the first sight of the *Yamato* and *Musashi*. And what targets they made! They even put on the spectacle of firing their main battery 18.1-inch guns at the American fliers, producing massive patterns of purple, pink and white, with silver phosphorus balls spilling from the centre of each burst. And the super-battleships themselves looked quite unsinkable. In these early strikes the dive-bombers made a hit on the *Yamato* and another battleship but they did not appear to do more than dent their thick armour.

Long before the advent of air power, back in the ironclad days, the battleship's first enemy had been 'the automobile torpedo'. All through this long and terrible war it was the torpedo which, aside from destroying hundreds of merchantmen of all nations, had sent to the bottom German, Italian, British, American and Japanese battleships. And so it was that Japan's latest and greatest battleship *Musashi*, finding herself the target for countless venomous American torpedo-bombers – as well as a few bombs – was shattered by no fewer than eight underwater explosions and brought to a stand-

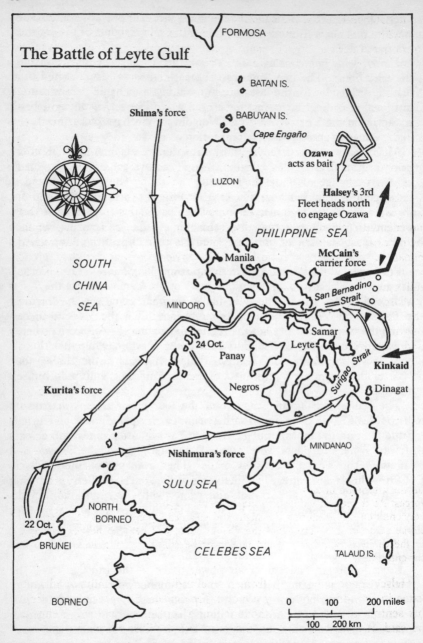

The Battle of Leyte Gulf

FORMOSA

BATAN IS.

BABUYAN IS.

Cape Engaño

Shima's force

Ozawa acts as bait

LUZON

Halsey's 3rd Fleet heads north to engage Ozawa

PHILIPPINE SEA

Manila

McCain's carrier force

SOUTH

CHINA

SEA

MINDORO

San Bernadino Strait

Samar

24 Oct.

Kinkaid

Leyte

Panay

Surigao Strait

Kurita's force

Negros

Dinagat

Nishimura's force

MINDANAO

SULU SEA

22 Oct.

NORTH BORNEO

BRUNEI

CELEBES SEA

TALAUD IS.

BORNEO

0   100   200 miles

100   200 km

still. Later in the day, the *Musashi*'s engines succeeded in providing some momentum to her 70,000 tons. Then soon after 3.00 p.m., torpedo-bombers from five American carriers again concentrated on her, pumping ten more torpedoes into her tortured carcass. At 7.35 p.m. she rolled over, never having fired her guns at the enemy, the biggest battleship ever to have been sunk.

The sinking of the *Musashi** was a great achievement but not only Japanese pilots exaggerated their claims. Besides this battleship, Air Group commanders reported four and probably five more enemy battleships and three heavy cruisers knocked out. This reassuring report was received by Admiral Halsey on his flagship *New Jersey*, at about the same time as a sighting report of Admiral Ozawa's carriers, the missing factor in the predicted sequence of the Japanese attack.

The Japanese carrier Admiral had been moving his force south in accordance with the decoy plan, increasingly surprised and then perturbed that no enemy air reconnaissance had spotted him, as Japanese seaplanes would by now certainly have picked up an enemy so close. Finally he despatched ahead of his carriers his two battleship-carriers, hoping that they would soon be spotted. And so they were, but not until they were less than 200 miles away.

Admiral Halsey rose to the bait like a trout in the mayfly season on the Test. Under the false impression that Admiral Kurita's powerful force of armoured ships had been neutralized by air power and submarine power, and confident that Kinkaid's battleships could comfortably cope with an attack up the Surigao Strait, the C-in-C determined to deliver an all-out attack on Ozawa's carriers with his own carriers and all his modern battleships. Was he taking a sledgehammer to crack a nut? With three task groups of the Third Fleet, sixty-five ships in all, he was taking on the six carriers and seventeen ships of Ozawa's force. Was this overkill?

Halsey himself, writing the following evening, tried to justify himself thus:

Searches by my carrier planes revealed the presence of the Northern carrier force on the afternoon of 24 October, which completed the picture of all enemy naval forces. As it seemed childish to me to guard statically San Bernardino Strait, I concentrated TF 38 during the night and steamed north to attack the Northern Force at dawn. I believed that the Center force had been so heavily damaged in the Sibuyan Sea that it could no longer be considered a serious menace to Seventh Fleet.[8]

Halsey ignored warnings from his subordinate commanders and later came in for some very heavy criticism for departing so precipitately from his sentry post off Leyte without telling a soul. But there was plenty to be said in favour of what he did even if his failure to tell anyone was

---

* Her twin, *Yamato*, was sunk on 11 April 1945 on a one-way suicide mission during the Okinawa operations.

unforgivable. The Pacific war had been dominated by carrier groups, Japanese and American, from Pearl Harbor to the Marianas operations. Sometimes the Americans had been lucky, sometimes fortune had favoured the Japanese. But while enemy carriers roamed the oceans, they could not be ignored; they had shown their sting too often. Six carriers was as many as Admiral Nagumo had employed at Pearl Harbor, and Halsey had no means of knowing that the carriers were almost empty of aircraft and that the pilots were as green as the Leyte jungle. He had been kept busy these last many hours with fiercely pressed-home enemy air attacks and he did not yet know that these were all land-based. As a carrier man he presumed that they were carrier-based. And time and again in the past, after seriously mauling Japanese carrier forces, some had got away to re-form and renew their threat.

On 24 October Halsey was like Hercules wielding his sword against the many-headed Hydra, determined once and for all to destroy the womb of reproduction. The result was that the Japanese achieved for the first time in a major engagement – and their last major engagement as it turned out – the degree of surprise for which they had so long been striving.

The man who suffered this unpleasant surprise was Rear-Admiral Thomas L. Sprague, a veteran naval aviator of fifty years, Commander of Northern Escort Carrier Group 77.4.31, now playing the role of platoon commander standing in as guard of a fort thought to be in no danger. Admiral Morison describes the gallant Admiral's moment of truth:

At 0645 strange things began to happen. Lookouts observed anti-aircraft fire to the northwestward. What could that be? Our own vessels shooting at friendly planes? At 0646 *Fanshaw Bay* made an 'unidentified surface contact' on her SG radar screen and her radio watch heard what sounded like 'Japs gabbling' on the inter-fighter direction set. Surely there could be no Japs around; somebody joking? At 0647 Ensign Jensen, pilot of an antisubmarine patrol plane from *Kadashan Bay*, encountered what he described as four Japanese battleships, eight cruisers, and a number of destroyers, 20 miles from Taffy 3; he made a glide-bombing attack on a cruiser, and reported that he was being fired upon. Admiral Sprague yelled 'Check identification!' at Air Plot, his unspoken thought being that the pilot had sighted part of Task Force 38. He got verification all right, and from his own lookouts: the unmistakable pagodalike masts of Japanese battleships and cruisers pricking up over the northern horizon. At 0658, when the Japanese ships were still hull-down, their guns opened fire. At 0650 colored splashes from their shells began rising astern of Taffy 3.

Admiral Kinkaid was preening himself in the early-morning sun of 25 October after the destruction of Nishimura's Surigao Strait attack when he received an emergency message from Sprague, three hours' steaming away, reporting that his tin-can 'Woolworth' carriers were being fired on by battleships. Kinkaid had no idea that the C-in-C had shot north with all his armour and fleet carriers to deal with a Japanese carrier threat.

The action which followed, the Battle off Samar, should have led to the total destruction of Sprague's escort carriers and destroyer escorts. Instead, it turned out a copybook example of how a hopelessly outnumbered and outgunned naval force is capable of holding its own against an enemy by a combination of determination, zeal, courage and effective use of resources. Any peacetime war game matching slow (17½-knot) almost defenceless carriers and a handful of destroyers against four battleships, eight cruisers and accompanying destroyers would have reckoned the carriers at the bottom of the sea within twenty minutes of contact, and the destroyers scattered or sunk, too. As a further handicap, in order to launch the few remaining planes not already operating with MacArthur ashore, the carriers had to steam almost at right angles to the enemy's pursuing course, making them even neater sitting targets.

Besides Admiral Sprague himself, the real heroes of the action that followed were the commanders of the three destroyers and four destroyer escorts, and the pilots who did succeed in getting airborne. The destroyers harried the Japanese monsters, making smoke, launching spreads of torpedoes which forced the enemy ships to comb the tracks and thus slow their pursuit; the Wildcats, Hellcats and Avengers, supported later by shore-based aircraft, distracted the enemy by making dummy torpedo and strafing runs when ammunition was exhausted.

It was an extraordinary and one-sided running battle during which at one point the mighty *Yamato* was forced by torpedo attacks to reverse course, taking the enemy out of range even of her 18.1-inch guns. But as the 16-inch and 14-inch shell bursts crept ever closer to the carriers, it did seem as if Admiral Kurita was about to score a great victory; and as the first hits were made on the *Gambier Bay*, Sprague recalled, 'At this point it did not appear that any of our ships could survive another five minutes.'

The destroyers, too, were paying the inevitable price for their repeated valiant attacks at close range. Take the *Johnston*, Commander Ernest Evans. All torpedoes fired, an engine knocked out, she was set upon by a Japanese destroyer squadron and several cruisers. One of her officers recalled:

For the next half hour this ship engaged first the cruiser on our port hand and then the destroyers on our starboard hand, alternating between the two groups in a somewhat desperate attempt to keep all of them from closing the carrier formation. The ship was getting hit with disconcerting frequency throughout this period.

At 0910 we had taken a hit which knocked out one forward gun and damaged the other. Fires had broken out. One of our 40-mm ready-lockers was hit and the exploding shells were causing as much damage as the Japs. The bridge was rendered untenable by the fires and explosions, and Commander Evans had been forced at 0920 to shift his command to the fantail, where he yelled his steering orders through an open hatch at the men who were turning the rudder by hand.[9]

By 9.45 a.m. the *Johnston* was dead in the water, surrounded by enemy cruisers and destroyers, one of which repeatedly circled her shooting 'like Indians attacking a prairie schooner'. Half an hour later she rolled over and began to sink. A survivor in the water believed he saw the Japanese captain salute. So it was as bad, or good, as that! At a cost of one destroyer and 186 officers and men, the carriers had been saved from a massive torpedo attack.

The Japanese were taking their losses, too. The cruisers *Chikuma* and *Chokai* were both sunk by a combination of destroyers' torpedoes and bombs, while in one case an escort carrier's 5-inch guns made their contribution to a cruiser's destruction. But two more of the carriers were receiving heavy shell damage when, to the astonishment of all who witnessed it, the entire Japanese force turned about at 9.15 a.m. and speedily disappeared over the horizon. As one officer demanded incredulously, 'What in hell's going on?' He might well ask.

Admiral Kurita's turn-about after sinking one carrier and three destroyers can be accounted for by poor intelligence, indecision and timidity, a fatal combination of demerits in any naval commander. His powerful armoured force, which could and should have wiped out Admiral Sprague's vulnerable force before breakfast, had the previous day witnessed the destruction of one of its two most powerful and allegedly 'unsinkable' ships, the *Musashi*, sent to the bottom with brisk American efficiency. Kurita's fear of American air power was greatly increased by this terrible spectacle. His lack of air cover was a further inhibiting factor.

When Kurita emerged from San Bernardino Strait his hope and expectation was to find transports, landing-craft and covering warships, with which he was equipped to deal. Instead, he sighted carriers which he misidentified as fleet carriers, with all their destructive potential, instead of 8,000-ton escort carriers designed to cover landings and not to indulge in fleet actions. His pursuit and attack was therefore hesitant and vulnerable to distractions from the air and from pressed-home destroyer attack. Although Kurita ordered a pursuit at best speed, his heart was never in the business, and when he sighted hull down the carriers of Rear-Admiral F.B.Stump (Southern Carrier Group 77.4.2), and misidentified them, too, as Admiral Halsey's fleet carriers, he decided that he had pushed his luck far enough. Imagine that decision in 1941–2!

There was only one more error of judgement that Admiral Kurita could commit: to hang about wondering what to do next. He did just that.

Admiral Clifton Sprague was not left in peace for long on this most fateful day for his escort carriers. Shortly before 11.00 a.m. Zeros suddenly began plummeting down from the heavens like hungry cormorants. Crews behind the sights of 5-inch, 40-mm, 20-mm, and .5s followed them down, firing on them all the way, waiting for the pull-out which would give them their best chance. Then they were astonished to see that there was to be no pull-out. They just went right on, like human bombs, which was what they were.

They were dealing with something quite new: the *kamikazes*, which were to become a feared factor in the closing months of the Pacific war. Nearly all of them were shot down before hitting, but it took only one to seal the fate of the *St Lo*, while three more carriers were cruelly hurt by these *kamikazes*.

Far distant north from the trials and tribulations of his subordinate, Clifton Sprague, Admiral Halsey was relishing the destruction of the last pathetic remnants of Japanese naval air power, Admiral Ozawa's six carriers. The one-sided engagement, to be named the Battle of Cape Engaño, began at 8.30 a.m. on 25 October, Ozawa's total force of nineteen remaining Zeros putting up a token resistance while waves of up to 200 American machines from Mitscher's carriers tore the carriers, including the flagship, to pieces. The result did indeed possess all the awful spectacle of Midway, with fires and explosions and billowing clouds of smoke rising to the heavens; but the glory and surprise and elation were somehow missing this time. The American air crews might not have realized it, but they were only nibbling live bait. When the *Zuikaku* was going down Admiral Ozawa shifted his flag to the light cruiser *Oyodo*; but even this move lacked the Wagnerian tragedy of Admiral Nagumo's escape from his flagship back in June 1942, which was not at all predicted.

Halsey received the first cry for help from Admiral Kinkaid at 8.22 a.m., minutes before this massacre began. Other messages followed, but three hours passed and an anxious enquiry 'Where are you?' had been received from Admiral Nimitz at Pearl Harbor, before Halsey despatched battleships at full speed. They arrived off San Bernardino Strait three hours after Kurita – who had at last made up his mind – escaped through it.

The Battle of Leyte Gulf was, in terms of the number of ships involved, the greatest naval battle of the Pacific war. But this must be qualified to the extent that the outcome was inevitable and resolved by the superior air power of the Americans at the preliminary engagement in the Philippine Sea. For the IJN Leyte was no more than a tragic epilogue to the bombing and dogfighting of 19–20 June 1944, and the later air raids on Formosa, Luzon and Okinawa. It would have made no difference to the outcome if Sprague had lost all his 'Woolworth' carriers, and Halsey had kept back his battleships and left Mitscher to finish off the enemy carriers on his own. Admiral Kurita was as incapable of losing as of winning any meaningful engagement; it was far too late for all that.

Mitscher's carrier 'victory' too was as hollow as the empty carriers he sent to the bottom. There was no command hero at Leyte on the American side, no great credit or discredit to be recorded for posterity. Kinkaid did well with his overwhelming power; Sprague did well with his overwhelming weakness. Halsey's action remains controversial but not discreditable and certainly not important: his war-winning record cannot be diminished, nor his heroic image be the least bit stained, by his action.

The only heroes of Leyte were the *kamikaze* pilots and the men who fought for the survival of those escort carriers, on the sea and in the air. As Admiral Morison put it succinctly: 'In no engagement of its entire history has the United States Navy shown more gallantry, guts and gumption than in those two morning hours ... off Samar.'[10]

As for the three Japanese senior commanders, Admiral Nishimura knew from the start that he was as fated to die as the *kamikaze* pilots of the following morning; Admiral Kurita added no glory to the brief annals of Imperial Japanese naval history; and Admiral Ozawa put a brave face, if nothing more, on the live-bait role cast for him in this whole tragic business.

Leyte Gulf really changed nothing, but as an exercise in the practice of sea power it is interesting because it included every form of twentieth-century naval engagement, some pointing to the past, some to the present and others to the future. There were close ship-to-ship destroyer actions – the bayonet attack of naval warfare – torpedo charges, gunnery duels the like of which had not been seen since the First World War, by night and by day, carrier-to-carrier actions, submarine attacks (*I-56* on the escort carrier *Santee* as well as those of the American submariners), and dive-bomber and torpedo-bomber operations against destroyers, cruisers, carriers and battleships, culminating in the destruction of the *Musashi*. No element was missing.

After the Battle of Leyte Gulf any further reinforcement of the American Pacific Fleet might appear to be an embarrassment of riches. But there are considerations of a non-military nature in a world war fought between allies which should be taken into account, for they cannot be ignored.

With the surrender of Italy and the opening up of the Mediterranean, the defeat of the U-boat in the Atlantic and the successful launching of Overlord in Europe, the responsibilities of the Royal Navy in home waters were much reduced. Churchill and the Joint Chiefs of Staff could now give greater attention to the naval war in the Indian Ocean and the Far East. This was to be one of the important items on the agenda at the second Quebec Conference convened in September 1944 at which Churchill and Roosevelt would once again thrash out their plans and problems. As Churchill wrote:

How, when, and where could we strike at Japan, and assure for Britain an honourable share in the final victory there? We had lost as much, if not more, than the United States. Over 160,000 British prisoners and civilian internees were in Japanese hands. Singapore must be redeemed and Malaya freed. For nearly three years we had persisted in the strategy of 'Germany First'. The time had now come for the liberation of Asia, and I was determined that we should play our full and equal part in it. What I feared most at this stage of the war was that the United

States would say in after-years, 'We came to your help in Europe and you left us alone to finish off Japan.' We had to regain on the field of battle our rightful possessions in the Far East, and not have them handed back to us at the peace table.[11]

Admiral King was, predictably, still the chief opponent of any British naval contribution to the war in the Pacific. The Australian and New Zealand contribution was a *fait accompli* and had been since the beginning, and the RAN and RNZN had shared the suffering and losses of the Guadalcanal campaign and Australian cruisers had become an integral part of Admiral Nimitz's fleet. But the idea of integrating a British fleet within either of the two main Pacific commands was something King could not stomach. He argued that the Royal Navy had no experience of the amphibious warfare developed by the US Navy over three years, its complex logistics, its self-sustaining fleet trains, its massive Task Forces with their sub-divisions into Task Groups.

There was indeed a certain validity to King's view of the RN's inexperience, and an understandable reluctance to allow a foreign navy to share, however modestly, in the credit for victory over the Japanese. But the manner of presentation of his case, and his widely recognized Anglophobia, aroused the President's suspicions that the head of his navy was not making a disinterested judgement. Admiral King also underestimated the flexibility of the RN and the speed with which it could adapt to new forms of warfare – a facility it had had to learn long before Pearl Harbor forced the United States into the war.

At Quebec Churchill raised the question of the British contribution generally to the defeat of Japan at the first plenary meeting on 13 September 1944, and dived in at the deep end by offering the British Eastern Fleet for service in the main operations against Japan. 'The President intervened', wrote Churchill, 'to say that the British Fleet was no sooner offered than accepted.'[12]

That was not the end of the matter by any means. When the discussion became more detailed, and Churchill asked King how the fleet could best be integrated, the American Admiral prevaricated, declared that the matter was under study and continued in this vein until Churchill, patience on the wane, demanded: 'The offer has been made. Is it accepted?' Before King could reply – and to his fury – the President chipped in: 'It is.'

Was that the end of the affair? It was not. The next day at a meeting of the Chiefs of Staff, King fought the battle all over again, in spite of lack of support from his fellow Americans, General Marshall especially, the language becoming so lurid that eventually the President's own Chief of Staff, Admiral William D. Leahy, had to intervene: 'I don't think we should wash our linen in public.' At last and with the worst possible grace King gave in – but, he said, there would be no assistance from the Americans: the British Fleet would have to be entirely self-subsisting. 'From this rather unhelpful attitude', wrote Admiral Cunningham, First Sea Lord since Dudley Pound's death, 'he never budged.'

Where it finally mattered however, at Pearl Harbor and at sea, co-operation could not have been closer or relations friendlier. Admiral Nimitz's welcome in particular could not have been warmer, and in the short time that the two navies worked together they got on extremely well at all levels, as they had when the modest-sized American battle fleet was integrated into the British Grand Fleet at the end of the First World War.

Whether Admiral King liked it or not, co-operation between the RN and the USN had been growing willy-nilly long before the Quebec Conference in September 1944. Admiral Somerville's Eastern Fleet had been growing and justifying its name by moving farther east since it had reinstalled itself at Ceylon in January 1944. Its first task was to deal with an enemy submarine campaign with both German and Japanese boats operating far from home. The Japanese, characteristically, employed their own brand of ruthlessness. Boats from sunk ships were rammed or crews machine-gunned, and in one case lined up on the submarine's casing and clubbed to death. In February the transport *Khedive Ismail*, packed with returning nurses, Wrens and ATS girls, was sunk off the Maldive Islands with the loss of 1,300 lives.

Somerville eventually mastered the menace by sinking the submarines by well-tested Atlantic methods, as soon as he could rustle up more escorts, and by sinking enemy tankers and 'milch cows', strangling the stranglers.

On 19 April 1944, with a powerful force of well-supported carriers, Somerville struck at the Japanese-held island of Sabang, and later co-operated with units of Admiral Halsey's Fleet operating with General MacArthur. These and other strikes, small by comparison with Nimitz's Pacific operations, were in support of the Fourteenth Army's advance into Burma towards the Chindwin River.

In August 1944 Admiral Somerville, who had borne the most demanding burdens of responsibility since the beginning of the war, was at last relieved by Admiral Sir Bruce Fraser – who had not been idle since 1939 either. Somerville would willingly have continued in command, as Churchill wished him to do, but Mountbatten failed to get on with him and insisted that he went. As a final flourish and final page to his war service record, Somerville laid on a massive new attack on Sabang, employing four battleships, seven cruisers and ten destroyers, while the Dutch cruiser *Tromp* and three more destroyers actually entered the harbour, guns blazing. Fighters from the carriers raked the Japanese airfields, destroying dozens of aircraft.

Fraser's command lasted barely a month. As a result of the Quebec Conference's decision to form a British Pacific Fleet and integrate it under Admiral Nimitz's command, Fraser was called back to London for consultations. On 22 November 1944, back in Ceylon, he hoisted his flag as C-in-C of this new fleet. It was, as yet, only a phantom fleet. The ships had still to arrive. The sinking of the *Tirpitz* by the RAF had expedited the release of the heavy ships the giant had pinned down for so long. Meanwhile, the old Eastern Fleet had been renamed East Indies Fleet, C-in-C Admiral Sir Arthur Power, and was to work with Mountbatten's South-East Asia Command exclusively, very much as Admiral Halsey had operated for so long with General MacArthur.

Hindsight is not always an advantage in considering naval history, or any other history for that matter. Most American and British civilians thought the war was over bar the shouting in November–December 1944. The Allied armies in Europe were on the borders of Germany, the Russians advancing on every front, and in the Pacific brilliantly conducted amphibious operations had brought both Nimitz's and MacArthur's commands to Japan's porch: all they had to do was to break in the door.

For the fighting men everywhere – a marine private on Guam, a carrier's gunner facing a diving Judy, a Fourteenth Army infantryman, bayonet fixed, in the Burma jungle, a pfc of the US First Army Group struggling through the frozen Hurtgen Forest east of the River Roer – for them and millions like them the war remained a prolonged, uncomfortable and dangerous business. The atomic bomb was many months away, and only a handful of people knew about 'Tube Alloys', certainly not Joseph Stalin, Admiral Nimitz or General MacArthur. Meanwhile, the attempt to jump the Rhine at Arnhem had failed at awful cost, the German armies had surprised and thrown back the Americans in the Ardennes, even threatening Paris – just like 1918 – and in the Pacific Americans were dying in *kamikaze* attacks on warships and the Japanese were fighting suicidally for every yard of their island bases.

The men of the new Pacific Fleet did not regard themselves as actors in some political drama; war for them was a reality, and sometimes it seemed an interminable one at that. Ships and men who had served perhaps in the North or South Atlantic, the Indian Ocean, the Mediterranean or the Arctic – perhaps in all these theatres – now had to prepare for more fighting in the Pacific, and adjust themselves to working with another navy of which, in spite of all the years they had been fighting on the same side, they knew little.

The problems which faced Admiral Fraser [wrote Captain Roskill] were extremely complex, and his position was probably unique in the long annals of the Royal Navy; for while he was under Admiral Nimitz for operational purposes, he was responsible to the Admiralty for the maintenance of his ships and the welfare of their crews; and the governments of Australia and New Zealand owned the rearward bases and shore installations on which he depended. Lastly nearly all his supplies had to be transported across some 12,000 miles of sea from the British Isles.[13]

Nor did Admiral Fraser receive all the co-operation he might expect from his own Admiralty. Admiral Cunningham was much more imaginative and effective as C-in-C Mediterranean than as First Sea Lord. As if Fraser had not got enough on his plate, he had to fight Their Lordships on any number of matters, from the wearing of khaki uniform instead of traditional tropical white, which would show the Americans how tradition-bound (and no doubt superior) they were, to the adoption of American signalling, which Cunningham opposed vehemently until forced to capitulate.

Then when Fraser began gathering his force about him, he had to face the Australians, who were socially welcoming as always but bloody-minded about doing any work on the ships. Union dockers and shipwrights reckoned they had had their war. After threatening to transfer his base from Sydney to Auckland, New Zealand, combining this with some subtle diplomacy, Fraser got his way here, too, and in due course was viewed with respect and affection.

During February 1945 Fraser was able to bring together the various units of his fleet – Vice-Admiral Sir Bernard Rawlings as VA2 flying his flag in the *King George V*, and Rear-Admiral Sir Philip Vian (nearly five years after Norway) with four modern armoured fleet carriers. On 10 February Fraser made a grand entry into Sydney harbour, the most beautiful and spectacular in the world, and the city went mad.

The British Pacific Fleet was to become a part of Admiral Spruance's 5th Fleet for the final assault, via Okinawa and Iwo Jima, on Japan. Fraser had already met Spruance at Pearl Harbor and was confident that the British force would be welcome and that co-operation would be wholehearted. Personally, he took to 'the reserved, silent mastermind of the decisive American carrier victories'. 'A great commander – but very austere,' Fraser commented. 'He gave me lunch: I think we had a couple of lettuces or something.'[14]

The British Pacific Fleet reached Manus on 7 March 1945, thoroughly Americanized and, by gigantic endeavours, ready for action. Rawlings signalled Nimitz, reporting this fact, adding: 'It is with a feeling of great pride and pleasure that the BPF joints the US Naval Forces under your command.' And Nimitz replied welcomingly and with equal grace.

The severe strictures laid down by Admiral King about total British independence broke down in the intimacy of personal contact, and there was a lot of exchange of hospitality as well as of spare parts. Fraser himself recounts:

At one moment we were short of three Avenger aircraft. I made a signal to Admiral Nimitz to ask if he could lend us three Avengers, and the reply came back, no. I sent for my American liaison officer: he couldn't understand this at first. And then he said, 'Ah, it has to go through Washington! I think you'll find that they'll provide you with some.' Sure enough, when we got up to Manus, the American CO there said, 'I'm sorry, but we don't issue less than six – and if you've got a bottle of whisky you can have a dozen!'[15]

The fully operational life of the BPF ran only from March to August 1945, but its Task Forces participated fully in the closing operations in the Okinawa–Formosa areas especially, taking their fair share of *kamikazes* (and the damage they could cause) and bombarding alongside American battleships. To the bitter end, King attempted to disrupt this integration and co-operation. He attempted to transfer the whole fleet to Borneo, but Nimitz intervened. The Americans were not only happy to have the British around, but were finding them increasingly useful. Many carrier captains envied the British carriers' armoured decks which made comparatively light of Japanese 550- and 1,100-pound bombs, and even shrugged off the occasional *kamikaze*.

Relations between Fraser and Nimitz were finally and irrevocably sealed on the day the Hiroshima bomb was dropped. Fraser in the battleship *Duke of York* happened to be making a call on the American Admiral at Guam, part of Fraser's duty being the presentation of the Order of the Bath to Nimitz onboard his flagship. This concluded, Nimitz expressed a wish to leave, and he asked, 'Can I have my barge now?'

I said, 'No, you've got to taste a bit of grog out of our grog-tub.' So he did that; then he said, 'Can I have my barge now?', and I said, 'No, you've got to visit the Wardroom, I'm afraid, and have a drink there.' And when we'd visited the Wardroom, he said, 'Can I have my barge now?' and I said, 'No, I'm sorry, you've got to come down to the Gunroom.' And after the visit to the Gunroom he said, 'Can I I have my barge *now*?' – getting a little bit heated – but I said, 'No, you've got to visit the Warrant Officers' Mess'.... We went through the lot, and finally, quite red-faced, he went over the side. He never forgave me for that, he said – a wonderful man.[16]

Admiral Fraser, at a more solemn ceremony, was present later as British naval representative on board Halsey's flagship *Missouri* in Tokyo Bay on 2 September 1945. Halsey had already been honoured with the KBE, presented two weeks earlier by Fraser, when they both signed the instrument of surrender – one autographed copy of which Nimitz presented to Fraser: 'with warmest regards and best wishes'.

And that seems, to this writer, to have been an appropriate conclusion, at an appropriate occasion, to five years of naval co-operation between allies.

APPENDIX A

Some Naval Commanders of the Second World War

Cunningham, Admiral of the Fleet Viscount (Andrew) (1883–1963): Entered RN 1898. First World War DSO and two bars. Deputy Chief of Naval Staff 1938–9. C-in-C Mediterranean 1939–43. Led British Admiralty Delegation to Washington 1942. First Sea Lord 1943–6. Britain's greatest fighting admiral since Nelson.

Doenitz, Grand Admiral Karl (1892–1980): Commissioned in German Navy 1910. Entered U-boat service 1916. Flag Officer U-boats. In 1943 succeeded Admiral Raeder (q.v.) as C-in-C German Navy. Succeeded Adolf Hitler as Fuehrer 1945. Sentenced to ten years' imprisonment at Nuremberg War Trials.

Fletcher, Fleet Admiral Frank (1885–1973): Came from an old naval family, serving in destroyers in the First World War, and commanded the battleship *New Mexico* later. At the outbreak of the European war commanded cruiser division. Was in tactical command at Midway, and from 1943 commanded the North Pacific Forces.

Forbes, Admiral of the Fleet Sir Charles (1880–1960): Entered RN 1894. Captain 1917. DSO for services at Battle of Jutland. C-in-C Home Fleet 1938–40. C-in-C Plymouth 1941–3.

Fraser, Admiral of the Fleet Lord (Bruce) (1888–1981): Entered RN 1902. Served at Gallipoli and in battleship *Resolution* First World War. Third Sea Lord 1939–42. C-in-C Home Fleet 1943–4 (sinking of *Scharnhorst*). C-in-C Eastern Fleet 1944, and Pacific Fleet 1945–6. First Sea Lord 1948–51.

Halsey, Fleet Admiral William F. (1882–1952): Entered USN and graduated 1904. Served in Atlantic on destroyers in First World War. Became closely acquainted with Franklin D. Roosevelt when he was Assistant Secretary of the Navy. Commanded Task Force 16 in April 1942 for General Doolittle's raid on Tokyo. Hospitalized at the time of Midway, he later became Supreme Commander South Pacific. Replaced Admiral Spruance (q.v.) as Supreme Commander in the central Pacific for Leyte Gulf operations. The formal Japanese surrender took place in Tokyo Bay on board his flagship *Missouri*.

Harwood, Admiral Sir Henry (1888–1950): Joined the RN 1904. As Commodore defeated the pocket-battleship *Admiral Graf Spee* at the action off the River Plate 1939. Briefly C-in-C Mediterranean 1942.

King, Fleet Admiral Ernest J. (1878–1956): C-in-C naval forces at outbreak of Pacific war. March 1942, Chief of Naval Operations, member of the US Joint

Chiefs of Staff and Combined Chiefs of Staff Committee. A powerful and inspiring figure, his record was flawed by his prejudices and narrow view of the world war in favour of Pacific operations to the detriment of all others.

Kinkaid, Fleet Admiral Thomas C. (1888–1972): At the Naval Academy 1908. Served in battleships, including Gunnery Officer USS *Arizona* 1918–20. Commanded Cruiser Division 6 at Coral Sea, and Task Force 16 at Battle of Santa Cruz. Commanded Northern Forces in Aleutian campaign, 7th Fleet at Leyte Gulf. Was especially praised for his development of previously neglected night-fighting abilities of the American Navy.

Mitscher, Fleet Admiral Marc (1887–1947): Aviation specialist who commanded the carrier *Hornet* from which the Doolittle bombers took off for Tokyo April 1942. Air Commander at Guadalcanal, and in January 1944 commanded Fast Carrier Force, Task Force 58, under Spruance (q.v.). From January through October 1944 his TF responsible for destroying 795 enemy ships and 4,425 aircraft. At the Philippine Sea action Mitscher took the risk of attacking the enemy at dusk at long range, which paid off handsomely. Provided air cover for the Iwo Jima and Okinawa operations.

Nagumo, Vice-Admiral Chuichi (1882–1944): Began the Pacific war heroically as the Commander of the First Carrier Strike Force, flying his flag in the carrier *Akagi* at Pearl Harbor and subsequent operations. Primarily a torpedo specialist and relying too heavily on his staff for guidance, his star fell into the descendant during the prolonged Guadalcanal operations. Demoted to ground commander on Saipan, he committed suicide 6 July 1944 when defeat was certain.

Nimitz, Fleet Admiral Chester W. (1885–1966): The *beau idéal* of an admiral, shrewd, forceful, tactful, and more responsible for winning the Pacific war with incredibly low casualties than any other officer. C-in-C Pacific Fleet 17 December 1941 until victory. Was the chief proponent of the 'leapfrogging' strategy followed latterly in the war.

Noble, Admiral Sir Percy (1880–1955): Entered RN 1894. Served in the Grand Fleet 1914–19. Fourth Sea Lord 1935–7. As C-in-C Western Approaches was responsible for the initiation and defence of Atlantic convoys during critical years 1941–2. Head of British Naval Delegation to Washington 1942–4.

Ozawa, Vice-Admiral Jisaburo (1896–1966): An aviation specialist and Commander of the Japanese Mobile Fleet from November 1942, after Nagumo (q.v.) had revealed his own shortcomings. It was perhaps as well for the American Pacific Fleet that this considerable strategist and organizer did not take over until the Japanese carrier force had been fatally weakened by losses. He commanded the 'live bait' carriers at the Leyte Gulf operations.

Pound, Admiral of the Fleet Sir Dudley (1877–1943): Commanded battleship *Colossus* at the Battle of Jutland. C-in-C Mediterranean Fleet 1936–9, when appointed First Sea Lord. Chairman Chiefs of Staff Committee until 1942. A steady and much admired officer who coped admirably with Churchill and saw the RN through some of its most difficult years. Was a firm centralist and poor delegator, which led to his taking the blame for the disastrous PQ17 convoy. Weakened by poor health until his death on Trafalgar Day 1943.

Raeder, Grand Admiral Erich (1876–1960): After early notable service in the First World War, Raeder was the architect of the new German Navy of the 1930s, and of the successful Norwegian invasion of April 1940. From this time Hitler's confidence in him went into decline, the spirit and record of the surface Fleet becoming increasingly disappointing. Was dismissed and replaced by Doenitz (q.v.) after the failure at the Battle of Barents Sea. Sentenced to ten years' imprisonment at the Nuremberg War Trials.

Ramsay, Admiral Sir Bertram (1883–1945): Entered RN 1898. Commanded HMS *Broke* of the Dover Patrol in the First World War. Rear-Admiral and Chief of Staff Home Fleet 1935. Retired but reinstated during Second World War. As Flag Officer, Dover organized the Dunkirk evacuation. Commanded naval forces at invasion of North Africa 1942 and Normandy 1944.

Somerville, Admiral of the Fleet Sir James (1882–1949): Entered RN 1898, served at Gallipoli (DSO). Commanded Force H at Gibraltar 1940–42, including the partial destruction of the French Fleet at Oran. C-in-C Eastern Fleet 1942–4. Head of British Admiralty Delegation to Washington 1944–5. Perhaps the second greatest fighting British admiral, after Cunningham (q.v.), of the Second World War. Relieved by Lord Mountbatten who considered he did not receive sufficient respect from him.

Spruance, Fleet Admiral Raymond A. (1886–1969): Graduated from the Naval Academy 1907. Became a specialist in engineering and gunfire control. At heart a battleship officer, he was in command of Admiral Halsey's (q.v.) cruisers when Halsey fell ill before Midway. Nimitz, at Halsey's recommendation, appointed him in his place as CO Task Force 16. He at once showed his decisiveness, anticipation and speed of thought at Midway, which made his name and fame. Became in succession Chief of Staff to Nimitz (q.v.), Commander of the 5th (Central Pacific) Fleet, and Commander of the naval side at the invasion of Okinawa and Iwo Jima.

Tovey, Admiral of the Fleet Sir John (1885–1971): Served in destroyers in First World War (DSO) and Rear-Admiral Destroyers with the Mediterranean Fleet 1938–40. C-in-C Home Fleet 1940–43 through the navy's most fateful years, including the *Bismarck* raid and destruction. Attracted equally admiration and affection.

Turner, Admiral Richmond Kelly (1885–1961): Served in battleships as gunnery officer in First World War. Later trained as a pilot and became Chief of Staff to Commander Aircraft Battle Force 1933–5. Appointed Commander Amphibious Force South Pacific 1942 for Guadalcanal invasion. His 'grizzled head, beetling black brows, tireless energy and ferocious language were to become almost legendary in the Pacific' (Morison). An amphibious specialist, Turner commanded at the taking of Kwajelein, Eniwetok and Iwo Jima.

Vian, Admiral of the Fleet Sir Philip (1894–1968): One of the most brilliant and aggressive commanders of the Second World War, gaining fame first for boarding the German supply ship *Altmark* off Norway and releasing 299 British prisoners. Later his destroyer *Afridi* was sunk during the evacuation of Norway. (Awarded DSO and two bars in that year alone.) Further embellished his reputation during the *Bismarck* action and in the Mediterranean where he relished fighting against impossible odds with his destroyers. Commanded British carriers during the assault on Okinawa.

Yamamoto, Fleet Admiral Isoroku (1884–1943): Japan's greatest strategist and naval hero, Yamamoto opposed war with the USA, and when he had to face the inevitable conceived a surprise attack on Pearl Harbor as the prelude to a short, sharp, decisive campaign. Shot down and killed by an American fighter.

APPENDIX B

Some Printed Works Consulted

Beach, E.L., *Submarine!* (1952)
Bekker, C., *The Luftwaffe War Diaries* (1964)
Brooke, G., *Alarm Starboard* (1982)
Buell, T.B., *Master of Sea Power: A Biography of Fleet Admiral Ernest J. King* (1981)
Chesnau, R., *Aircraft Carriers of the World* (1984)
Churchill, W.S., *The Second World War*, Vols I–VI (1948–54)
Cremer, P., *U333: The Story of a U-boat Ace* (1984)
Cunningham, A., *A Sailor's Odyssey* (1951)
Doenitz, C., *Memoirs* (1959)
Frank, P., and Harrington, J.D., *Rendezvous at Midway* (1960)
Frank, W., *The Sea Wolves* (1955)
Hinsley, F.H., *British Intelligence in the Second World War*, Vols I–III (1979–84)
Hough, R., *The Hunting of Force Z* (1963)
Kemp, P., *Victory at Sea* (1957)
Lord, W., *Incredible Victory: The Battle of Midway* (1968)
Macintyre, D., *The Battle of the Atlantic* (1961)
Macintyre, D., *The Battle for the Mediterranean* (1964)
Macintyre, D., *The Battle for the Pacific* (1966)
Macintyre, D., *The Naval War Against Hitler* (1971)
Marder, A.J., *Old Friends, New Enemies: The Royal Navy and the Imperial Japanese Navy* (1981)
Middlebrook, M., *Convoy* (1976)
Middlebrook, M., and Mahoney, P., *Battleship: The Loss of the Prince of Wales and Repulse* (1977)
Morison, S.E., *History of United States Naval Operations in World War II*, Vols I–XV (1948–64)
Müllenheim-Rechberg, B., *Battleship Bismarck: A Survivor's Story* (1980)
Okumiya, M., and Horikoshi, J., *Zero!* (1957)
Pope, D., *Flag 4: The Battle of Coastal Forces in the Mediterranean* (1954)
Roskill, S.W., *The War at Sea 1939–1945*, Vols I–III (1954–61)
Roskill, S.W., *HMS Warspite* (1957)
Ruge, F., *Sea Warfare: A German Concept* (1957)
Scott, P., *The Battle of the Narrow Seas* (1945)
Spector, R.H., *Eagle Against the Sun* (1985)
Sturtivant, R., *Fleet Air Arm at War* (1982)
Tuleja, T., *Climax at Midway* (1960)
Werner, H.A., *Iron Coffins* (1969)
Winton, J. (ed.), *Freedom's Battle*: Vol I: *The War at Sea 1939–1945* (1967)
Young, E., *One of our Submarines* (1952)

APPENDIX C

Representative Aircraft Carriers

HMS *Ark Royal*
Laid down: 15 September 1935
Launched: 13 April 1937
Commissioned: 16 November 1938
Displacement: 22,000 tons standard
Dimensions: 800 ft long overall, max. beam 94 ft, mean draught 22 ft 9 in.
Machinery: 3-shaft Parsons geared turbines, 6 Admiralty 3-drum boilers, 102,000 shaft horsepower = 31 kts
Oil fuel: 4,443 tons
Range: 7,600 nautical miles @ 12 kts, 4,300 nm @ 20 kts
Armour: $2\frac{1}{2}$–$3\frac{1}{2}$-in. armoured deck, $4\frac{1}{2}$-in. belt
Armament: 8×4.5 in., 48×2 pdr, $32 \times .5$ in.
Aircraft: 72

USS *Enterprise*
Laid down: 21 May 1934
Launched: 4 April 1936
Commissioned: 30 September 1937
Displacement: 19,872 tons standard
Dimensions: 770 ft long overall, max. beam 86 ft, mean draught 21 ft 6 in.
Machinery: 3-shaft Parsons geared turbines, 9 Babcock & Wilcox boilers, 120,000 shaft horsepower = 32.5 kts
Oil fuel: 4,360 tons
Range: 12,000 nm @ 15 kts
Armour: $1\frac{1}{2}$-in. armoured deck, $2\frac{1}{2}$–$4\frac{1}{2}$-in. belt
Armament (original): 8×5 in., 16×1.1 in., $16 \times .5$ in.
Aircraft: 96

IJN *Soryu*
Laid down: 20 November 1934
Launched: 21 December 1935
Commissioned: 29 January 1937
Displacement: 15,900 tons standard
Dimensions: 728 ft long overall, max. beam 85 ft, mean draught 25 ft
Machinery: 4-shaft geared turbines, 8 Kampon boilers, 152,000 shaft horsepower = 34 kts

Oil fuel: 3,670 tons
Range: 7,750 nm @ 18 kts
Armour: 1-in. deck, 2.2-in. over magazines
Armament: 12 × 5 in., 28 × 25 mm, ? smaller calibre
Aircraft: 71

APPENDIX D

Representative Naval Guns

		Weight of shell in pounds	Rate of fire per min.
18.1-inch	(Japanese)	3,200	2
16-inch	(British)	2,461	2
16-inch	(American)	2,100	2
15-inch	(German)	1,675	2–3
15-inch	(British)	1,920	2
14-inch	(British)	1,560	3
14-inch	(American)	1,400	2
11-inch	(German)	670	3
8-inch	(British)	256	4
8-inch	(American)	260	4
6-inch	(British)	100	8–12
6-inch	(American)	105	10–15
5.9-inch	(German)	100	6–10
5.25-inch	(British)	85	15
5-inch	(American)	50	15
40-mm	(British Vickers)	2	100
20-mm	(Hispano)		650–750
20-mm	(Oerlikon)		520

APPENDIX E

Representative Aircraft of the Naval War

Avenger (Grumman) Torpedo/Bomber/Reconnaissance
First Flew: 1 August 1941
Engine: 1,600 hp giving max. speed: 266 mph
Armament: 5 × .5-in. machine-guns, 1 × 22-in. torpedo/2,000-pound bombs

B-17 (Boeing) Heavy bomber
28 July 1935
4 × 1,200 hp = 300 mph
6 × .5-in., 1 × .3-in., 4,000-pound bombs (armament varied widely)

Betty (Mitsubishi G4M) Torpedo/Bomber
October 1939
2 × 1,530 hp = 265 mph
3 × 7.7-mm, 1 × 20-mm cannon, 1,765-pound bombs or torpedo

Buffalo (Brewster) Fighter
January 1938
1,000 hp = 280 mph
1 × .3-in., 1 × .5-in. (later 4 × .5-in.)

Catalina (Consolidated PBY) Patrol/Anti-submarine
28 March 1935
2 × 825 hp = 175 mph
4 × .3-in., 4,500-pound bombs or torpedoes or depth-charges

Corsair (Vought F4U) Fighter/Fighter-bomber
29 May 1940
2,000 hp = 395 mph
4 × .5-in, 2,000-pound bombs or 8 × 5-in. rockets

Dauntless (Douglas SBD) Scout/Bomber
1936
1,000 hp = 250 mph
2 × .5-in., 1 × .3-in., 1,000-pound bombs (later 1,600 pounds)

Devastator (Douglas TBD) Torpedo-bomber
24 April 1935
900 hp = 125 mph (loaded), 175 mph (unloaded)
2 × .3-in., 1,000-pound torpedo

Fulmar (Fairey) Fighter
4 January 1940
1,060 hp = 270 mph
8 × .303-in.

Hellcat (Grumman F6F) Fighter
26 June 1942
1,675 hp = 375 mph
6 × .5-in. (cannon armament and 1 × 1,000-pound bomb later)

Hurricane (Hawker Sea-) Fighter
6 November 1935
1,030 hp = 300 mph
8 × .303-in. (cannon armament and 500-pound bombs later)

Ju87 (Junkers) Dive-bomber
1936
1,400 hp = 250 mph (loaded)
3 × 7.92-mm, 2,200-pound bombs

Ju88 (Junkers) Dive-bomber/Level-bomber/Torpedo-bomber
21 December 1936
2 × 1,200 hp = 290 mph
4 × 7.9-mm (later increased), 4,000-pound bombs

Judy (Yokosuka D4Y2) Dive-bomber
November 1940
1 × 1,380 hp = 350 mph
3 × 7.7-mm, 1,100-pound bombs

Kate (Nakajima B5N2) Torpedo-bomber
January 1937
1,000 hp = 225 mph
3 × 7.7-mm, 1,764-pound torpedo

Liberator (Consolidated) Bomber
29 December 1939
4 × 1,350 hp = 310 mph
Various 20-mm cannon and .5-in. machine-gun defensive armament
Bomb or depth-charge load, 12,800-pound bombs

Messerschmitt Bf 110 Fighter/Fighter-bomber
12 May 1936

2 × 1,100 hp = 350 mph
2 × 20-mm cannon, 4 × 7.9-mm, 2,200-pound bombs

Swordfish (Fairey) Torpedo-bomber/Bomber/Reconnaissance
17 April 1934
690 hp = 115 mph
2 × .303-in., 1 × 1,610-pound torpedo or 1,500-pound bombs or depth-charges

Val (Aichi D3A) Dive-bomber
1937
1,075 hp = 240 mph
3 × 7.7-mm, 900-pound bombs

Wildcat (Grumman F4F) Fighter
2 September 1937
1,100 hp = 320 mph
6 × .5-in.

Zero (Mitsubishi A6M) Fighter/Fighter-bomber
1 April 1939
925 hp = 330 mph
2 × 20-mm cannon, 2 × 13-mm, 260-pound bombs
(Developed versions known as Zeke or Hamp. Zero-Sen made up half all *kamikazes* with up to 1,100-pound bomb)

Notes

1: '... business in great waters'

1 Lieutenant-Commander P.K. Kemp RN to the author, 17 December 1985
2 Conversation with Admiral Tennant, 18 June 1961
3 W.S.Churchill, *The Second World War* (VI vols, 1948–54), Vol. II, p. 402
4 Purnell's *History of The Second World War*, 'The Battle of the River Plate', p. 110
5 *Ibid.*
6 Conversation with Lord Mountbatten, 16 February 1971
7 S.W.Roskill, *The Navy at War* (1960), p. 40
8 Churchill, *Second World War*, Vol. I, p. 479
9 *Ibid.*, p. 470
10 Lieutenant-Commander P.K. Kemp, *Victory at Sea* (1958), p. 58
11 R.Hough, *Mountbatten: Hero of our Time* (1980), p. 121
12 C.de Wiart, *Happy Odyssey* (1950), p. 174
13 Captain D.Macintyre, *The Naval War Against Hitler* (1971), p. 27
14 A.C.Hardy, *Everyman's History of the Sea War*, Vol. I (1948), pp. 153–4
15 *Ibid.*, p. 155
16 Macintyre, *Naval War Against Hitler*, p. 38
17 R.Healiss, *Adventure Glorious* (1957), p. 52
18 Churchill, *Second World War*, Vol. I, p. 517
19 *Ibid.*, pp. 518–19
20 Roskill, *Navy at War*, p. 71

2: Amphibious Warfare

1 B.H.Liddell-Hart, *History of the Second World War* (1970), p. 66
2 N.Harman, *Dunkirk: The Necessary Myth* (1980), p. 142 (paperback edn)
3 *Ibid.*, pp. 224–5
4 W.Lord, *The Miracle of Dunkirk* (1983), p. 261
5 Churchill, *Second World War*, Vol. II, p. 213
6 *Ibid.*, p. 145
7 P.Halpern (ed.), *The Keyes Papers*, Vol. III (1981), p. 72
8 *Ibid.*, p. 88
9 Conversation with Lord Mountbatten, July 1972
10 Commander Robert Ryder VC, RN, *The Attack on St Nazaire* (1947), p. 187
11 T.Robertson, *Dieppe: The Shame and the Glory* (1963), p. 299
12 *Ibid.*, p. 288
13 Kemp, *Victory at Sea*, p. 267

3: U-boat Warfare,
September 1939–March 1943

1 Löthar-Günther Buchheim, *U-Boat War* (translated by G. Lawaetz, 1978), unpaged
2 Admiral Sir Arthur Wilson
3 Macintyre, *Naval War Against Hitler*, p. 49
4 *Ibid.*
5 *Ibid.*, pp. 61–2

6 Churchill, *Second World War*, Vol. II, p. 537

7 Quoted R.Barker, *The Hurricats* (1978), p. 17

8 *Ibid.*, pp. 176–9

9 Macintyre, *Naval War Against Hitler*, pp. 100–101

10 S.E.Morison, *History of the U.S. Navy in World War II*, XV vols (1947–62), Vol. I, p. 56

11 P.Cremer, *U-333* (1984), pp. 68–9

12 Quoted M.Middlebrook, *Convoy* (1976), p. 71

13 *Ibid.*, p. 146

14 *Ibid.*, p. 174

15 *Ibid.*, p. 175

16 Churchill, *Second World War*, Vol. III, p. 331

17 *Ibid.*, Vol. IV, p. 233

18 *Ibid.*

19 John Winton (ed.), *Freedom's Battle*, Vol. I, p. 241

20 G.Winn, *PQ17*, pp. 86–7

21 Roskill, *Navy at War*, p. 208

22 Macintyre, *Naval War Against Hitler*, p. 222

23 Kemp, *Victory at Sea*, pp. 239–40

4: Folly and Infamy

1 Vice-Admiral Homer N. Wallin, *Pearl Harbor: Why, How, Fleet Salvage and Final Appraisal* (1968), pp. 126–7

2 Walter Lord, *Day of Infamy* (1957), pp. 72–3

3 Wallin, *Pearl Harbor*, p. 234

4 *Ibid.*, p. 131

5 *Ibid.*, p. 133

6 *Ibid.*, p. 150

7 Commander W.Karig and Lieutenant W.Kelley, *Battle Report: Pearl Harbor to Coral Sea* (1944), p. 81

8 Lord, *Day of Infamy*, p. 25

5: Battleships in the North Atlantic

1 US Senate Sub-Committee on Military Affairs report, 12 September 1919

2 C.MacNeil, *San Demetrio* (1967), p. 147

3 L. Kennedy, *Pursuit* (1974), p. 29

4 Conversation with Captain A.J.L. Phillips, 17 July 1943

5 B. von Müllenheim-Rechberg, *Battleship Bismarck: A Survivor's Story* (1981), p. 84

6 *Ibid.*, p. 88

7 T.J.Cain, *HMS Electra* (1959), pp. 70–71

8 Kennedy, *Pursuit*, p. 69

9 Cain, *Electra*, pp. 79–80

10 Müllenheim-Rechberg, *Battleship Bismarck*, pp. 103–4

11 *Ibid.*, p. 110

12 E.Knight, 'Enemy in Sight' (article in *Blackwood's Magazine*)

13 Müllenheim-Rechberg, *Battleship Bismarck*, p. 133

14 Conversation with Captain Phillips

6: 'A bloody tumult of destruction ...'

1 Müllenheim-Rechberg, *Battleship Bismarck*, p. 151

2 J.Colville, *The Fringes of Power: Downing Street Diaries 1939–45* (1985), p. 391

3 G.Woods, *Wings at Sea* (1985), pp. 94–5

4 Müllenheim-Rechberg, *Battleship Bismarck*, pp. 168–70

5 *Ibid.*, p. 214

6 Churchill, *Second World War*, Vol. III, p. 283

7 K.Doenitz, *Memoirs* (1959), p. 170

8 Churchill, *Second World War*, Vol. III, p. 286

9 W.F.Kimball (ed.), *Churchill and Roosevelt: The Complete Correspondence*, Vol. I (1984), p. 263

10 W.R.Fell, *The Sea our Shield* (1966), p. 187

11 F-Otto Busch, *The Sinking of the Scharnhorst* (1956), p. 15 (paperback edn)

12 *Ibid.*, p. 51

13 *Ibid.*, p. 106

14 Doenitz, *Memoirs*, p. 380

15 Quoted *ibid.*, pp. 382-3
16 Busch, *Sinking of the Scharnhorst*, p. 137
17 B.B.Ramsden, 'The Sinking of the *Scharnhorst*' (article in *Blackwood's Magazine*)

7: Catastrophe in the Far East
1 Churchill, *Second World War*, Vol. III, p. 469
2 *Ibid.*, p. 525
3 *Ibid.*, p. 547
4 Kemp to author, 15 September 1985
5 *Ibid.*
6 M.Okumiya and J.Horikoshi, *Zero: The Story of the Japanese Navy Air Force* (1957), p. 73
7 M.Middlebrook and P.Mahoney, *Battleship: The Loss of the Prince of Wales and Repulse* (1977), p. 136
8 *Ibid.*, p. 185
9 *Ibid.*, p. 186
10 *Daily Express*
11 Middlebrook and Mahoney, *Battleship*, pp. 192-3
12 Okumiya and Horikoshi, *Zero*, p. 82
13 *Daily Express*
14 G.Brooke, *Alarm Starboard* (1982), p. 108
15 Conversation with Admiral Tennant, 18 June 1961
16 Kemp to author, 15 September 1985
17 Churchill, *Second World War*, Vol. III, p. 551
18 A.C.Hardy, *Everyman's History of the Sea War*, Vol. II (1948), p. 53

8: 'The lowest ebb ...'
1 Okumiya and Horikoshi, *Zero*, p. 46
2 *Ibid.*, p. 87
3 D.Macintyre, *The Battle for the Pacific* (1966), p. 51
4 Quoted from *Hornet* action report in Morison, *History of the U.S. Navy*, Vol. III, p. 391
5 Q.Reynolds, *The Amazing Mr Doolittle* (1954), pp. 205-6
6 E.B.Potter and ChesterW.Nimitz (eds), *The Great Sea War: The Story of Naval Action in World War II* (1961), p. 215
7 P.Frank and J.D.Harrison, *Rendezvous at Midway* (1967), p. 67 (paperback edn)
8 *Ibid.*, p. 71
9 Okumiya and Horikoshi, *Zero*, p. 109
10 Frank and Harrison, *Rendezvous at Midway*, pp. 77-8
11 *Ibid.*, p. 84
12 *Ibid.*, p. 87
13 Morison, *History of the U.S. Navy*, Vol. IV, p. 60

9: Midway: The Invisible Enemy
1 Morison, *History of the U.S. Navy*, Vol. IV, p. 71
2 W.Lord, *Incredible Victory* (1958), pp. 36-7
3 *Ibid.*, p. 133
4 Morison, *History of the U.S. Navy*, Vol. IV, p. 125
5 T.V.Tuleja, *Climax at Midway* (1960), pp. 148-9
6 Morison, *History of the U.S. Navy*, Vol. IV, p. 128
7 *Ibid.*, p. 129
8 Conversation with Lieutenant Rikivini, 19 September 1961
9 Lord, *Incredible Victory*, p. 197
10 Morison, *History of the U.S. Navy*, Vol. IV, p. 142

10: The Long Struggle for the Midland Sea
1 Conversation with Admiral Collins, 16 February 1985
2 Admiral Andrew Cunningham, *Sailor's Odyssey* (1950), p. 266
3 *Ibid.*, p. 282
4 M.R.Maund, 'A Taranto Diary' (article in *Blackwood's Magazine*)
5 M.A.Brigadin, *The Italian Navy in World War II* (1967), p. 45
6 Cunningham, *Sailor's Odyssey*, p. 302
7 *Ibid.*, p. 303

8 *Ibid.*, 362
9 D.Macintyre, *The Battle for the Mediterranean* (1964), pp. 89–90
10 S.W.C.Pack, *The Battle of Matapan* (1961), p. 52
11 *Ibid.*, p. 75
12 *Ibid.*
13 *Ibid.*, p. 78
14 *Ibid.*
15 Cunningham, *Sailor's Odyssey*, p. 332
16 Churchill, *Second World War*, Vol. III, p. 218
17 Conversation with Admiral Mountbatten, 23 July 1972
18 E.Bush, *Bless our Ship* (1958), p. 227
19 *Ibid.*, pp. 228–9
20 J.B.Clegg to author, 15 January 1985
21 H.Popham, *Sea Flight* (1954), pp. 126–8
22 A.Kimmins, *The Listener* (1961), p. 217

11: Guadalcanal
1 R.F.Newcomb, *Savo* (1963), p. 59
2 Morison, *History of the U.S. Navy*, Vol. V, p. 46
3 R.Leckie, *Challenge for the Pacific* (1966), p. 100
4 Morison, *History of the U.S. Navy*, Vol. V, pp. 91–2
5 J.G.Finch to author, 17 September 1982
6 Morison, *History of the U.S. Navy*, Vol. V, p. 96
7 *Ibid.*, p. 107
8 *Ibid.*, p. 132
9 Macintyre, *Battle for Pacific*, p. 96
10 R.Hough, *The Great Admirals* (1977), p. 251
11 Morison, *History of the U.S. Navy*, Vol. V, pp. 220–21

12: The War of the Boats
1 Quoted Macintyre, *Naval War Against Hitler*, p. 318
2 *Ibid.*, p. 322
3 Lindemann Report, 3 March 1943
4 Roskill, *Navy at War*, p. 272

5 P.Cremer, *U-333: The Story of a U-boat Ace* (1984), p. 117
6 Doenitz, *Memoirs*, p. 34
7 H.Warner, *Iron Coffins* (1969), pp. 130–31
8 C.Anscomb, *Submariner* (1957) p. 122
9 *Ibid.*, p. 125
10 E.Young, *One of Our Submarines* (1952), pp. 236–7
11 Morison, *History of the U.S. Navy*, Vol. IV, p. 188
12 Comsubforce, *Current Doctrine on Submarines*, 1939
13 E.L.Beach, *Submarine!* (1956), pp. 280–81 (paperback edn)
14 Message originally proposed to the Admiralty, 2 May 1943
15 Coastal Forces Periodical Review, 1945
16 Conversation with Lieutenant Walter Blount DSC, 12 December 1985
17 P.Scott, *The Battle of the Narrow Seas* (1945), p. 21
18 *Ibid.*, p. 138
19 D.Pope, *Flag 4* (1954), p. 45
20 Conversation with Blount
21 *Ibid.*
22 Pope, *Flag 4*, p. 200
23 *Ibid.*

13: The Central Thrust: Tarawa
1 Minutes of King–Nimitz Conference, 30 July–1 August 1943
2 Morison, *History of the U.S. Navy*, Vol. VII, p. 69
3 *Ibid.*, p. 140
4 Quoted *ibid.*, p. 148
5 Stouffer and others, *Combat and its Aftermath*, Spector 265, p. 90
6 Quoted Morison, *History of the U.S. Navy*, Vol. VII, pp. 148–9

14: Overlord and After
1 Churchill, *Second World War*, Vol. V, p. 557
2 Kemp, *Victory at Sea*, p. 331

3 From a privately printed narrative quoted M. Hastings, *Overlord* (1984), p. 98 (paperback edn)

15: The Pacific: The Curtain Falls

1 Okumiya and Horikoshi, *Zero*, p. 172
2 *Ibid.*, p. 165
3 R. Chesneau, *Aircraft Carriers of the World* (1984), p. 180
4 Okumiya and Horikoshi, *Zero*, pp. 230–31
5 Macintyre, *Battle for Pacific*, p. 169
6 Report to author from John C. Date RANVR, February 1985

7 Morison, *History of the U.S. Navy*, Vol. XII, p. 172
8 *Ibid.*, p. 246
9 *Ibid.*, pp. 273–4
10 *Ibid.*, p. 275
11 Churchill, *Second World War*, Vol. VI, pp. 129–30
12 *Ibid.*, p. 134
13 S. Roskill, *The War at Sea*, 3 vols (1954–61), Vol. III (Part 2), p. 203
14 R. Humble, *Fraser of North Cape* (1983), p. 261
15 *Ibid.*, p. 262
16 *Ibid.*, pp. 276–7

Index

by Douglas Matthews